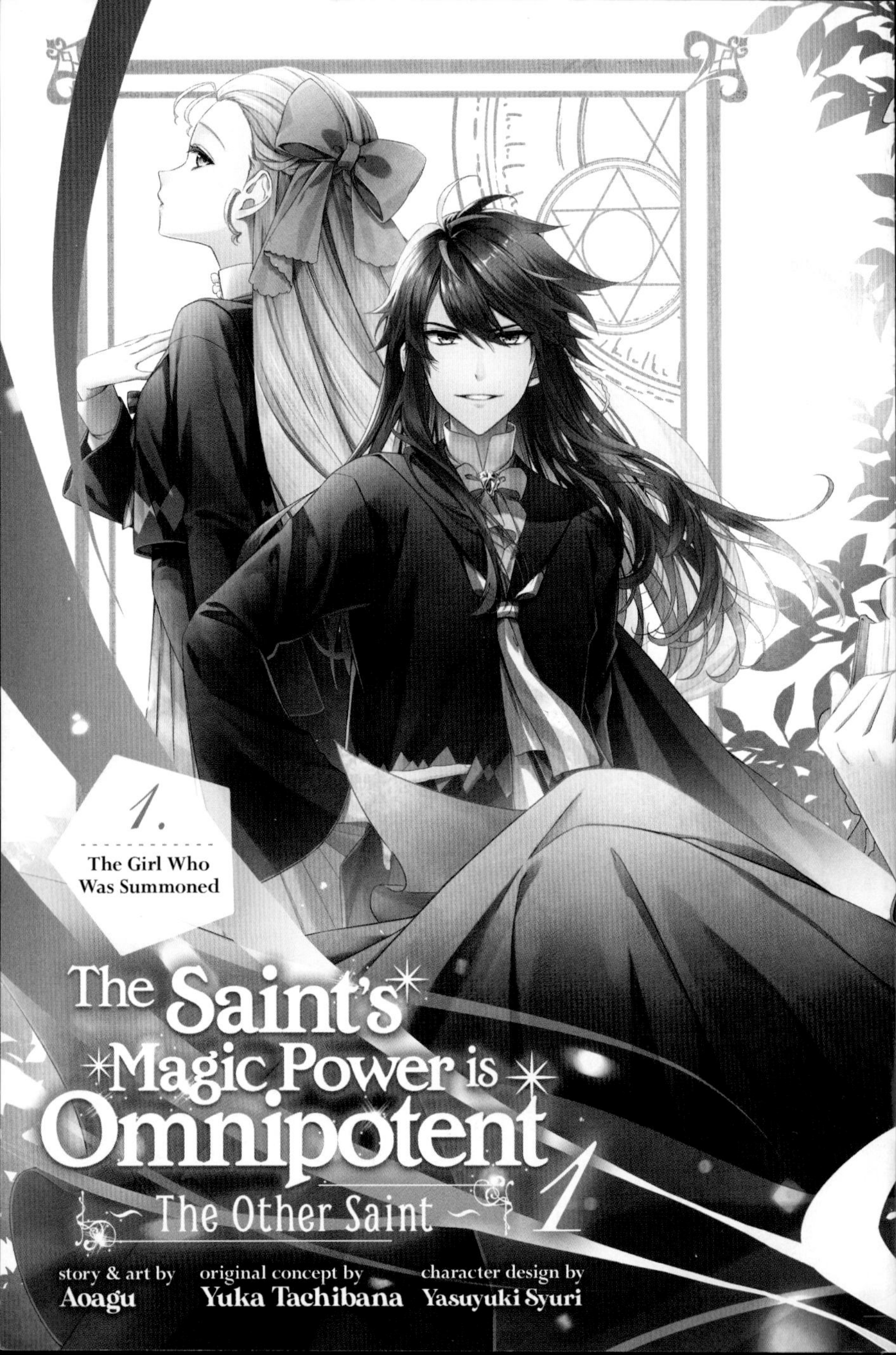
1.
The Girl Who Was Summoned
The Saint's Magic Power is Omnipotent
The Other Saint
1
story & art by
Aoagu
original concept by
Yuka Tachibana
character design by
Yasuyuki Syuri

Contents

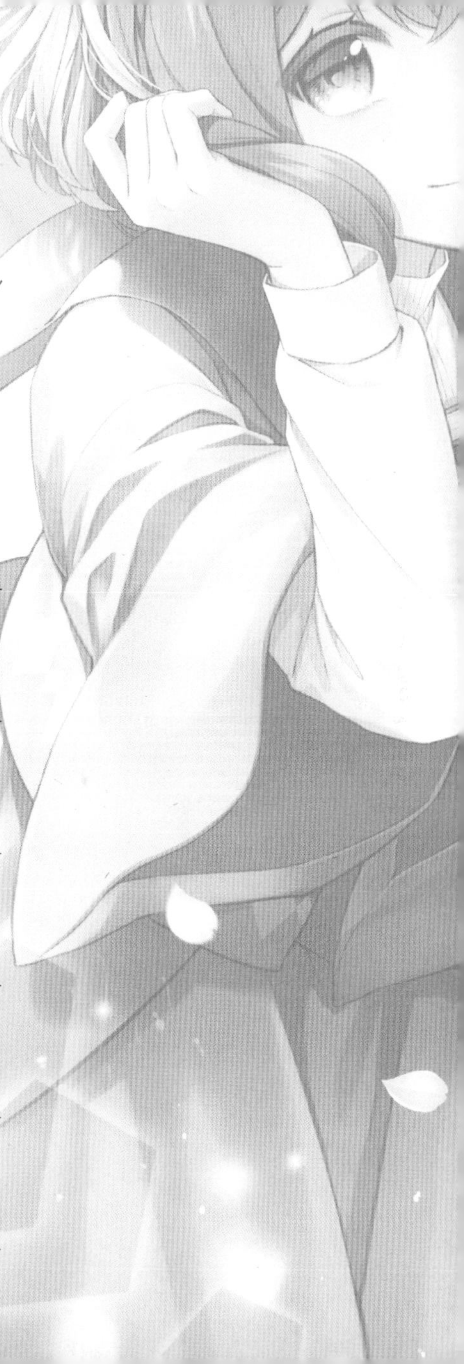

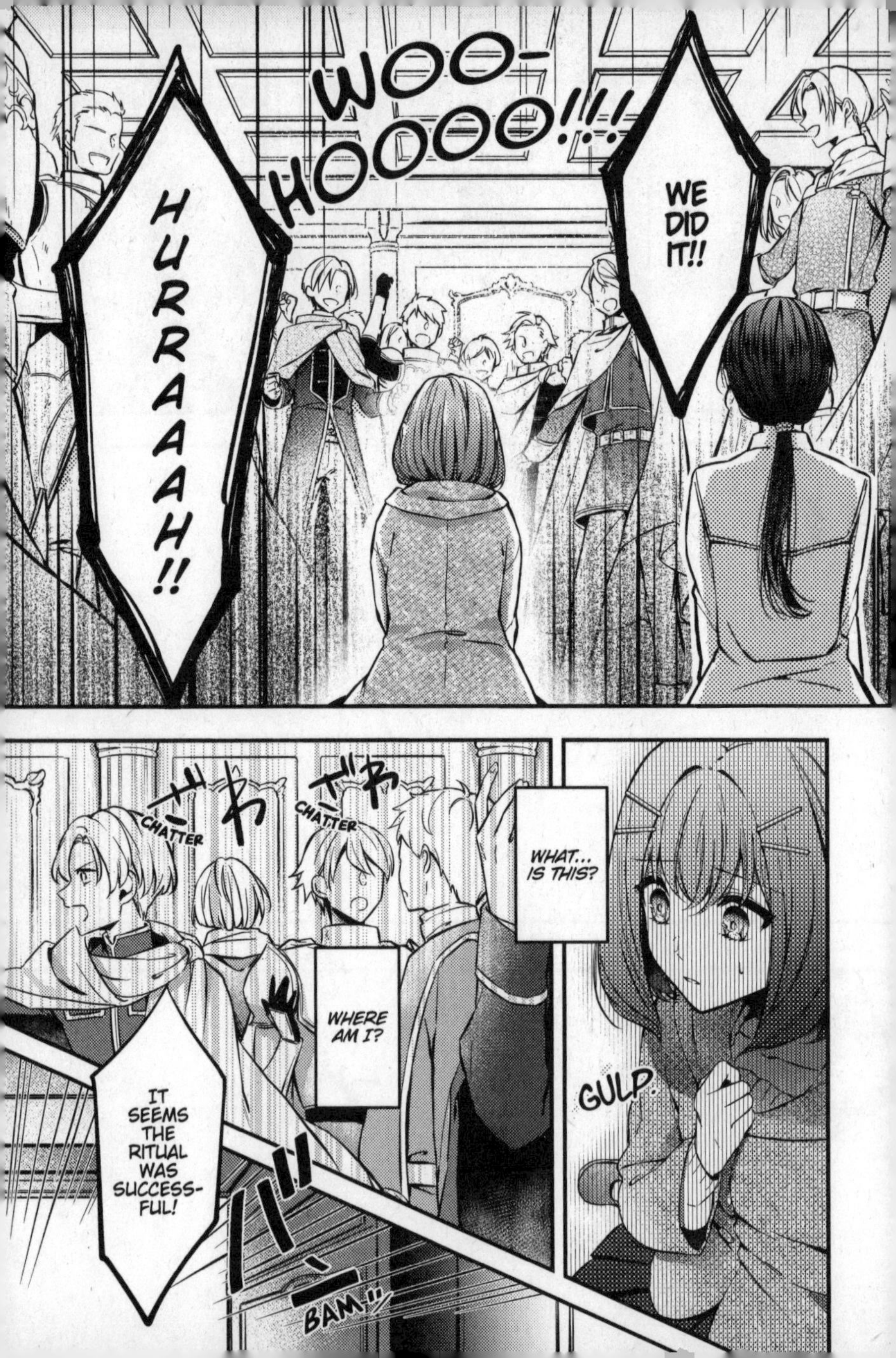
WE DID IT!!
WOO-HOOOOO!!!
HURRAAAAH!!
WHAT... IS THIS?
GULP.
WHERE AM I?
ざわ ざわ
CHATTER
CHATTER
IT SEEMS THE RITUAL WAS SUCCESSFUL!
BAM

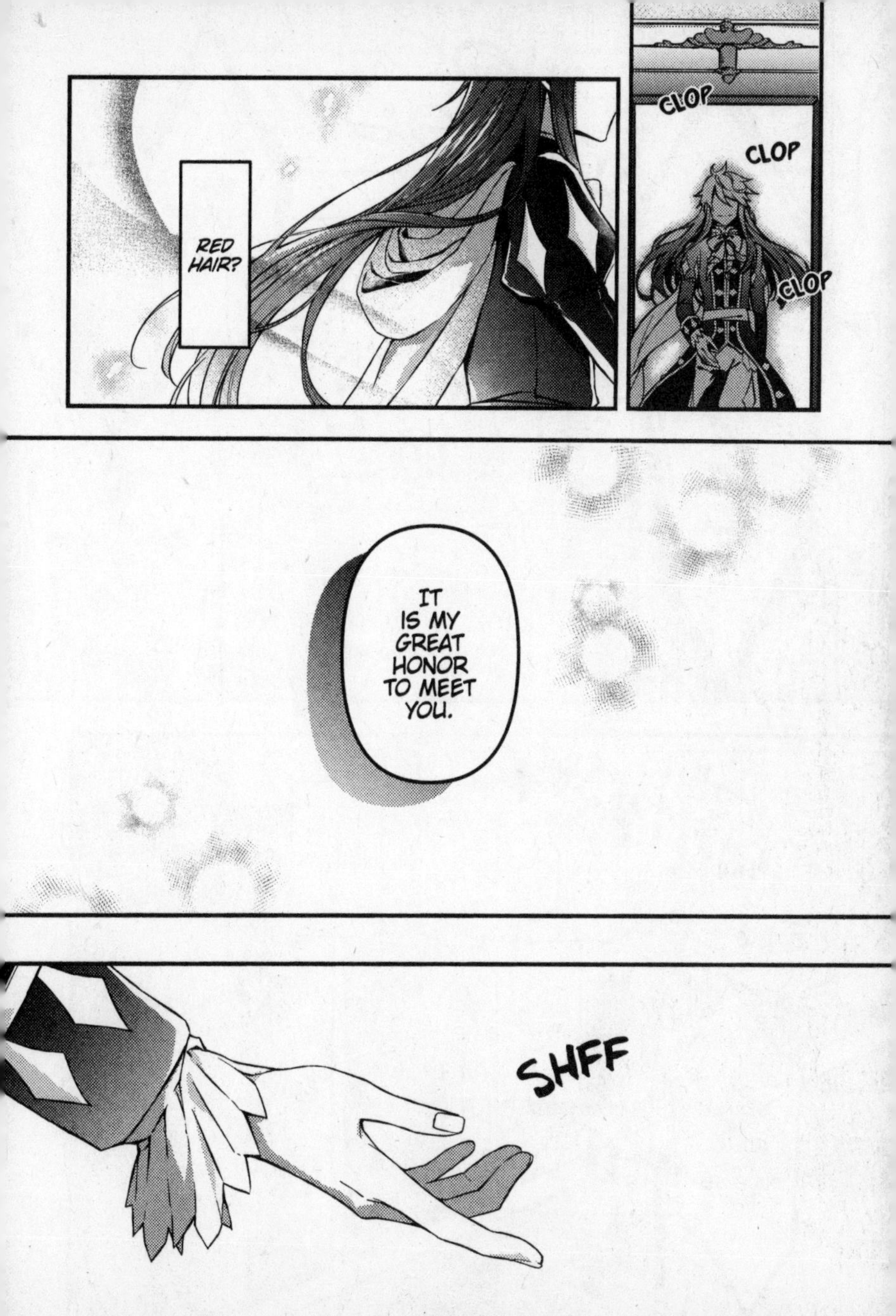
CLOP
CLOP
CLOP
RED HAIR?
IT IS MY GREAT HONOR TO MEET YOU.
SHFF

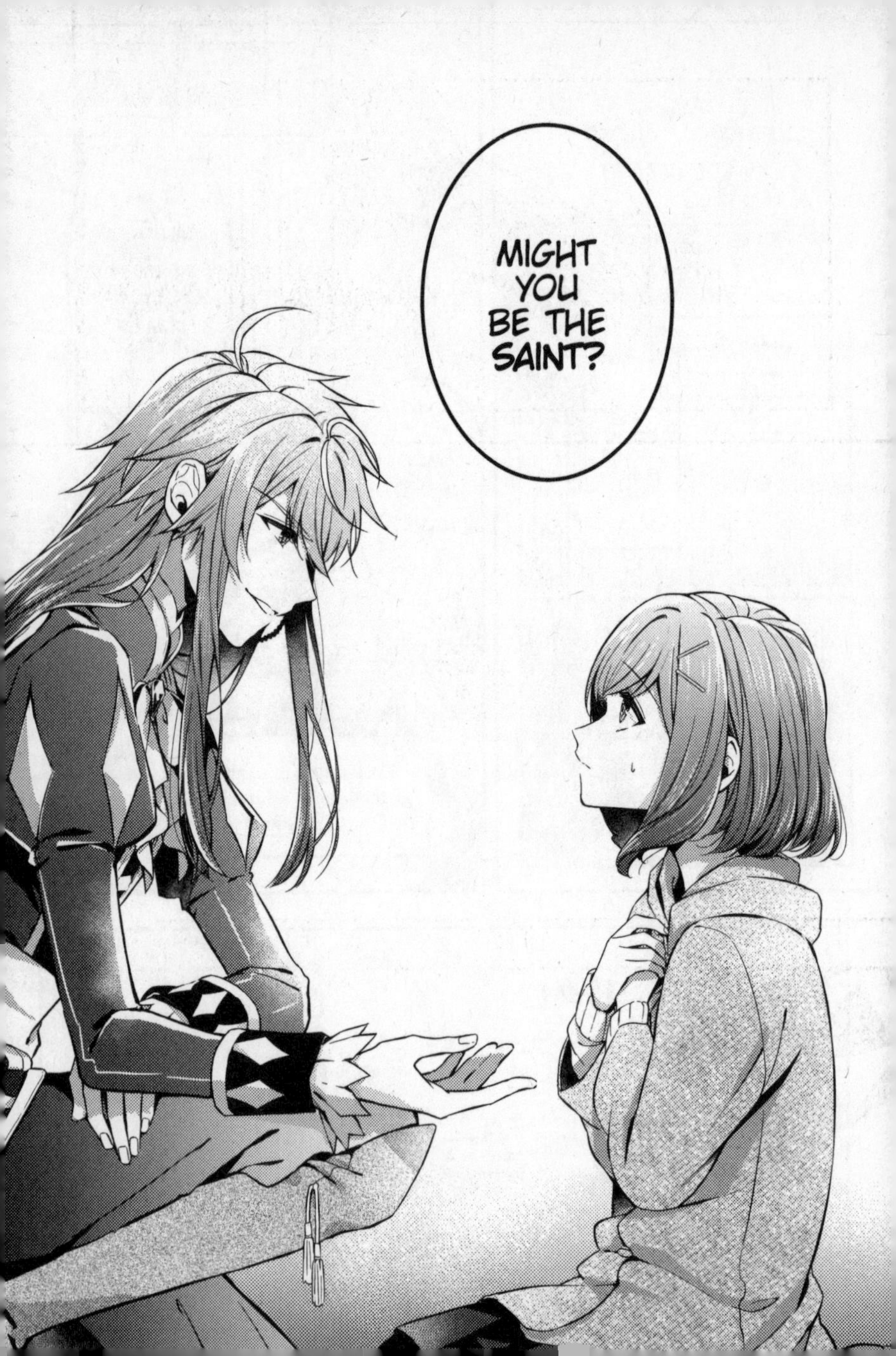
MIGHT YOU BE THE SAINT?

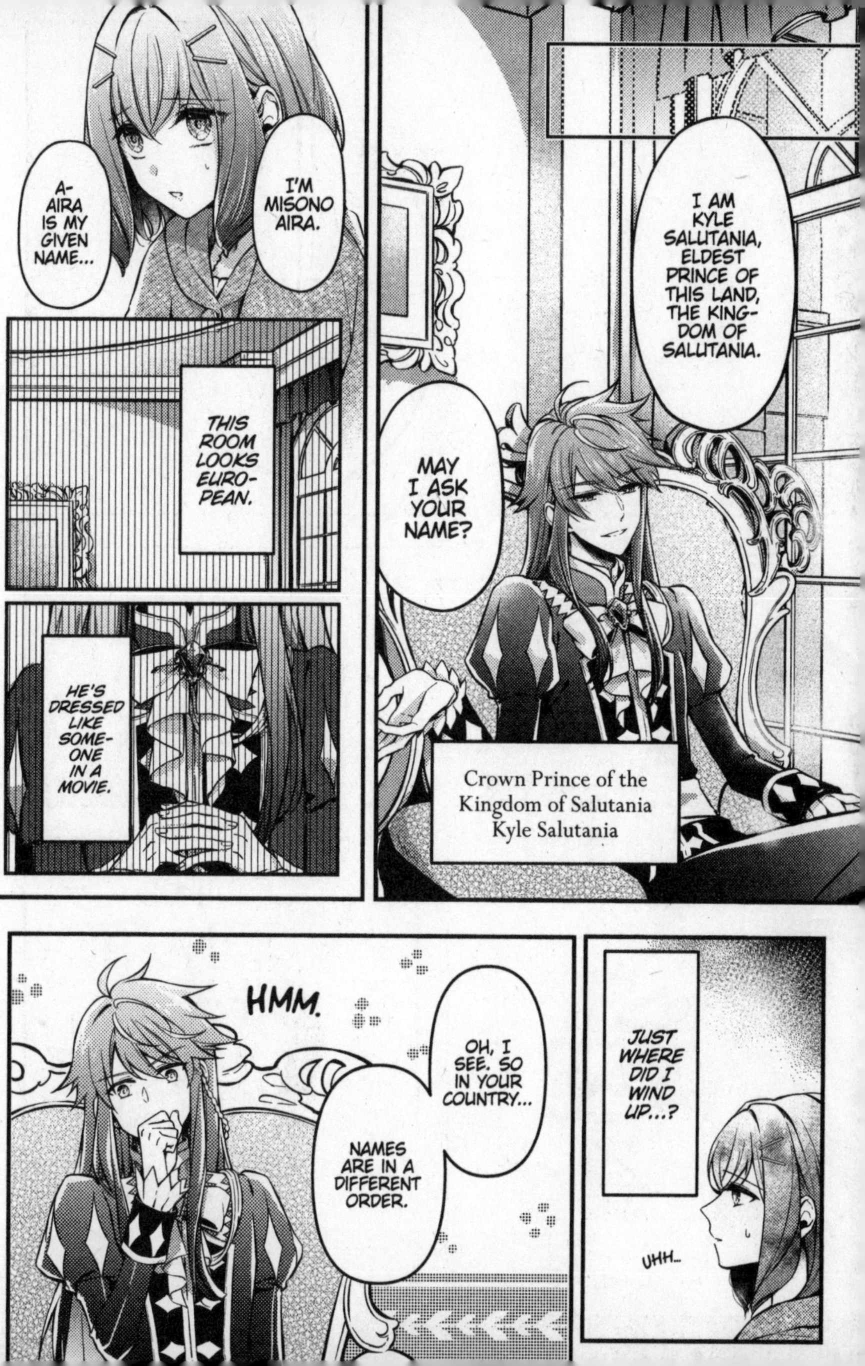
I AM KYLE SALUTANIA, ELDEST PRINCE OF THIS LAND, THE KING-DOM OF SALUTANIA.
MAY I ASK YOUR NAME?
Crown Prince of the Kingdom of Salutania Kyle Salutania
I'M MISONO AIRA.
A-AIRA IS MY GIVEN NAME...
THIS ROOM LOOKS EURO-PEAN.
HE'S DRESSED LIKE SOME-ONE IN A MOVIE.
JUST WHERE DID I WIND UP...?
UHH...
HMM.
OH, I SEE. SO IN YOUR COUNTRY...
NAMES ARE IN A DIFFERENT ORDER.

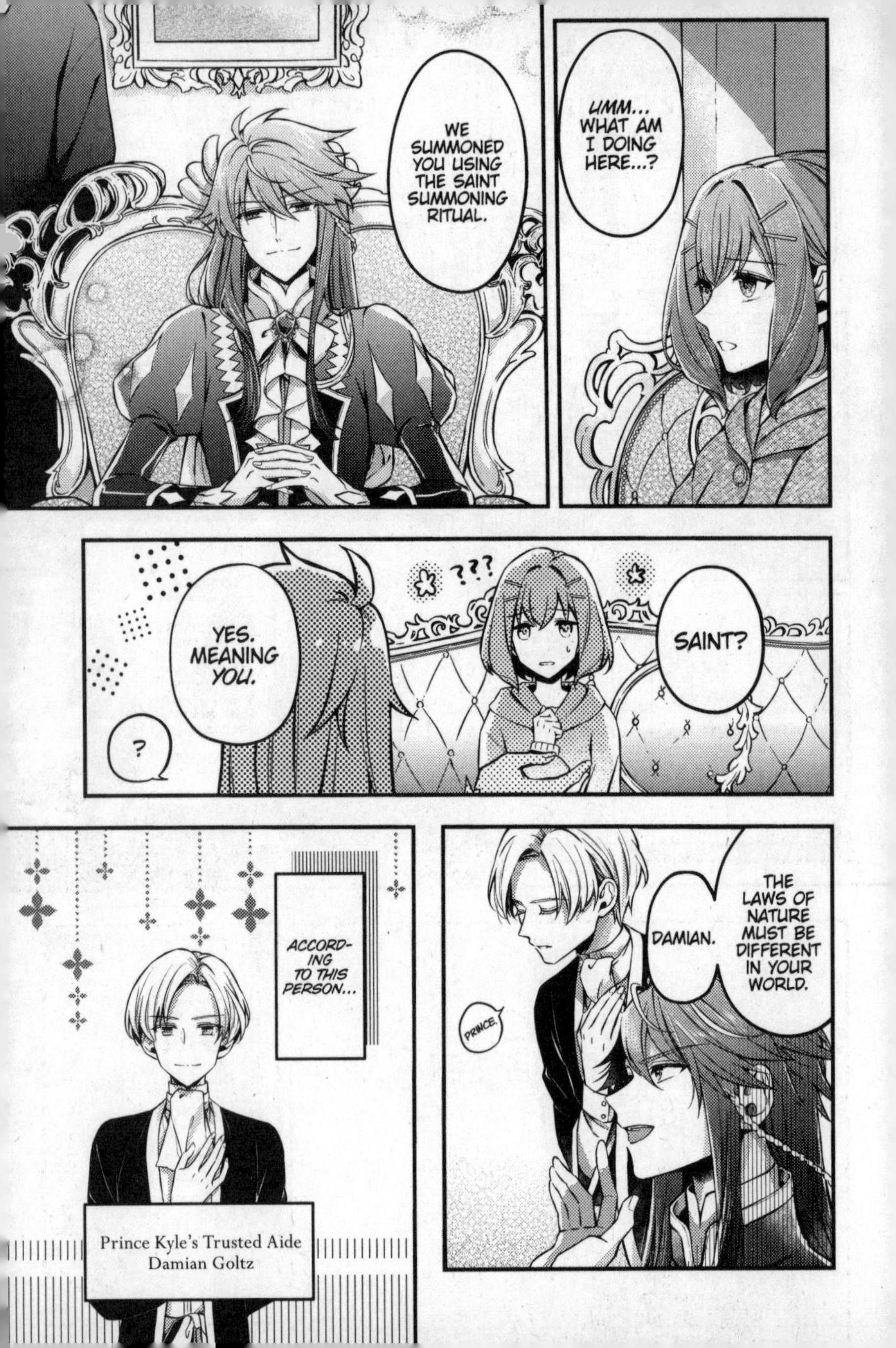
UMM... WHAT AM I DOING HERE...?
WE SUMMONED YOU USING THE SAINT SUMMONING RITUAL.
SAINT?
???
YES. MEANING YOU.
?
THE LAWS OF NATURE MUST BE DIFFERENT IN YOUR WORLD.
DAMIAN.
PRINCE.
ACCORDING TO THIS PERSON...
Prince Kyle's Trusted Aide
Damian Goltz

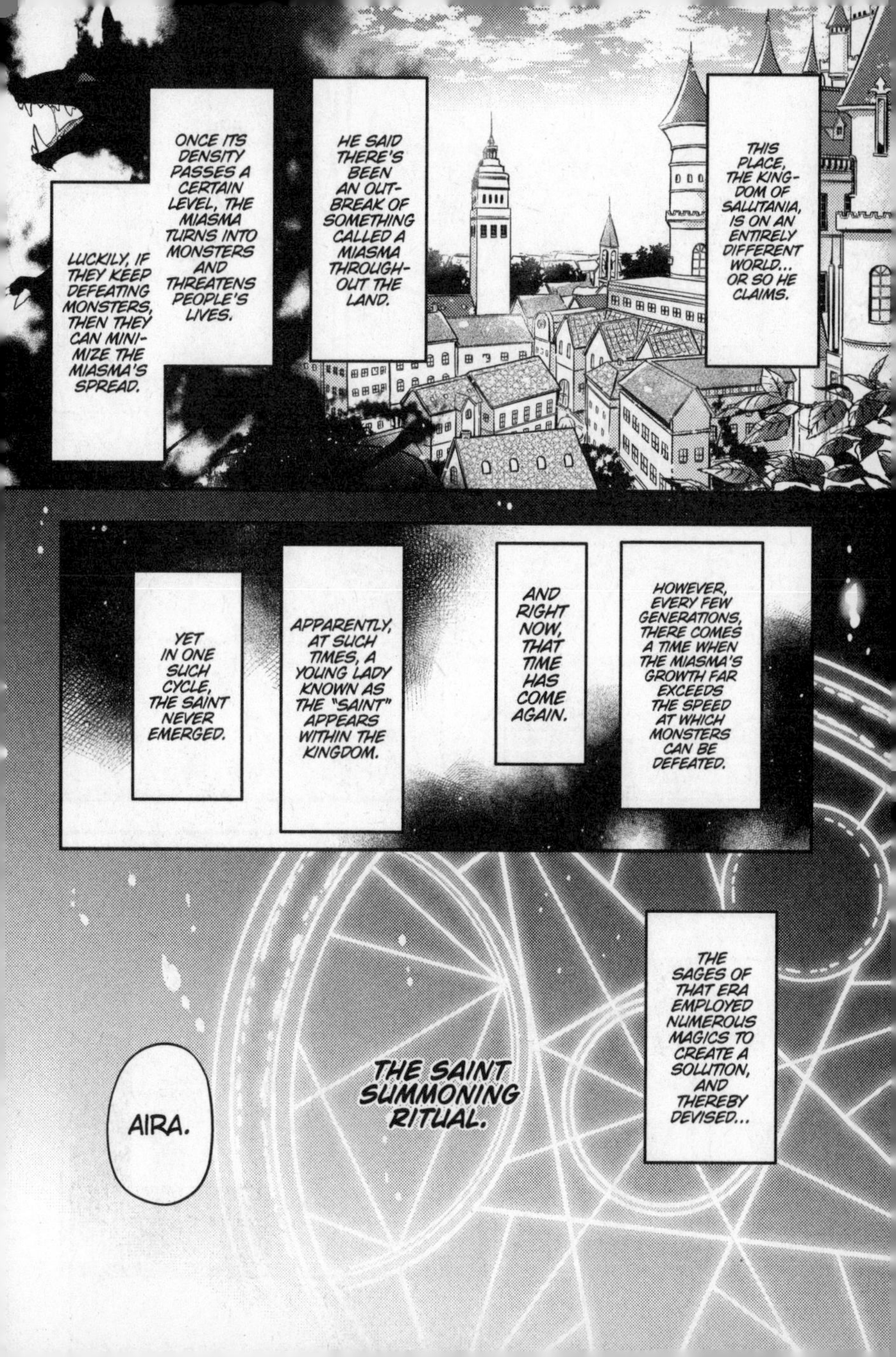
THIS PLACE, THE KINGDOM OF SALUTANIA, IS ON AN ENTIRELY DIFFERENT WORLD... OR SO HE CLAIMS.
HE SAID THERE'S BEEN AN OUTBREAK OF SOMETHING CALLED A MIASMA THROUGHOUT THE LAND.
ONCE ITS DENSITY PASSES A CERTAIN LEVEL, THE MIASMA TURNS INTO MONSTERS AND THREATENS PEOPLE'S LIVES.
LUCKILY, IF THEY KEEP DEFEATING MONSTERS, THEN THEY CAN MINIMIZE THE MIASMA'S SPREAD.
HOWEVER, EVERY FEW GENERATIONS, THERE COMES A TIME WHEN THE MIASMA'S GROWTH FAR EXCEEDS THE SPEED AT WHICH MONSTERS CAN BE DEFEATED.
AND RIGHT NOW, THAT TIME HAS COME AGAIN.
APPARENTLY, AT SUCH TIMES, A YOUNG LADY KNOWN AS THE "SAINT" APPEARS WITHIN THE KINGDOM.
YET IN ONE SUCH CYCLE, THE SAINT NEVER EMERGED.
THE SAGES OF THAT ERA EMPLOYED NUMEROUS MAGICS TO CREATE A SOLUTION, AND THEREBY DEVISED...
THE SAINT SUMMONING RITUAL.
AIRA.

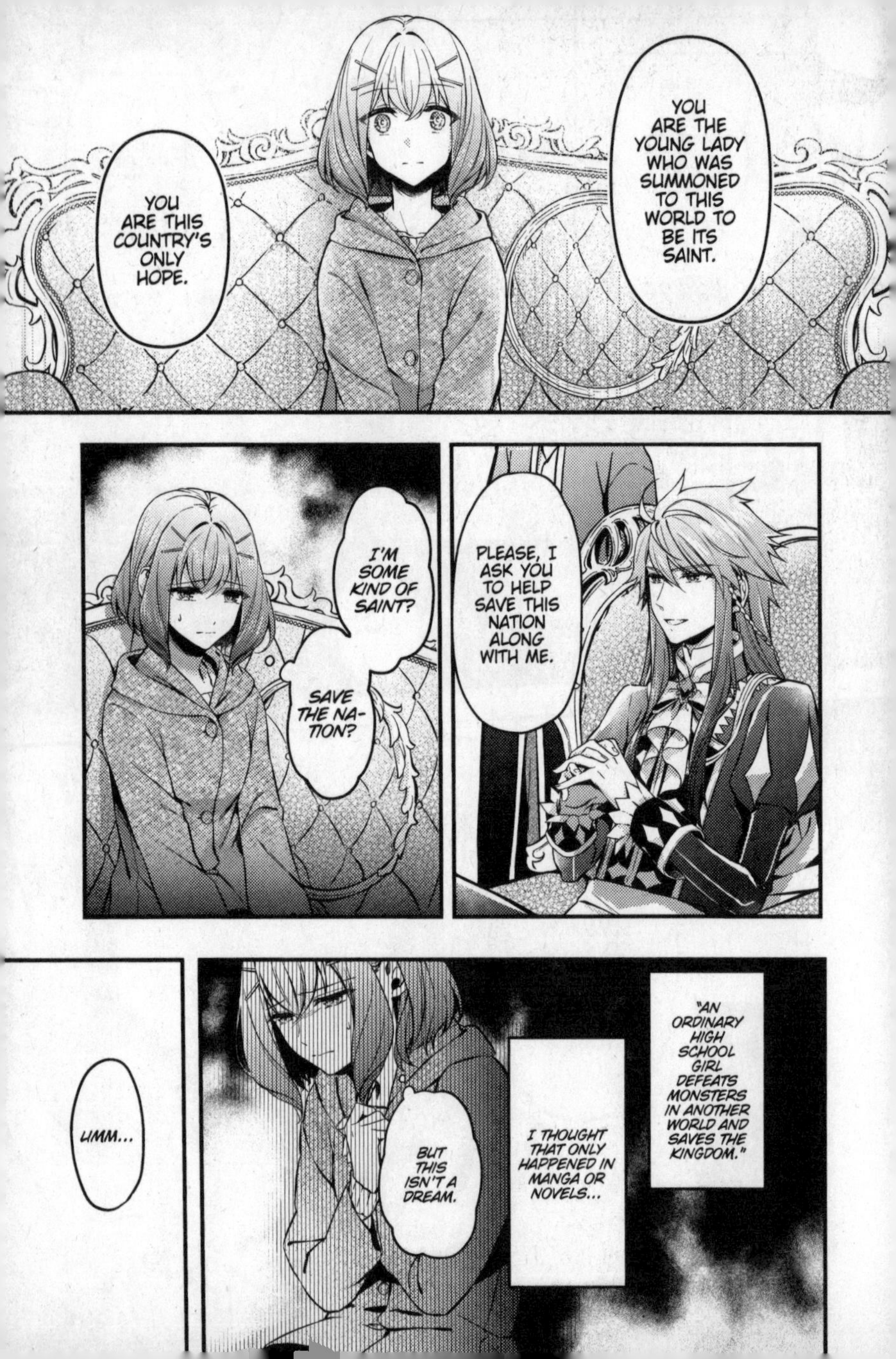
YOU ARE THE YOUNG LADY WHO WAS SUMMONED TO THIS WORLD TO BE ITS SAINT.
YOU ARE THIS COUNTRY'S ONLY HOPE.
PLEASE, I ASK YOU TO HELP SAVE THIS NATION ALONG WITH ME.
I'M SOME KIND OF SAINT?
SAVE THE NA-TION?
"AN ORDINARY HIGH SCHOOL GIRL DEFEATS MONSTERS IN ANOTHER WORLD AND SAVES THE KINGDOM."
I THOUGHT THAT ONLY HAPPENED IN MANGA OR NOVELS...
BUT THIS ISN'T A DREAM.
UMM...

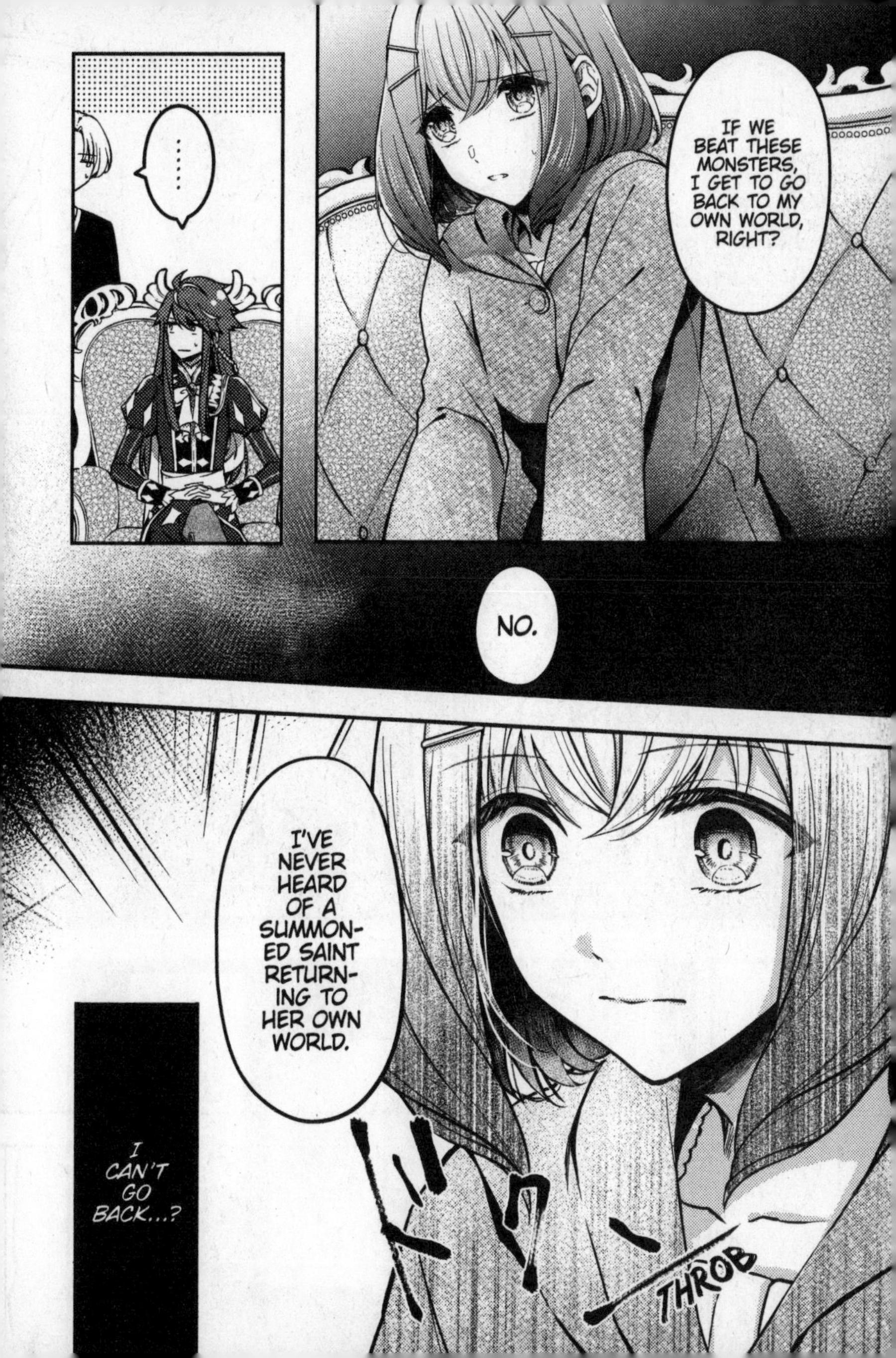
IF WE BEAT THESE MONSTERS, I GET TO GO BACK TO MY OWN WORLD, RIGHT?
......
NO.
I'VE NEVER HEARD OF A SUMMON-ED SAINT RETURN-ING TO HER OWN WORLD.
I CAN'T GO BACK...?
THROB

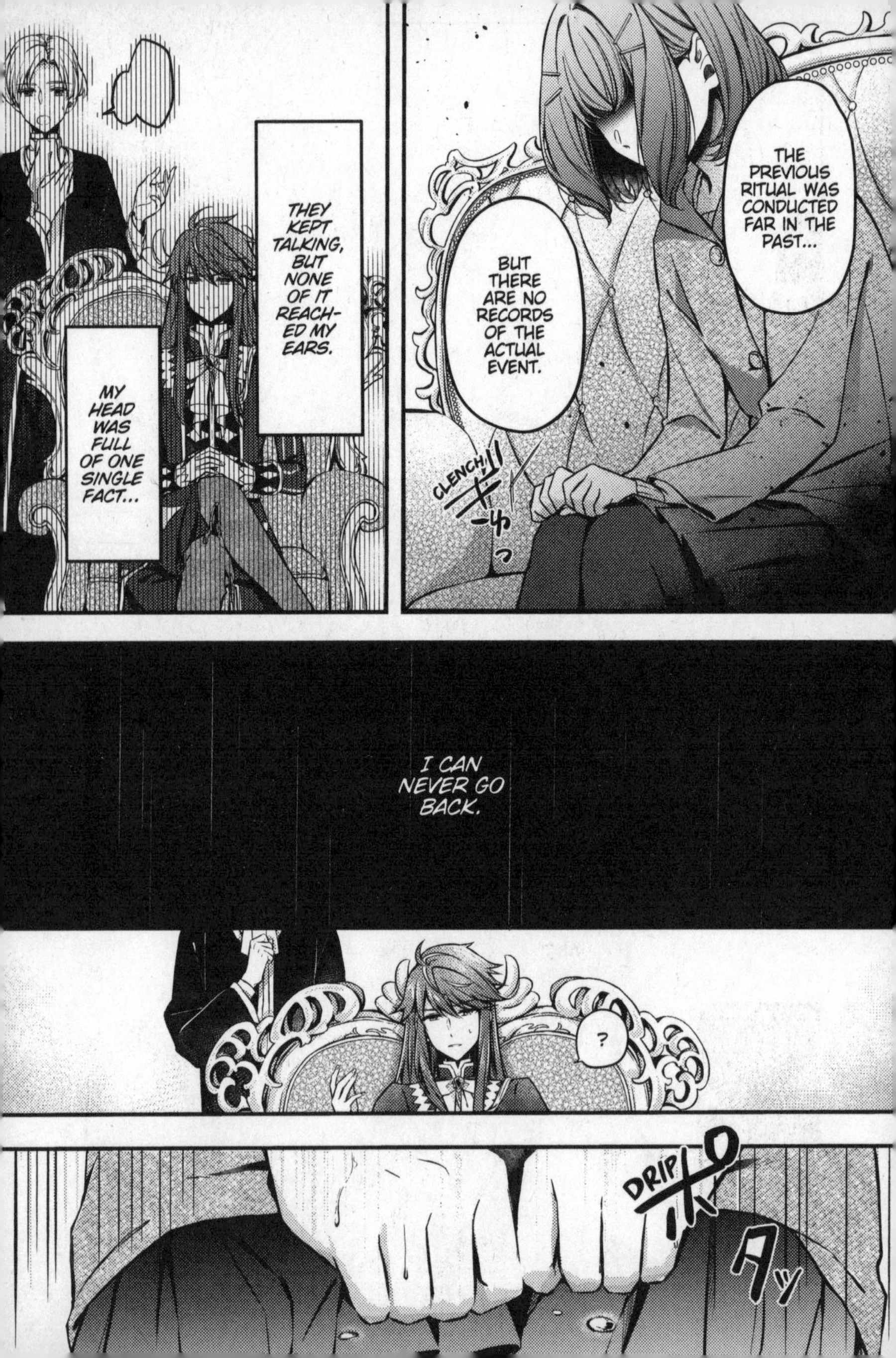

THE PREVIOUS RITUAL WAS CONDUCTED FAR IN THE PAST...
BUT THERE ARE NO RECORDS OF THE ACTUAL EVENT.
CLENCH
THEY KEPT TALKING, BUT NONE OF IT REACHED MY EARS.
MY HEAD WAS FULL OF ONE SINGLE FACT...
I CAN NEVER GO BACK.
?
DRIP

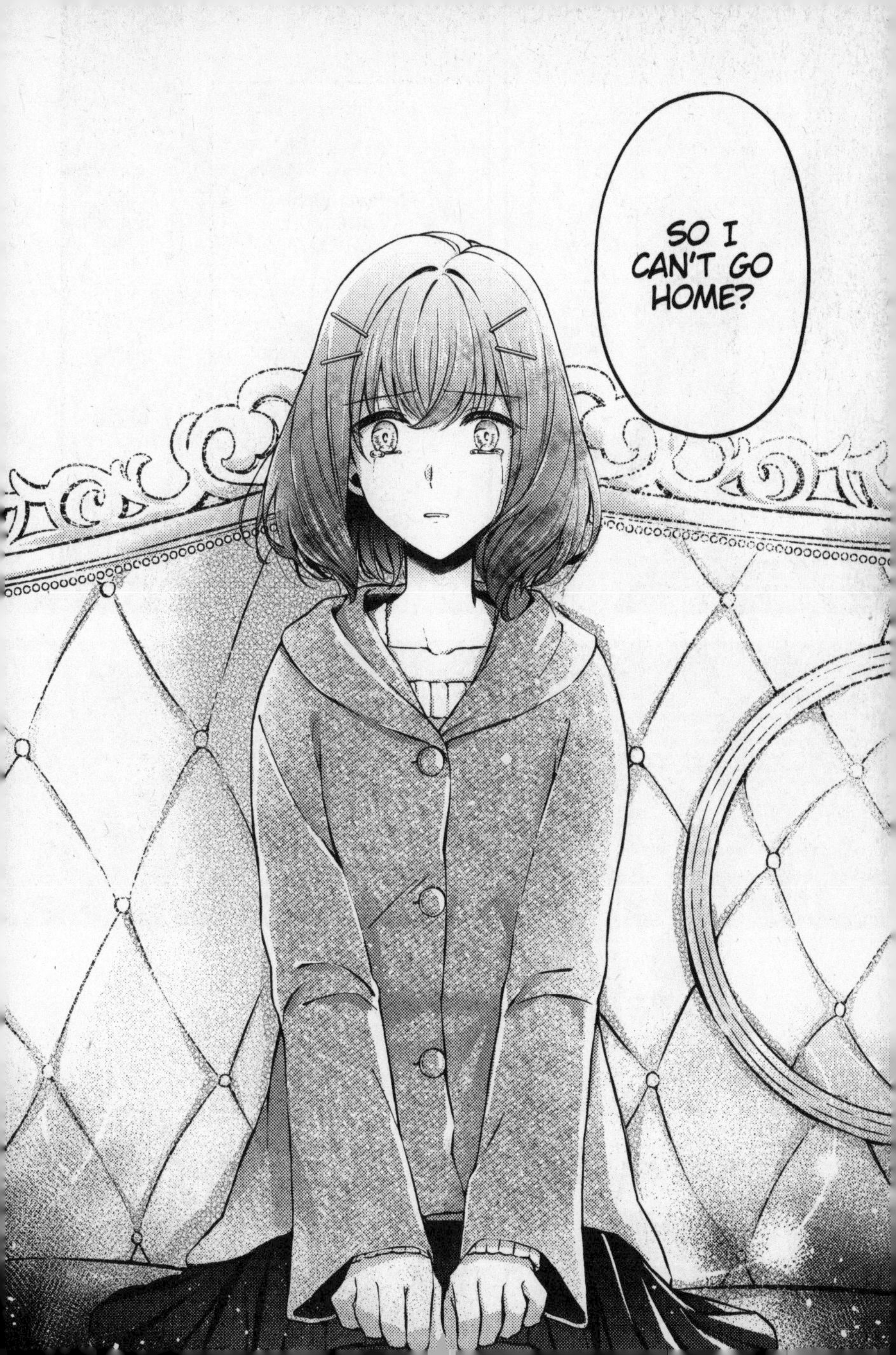
SO I CAN'T GO HOME?

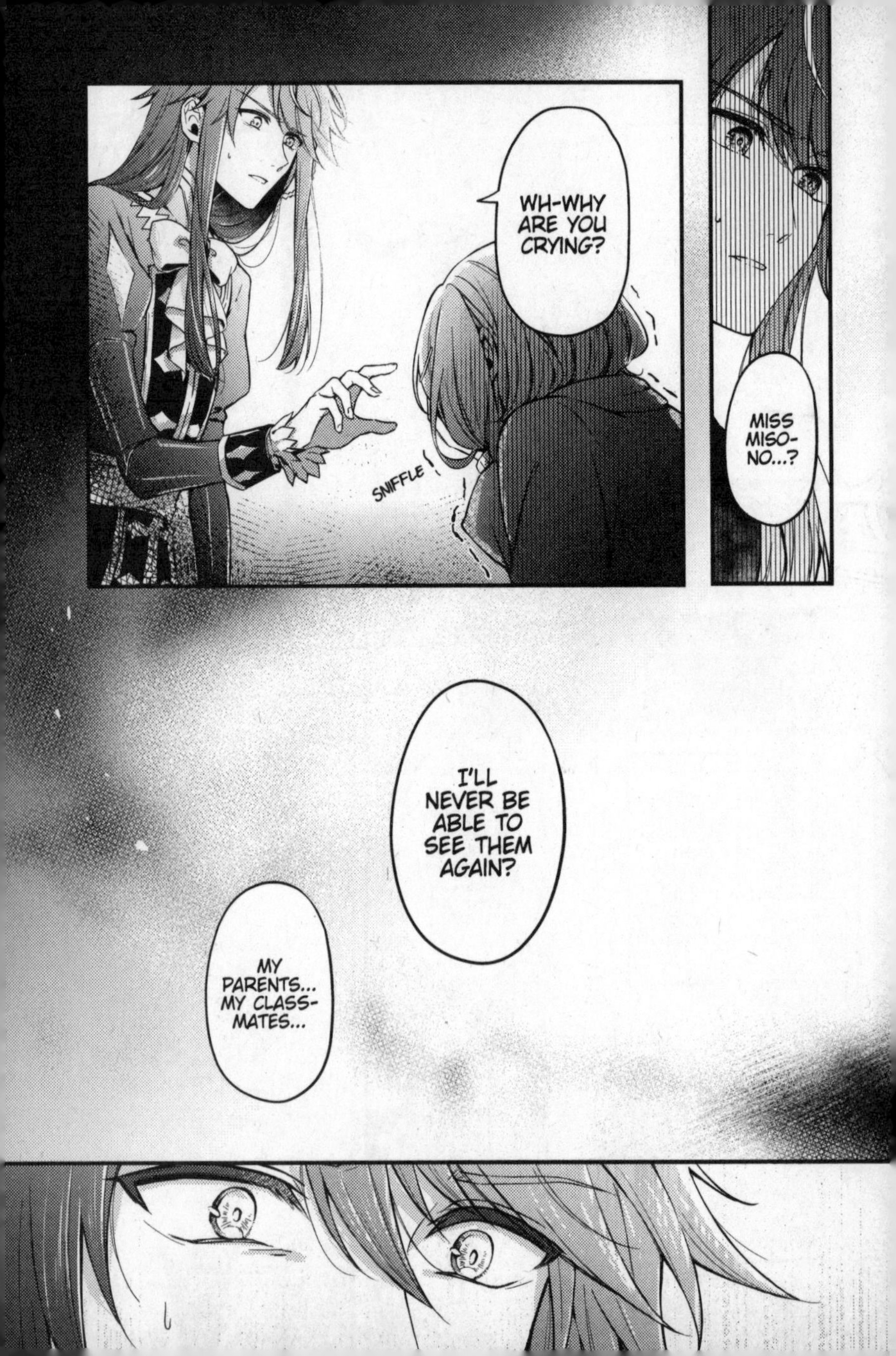
MISS MISO-NO...?
WH-WHY ARE YOU CRYING?
SNIFFLE
I'LL NEVER BE ABLE TO SEE THEM AGAIN?
MY PARENTS... MY CLASS-MATES...

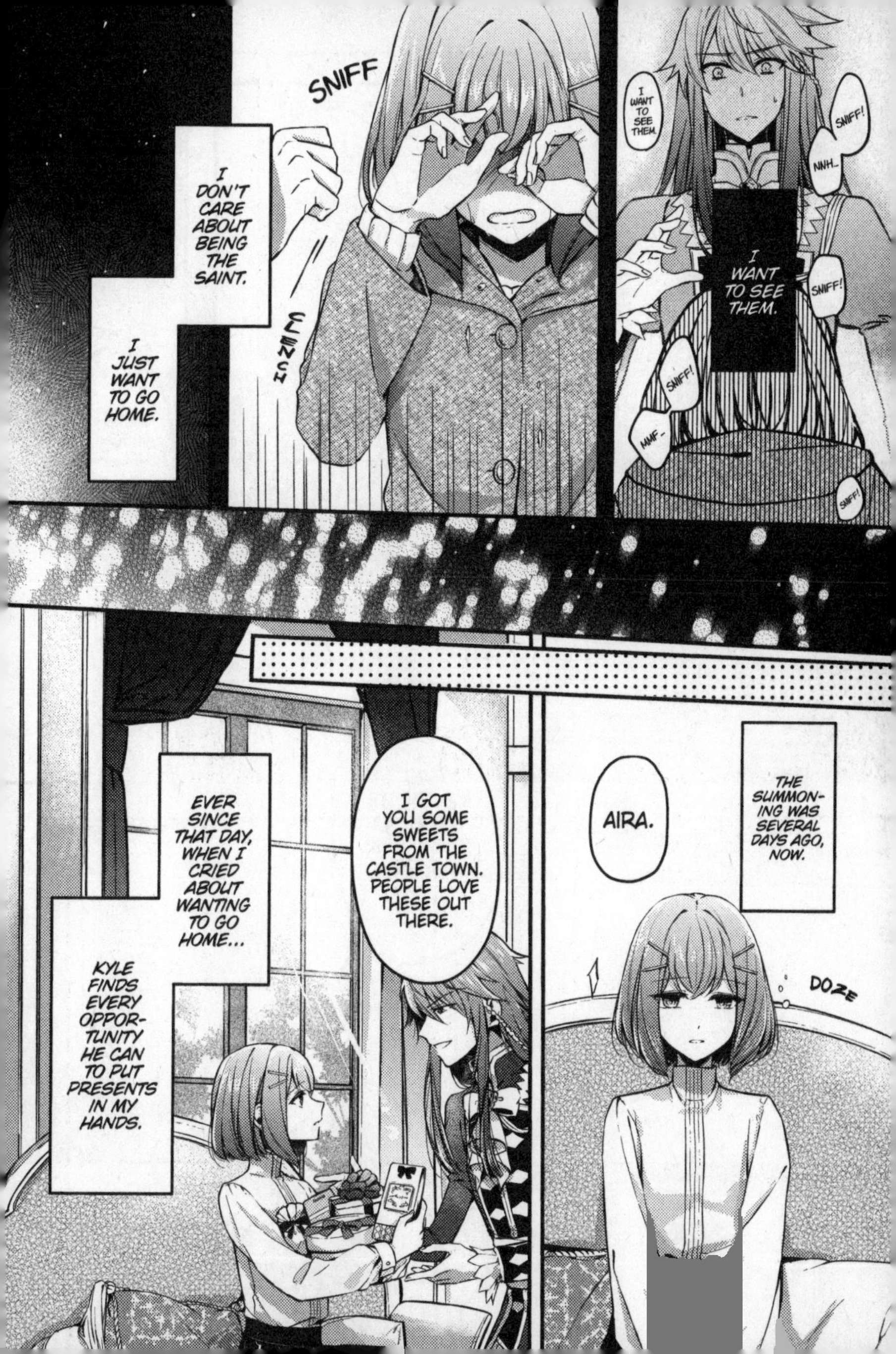
I WANT TO SEE THEM.
SNIFF!
NNH...
I WANT TO SEE THEM.
SNIFF!
SNIFF!
MMF...
SNIFF!
SNIFF
I DON'T CARE ABOUT BEING THE SAINT.
CLENCH
I JUST WANT TO GO HOME.
THE SUMMONING WAS SEVERAL DAYS AGO, NOW.
AIRA.
DOZE
EVER SINCE THAT DAY, WHEN I CRIED ABOUT WANTING TO GO HOME...
I GOT YOU SOME SWEETS FROM THE CASTLE TOWN. PEOPLE LOVE THESE OUT THERE.
KYLE FINDS EVERY OPPORTUNITY HE CAN TO PUT PRESENTS IN MY HANDS.

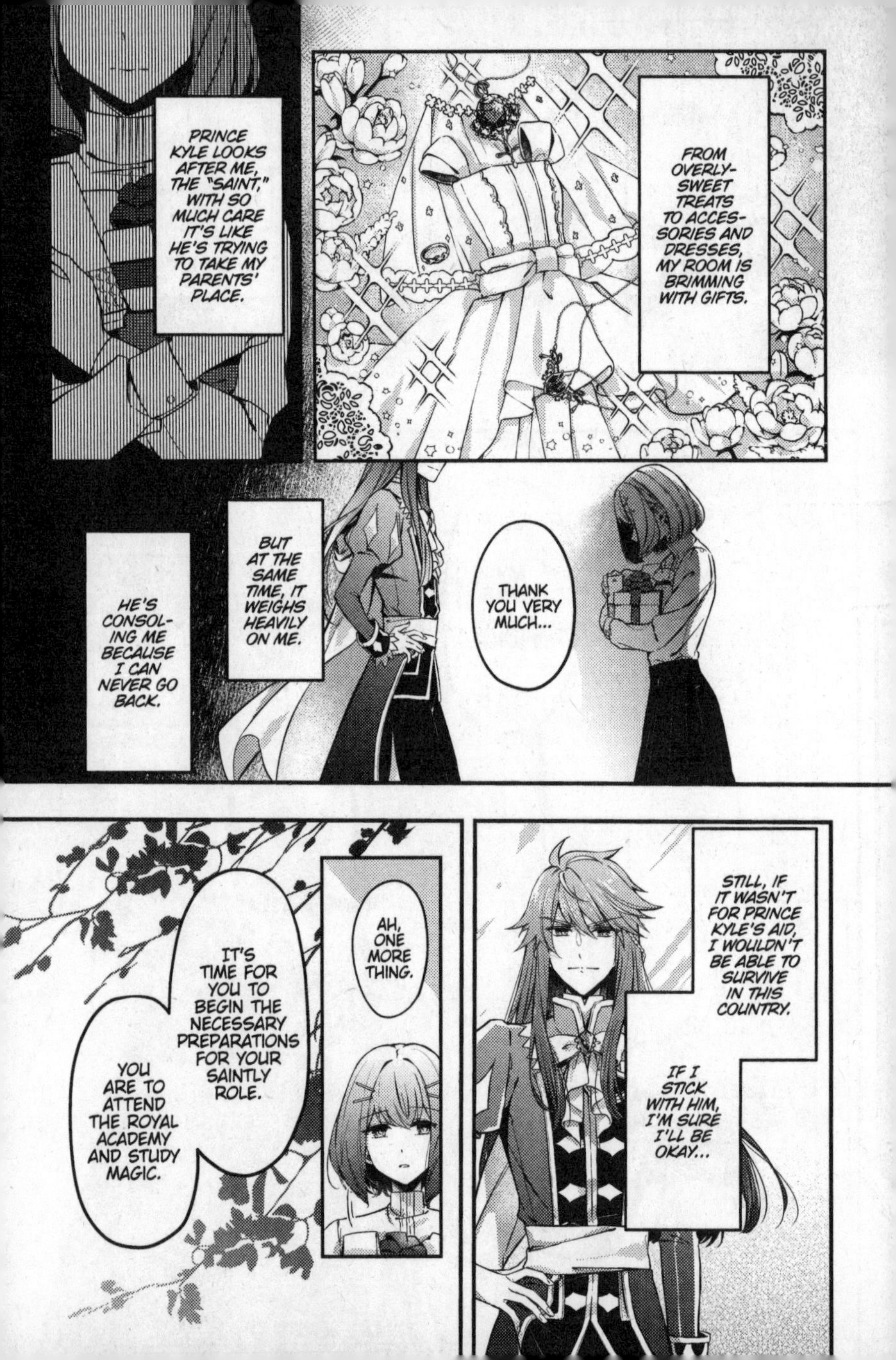
FROM OVERLY-SWEET TREATS TO ACCES-SORIES AND DRESSES, MY ROOM IS BRIMMING WITH GIFTS.
PRINCE KYLE LOOKS AFTER ME, THE "SAINT," WITH SO MUCH CARE IT'S LIKE HE'S TRYING TO TAKE MY PARENTS' PLACE.
THANK YOU VERY MUCH...
BUT AT THE SAME TIME, IT WEIGHS HEAVILY ON ME.
HE'S CONSOL-ING ME BECAUSE I CAN NEVER GO BACK.
STILL, IF IT WASN'T FOR PRINCE KYLE'S AID, I WOULDN'T BE ABLE TO SURVIVE IN THIS COUNTRY.
IF I STICK WITH HIM, I'M SURE I'LL BE OKAY...
AH, ONE MORE THING.
IT'S TIME FOR YOU TO BEGIN THE NECESSARY PREPARATIONS FOR YOUR SAINTLY ROLE.
YOU ARE TO ATTEND THE ROYAL ACADEMY AND STUDY MAGIC.

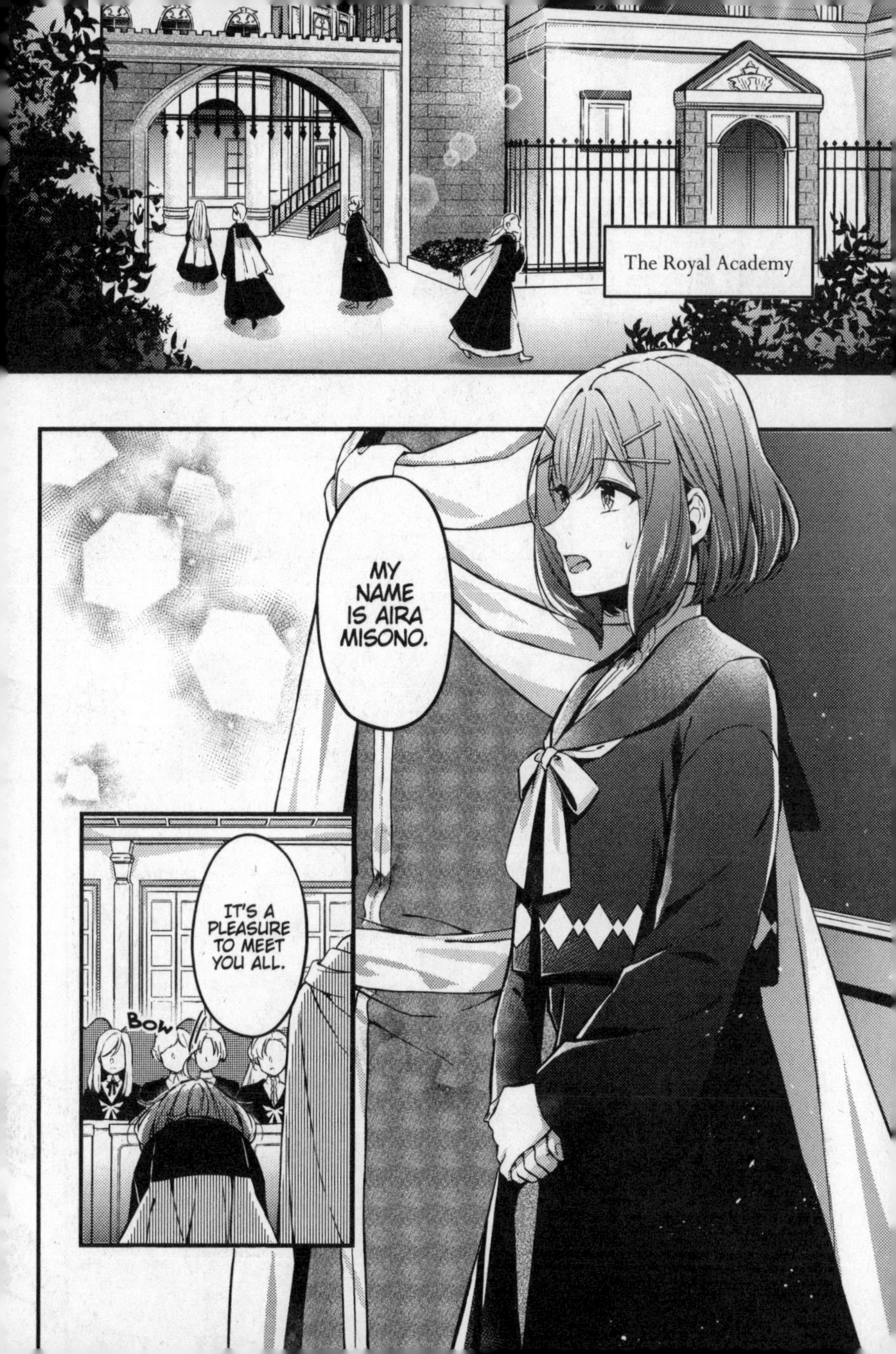
The Royal Academy
MY NAME IS AIRA MISONO.
IT'S A PLEASURE TO MEET YOU ALL.
BOW

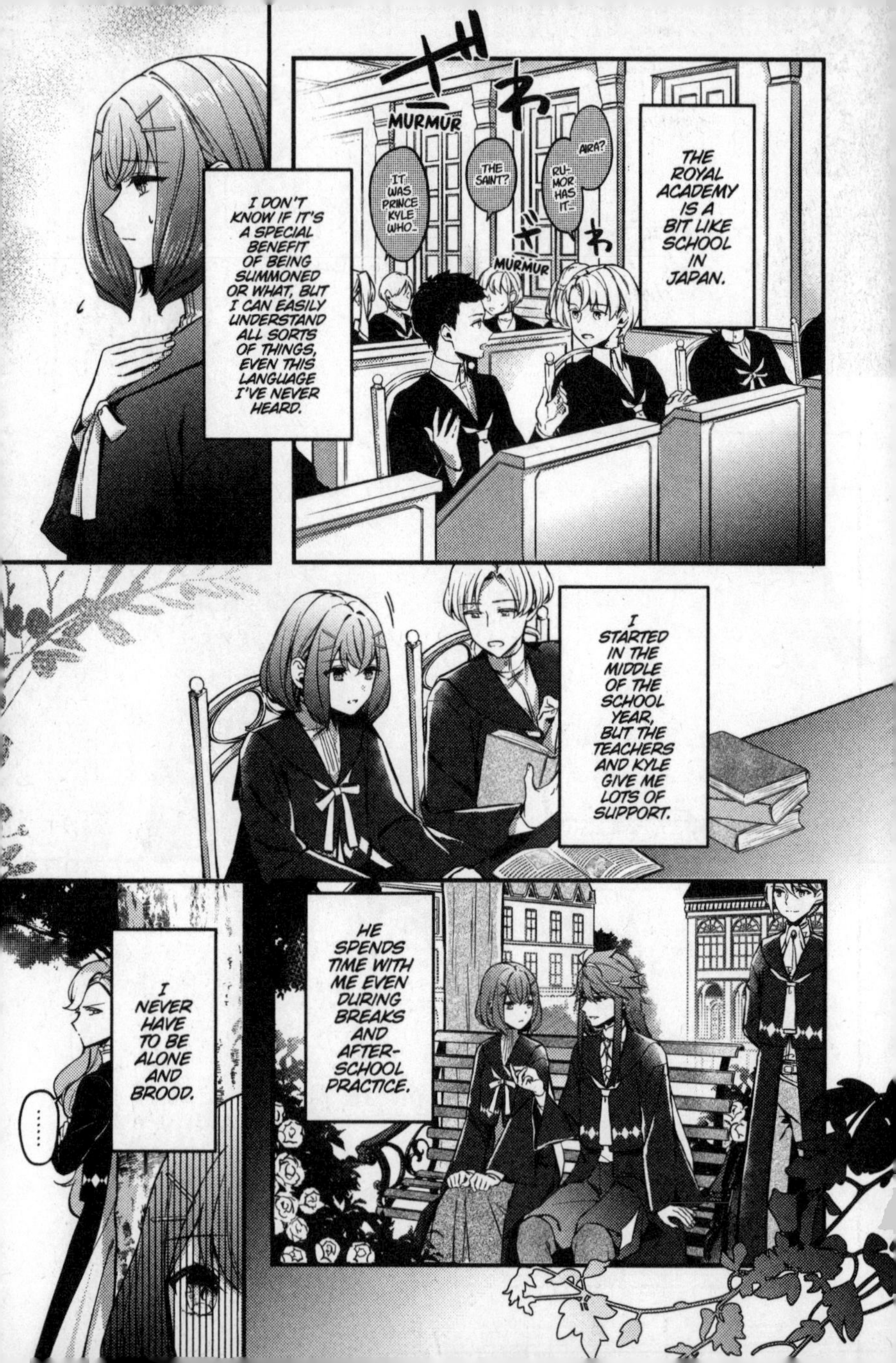

THE ROYAL ACADEMY IS A BIT LIKE SCHOOL IN JAPAN.
ザワ
MURMUR
AIRA?
RU-MOR HAS IT...
THE SAINT?
IT WAS PRINCE KYLE WHO...
ザワ
MURMUR
I DON'T KNOW IF IT'S A SPECIAL BENEFIT OF BEING SUMMONED OR WHAT, BUT I CAN EASILY UNDERSTAND ALL SORTS OF THINGS, EVEN THIS LANGUAGE I'VE NEVER HEARD.
I STARTED IN THE MIDDLE OF THE SCHOOL YEAR, BUT THE TEACHERS AND KYLE GIVE ME LOTS OF SUPPORT.
HE SPENDS TIME WITH ME EVEN DURING BREAKS AND AFTER-SCHOOL PRACTICE.
I NEVER HAVE TO BE ALONE AND BROOD.
......

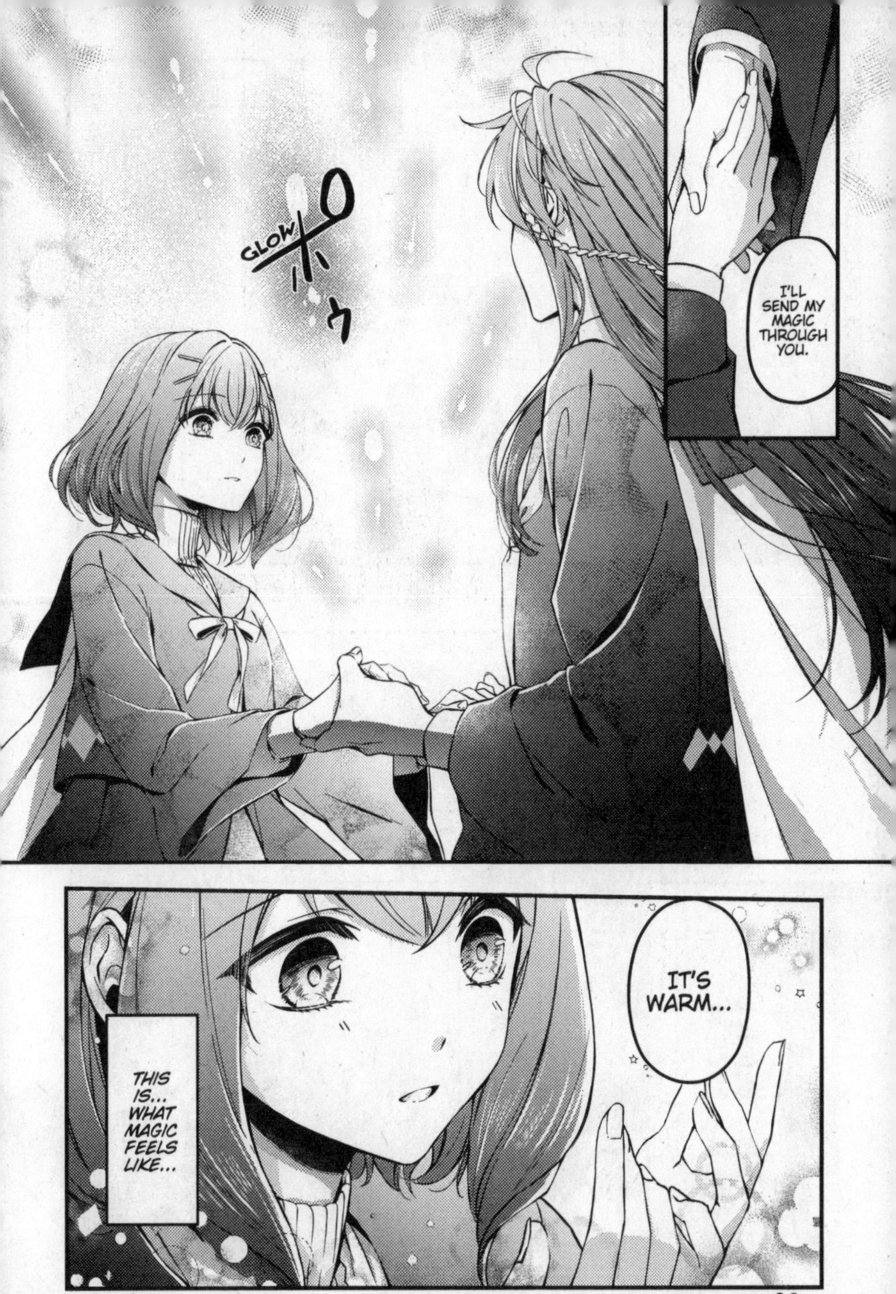
I'LL SEND MY MAGIC THROUGH YOU.
GLOW
IT'S WARM...
THIS IS... WHAT MAGIC FEELS LIKE...

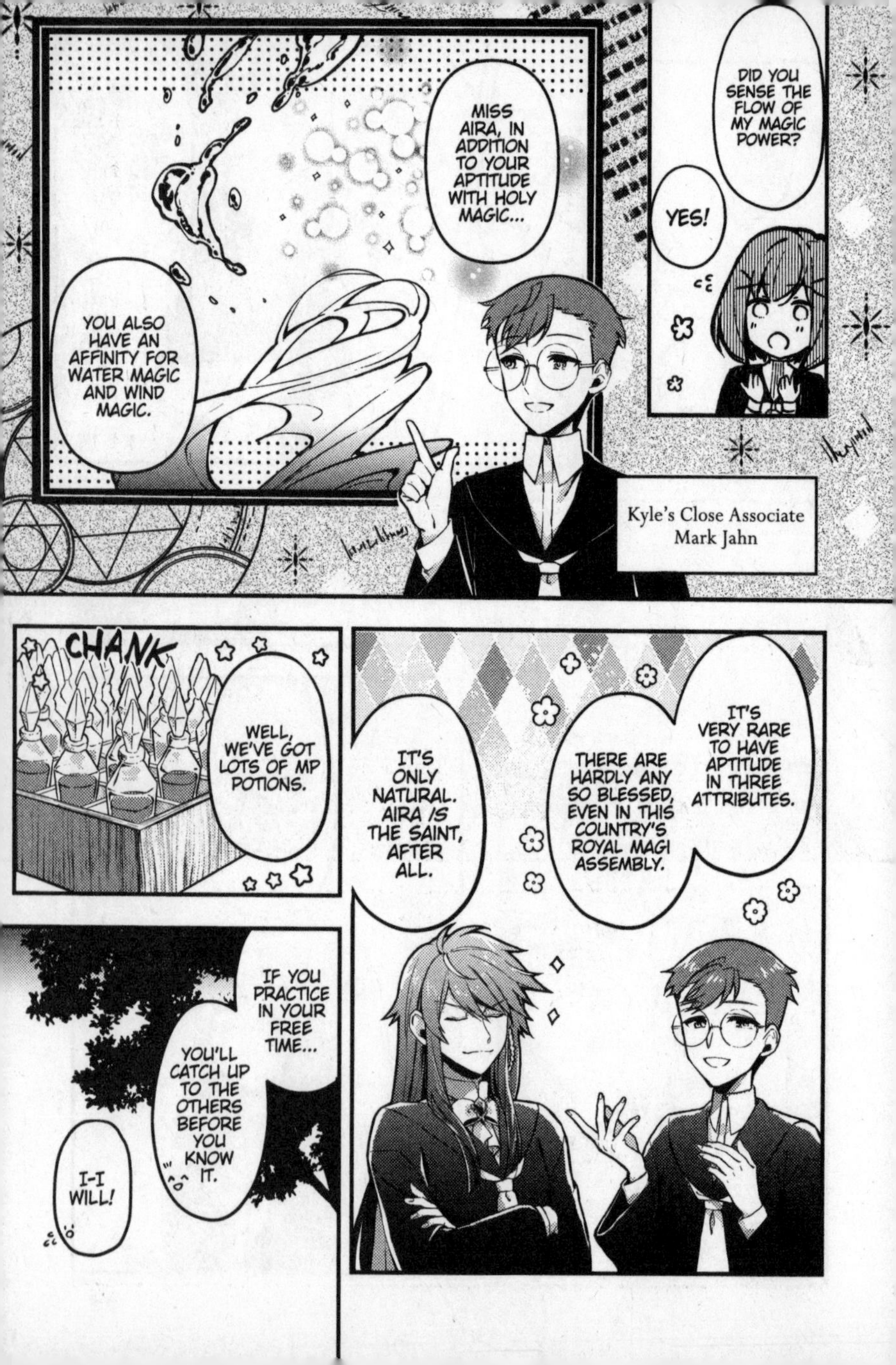
DID YOU SENSE THE FLOW OF MY MAGIC POWER?
YES!
MISS AIRA, IN ADDITION TO YOUR APTITUDE WITH HOLY MAGIC...
YOU ALSO HAVE AN AFFINITY FOR WATER MAGIC AND WIND MAGIC.
Kyle's Close Associate
Mark Jahn
IT'S VERY RARE TO HAVE APTITUDE IN THREE ATTRIBUTES.
THERE ARE HARDLY ANY SO BLESSED, EVEN IN THIS COUNTRY'S ROYAL MAGI ASSEMBLY.
IT'S ONLY NATURAL. AIRA *IS* THE SAINT, AFTER ALL.
CHANK
WELL, WE'VE GOT LOTS OF MP POTIONS.
IF YOU PRACTICE IN YOUR FREE TIME...
YOU'LL CATCH UP TO THE OTHERS BEFORE YOU KNOW IT.
I-I WILL!

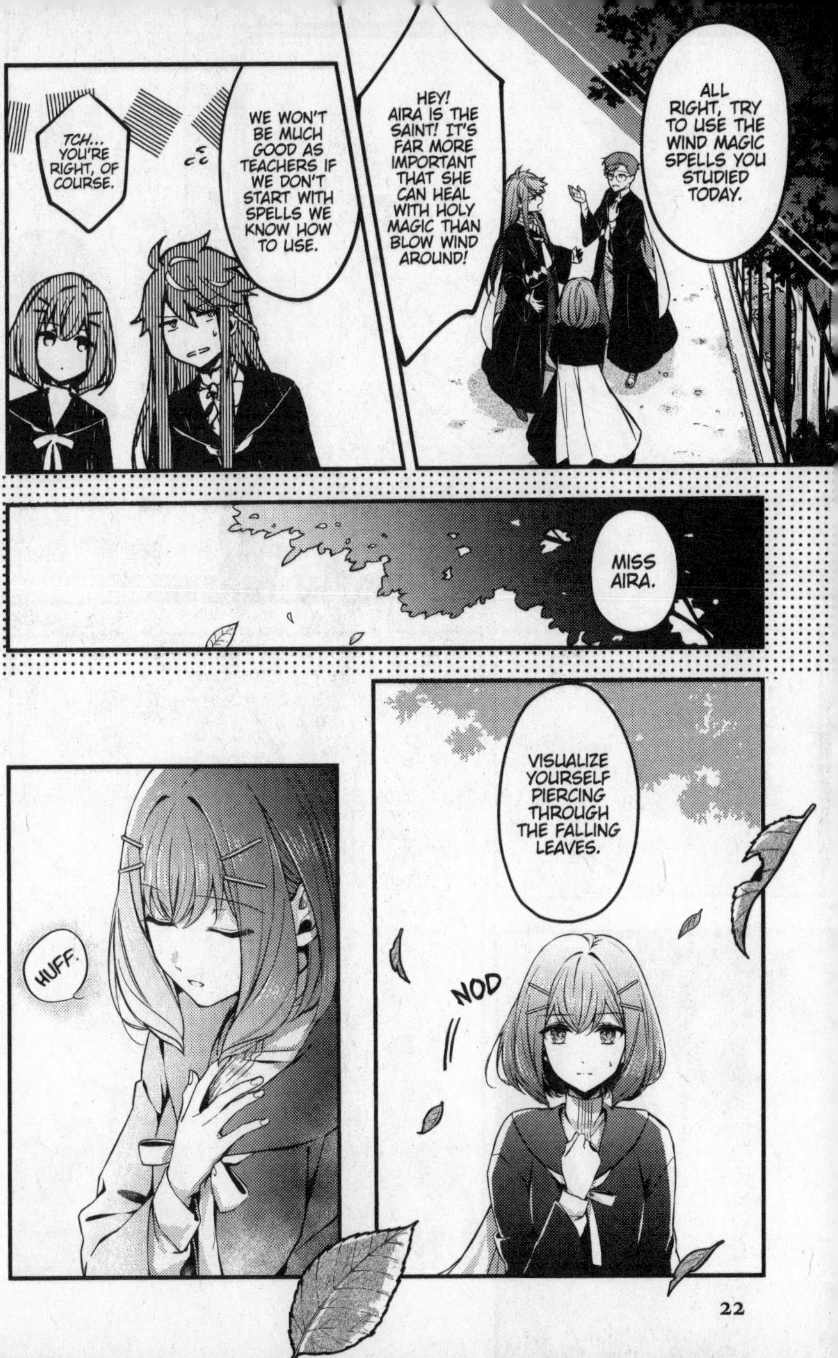
ALL RIGHT, TRY TO USE THE WIND MAGIC SPELLS YOU STUDIED TODAY.
HEY! AIRA IS THE SAINT! IT'S FAR MORE IMPORTANT THAT SHE CAN HEAL WITH HOLY MAGIC THAN BLOW WIND AROUND!
WE WON'T BE MUCH GOOD AS TEACHERS IF WE DON'T START WITH SPELLS WE KNOW HOW TO USE.
TCH... YOU'RE RIGHT, OF COURSE.
MISS AIRA.
VISUALIZE YOURSELF PIERCING THROUGH THE FALLING LEAVES.
NOD
HUFF.

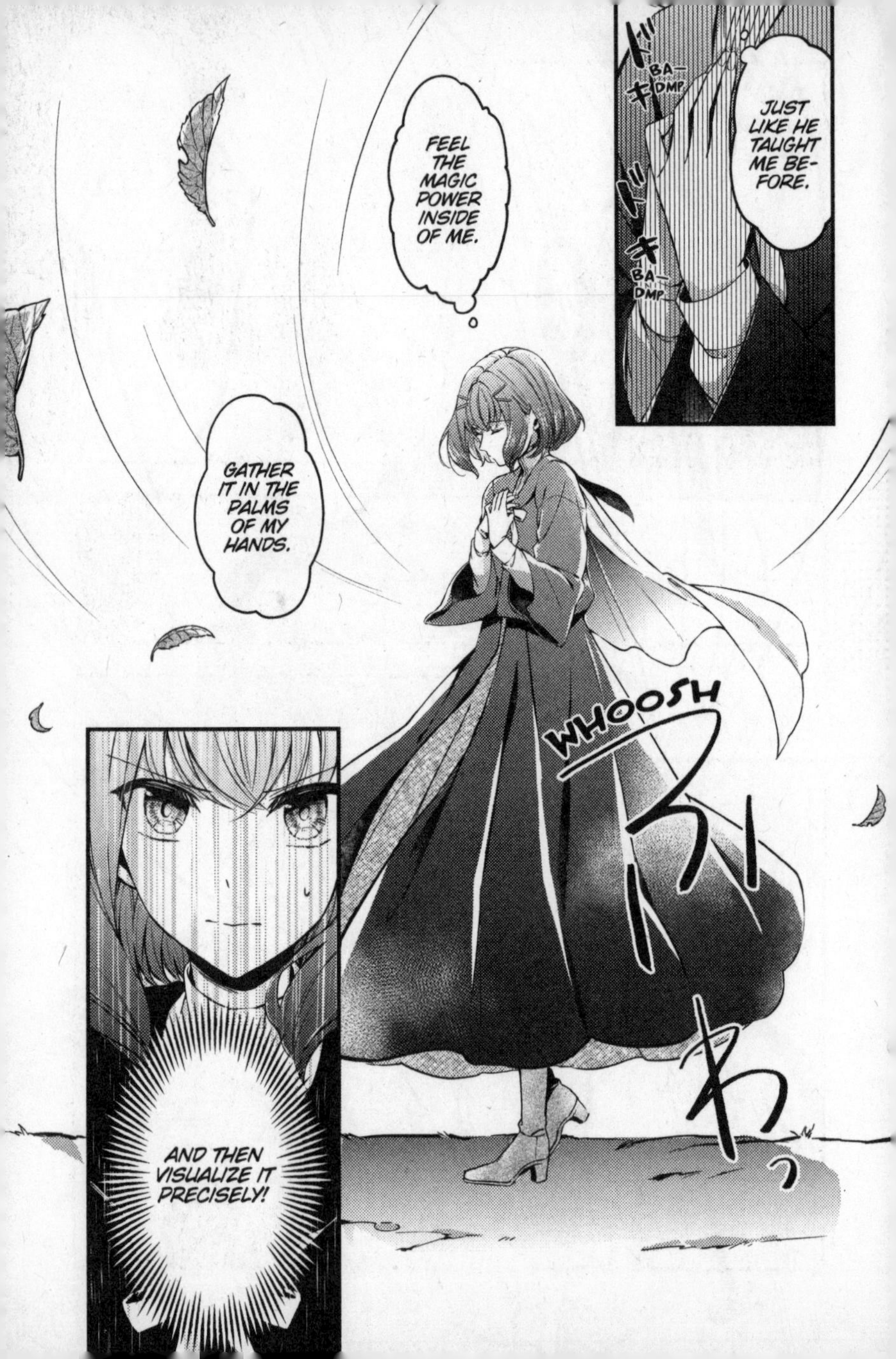
BA-DMP
JUST LIKE HE TAUGHT ME BE-FORE.
BA-DMP
FEEL THE MAGIC POWER INSIDE OF ME.
GATHER IT IN THE PALMS OF MY HANDS.
WHOOSH
AND THEN VISUALIZE IT PRECISELY!

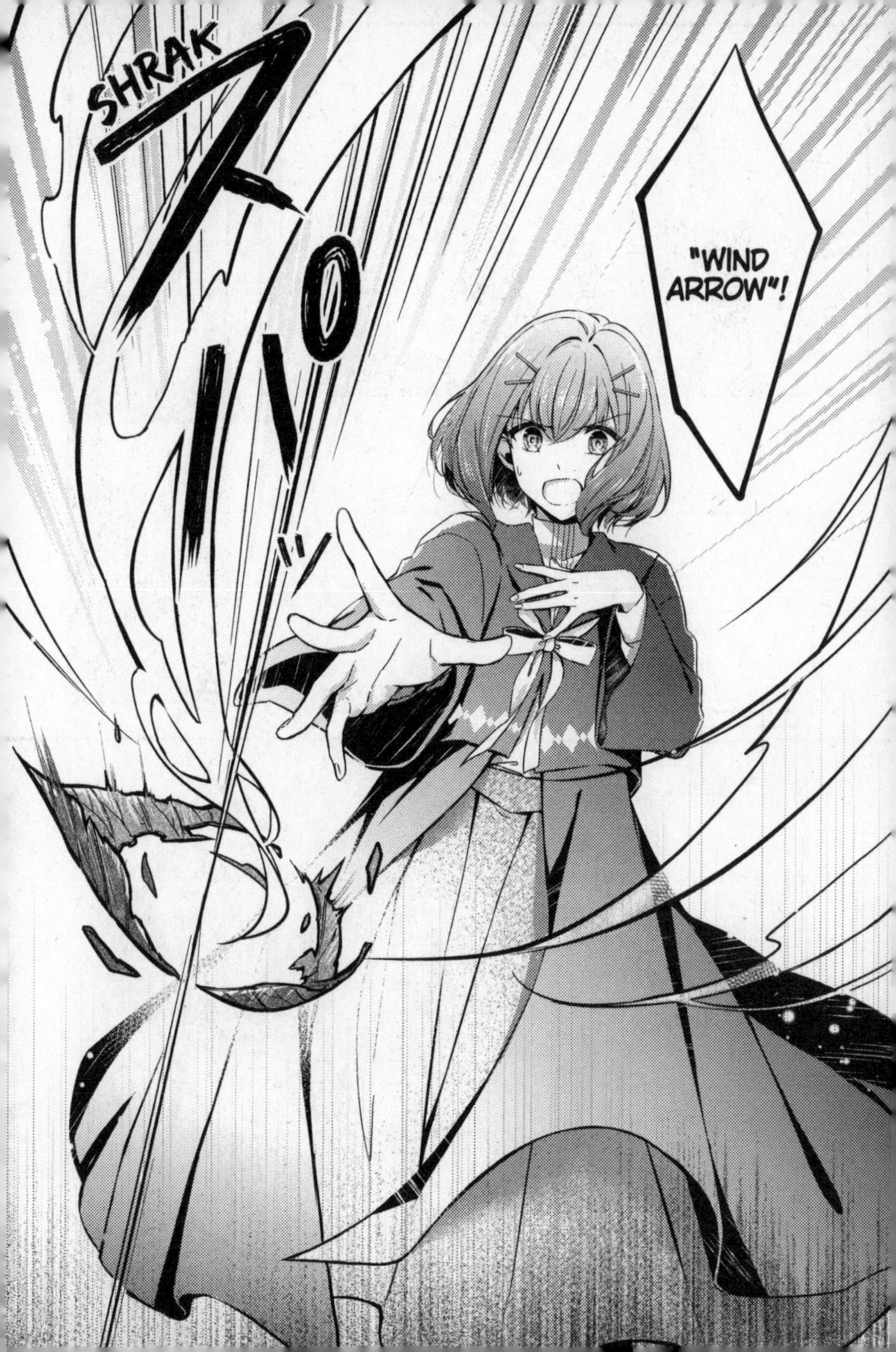
"WIND ARROW"!
SHRAK

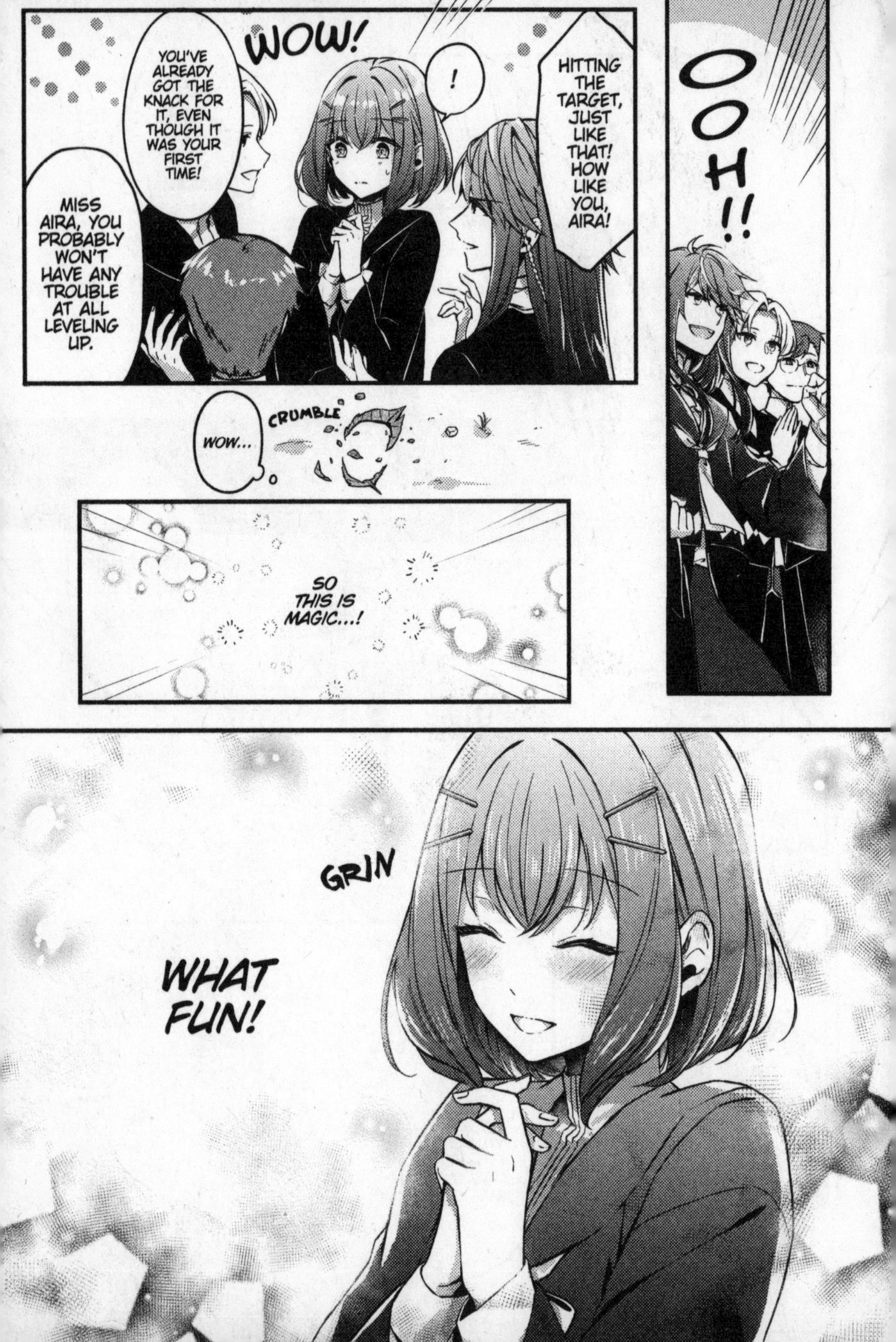
OOH!!
HITTING THE TARGET, JUST LIKE THAT! HOW LIKE YOU, AIRA!
!
WOW!
YOU'VE ALREADY GOT THE KNACK FOR IT, EVEN THOUGH IT WAS YOUR FIRST TIME!
MISS AIRA, YOU PROBABLY WON'T HAVE ANY TROUBLE AT ALL LEVELING UP.
CRUMBLE
WOW...
SO THIS IS MAGIC...!
GRIN
WHAT FUN!

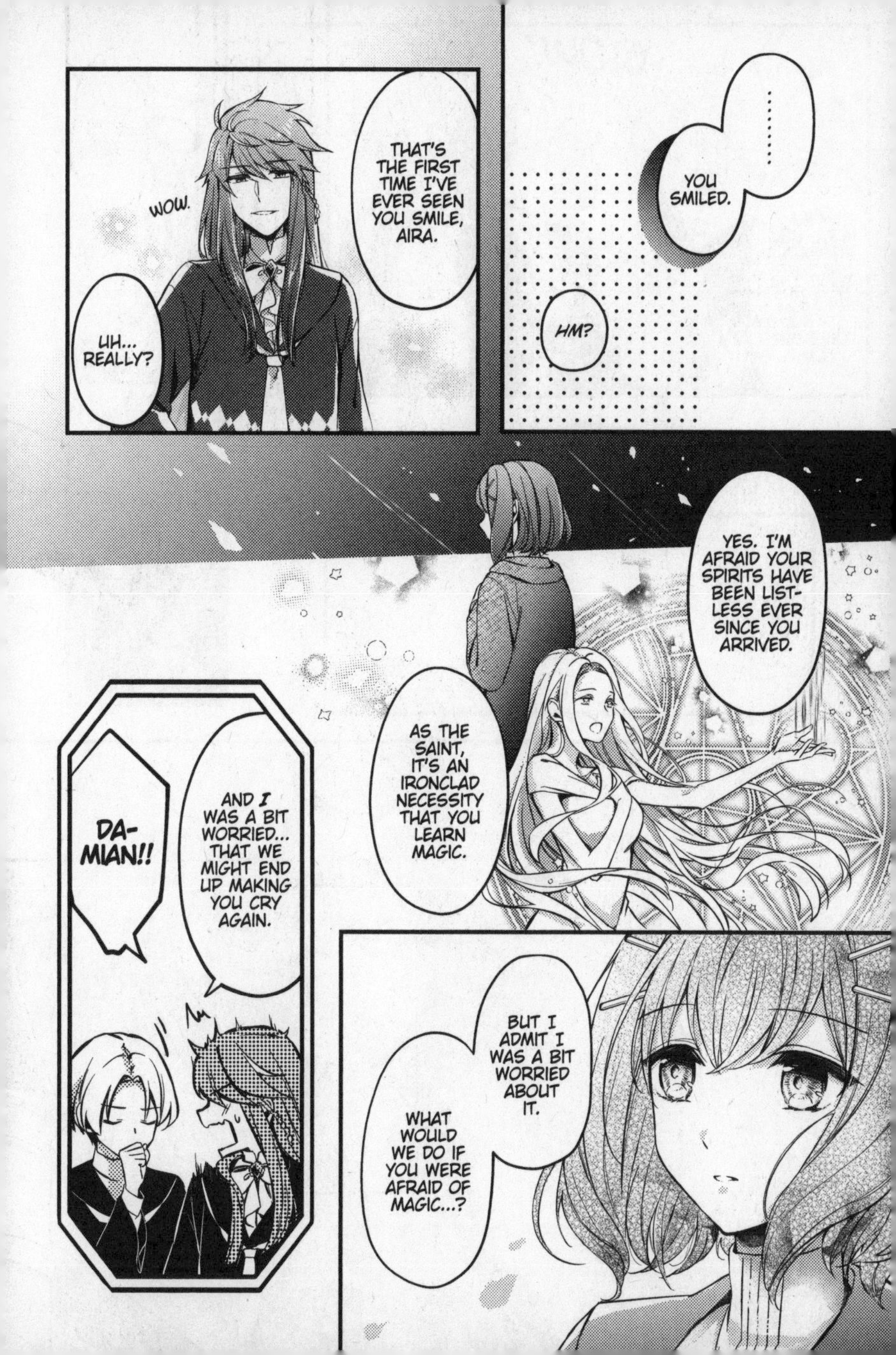
......
YOU SMILED.
HM?
THAT'S THE FIRST TIME I'VE EVER SEEN YOU SMILE, AIRA.
WOW.
UH... REALLY?
YES. I'M AFRAID YOUR SPIRITS HAVE BEEN LIST-LESS EVER SINCE YOU ARRIVED.
AS THE SAINT, IT'S AN IRONCLAD NECESSITY THAT YOU LEARN MAGIC.
BUT I ADMIT I WAS A BIT WORRIED ABOUT IT.
WHAT WOULD WE DO IF YOU WERE AFRAID OF MAGIC...?
AND I WAS A BIT WORRIED... THAT WE MIGHT END UP MAKING YOU CRY AGAIN.
DA-MIAN!!

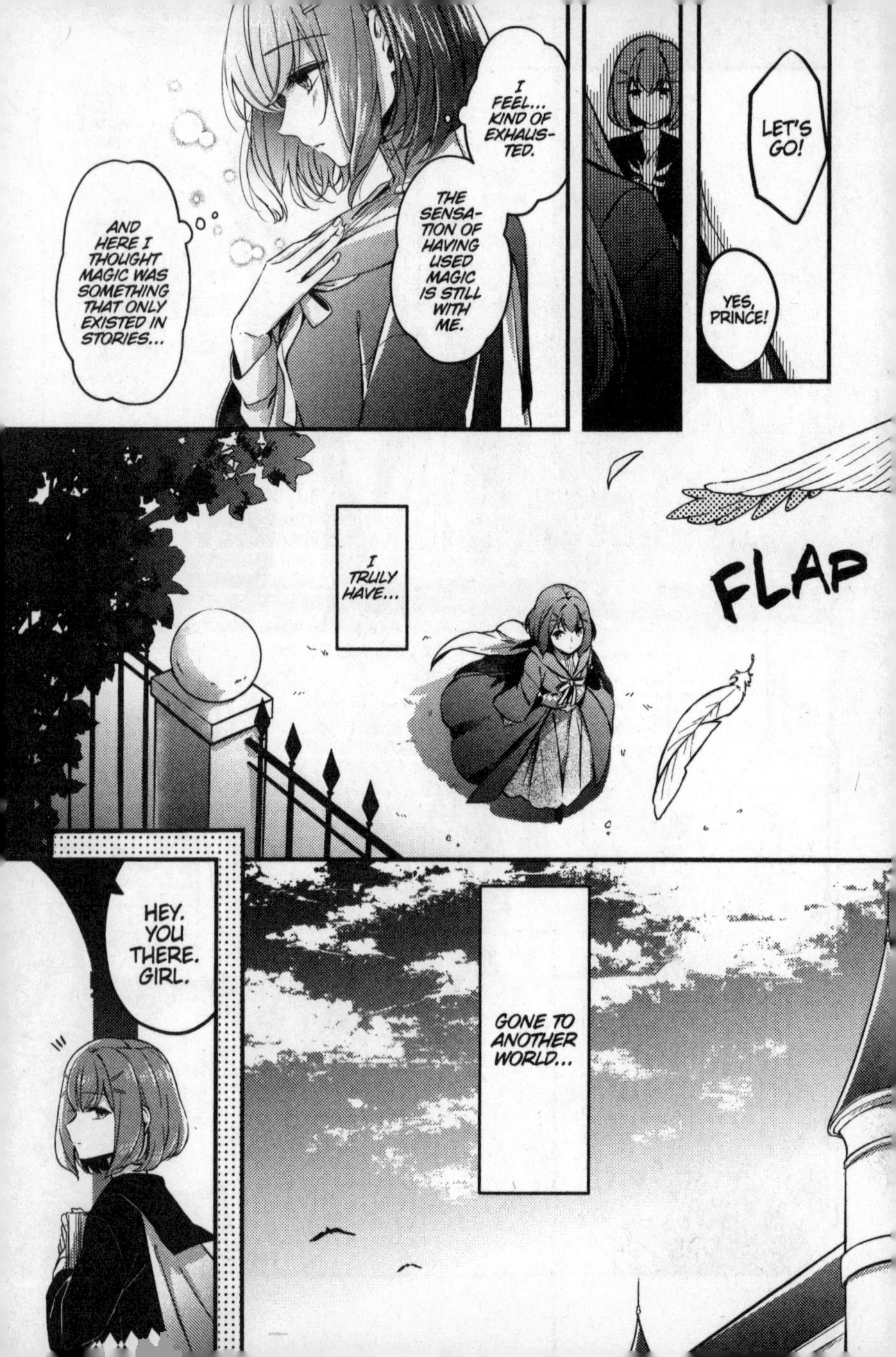
LET'S GO!
YES, PRINCE!
I FEEL... KIND OF EXHAUSTED.
THE SENSATION OF HAVING USED MAGIC IS STILL WITH ME.
AND HERE I THOUGHT MAGIC WAS SOMETHING THAT ONLY EXISTED IN STORIES...
FLAP
I TRULY HAVE...
GONE TO ANOTHER WORLD...
HEY. YOU THERE. GIRL.

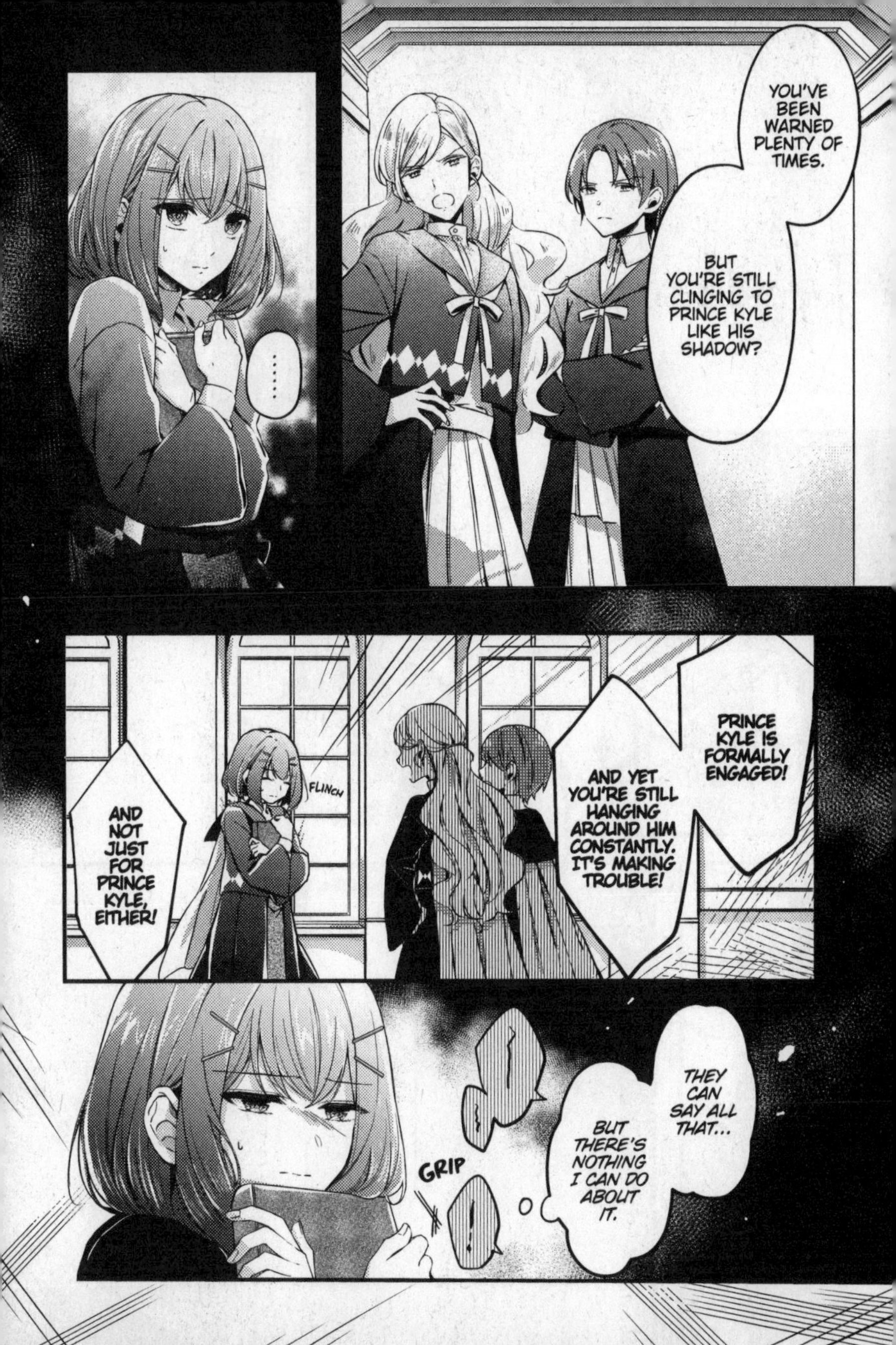
YOU'VE BEEN WARNED PLENTY OF TIMES.
BUT YOU'RE STILL CLINGING TO PRINCE KYLE LIKE HIS SHADOW?
......
PRINCE KYLE IS FORMALLY ENGAGED!
AND YET YOU'RE STILL HANGING AROUND HIM CONSTANTLY. IT'S MAKING TROUBLE!
FLINCH
AND NOT JUST FOR PRINCE KYLE, EITHER!
THEY CAN SAY ALL THAT...
BUT THERE'S NOTHING I CAN DO ABOUT IT.
!
GRIP

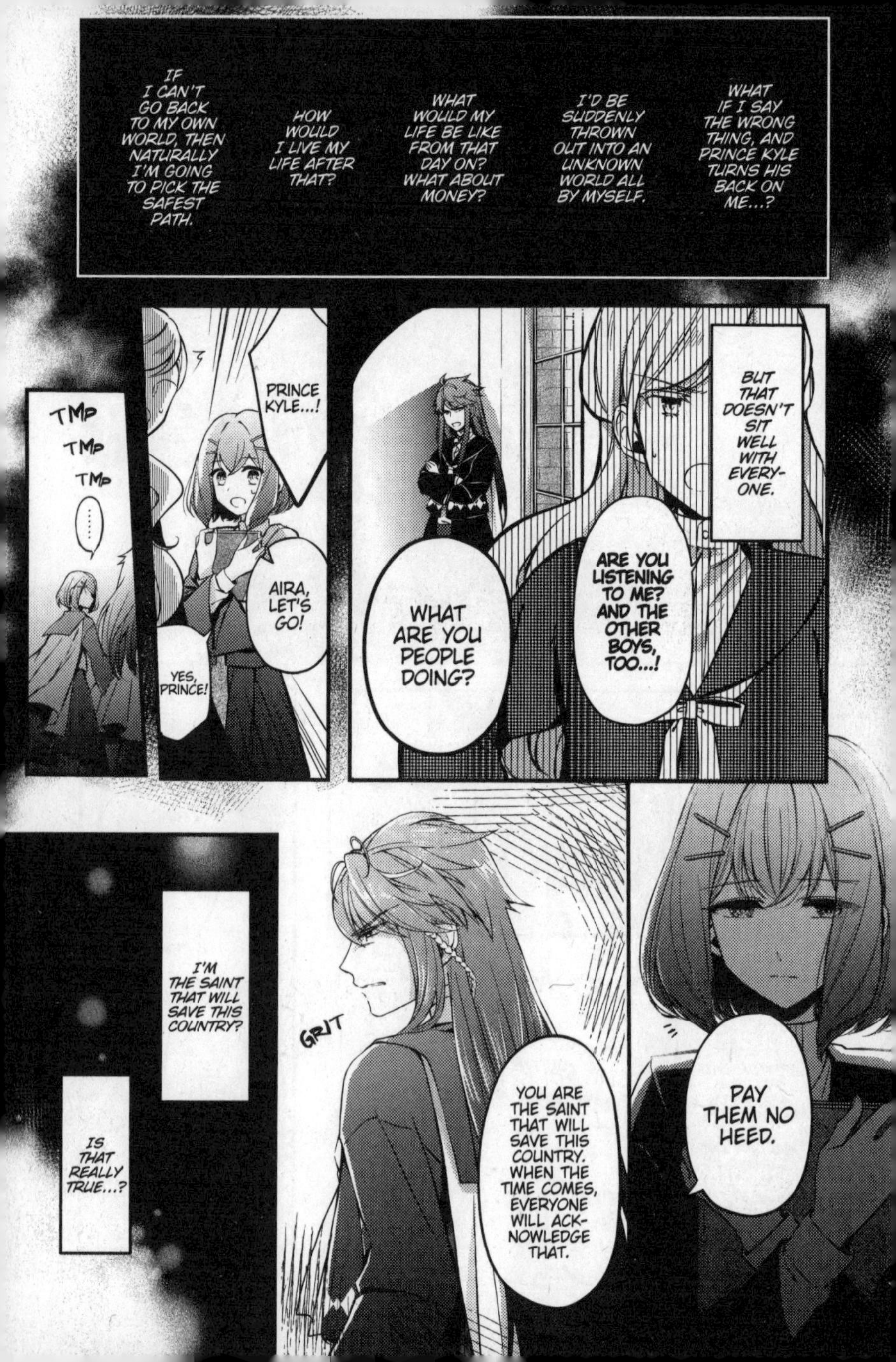
WHAT IF I SAY THE WRONG THING, AND PRINCE KYLE TURNS HIS BACK ON ME...?
I'D BE SUDDENLY THROWN OUT INTO AN UNKNOWN WORLD ALL BY MYSELF.
WHAT WOULD MY LIFE BE LIKE FROM THAT DAY ON? WHAT ABOUT MONEY?
HOW WOULD I LIVE MY LIFE AFTER THAT?
IF I CAN'T GO BACK TO MY OWN WORLD, THEN NATURALLY I'M GOING TO PICK THE SAFEST PATH.
BUT THAT DOESN'T SIT WELL WITH EVERYONE.
ARE YOU LISTENING TO ME? AND THE OTHER BOYS, TOO...!
WHAT ARE YOU PEOPLE DOING?
PRINCE KYLE...!
AIRA, LET'S GO!
YES, PRINCE!
TMP
TMP
TMP
......
PAY THEM NO HEED.
YOU ARE THE SAINT THAT WILL SAVE THIS COUNTRY. WHEN THE TIME COMES, EVERYONE WILL ACKNOWLEDGE THAT.
GRIT
I'M THE SAINT THAT WILL SAVE THIS COUNTRY?
IS THAT REALLY TRUE...?

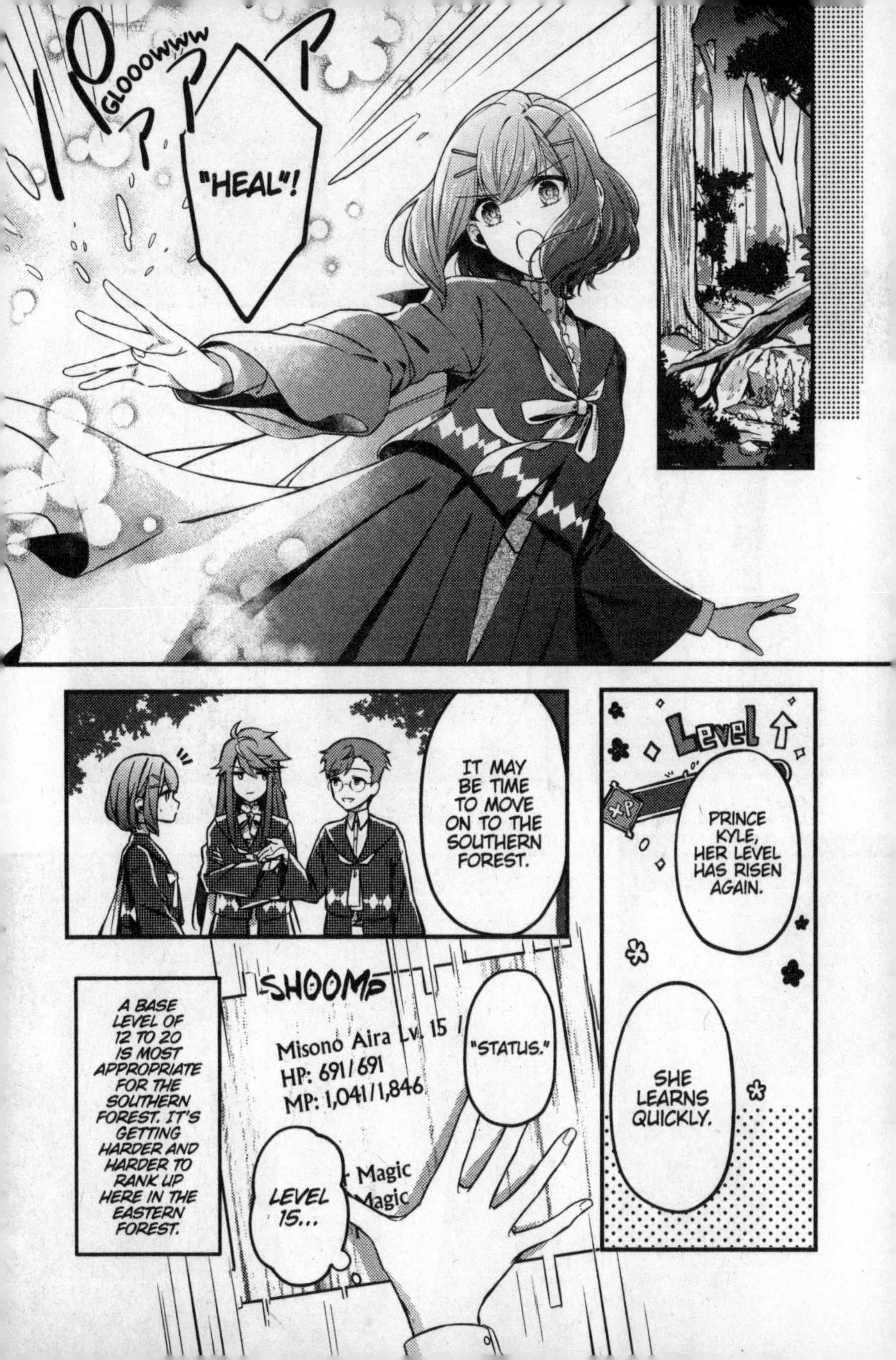
GLOOOWWW
"HEAL"!
Level
PRINCE KYLE, HER LEVEL HAS RISEN AGAIN.
SHE LEARNS QUICKLY.
IT MAY BE TIME TO MOVE ON TO THE SOUTHERN FOREST.
"STATUS."
SHOOMP
Misono Aira Lv. 15
HP: 691/691
MP: 1,041/1,846
LEVEL 15...
A BASE LEVEL OF 12 TO 20 IS MOST APPROPRIATE FOR THE SOUTHERN FOREST. IT'S GETTING HARDER AND HARDER TO RANK UP HERE IN THE EASTERN FOREST.

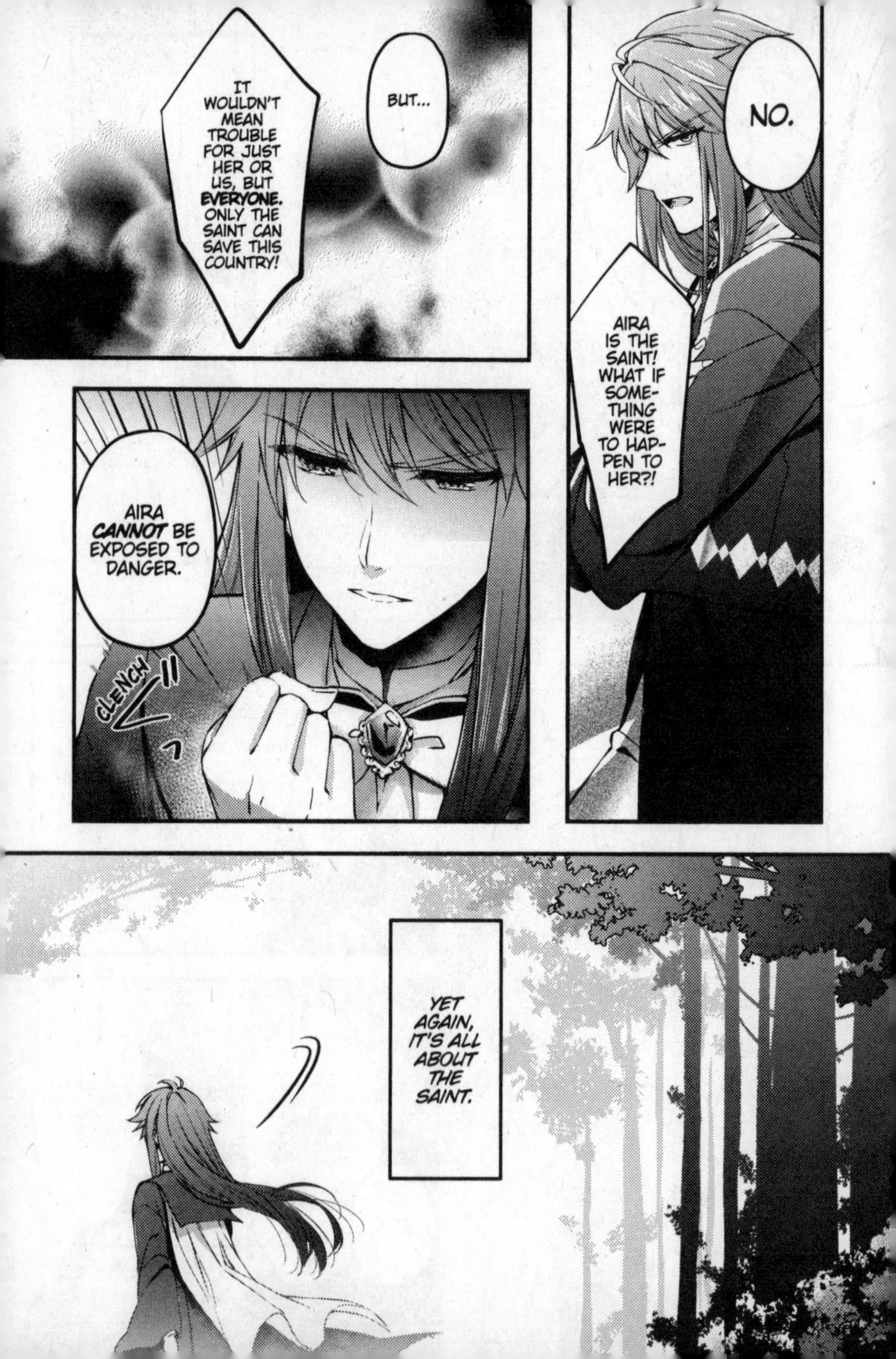
NO.
AIRA IS THE SAINT! WHAT IF SOMETHING WERE TO HAPPEN TO HER?!
BUT...
IT WOULDN'T MEAN TROUBLE FOR JUST HER OR US, BUT EVERYONE. ONLY THE SAINT CAN SAVE THIS COUNTRY!
AIRA CANNOT BE EXPOSED TO DANGER.
CLENCH
YET AGAIN, IT'S ALL ABOUT THE SAINT.

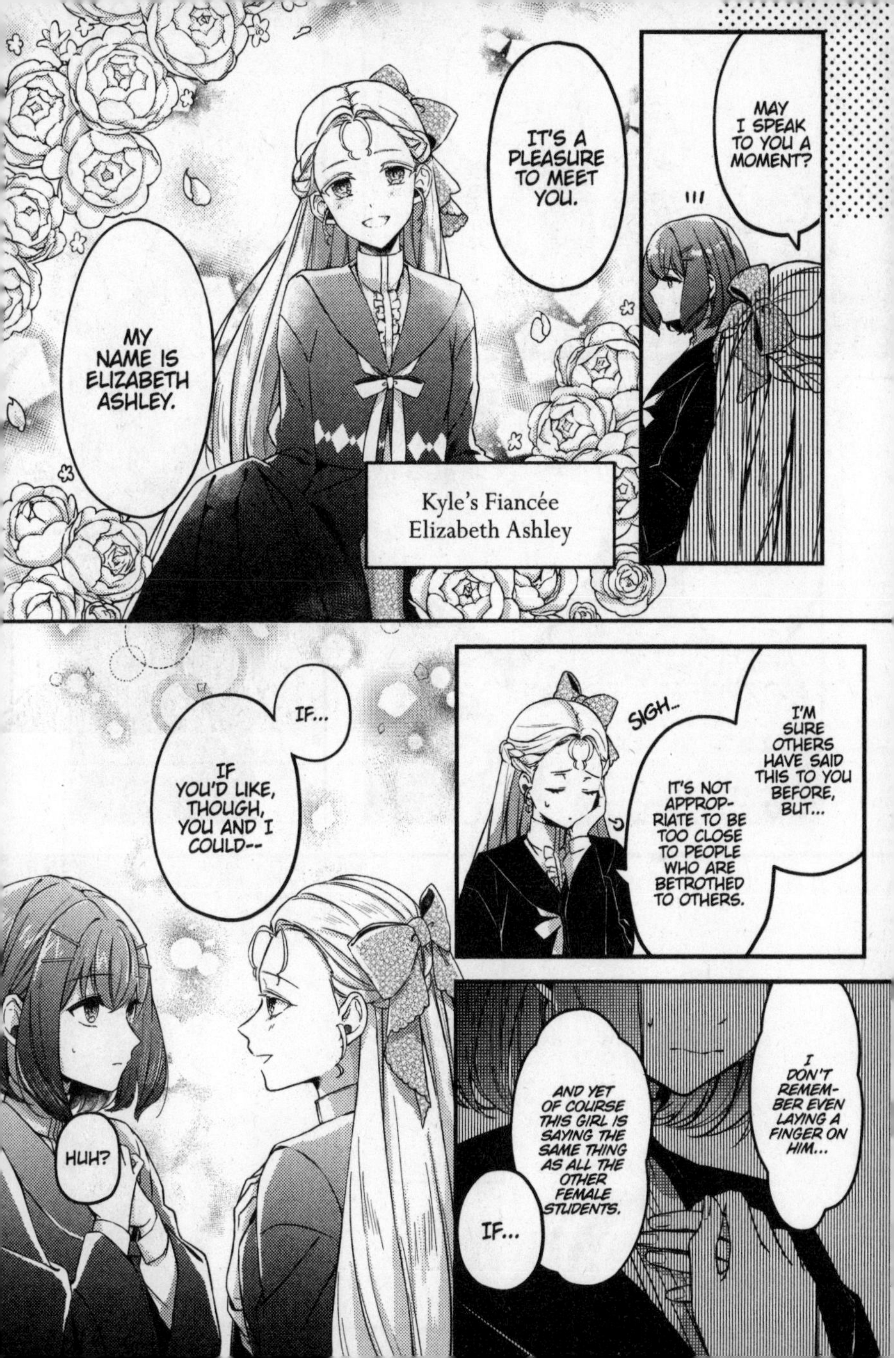
MAY I SPEAK TO YOU A MOMENT?
IT'S A PLEASURE TO MEET YOU.
MY NAME IS ELIZABETH ASHLEY.
Kyle's Fiancée
Elizabeth Ashley
SIGH...
I'M SURE OTHERS HAVE SAID THIS TO YOU BEFORE, BUT...
IT'S NOT APPROP-RIATE TO BE TOO CLOSE TO PEOPLE WHO ARE BETROTHED TO OTHERS.
I DON'T REMEM-BER EVEN LAYING A FINGER ON HIM...
AND YET OF COURSE THIS GIRL IS SAYING THE SAME THING AS ALL THE OTHER FEMALE STUDENTS.
IF...
IF...
IF YOU'D LIKE, THOUGH, YOU AND I COULD--
HUH?

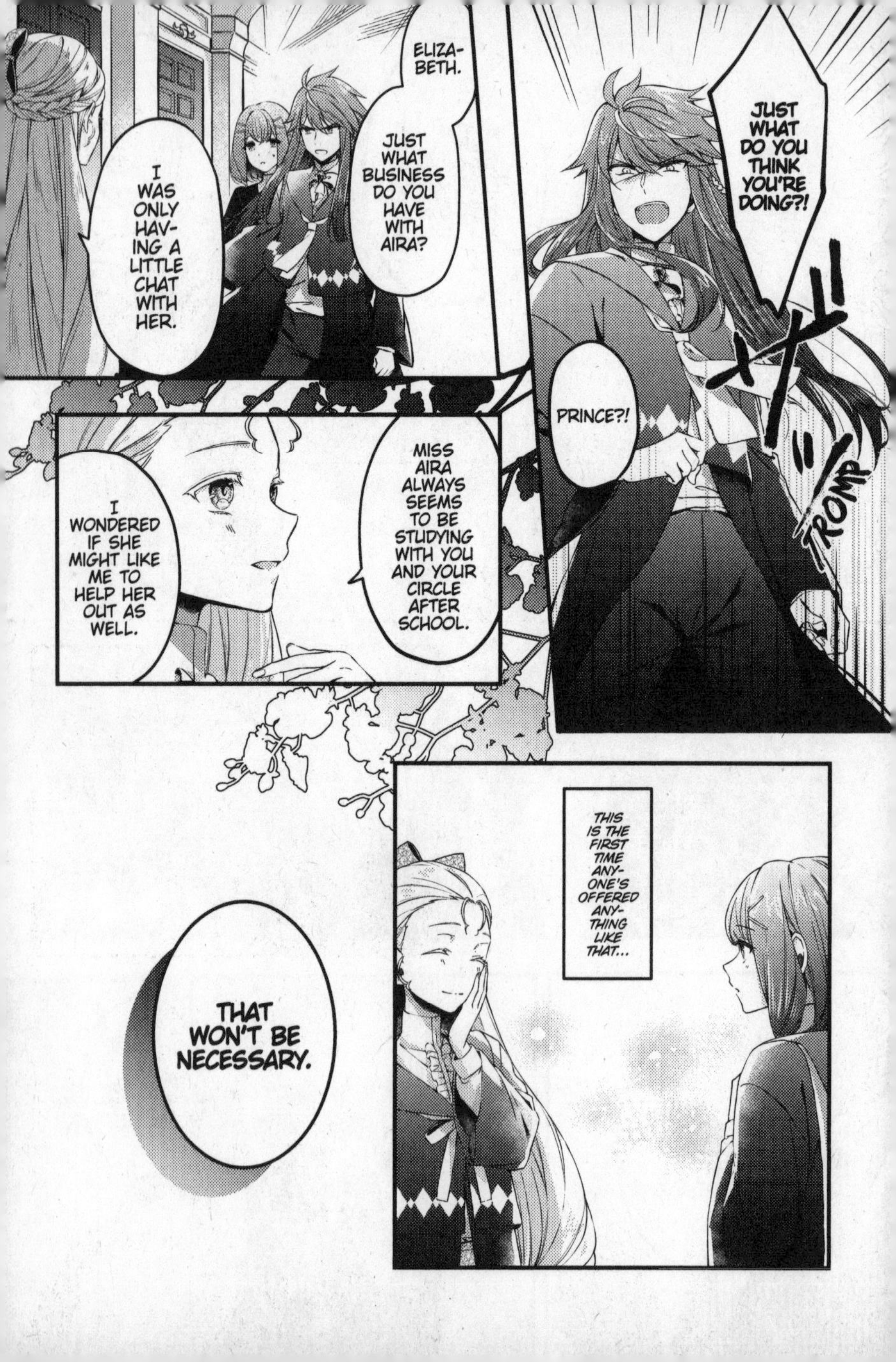
JUST WHAT DO YOU THINK YOU'RE DOING?!
TROMP
PRINCE?!
ELIZA-BETH.
JUST WHAT BUSINESS DO YOU HAVE WITH AIRA?
I WAS ONLY HAV-ING A LITTLE CHAT WITH HER.
MISS AIRA ALWAYS SEEMS TO BE STUDYING WITH YOU AND YOUR CIRCLE AFTER SCHOOL.
I WONDERED IF SHE MIGHT LIKE ME TO HELP HER OUT AS WELL.
THIS IS THE FIRST TIME ANY-ONE'S OFFERED ANY-THING LIKE THAT...
THAT WON'T BE NECESSARY.

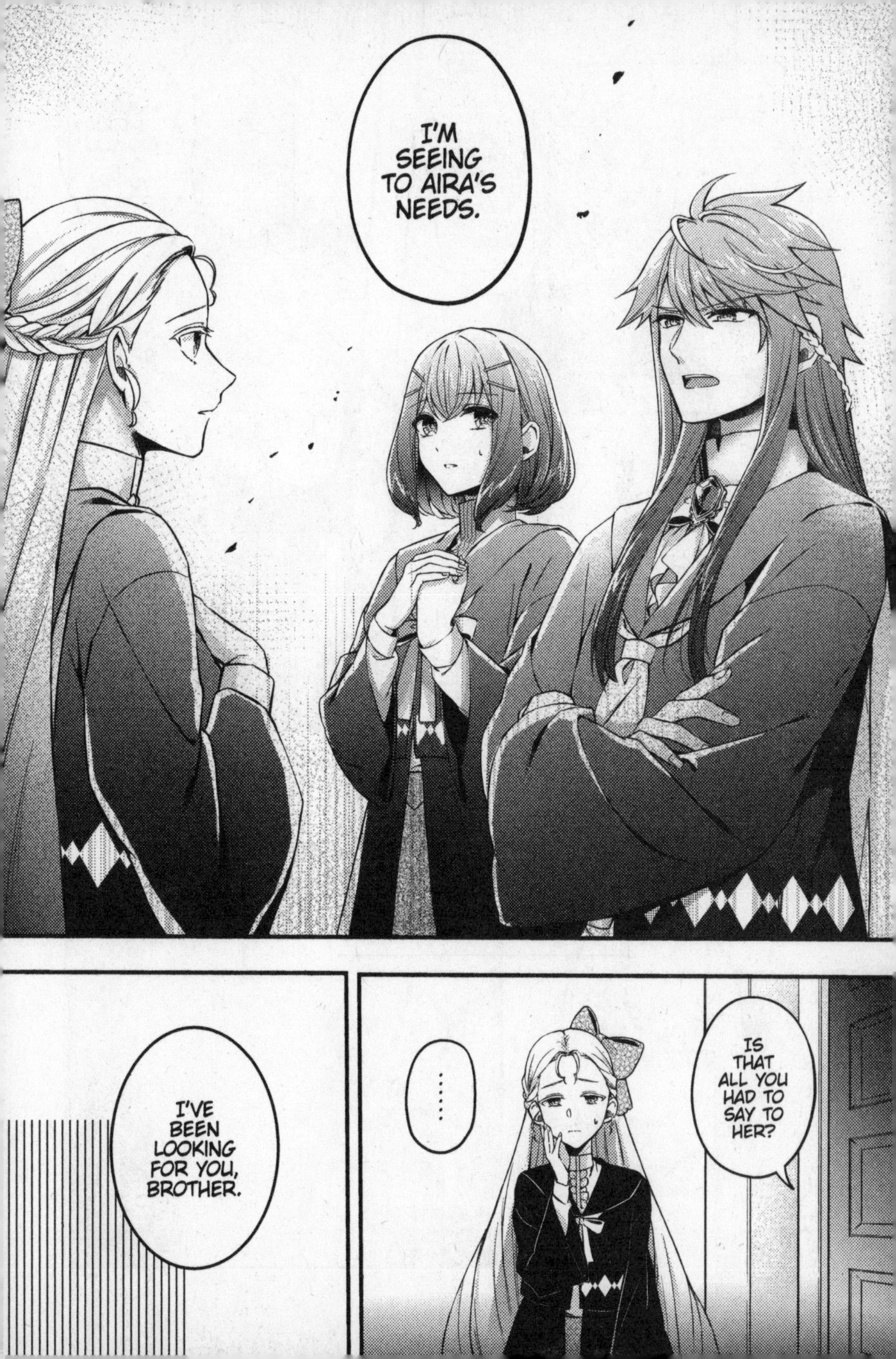
I'M SEEING TO AIRA'S NEEDS.
IS THAT ALL YOU HAD TO SAY TO HER?
......
I'VE BEEN LOOKING FOR YOU, BROTHER.

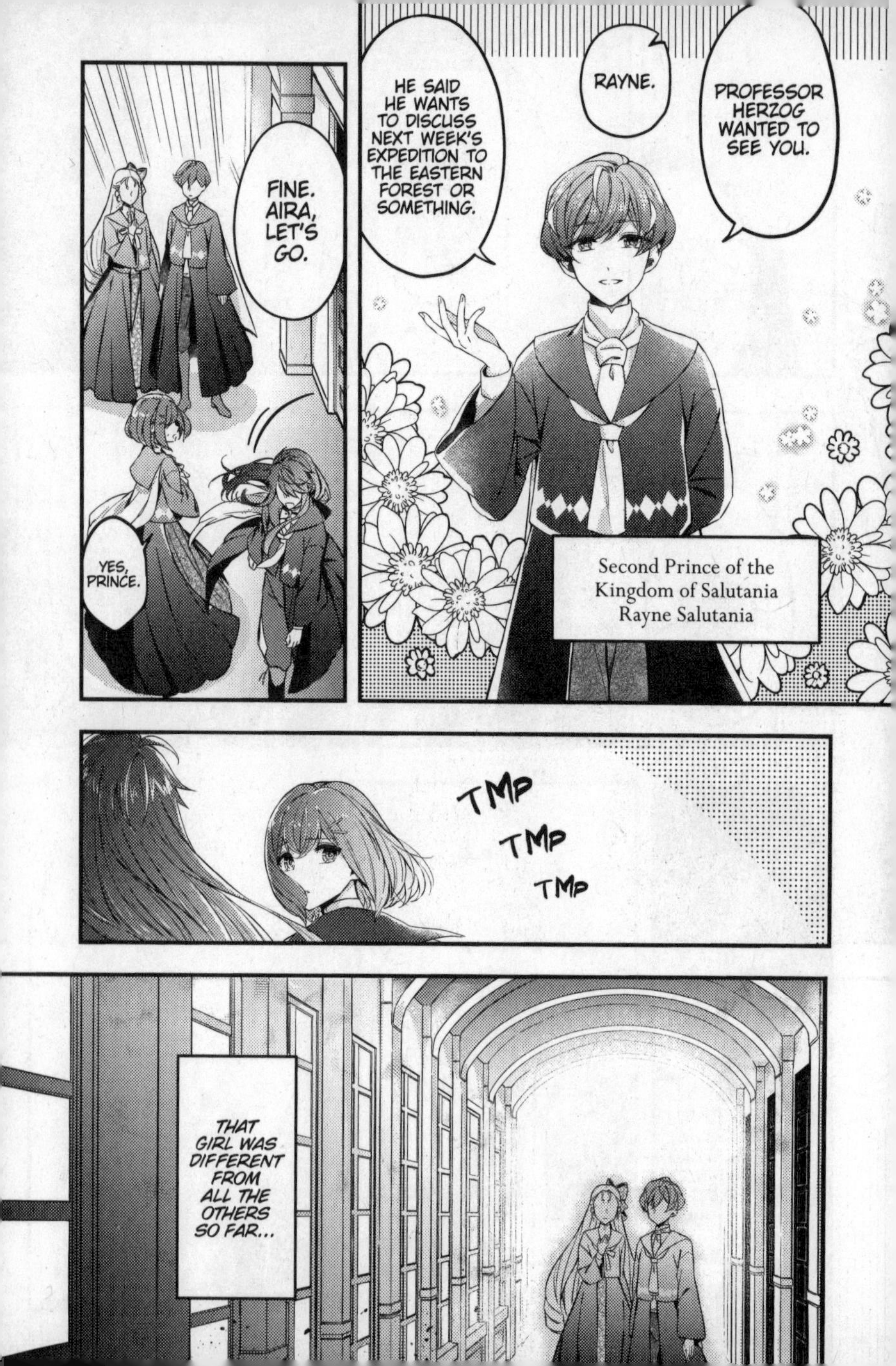
RAYNE.
PROFESSOR HERZOG WANTED TO SEE YOU.
HE SAID HE WANTS TO DISCUSS NEXT WEEK'S EXPEDITION TO THE EASTERN FOREST OR SOMETHING.
Second Prince of the Kingdom of Salutania Rayne Salutania
FINE. AIRA, LET'S GO.
YES, PRINCE.
TMP
TMP
TMP
THAT GIRL WAS DIFFERENT FROM ALL THE OTHERS SO FAR...

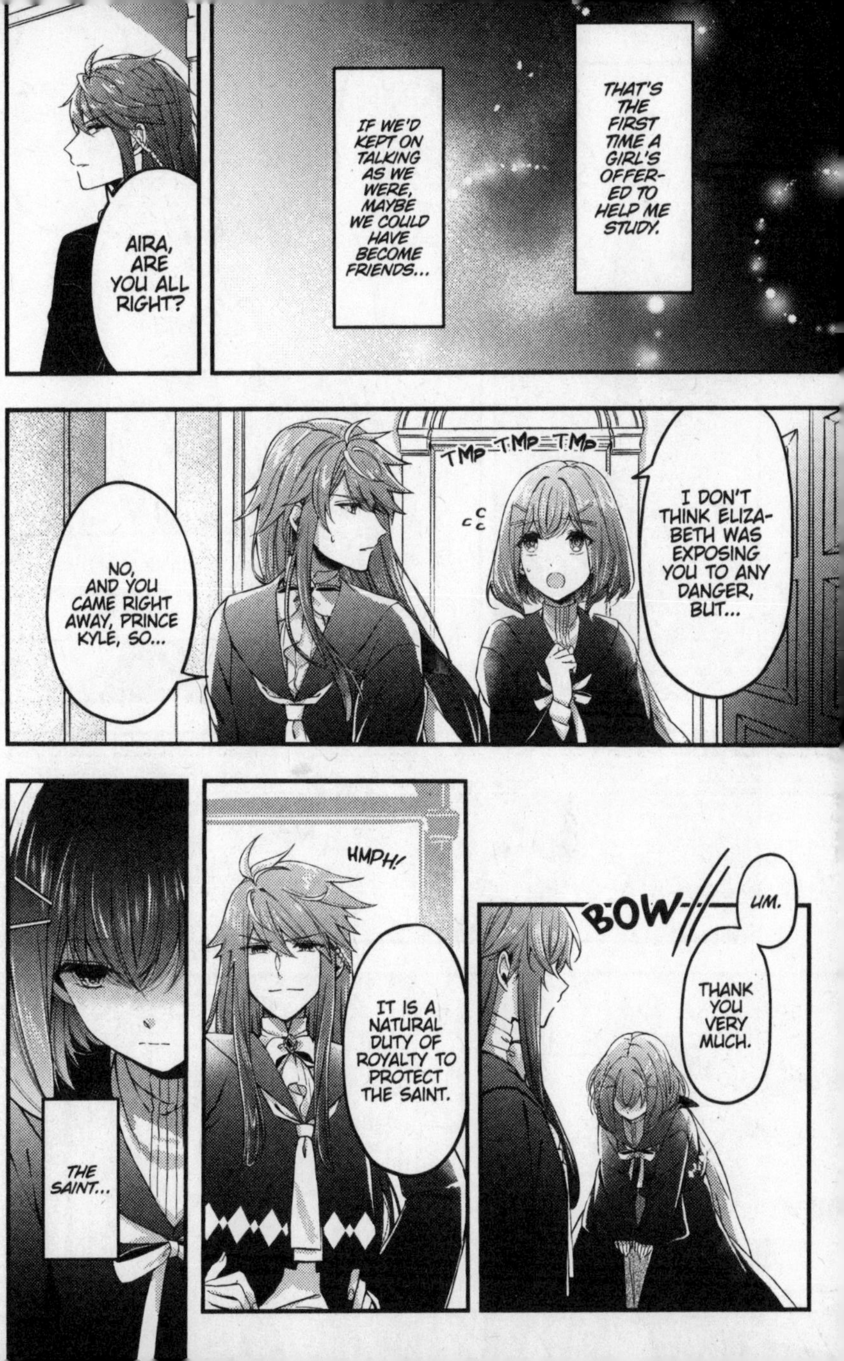
THAT'S THE FIRST TIME A GIRL'S OFFERED TO HELP ME STUDY.
IF WE'D KEPT ON TALKING AS WE WERE, MAYBE WE COULD HAVE BECOME FRIENDS...
AIRA, ARE YOU ALL RIGHT?
I DON'T THINK ELIZABETH WAS EXPOSING YOU TO ANY DANGER, BUT...
TMP TMP TMP
NO, AND YOU CAME RIGHT AWAY, PRINCE KYLE, SO...
UM.
BOW
THANK YOU VERY MUCH.
HMPH!
IT IS A NATURAL DUTY OF ROYALTY TO PROTECT THE SAINT.
THE SAINT...

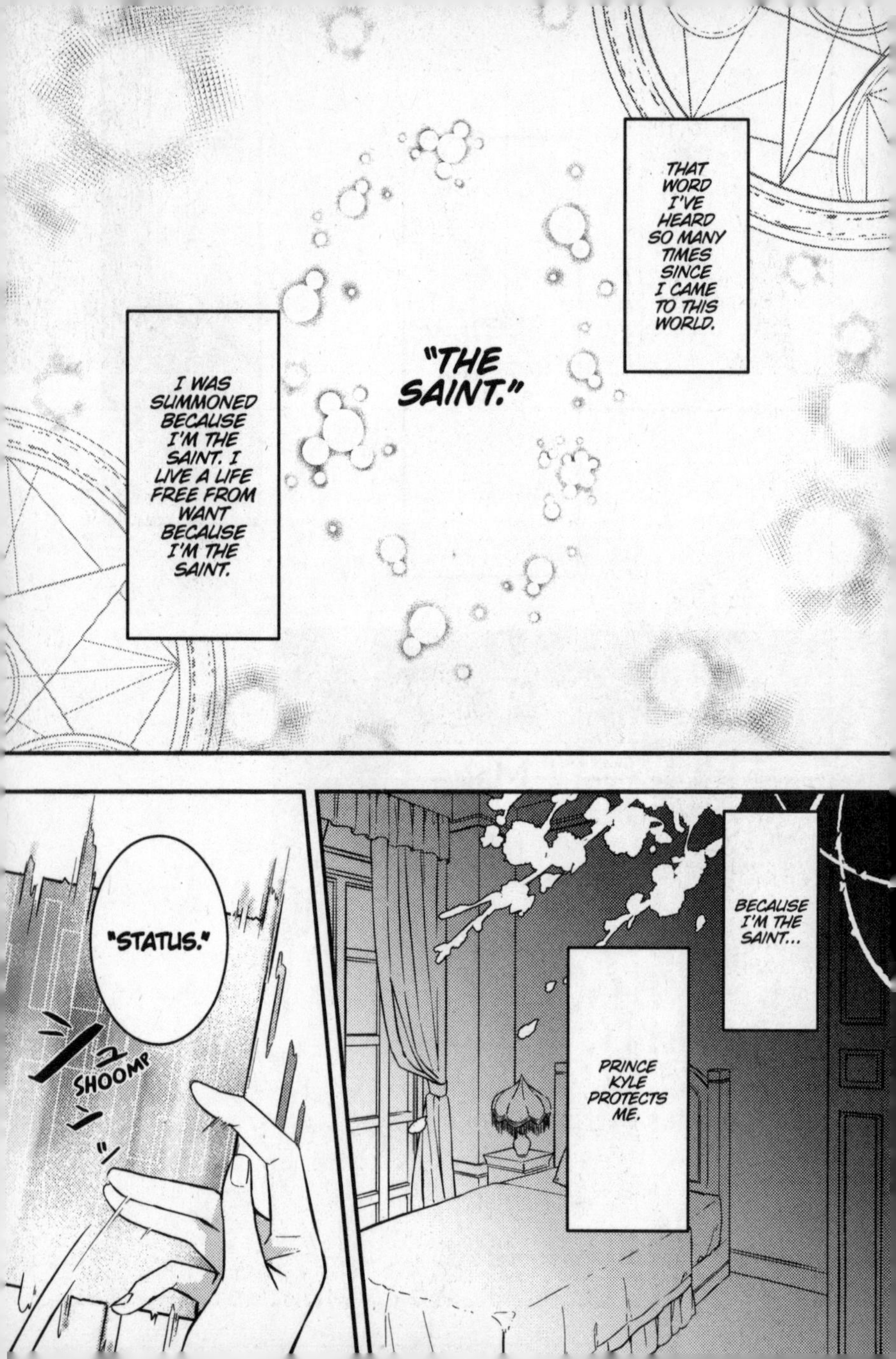
THAT WORD I'VE HEARD SO MANY TIMES SINCE I CAME TO THIS WORLD.
"THE SAINT."
I WAS SUMMONED BECAUSE I'M THE SAINT. I LIVE A LIFE FREE FROM WANT BECAUSE I'M THE SAINT.
BECAUSE I'M THE SAINT...
PRINCE KYLE PROTECTS ME.
"STATUS."
SHOOMP

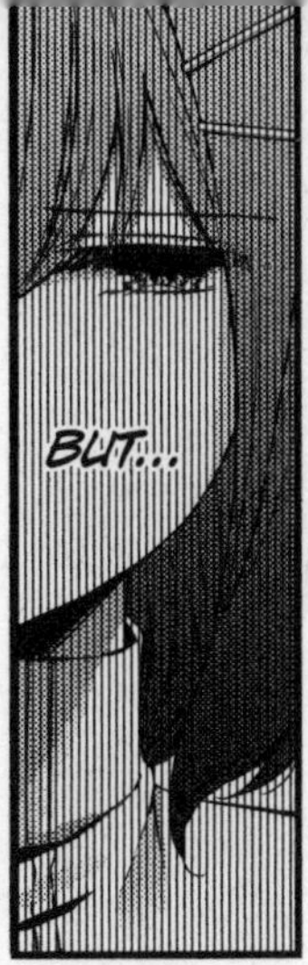
BUT...

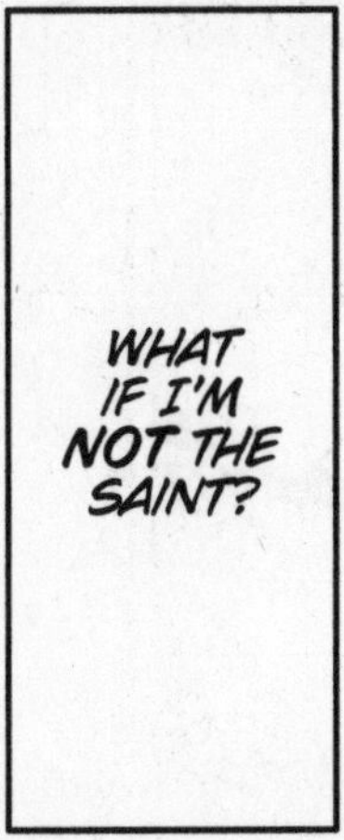
WHAT IF I'M NOT THE SAINT?

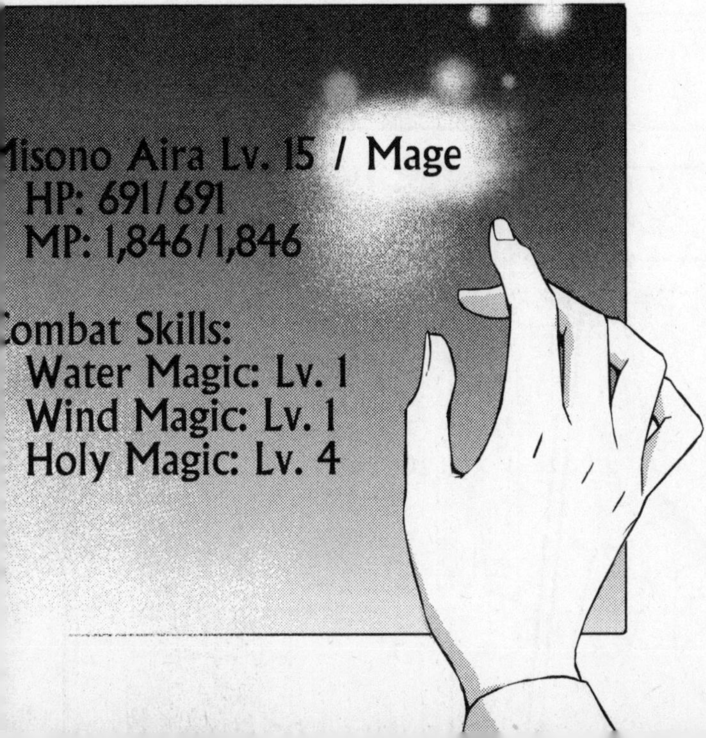
Misono Aira Lv. 15 / Mage
HP: 691/691
MP: 1,846/1,846
Combat Skills:
Water Magic: Lv. 1
Wind Magic: Lv. 1
Holy Magic: Lv. 4

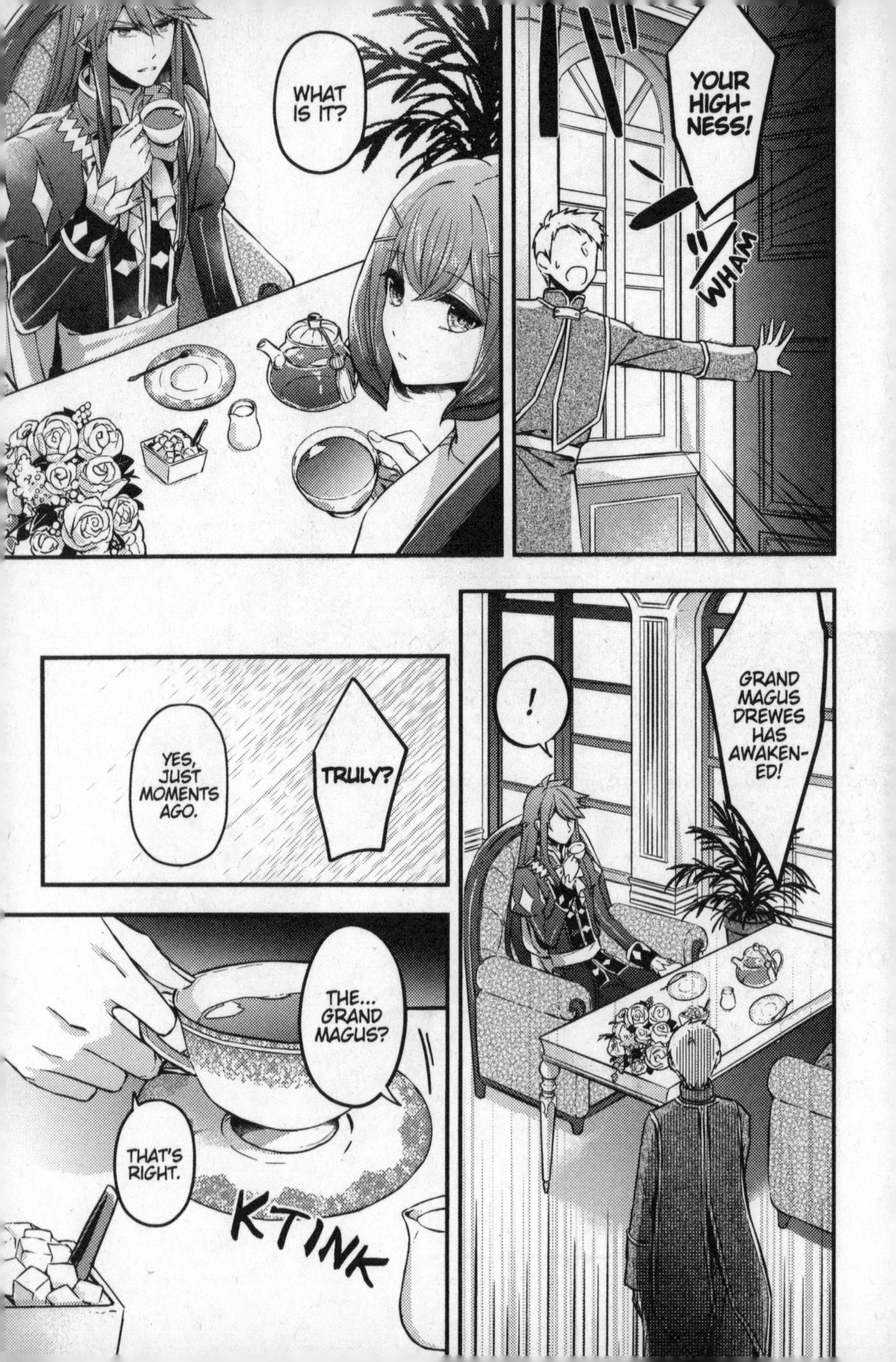

YOUR HIGH-NESS!
WHAM
WHAT IS IT?
GRAND MAGUS DREWES HAS AWAKEN-ED!
!
TRULY?
YES, JUST MOMENTS AGO.
THE... GRAND MAGUS?
THAT'S RIGHT.
KTINK

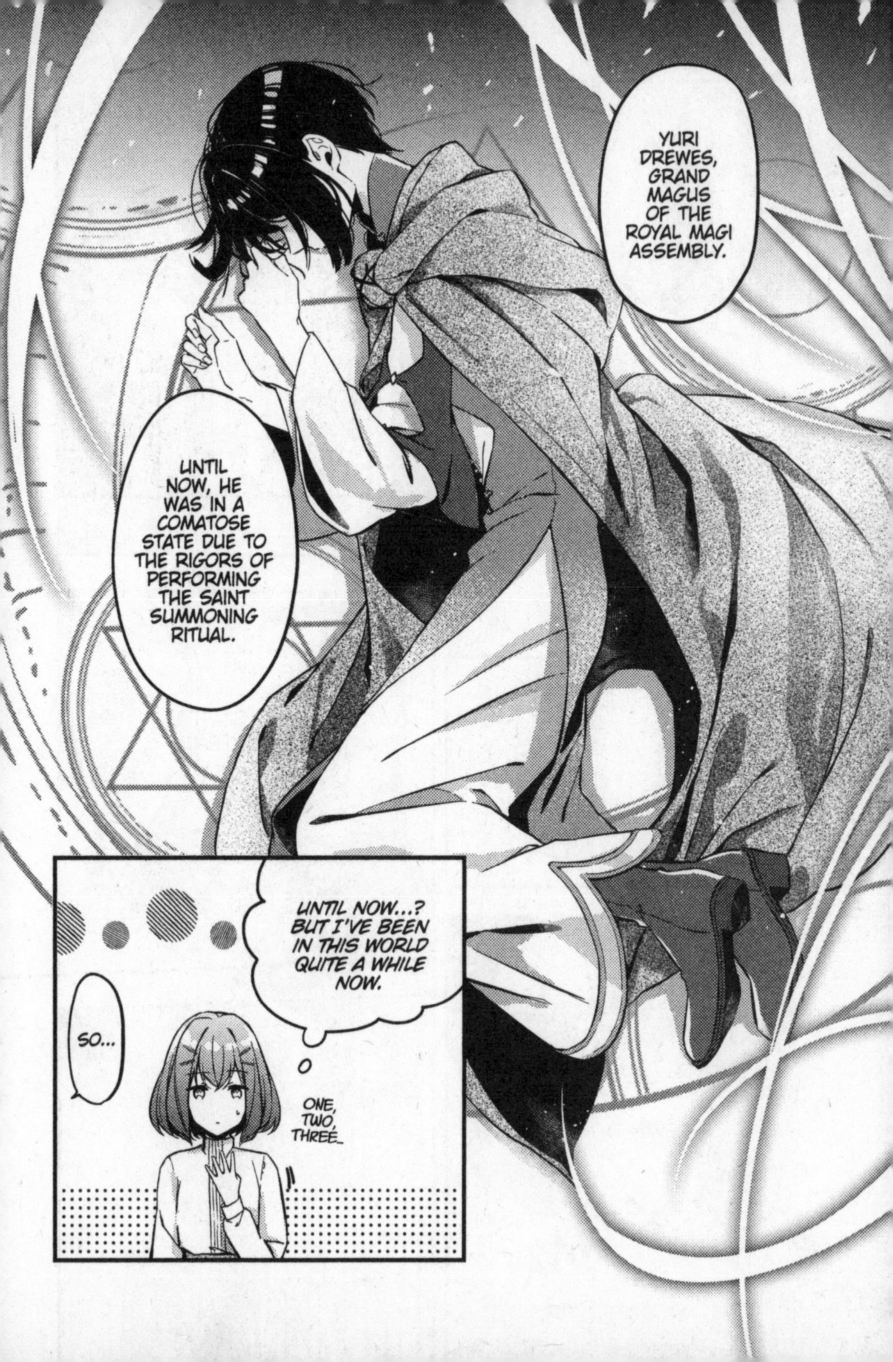
YURI DREWES, GRAND MAGUS OF THE ROYAL MAGI ASSEMBLY.
UNTIL NOW, HE WAS IN A COMATOSE STATE DUE TO THE RIGORS OF PERFORMING THE SAINT SUMMONING RITUAL.
UNTIL NOW...? BUT I'VE BEEN IN THIS WORLD QUITE A WHILE NOW.
SO...
ONE, TWO, THREE_

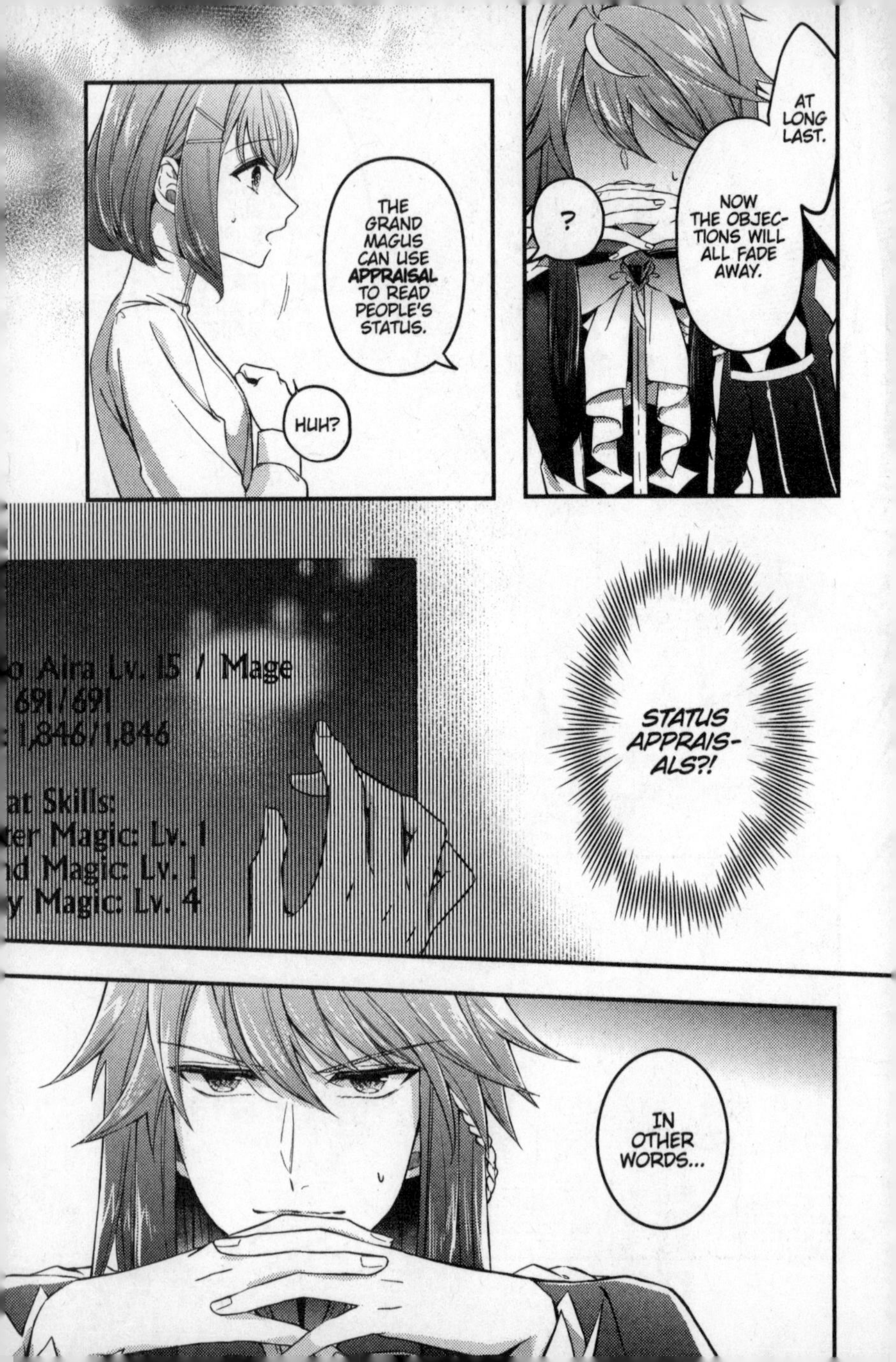
AT LONG LAST.
NOW THE OBJECTIONS WILL ALL FADE AWAY.
?
THE GRAND MAGUS CAN USE **APPRAISAL** TO READ PEOPLE'S STATUS.
HUH?
STATUS APPRAISALS?!
o Aira Lv. 15 / Mage
691/691
1,846/1,846
at Skills:
ter Magic: Lv. 1
nd Magic: Lv. 1
y Magic: Lv. 4
IN OTHER WORDS...

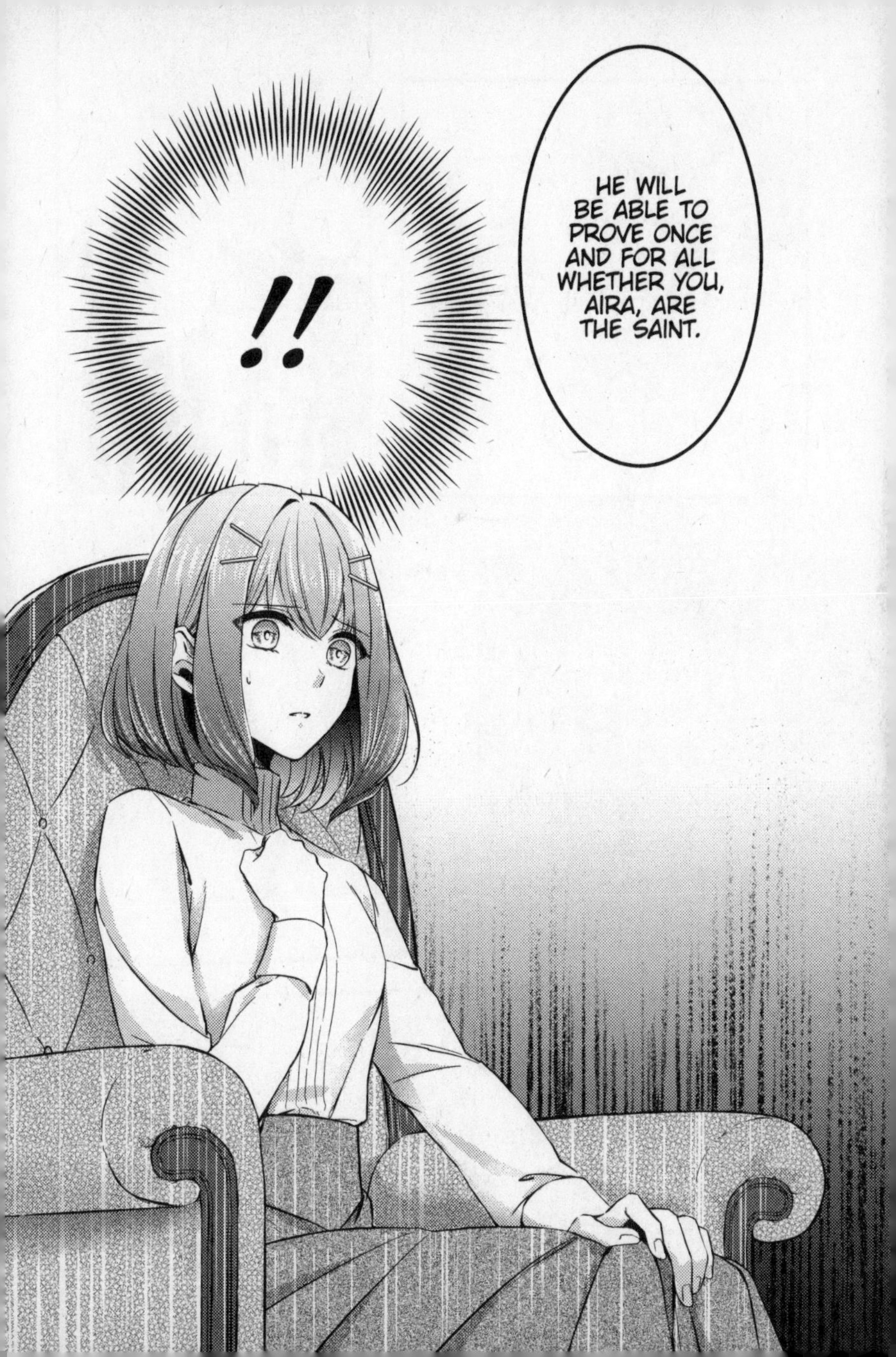
HE WILL BE ABLE TO PROVE ONCE AND FOR ALL WHETHER YOU, AIRA, ARE THE SAINT.
!!

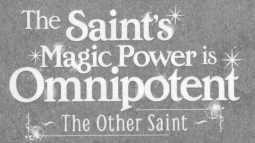

The Saint's Magic Power is
Omnipotent
~ The Other Saint ~

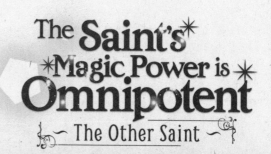

The Saint's
Magic Power is
Omnipotent
The Other Saint

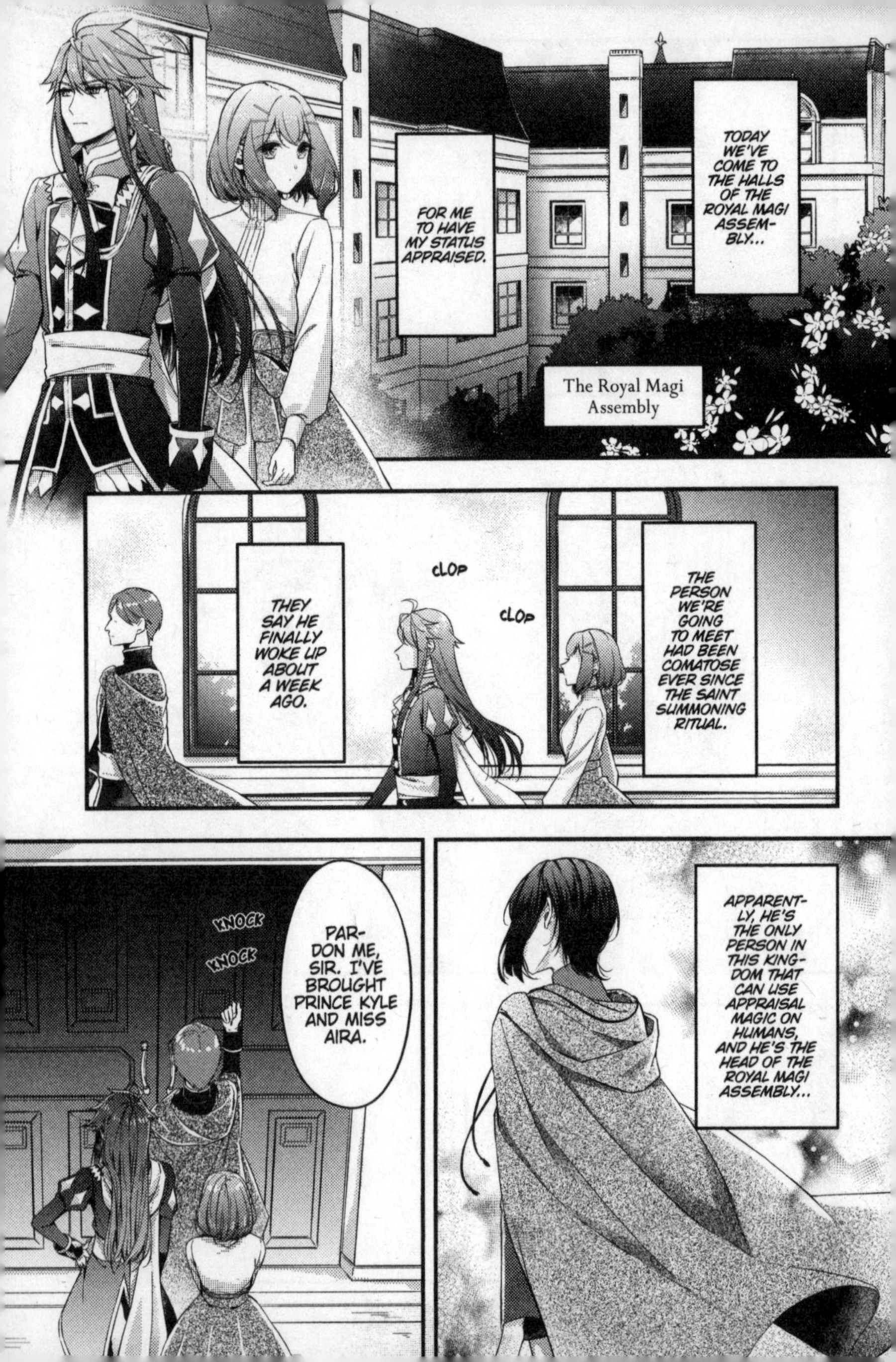
TODAY WE'VE COME TO THE HALLS OF THE ROYAL MAGI ASSEMBLY...
FOR ME TO HAVE MY STATUS APPRAISED.
The Royal Magi Assembly
THE PERSON WE'RE GOING TO MEET HAD BEEN COMATOSE EVER SINCE THE SAINT SUMMONING RITUAL.
CLOP
CLOP
THEY SAY HE FINALLY WOKE UP ABOUT A WEEK AGO.
APPARENTLY, HE'S THE ONLY PERSON IN THIS KINGDOM THAT CAN USE APPRAISAL MAGIC ON HUMANS, AND HE'S THE HEAD OF THE ROYAL MAGI ASSEMBLY...
KNOCK
KNOCK
PARDON ME, SIR. I'VE BROUGHT PRINCE KYLE AND MISS AIRA.

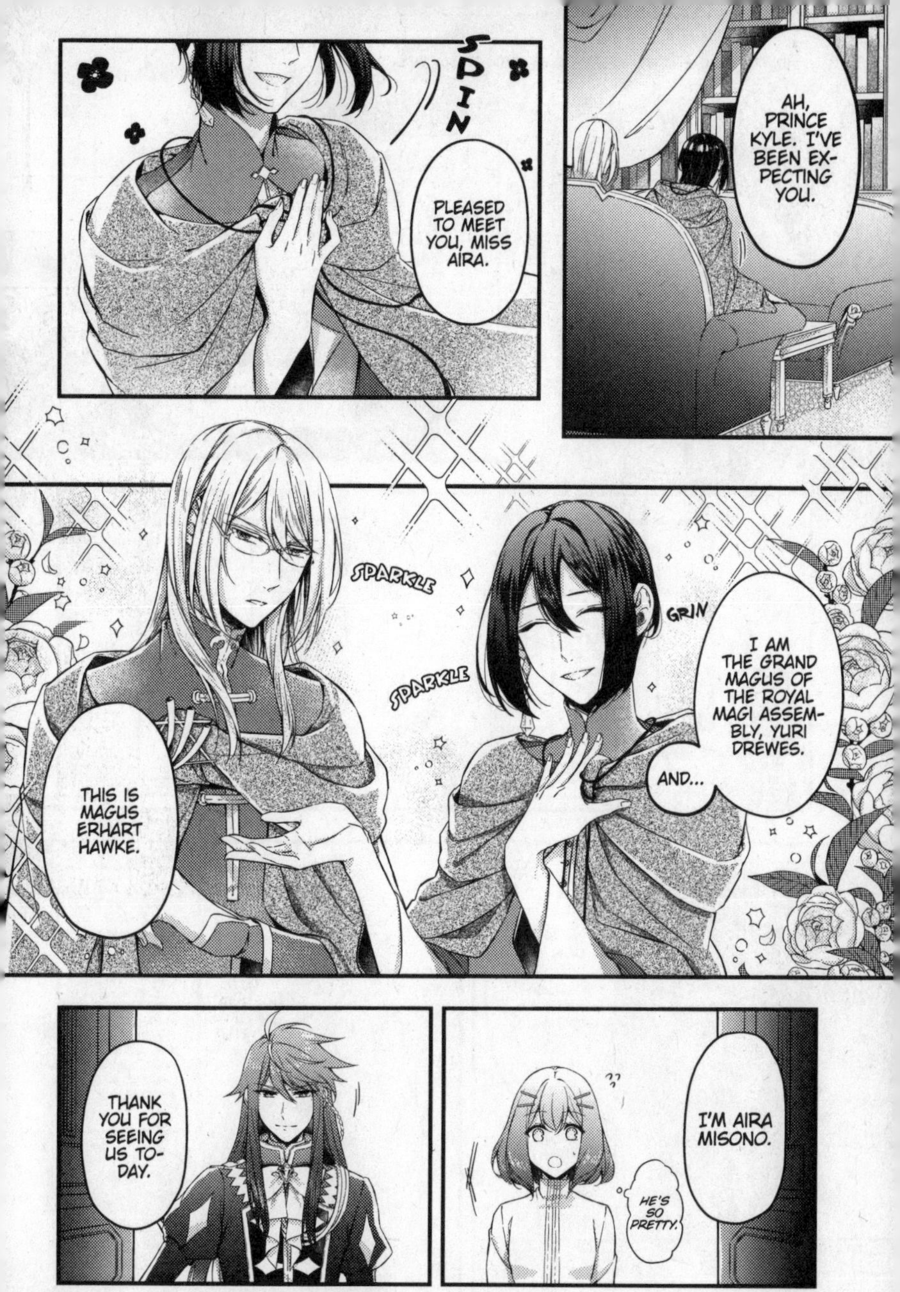
AH, PRINCE KYLE. I'VE BEEN EXPECTING YOU.
SPIN
PLEASED TO MEET YOU, MISS AIRA.
GRIN
I AM THE GRAND MAGUS OF THE ROYAL MAGI ASSEMBLY, YURI DREWES.
AND...
SPARKLE
SPARKLE
THIS IS MAGUS ERHART HAWKE.
I'M AIRA MISONO.
HE'S SO PRETTY.
THANK YOU FOR SEEING US TODAY.

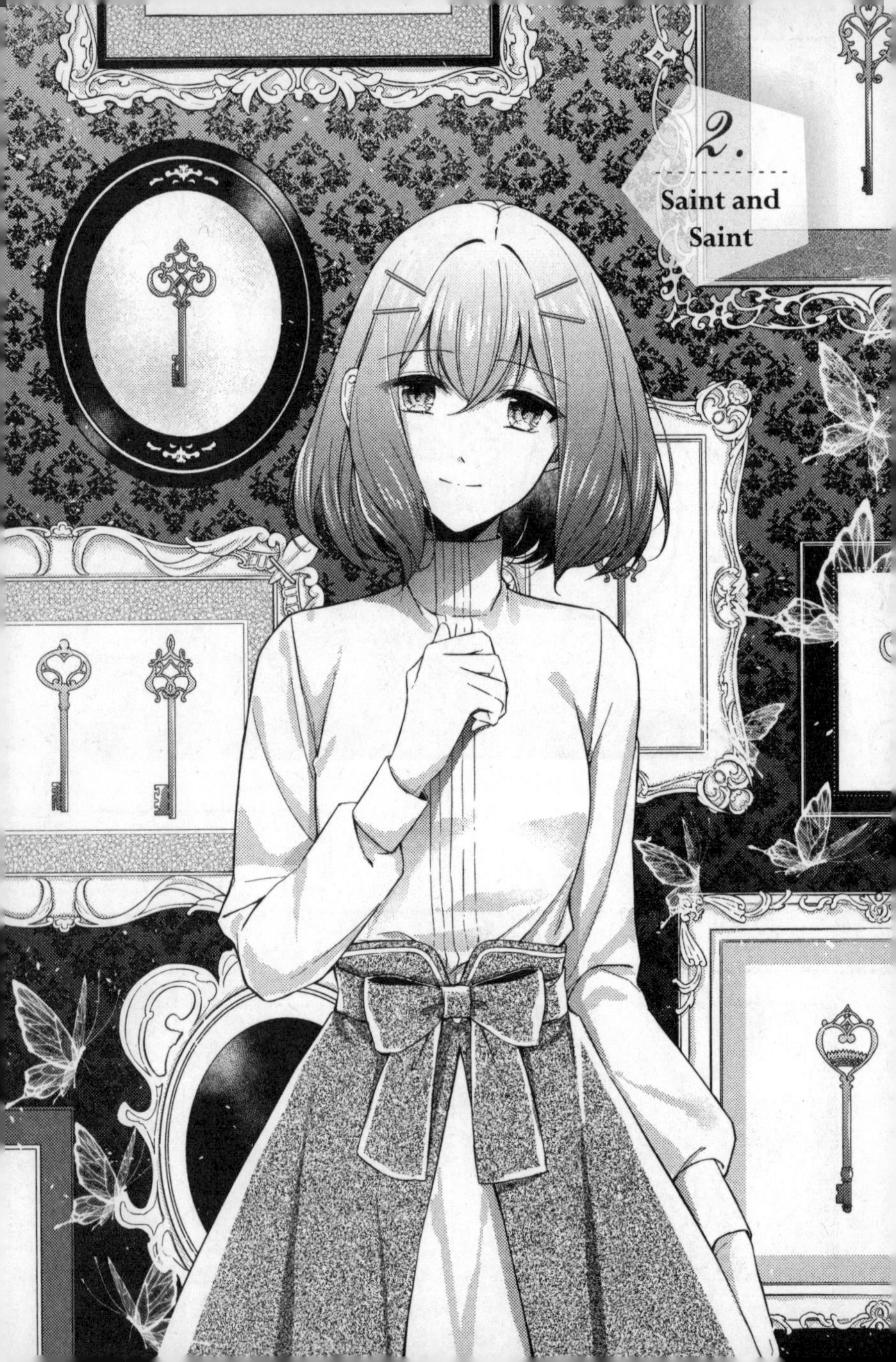
2.
Saint and Saint

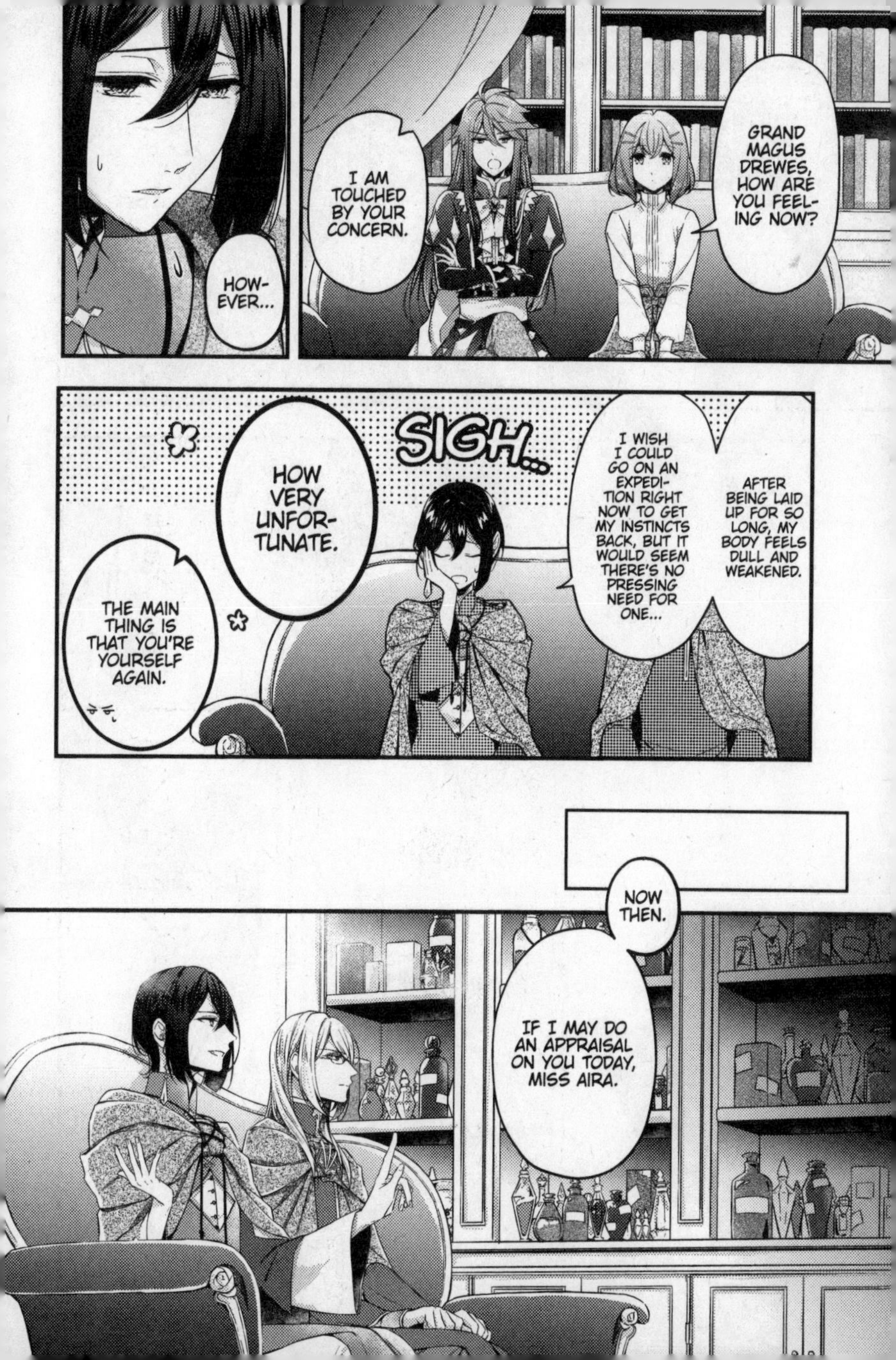
GRAND MAGUS DREWES, HOW ARE YOU FEEL-ING NOW?
I AM TOUCHED BY YOUR CONCERN.
HOW-EVER...
AFTER BEING LAID UP FOR SO LONG, MY BODY FEELS DULL AND WEAKENED.
I WISH I COULD GO ON AN EXPEDI-TION RIGHT NOW TO GET MY INSTINCTS BACK, BUT IT WOULD SEEM THERE'S NO PRESSING NEED FOR ONE...
SIGH...
HOW VERY UNFOR-TUNATE.
THE MAIN THING IS THAT YOU'RE YOURSELF AGAIN.
NOW THEN.
IF I MAY DO AN APPRAISAL ON YOU TODAY, MISS AIRA.

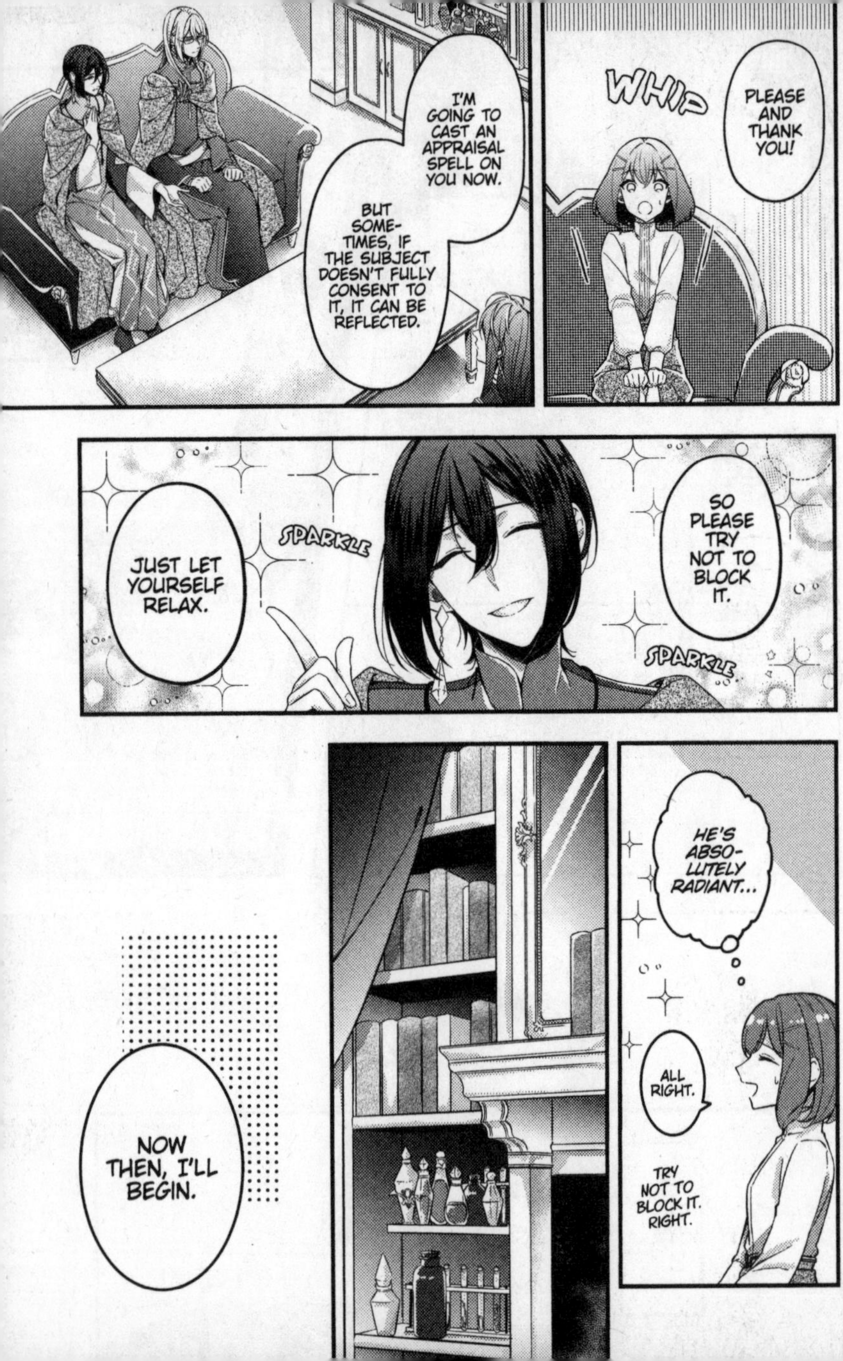
PLEASE AND THANK YOU!
WHIP
I'M GOING TO CAST AN APPRAISAL SPELL ON YOU NOW.
BUT SOME-TIMES, IF THE SUBJECT DOESN'T FULLY CONSENT TO IT, IT CAN BE REFLECTED.
SO PLEASE TRY NOT TO BLOCK IT.
SPARKLE
SPARKLE
JUST LET YOURSELF RELAX.
HE'S ABSO-LUTELY RADIANT...
ALL RIGHT.
TRY NOT TO BLOCK IT. RIGHT.
NOW THEN, I'LL BEGIN.

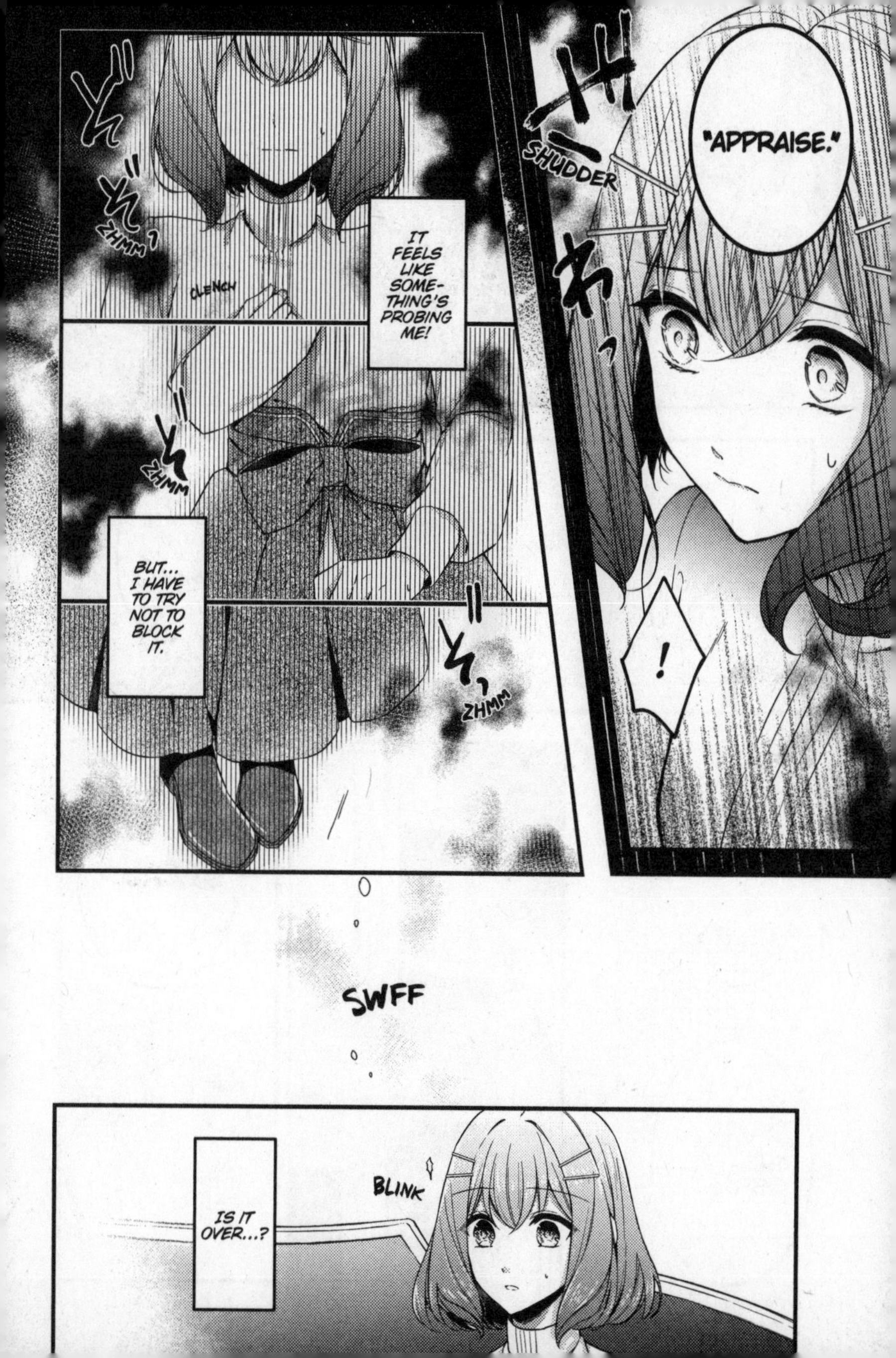
"APPRAISE."
SHUDDER
!
IT FEELS LIKE SOME-THING'S PROBING ME!
ZHMM
CLENCH
ZHMM
BUT... I HAVE TO TRY NOT TO BLOCK IT.
ZHMM
SWFF
BLINK
IS IT OVER...?

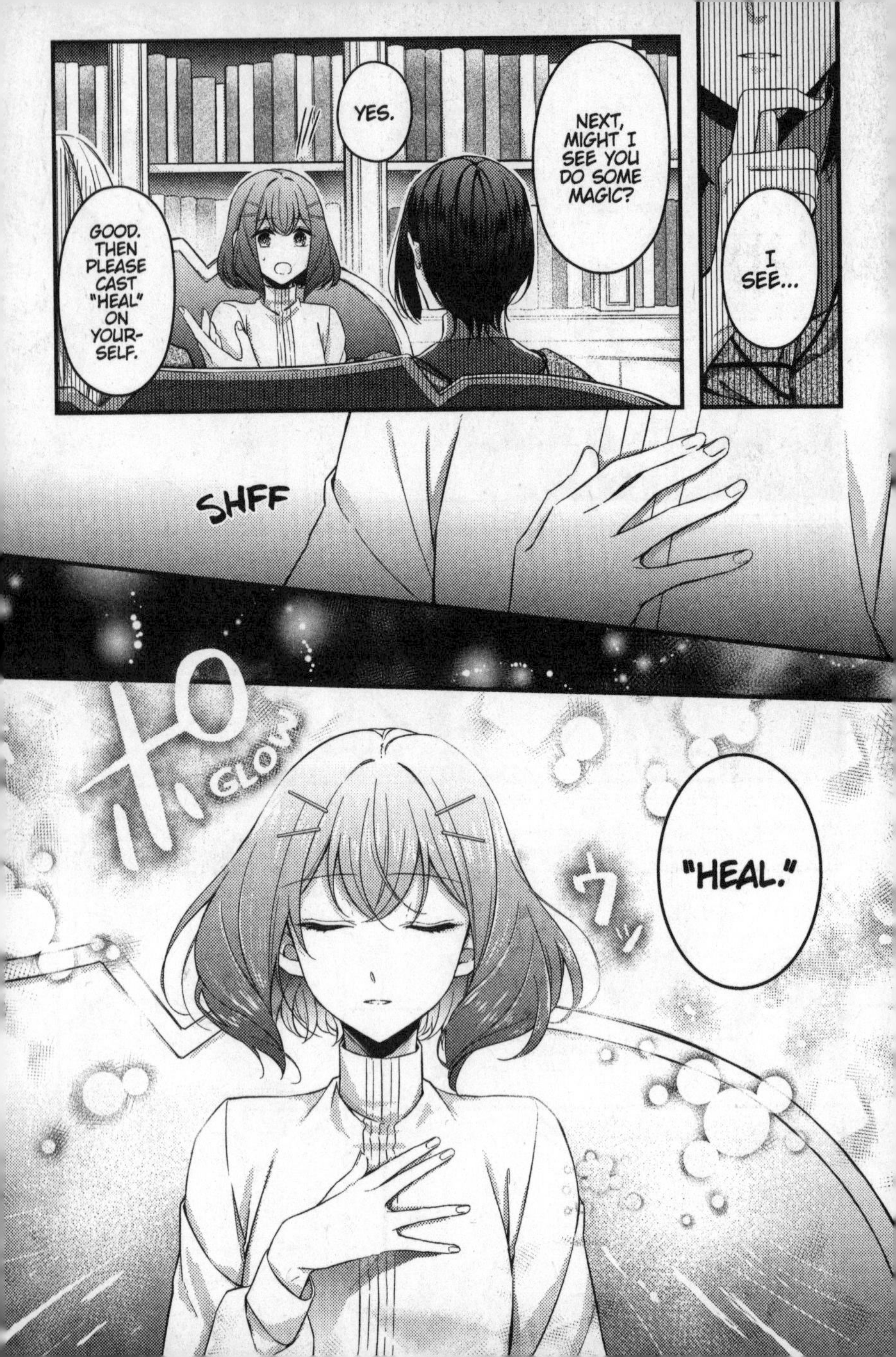
I SEE...
NEXT, MIGHT I SEE YOU DO SOME MAGIC?
YES.
GOOD. THEN PLEASE CAST "HEAL" ON YOURSELF.
SHFF
"HEAL."
GLOW

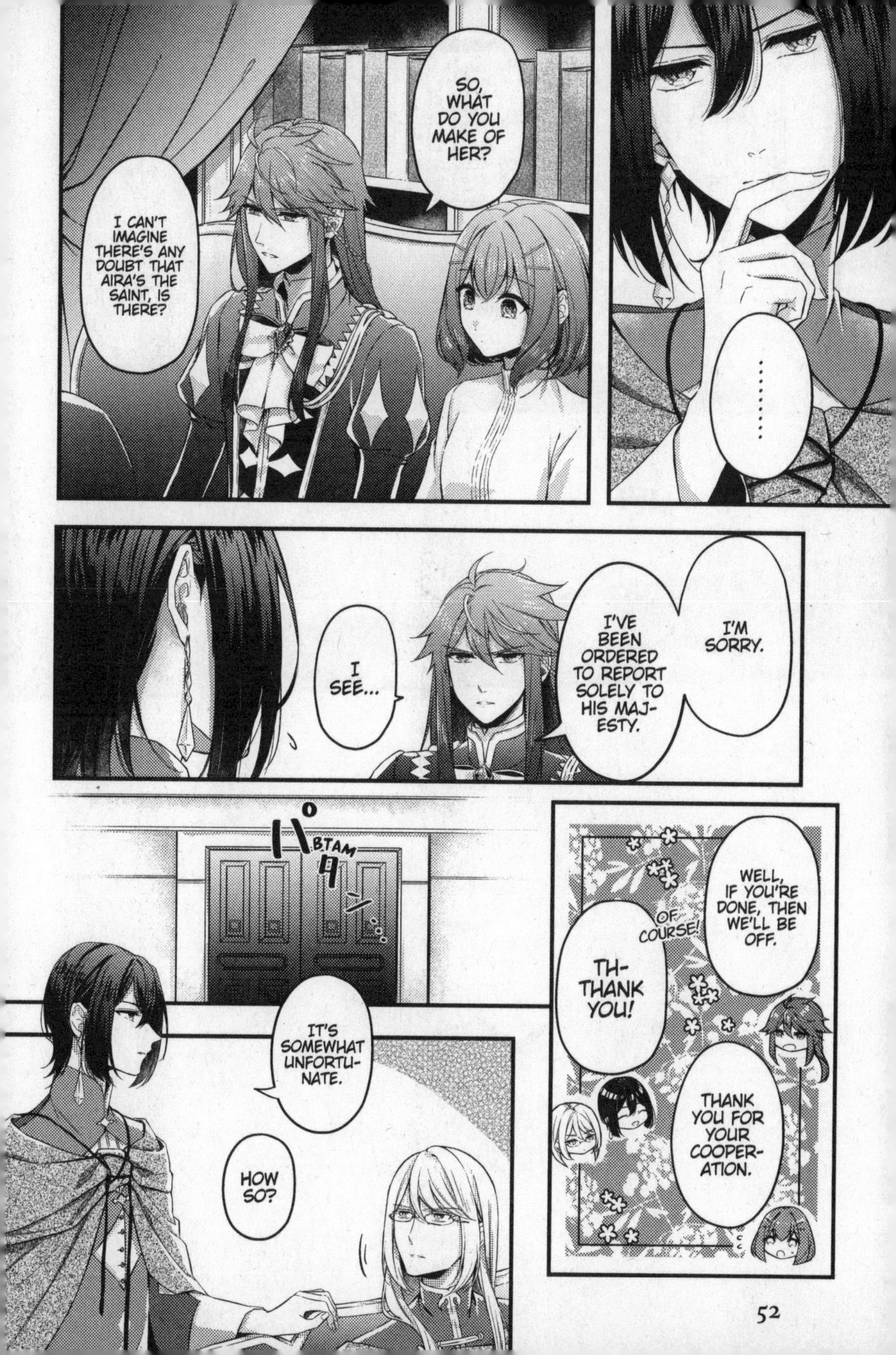
......
SO, WHAT DO YOU MAKE OF HER?
I CAN'T IMAGINE THERE'S ANY DOUBT THAT AIRA'S THE SAINT, IS THERE?
I'M SORRY.
I'VE BEEN ORDERED TO REPORT SOLELY TO HIS MAJ-ESTY.
I SEE...
WELL, IF YOU'RE DONE, THEN WE'LL BE OFF.
OF COURSE!
TH-THANK YOU!
THANK YOU FOR YOUR COOPER-ATION.
BTAM
IT'S SOMEWHAT UNFORTU-NATE.
HOW SO?

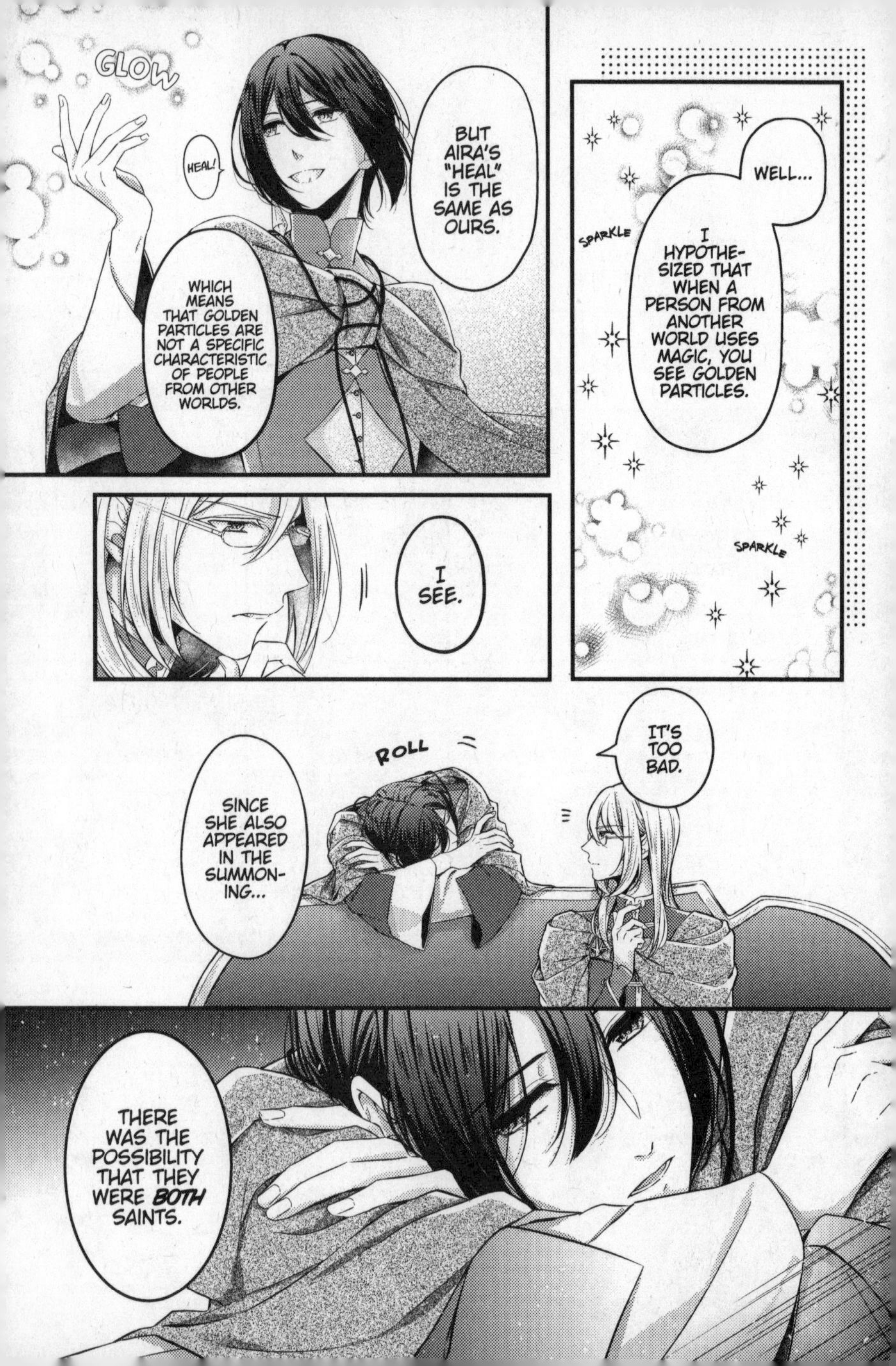
WELL...
SPARKLE
I HYPOTHESIZED THAT WHEN A PERSON FROM ANOTHER WORLD USES MAGIC, YOU SEE GOLDEN PARTICLES.
SPARKLE
BUT AIRA'S "HEAL" IS THE SAME AS OURS.
GLOW
HEAL!
WHICH MEANS THAT GOLDEN PARTICLES ARE NOT A SPECIFIC CHARACTERISTIC OF PEOPLE FROM OTHER WORLDS.
I SEE.
IT'S TOO BAD.
ROLL
SINCE SHE ALSO APPEARED IN THE SUMMONING...
THERE WAS THE POSSIBILITY THAT THEY WERE *BOTH* SAINTS.

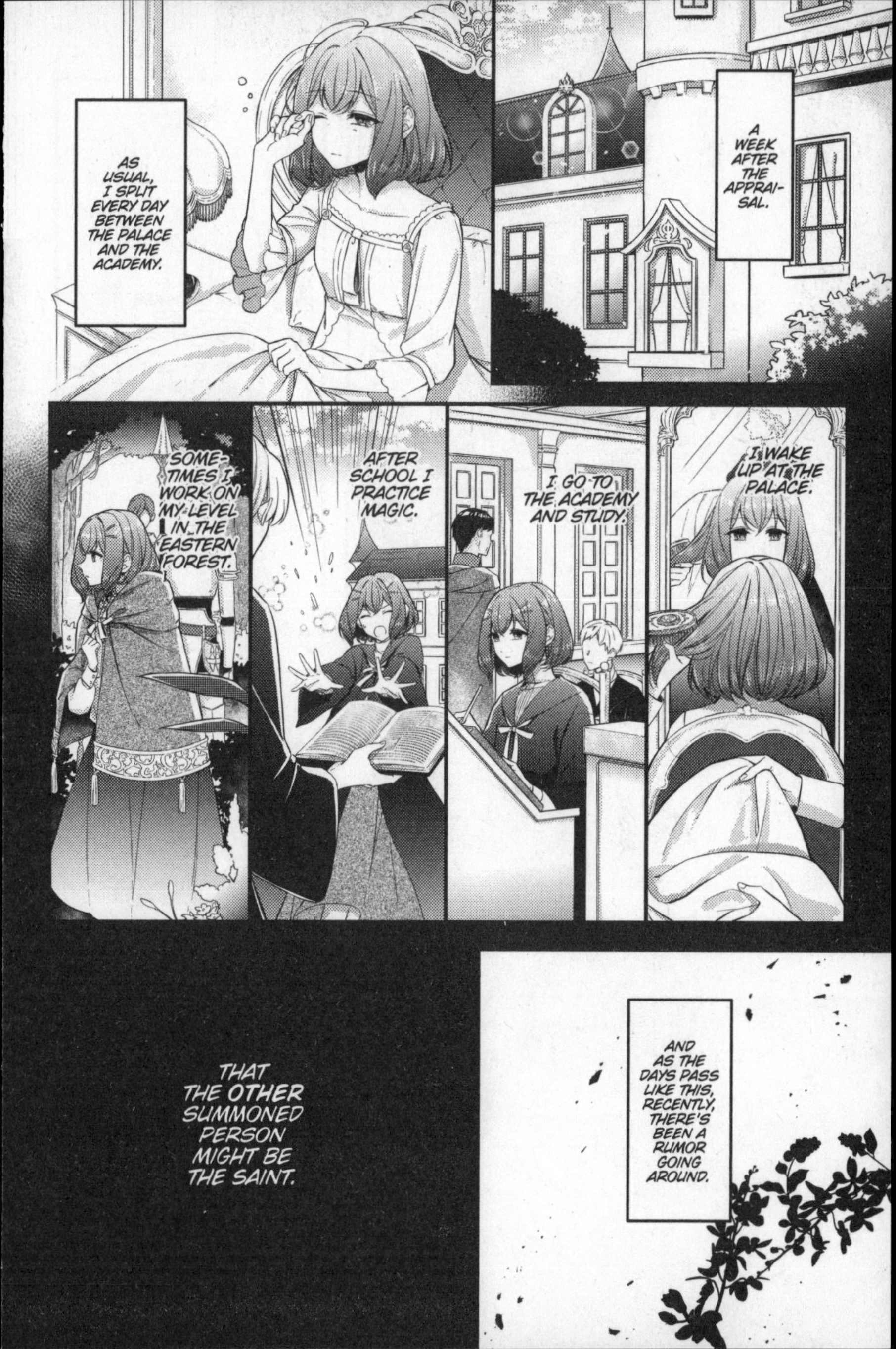
A WEEK AFTER THE APPRAI-SAL.
AS USUAL, I SPLIT EVERY DAY BETWEEN THE PALACE AND THE ACADEMY.
I WAKE UP AT THE PALACE.
I GO TO THE ACADEMY AND STUDY.
AFTER SCHOOL I PRACTICE MAGIC.
SOME-TIMES I WORK ON MY LEVEL IN THE EASTERN FOREST.
AND AS THE DAYS PASS LIKE THIS, RECENTLY, THERE'S BEEN A RUMOR GOING AROUND.
THAT THE OTHER SUMMONED PERSON MIGHT BE THE SAINT.

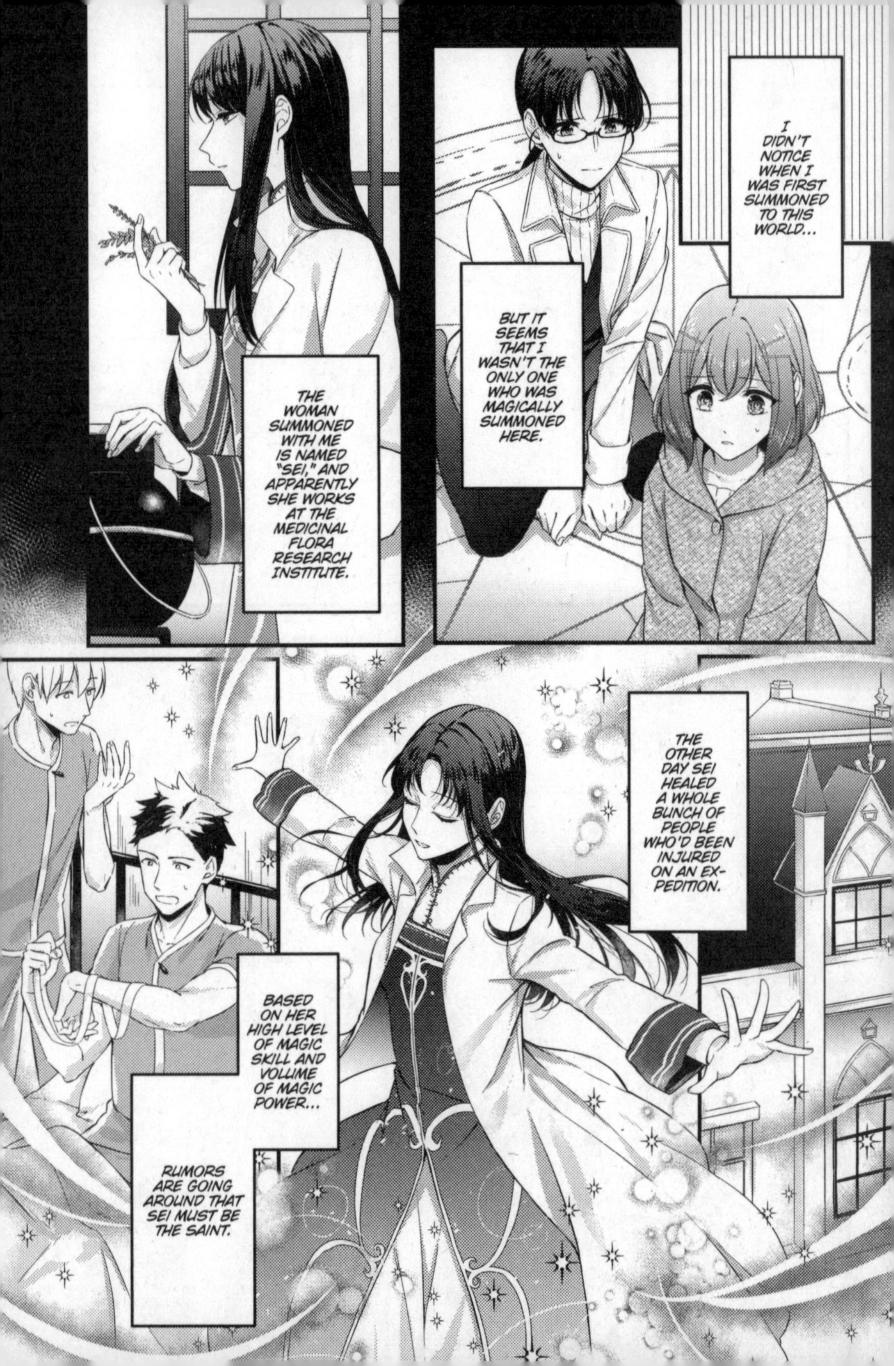
I DIDN'T NOTICE WHEN I WAS FIRST SUMMONED TO THIS WORLD...
BUT IT SEEMS THAT I WASN'T THE ONLY ONE WHO WAS MAGICALLY SUMMONED HERE.
THE WOMAN SUMMONED WITH ME IS NAMED "SEI," AND APPARENTLY SHE WORKS AT THE MEDICINAL FLORA RESEARCH INSTITUTE.
THE OTHER DAY SEI HEALED A WHOLE BUNCH OF PEOPLE WHO'D BEEN INJURED ON AN EX-PEDITION.
BASED ON HER HIGH LEVEL OF MAGIC SKILL AND VOLUME OF MAGIC POWER...
RUMORS ARE GOING AROUND THAT SEI MUST BE THE SAINT.

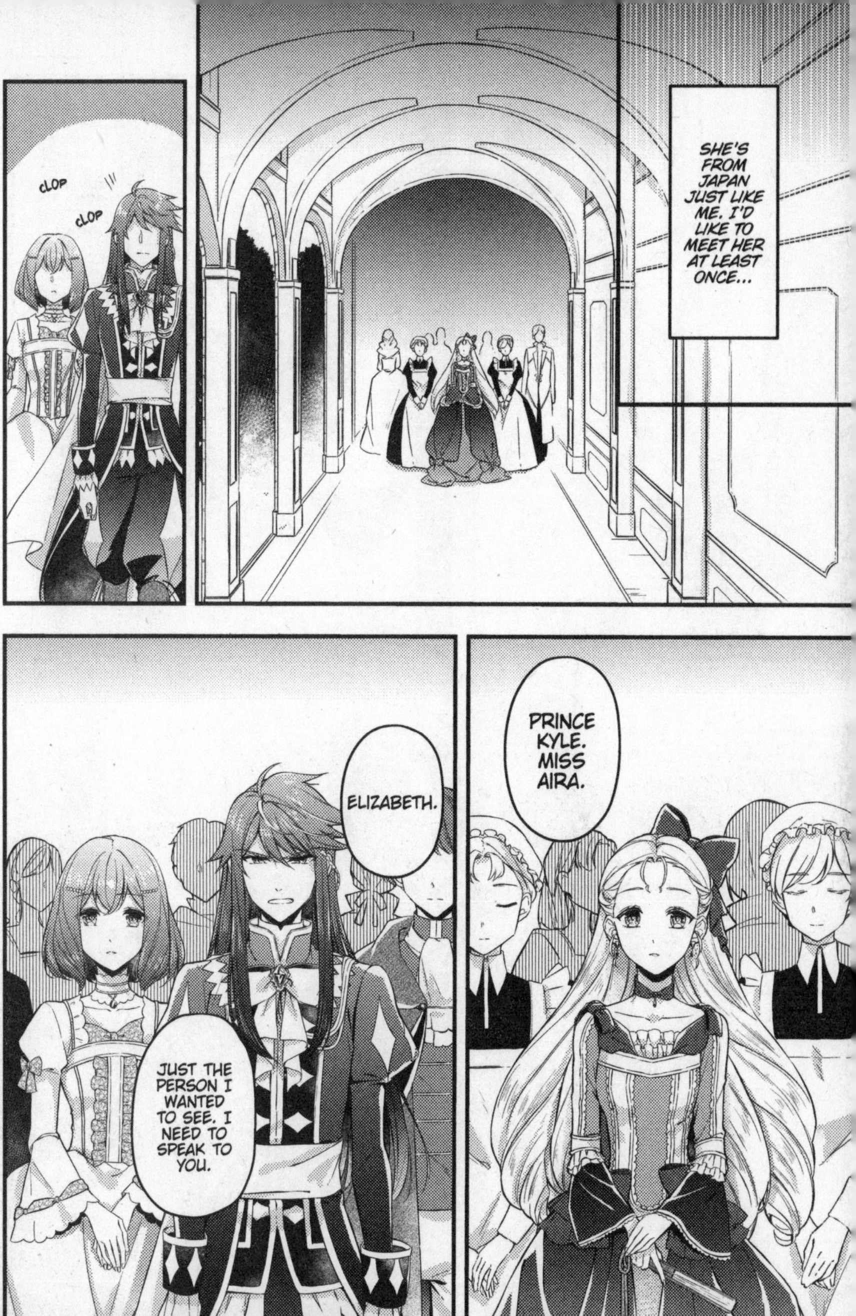
SHE'S FROM JAPAN JUST LIKE ME. I'D LIKE TO MEET HER AT LEAST ONCE...
CLOP
CLOP
PRINCE KYLE. MISS AIRA.
ELIZABETH.
JUST THE PERSON I WANTED TO SEE. I NEED TO SPEAK TO YOU.

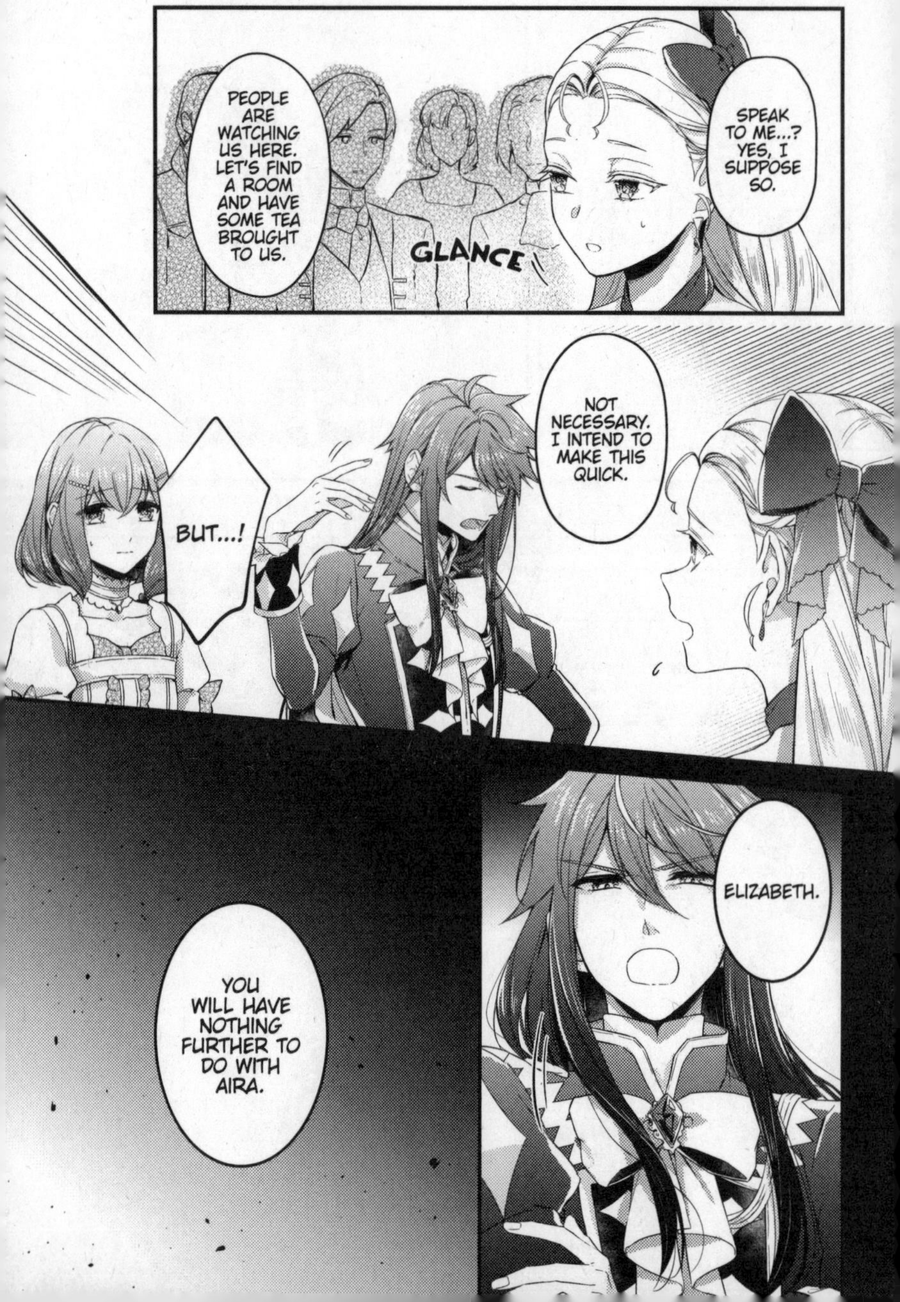
SPEAK TO ME...? YES, I SUPPOSE SO.
PEOPLE ARE WATCHING US HERE. LET'S FIND A ROOM AND HAVE SOME TEA BROUGHT TO US.
GLANCE
NOT NECESSARY. I INTEND TO MAKE THIS QUICK.
BUT...!
ELIZABETH.
YOU WILL HAVE NOTHING FURTHER TO DO WITH AIRA.

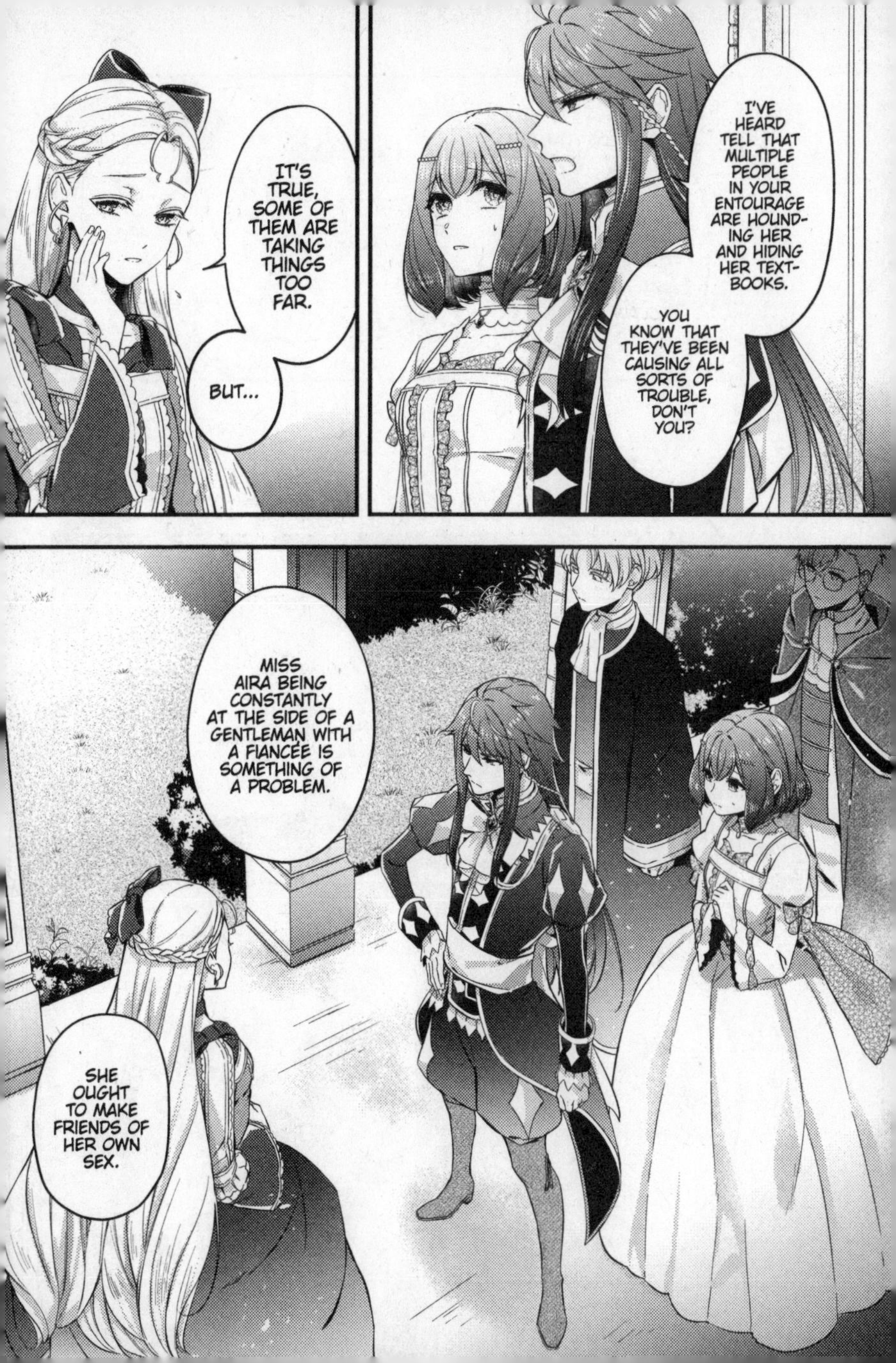
I'VE HEARD TELL THAT MULTIPLE PEOPLE IN YOUR ENTOURAGE ARE HOUNDING HER AND HIDING HER TEXTBOOKS.
YOU KNOW THAT THEY'VE BEEN CAUSING ALL SORTS OF TROUBLE, DON'T YOU?
IT'S TRUE, SOME OF THEM ARE TAKING THINGS TOO FAR.
BUT...
MISS AIRA BEING CONSTANTLY AT THE SIDE OF A GENTLEMAN WITH A FIANCÉE IS SOMETHING OF A PROBLEM.
SHE OUGHT TO MAKE FRIENDS OF HER OWN SEX.

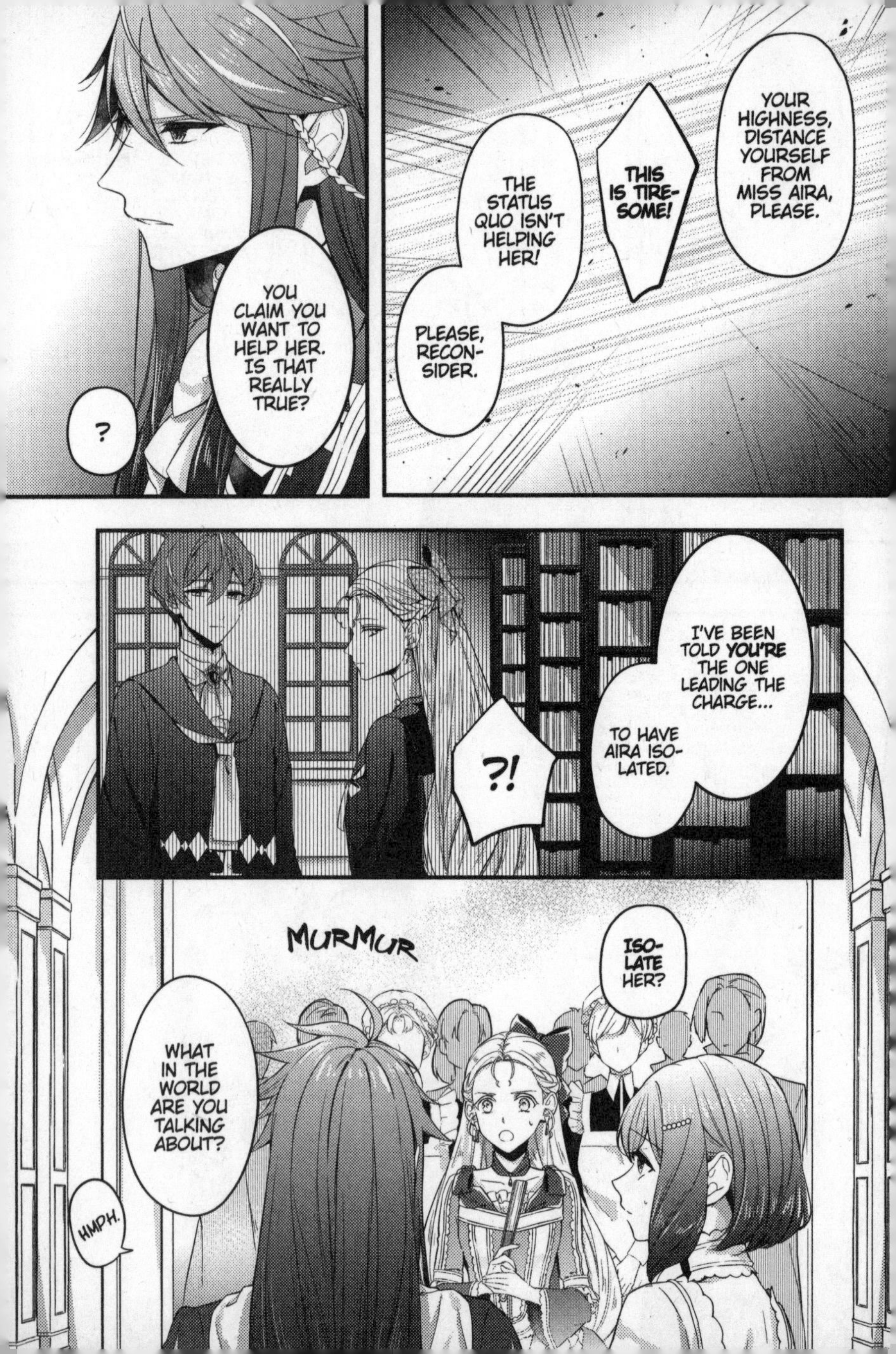
YOUR HIGHNESS, DISTANCE YOURSELF FROM MISS AIRA, PLEASE.
THIS IS TIRESOME!
THE STATUS QUO ISN'T HELPING HER!
PLEASE, RECONSIDER.
YOU CLAIM YOU WANT TO HELP HER. IS THAT REALLY TRUE?
?
I'VE BEEN TOLD YOU'RE THE ONE LEADING THE CHARGE...
TO HAVE AIRA ISOLATED.
?!
ISOLATE HER?
MURMUR
WHAT IN THE WORLD ARE YOU TALKING ABOUT?
HMPH.

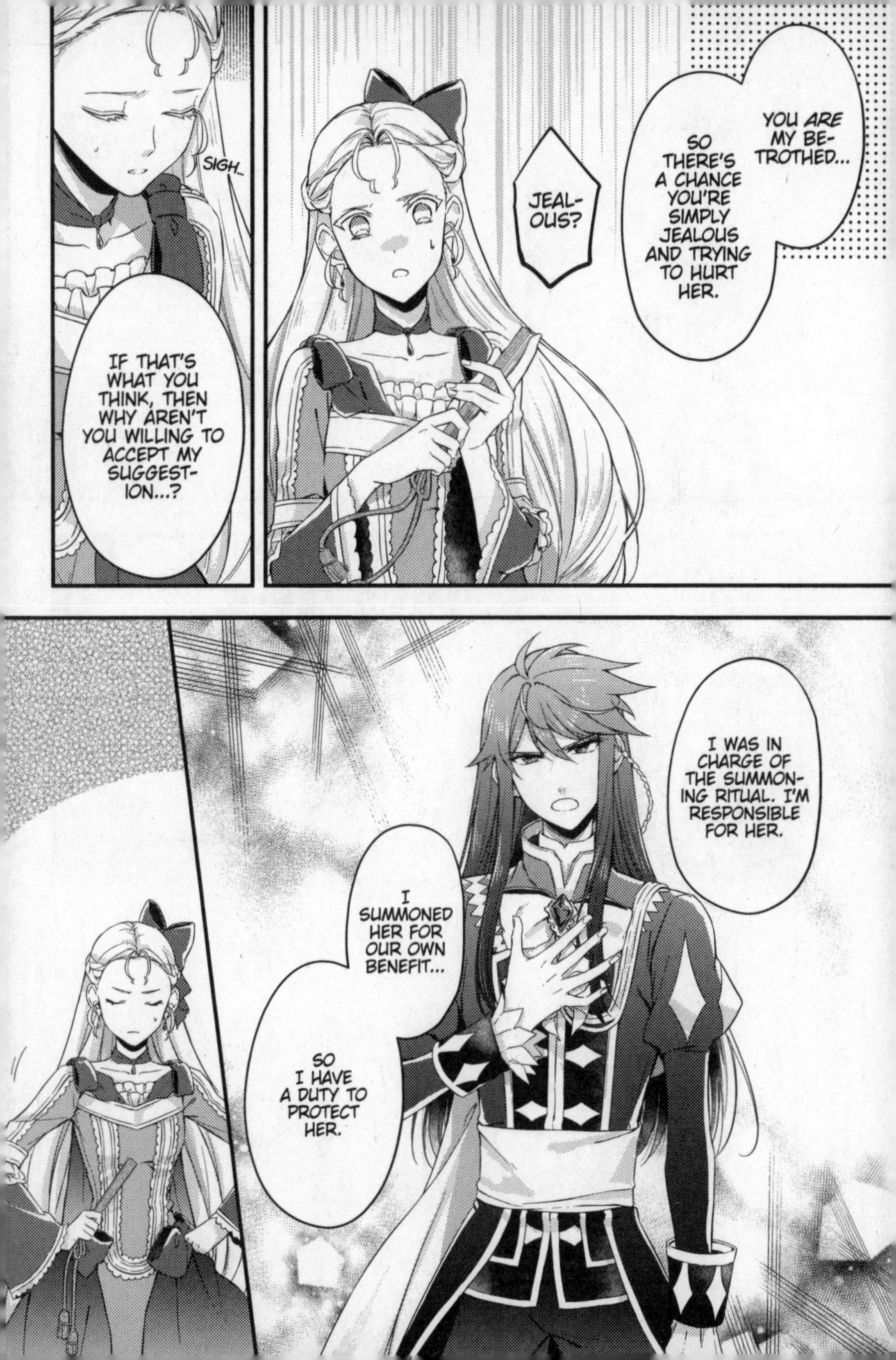
YOU ARE MY BE-TROTHED...
SO THERE'S A CHANCE YOU'RE SIMPLY JEALOUS AND TRYING TO HURT HER.
JEAL-OUS?
SIGH..
IF THAT'S WHAT YOU THINK, THEN WHY AREN'T YOU WILLING TO ACCEPT MY SUGGEST-ION...?
I WAS IN CHARGE OF THE SUMMON-ING RITUAL. I'M RESPONSIBLE FOR HER.
I SUMMONED HER FOR OUR OWN BENEFIT...
SO I HAVE A DUTY TO PROTECT HER.

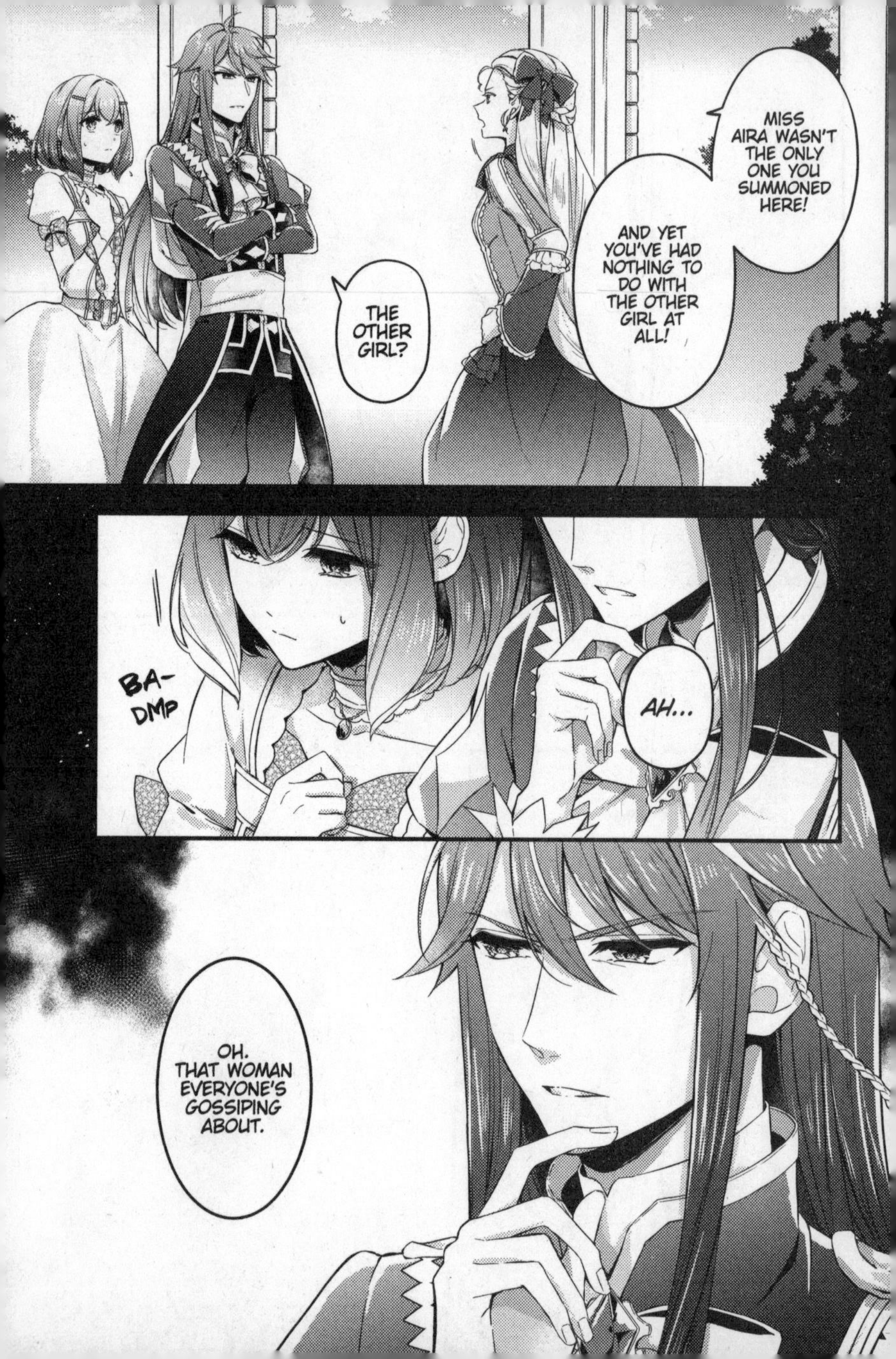
MISS AIRA WASN'T THE ONLY ONE YOU SUMMONED HERE!
AND YET YOU'VE HAD NOTHING TO DO WITH THE OTHER GIRL AT ALL!
THE OTHER GIRL?
AH...
BA-DMP
OH. THAT WOMAN EVERYONE'S GOSSIPING ABOUT.

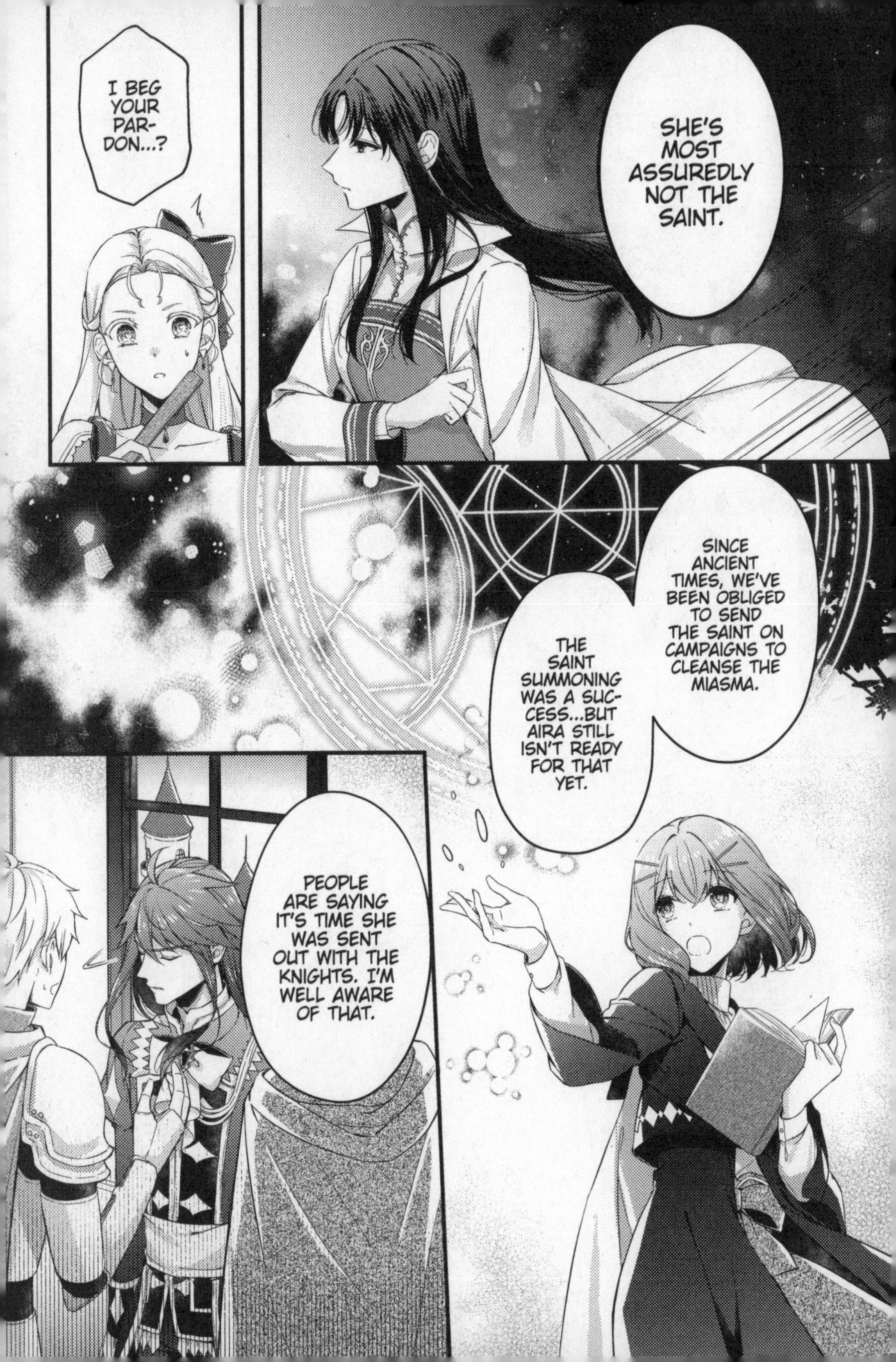
SHE'S MOST ASSUREDLY NOT THE SAINT.
I BEG YOUR PAR-DON...?
SINCE ANCIENT TIMES, WE'VE BEEN OBLIGED TO SEND THE SAINT ON CAMPAIGNS TO CLEANSE THE MIASMA.
THE SAINT SUMMONING WAS A SUC-CESS...BUT AIRA STILL ISN'T READY FOR THAT YET.
PEOPLE ARE SAYING IT'S TIME SHE WAS SENT OUT WITH THE KNIGHTS. I'M WELL AWARE OF THAT.

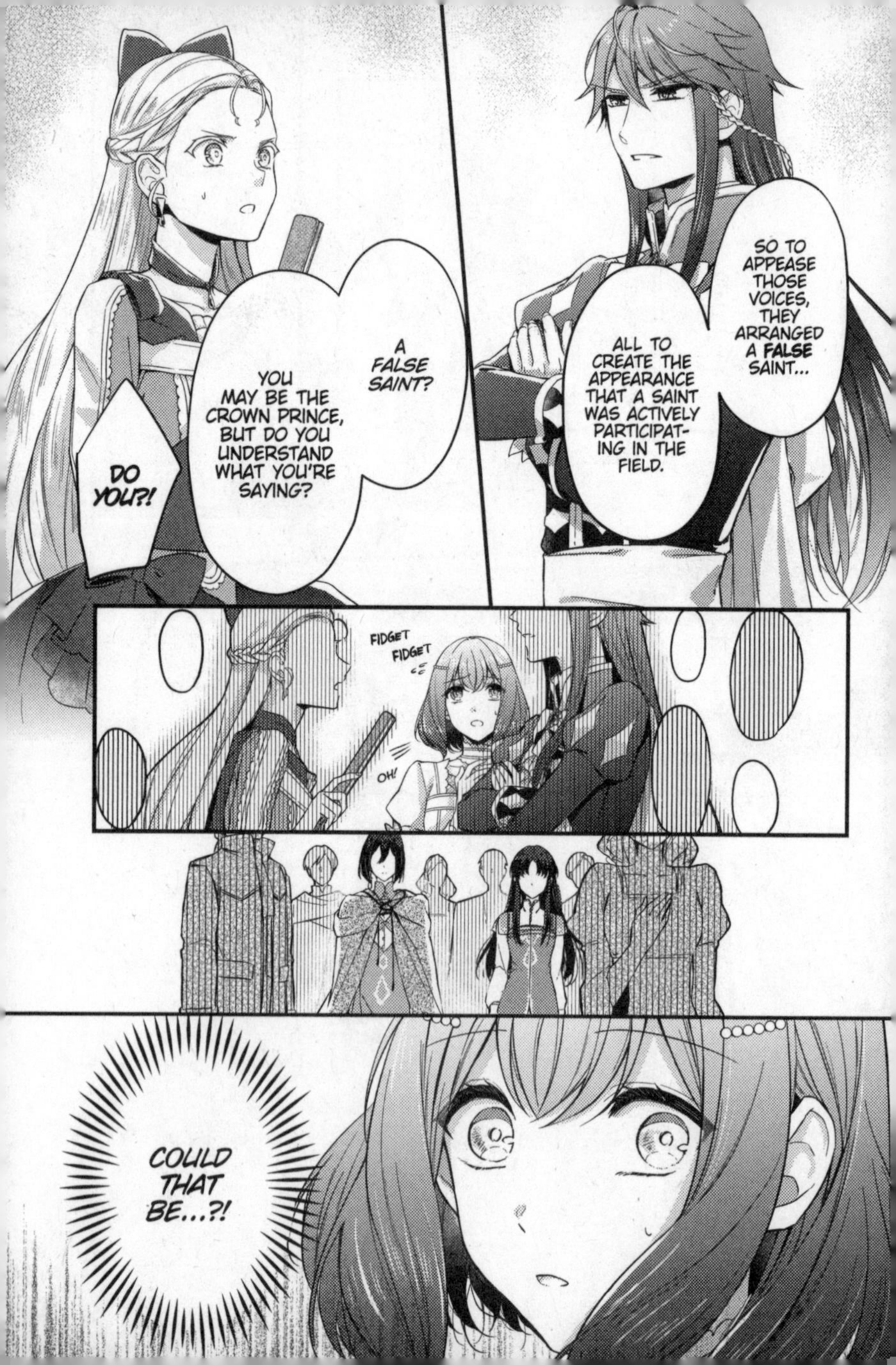

SO TO APPEASE THOSE VOICES, THEY ARRANGED A FALSE SAINT...
ALL TO CREATE THE APPEARANCE THAT A SAINT WAS ACTIVELY PARTICIPATING IN THE FIELD.
A FALSE SAINT?
YOU MAY BE THE CROWN PRINCE, BUT DO YOU UNDERSTAND WHAT YOU'RE SAYING?
DO YOU?!
FIDGET FIDGET
OH!
COULD THAT BE...?!

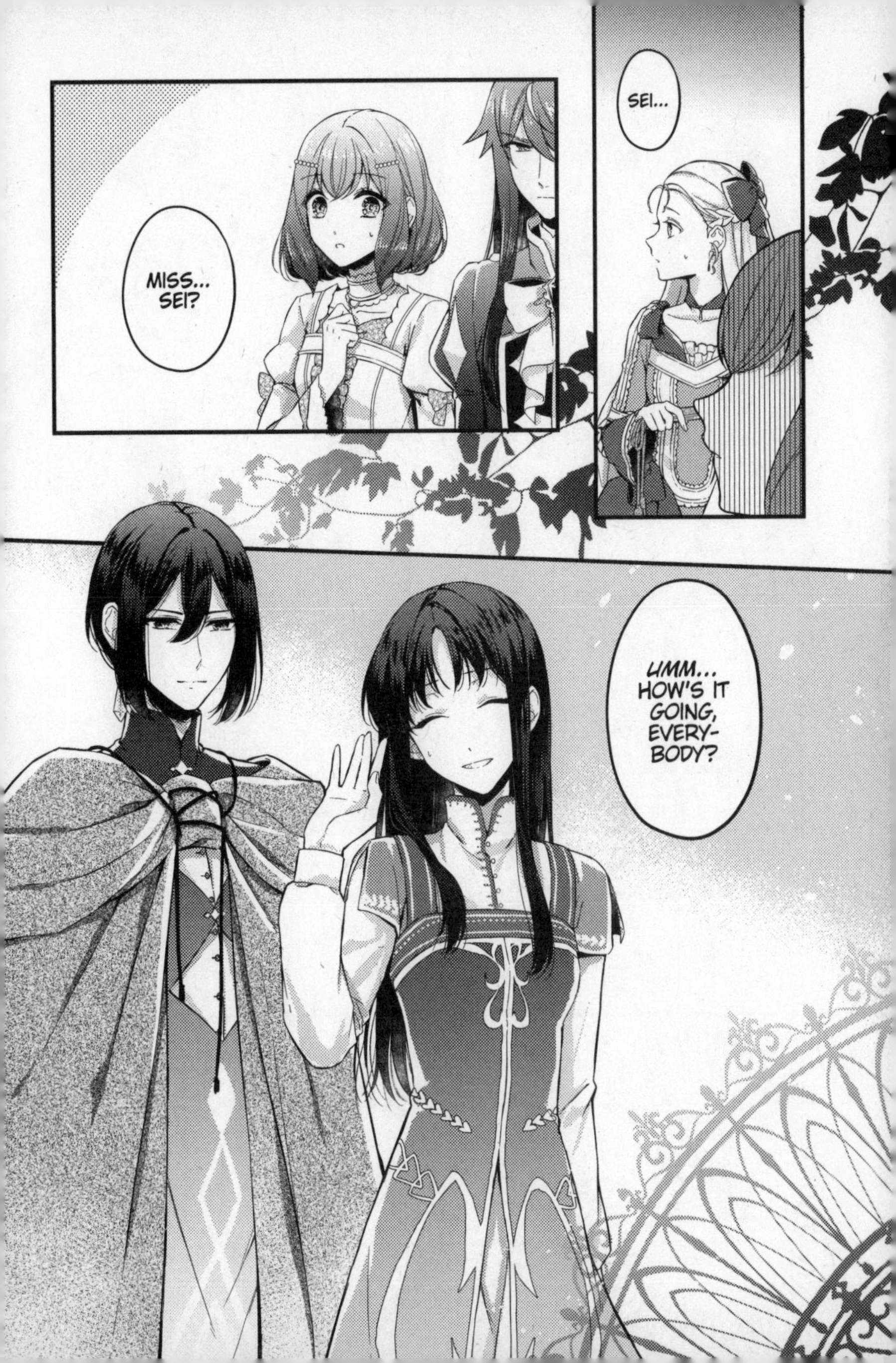
SEI...
MISS... SEI?
UMM... HOW'S IT GOING, EVERY-BODY?

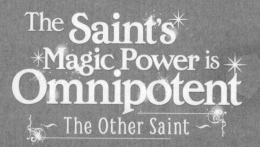

The Saint's
Magic Power is
Omnipotent
The Other Saint

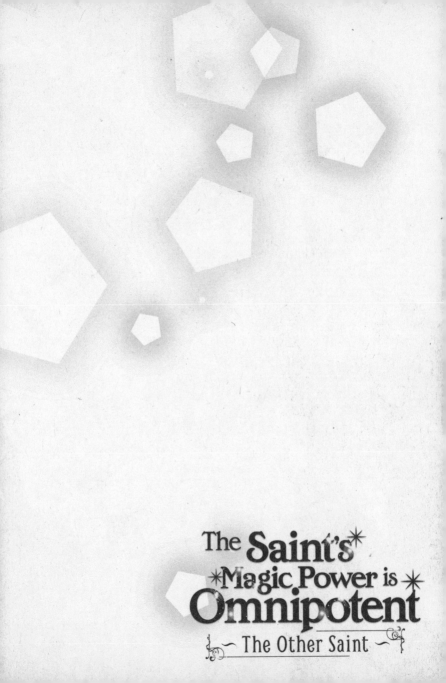

The Saint's
Magic Power is
Omnipotent
~ The Other Saint ~

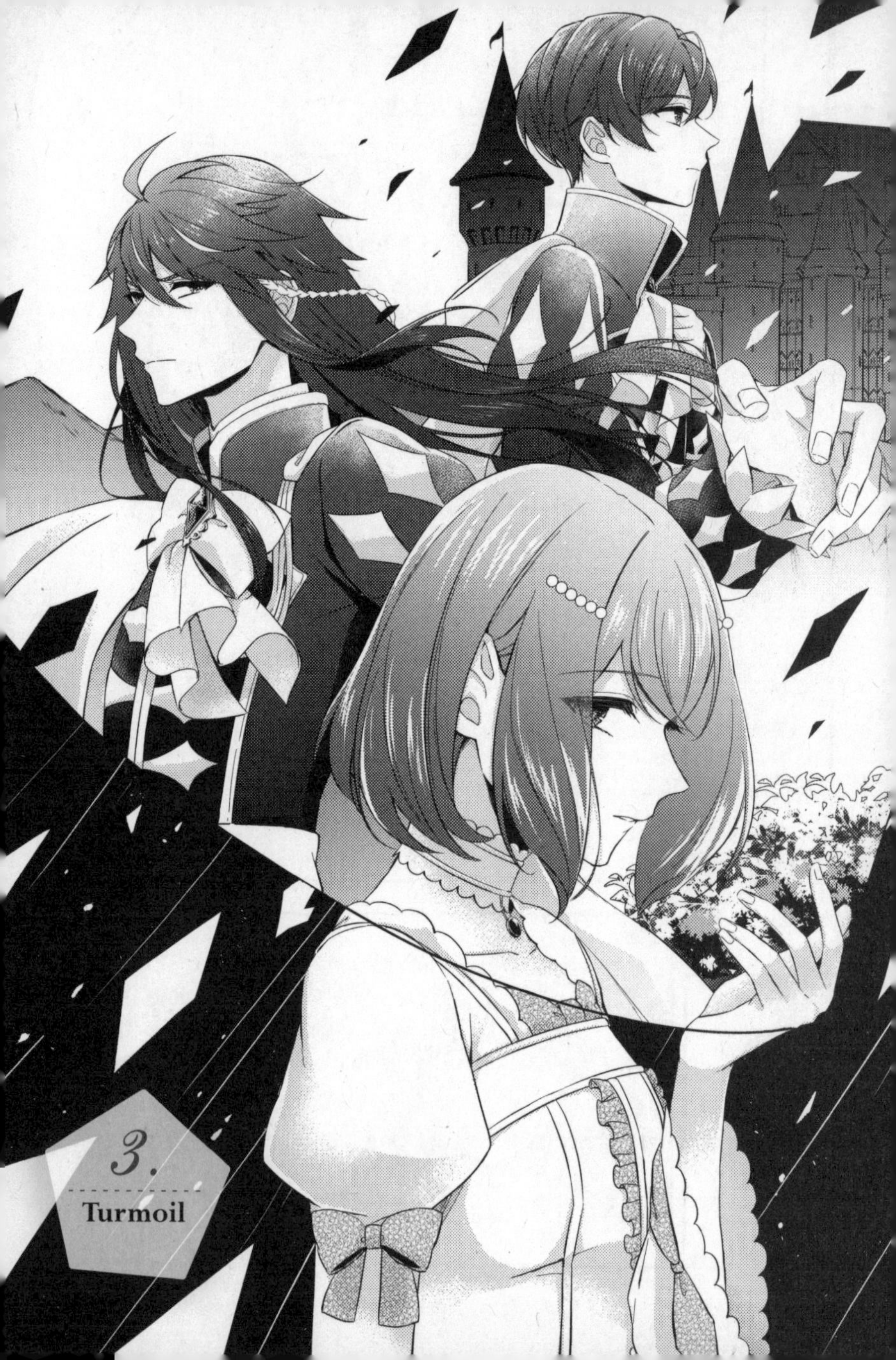
3.
Turmoil

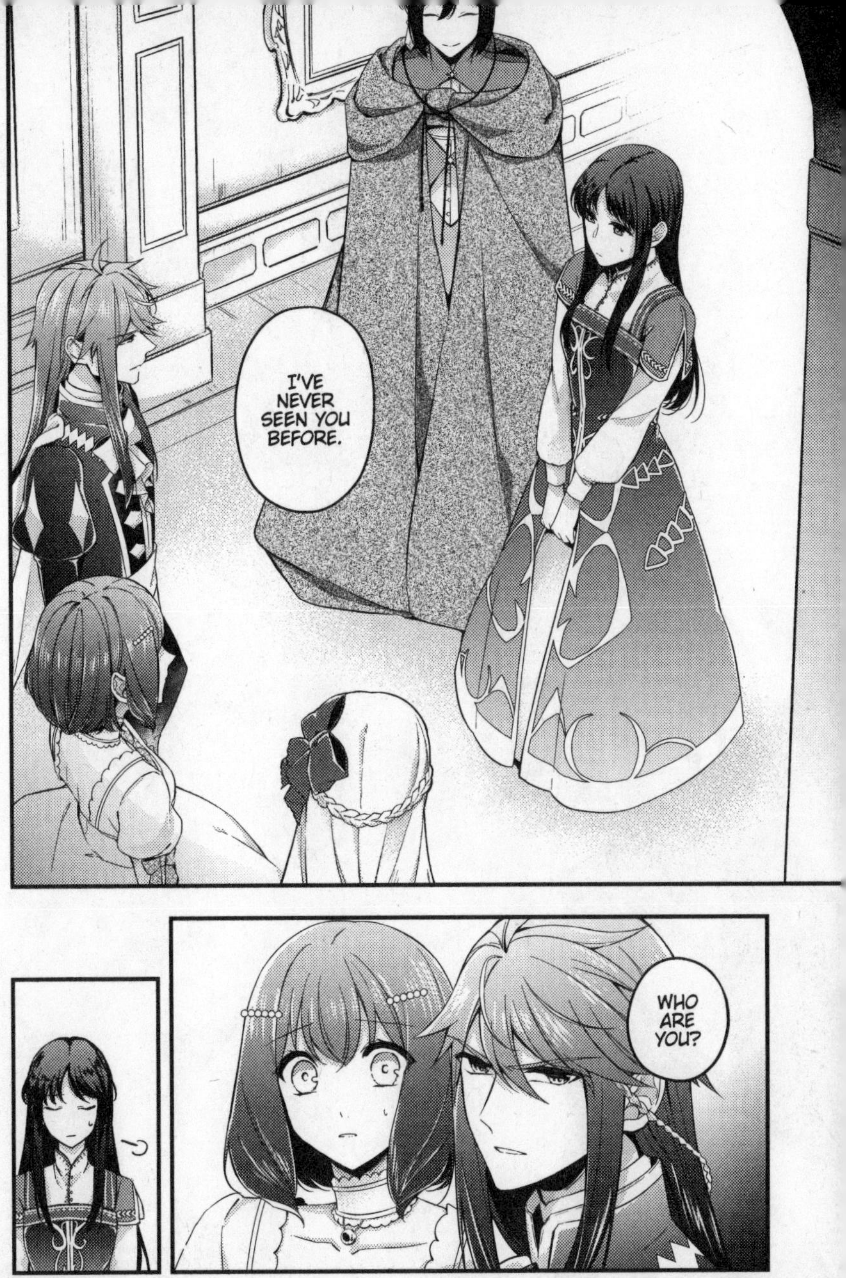
I'VE NEVER SEEN YOU BEFORE.
WHO ARE YOU?

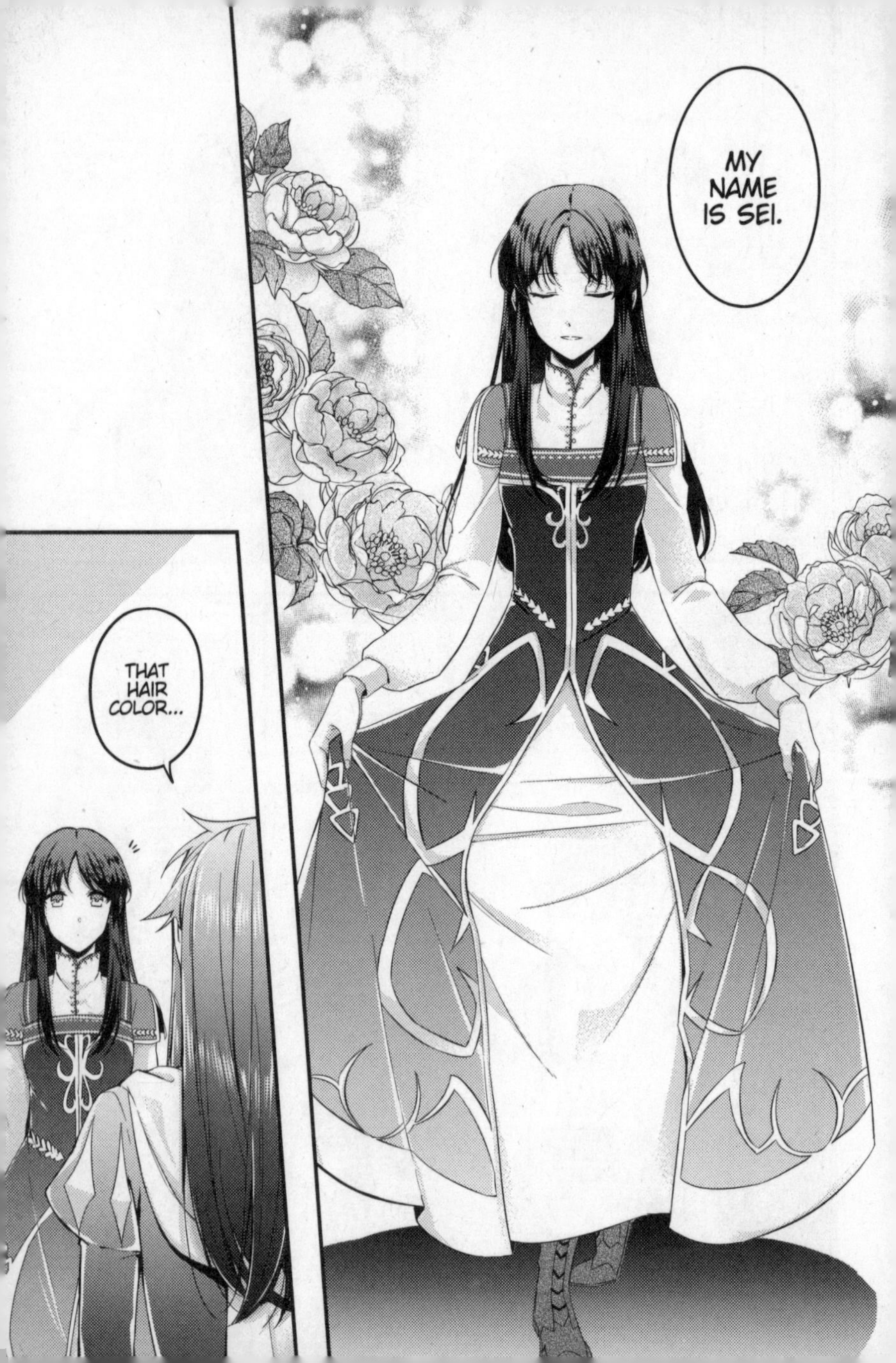
MY NAME IS SEI.
THAT HAIR COLOR...

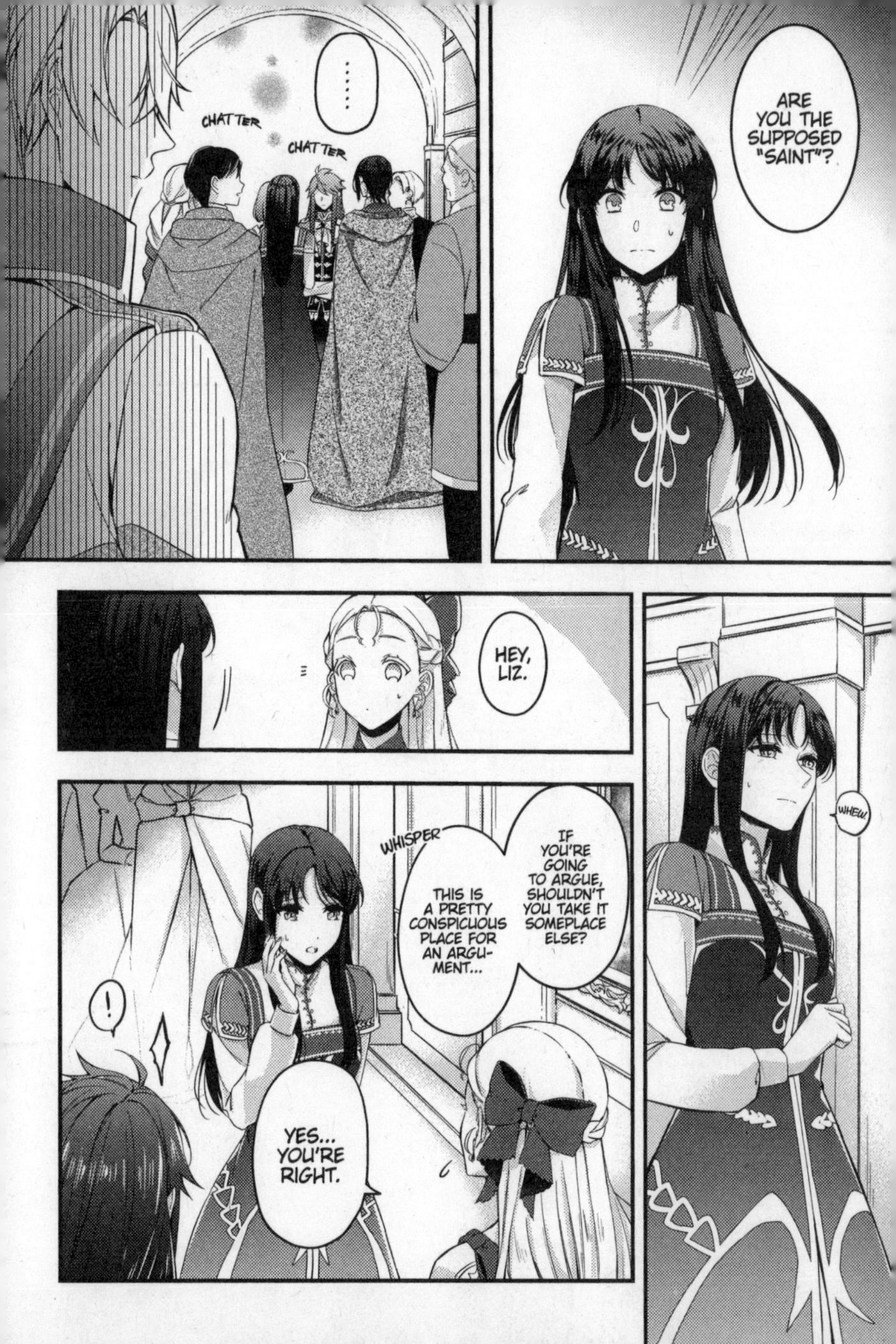
ARE YOU THE SUPPOSED "SAINT"?
......
CHATTER
CHATTER
WHEW
HEY, LIZ.
WHISPER
IF YOU'RE GOING TO ARGUE, SHOULDN'T YOU TAKE IT SOMEPLACE ELSE?
THIS IS A PRETTY CONSPICUOUS PLACE FOR AN ARGU-MENT...
!
YES... YOU'RE RIGHT.

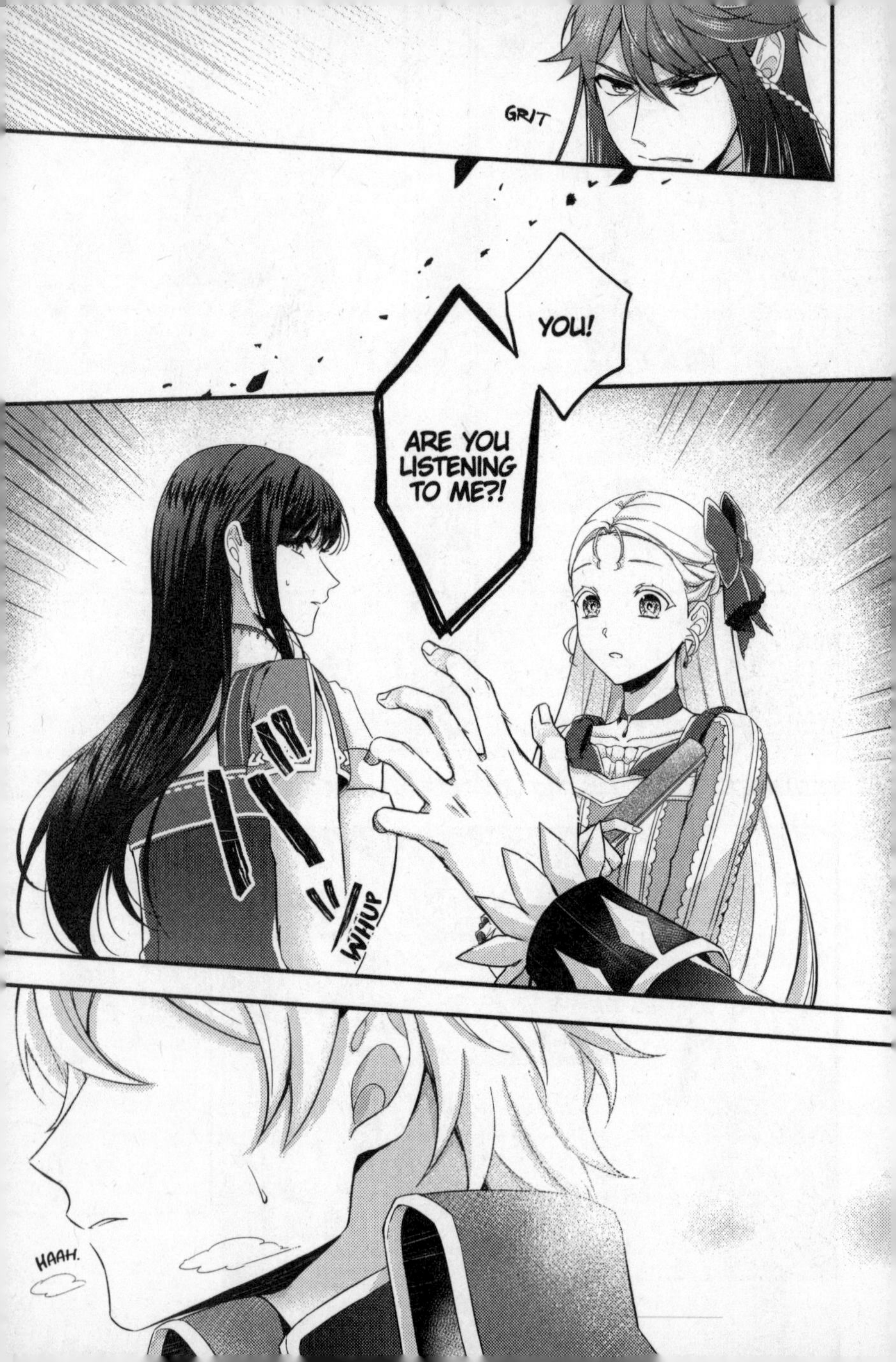
GRIT
YOU!
ARE YOU LISTENING TO ME?!
WHUP
HAAH.

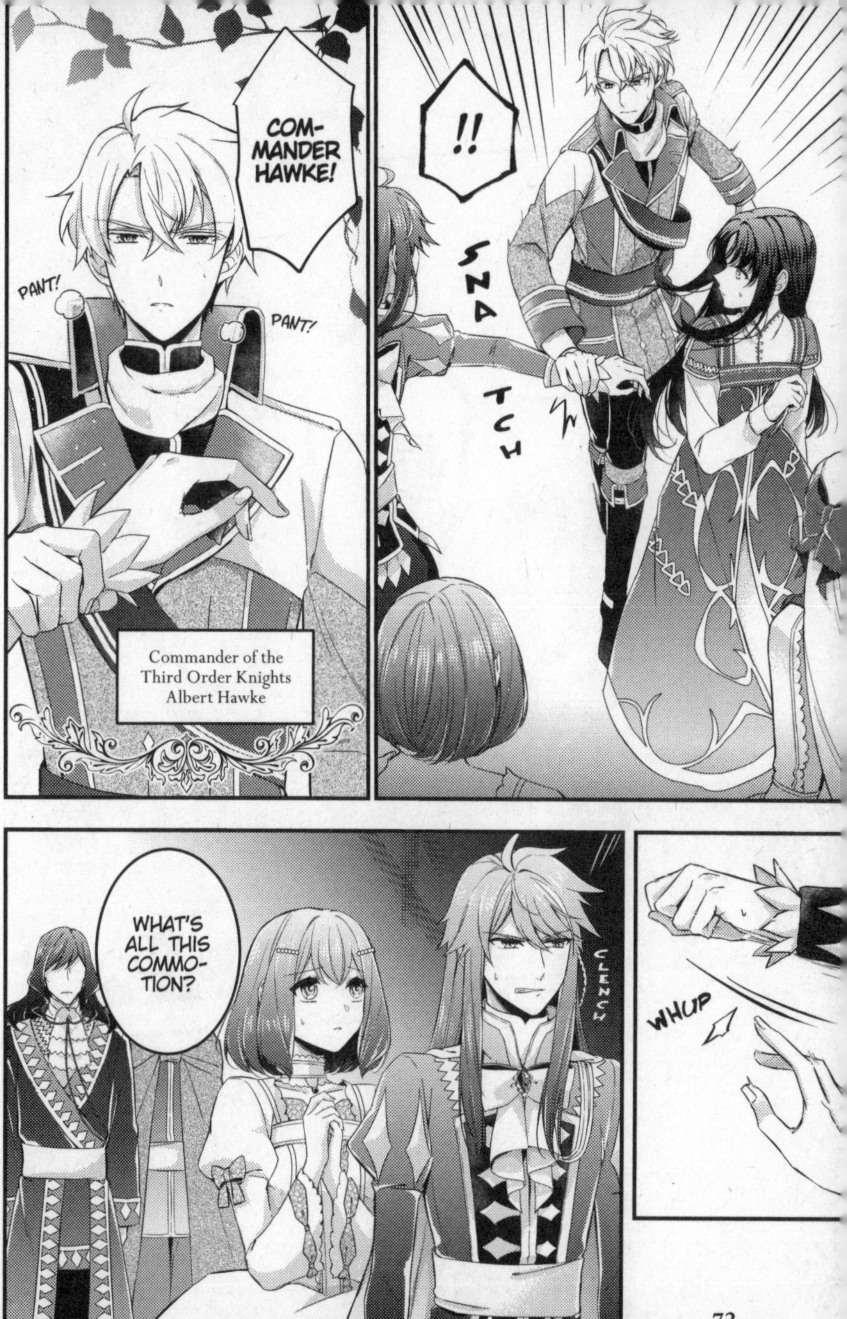
!!
SNATCH
COMMANDER HAWKE!
PANT!
PANT!
Commander of the Third Order Knights Albert Hawke
WHUP
WHAT'S ALL THIS COMMOTION?
CLENCH

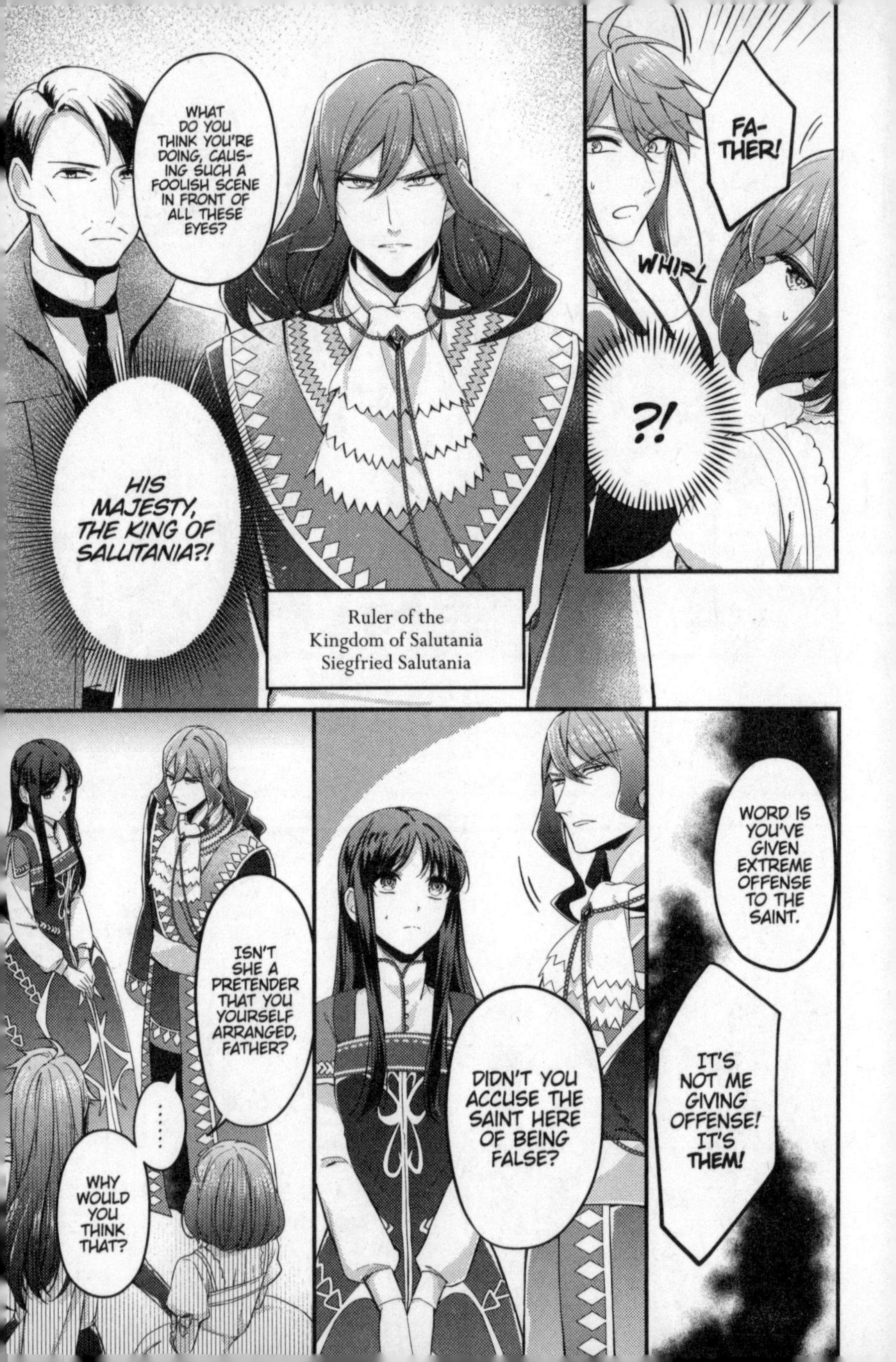

FA-THER!
WHIRL
?!
WHAT DO YOU THINK YOU'RE DOING, CAUSING SUCH A FOOLISH SCENE IN FRONT OF ALL THESE EYES?
HIS MAJESTY, THE KING OF SALUTANIA?!
Ruler of the Kingdom of Salutania Siegfried Salutania
WORD IS YOU'VE GIVEN EXTREME OFFENSE TO THE SAINT.
IT'S NOT ME GIVING OFFENSE! IT'S THEM!
DIDN'T YOU ACCUSE THE SAINT HERE OF BEING FALSE?
ISN'T SHE A PRETENDER THAT YOU YOURSELF ARRANGED, FATHER?
......
WHY WOULD YOU THINK THAT?

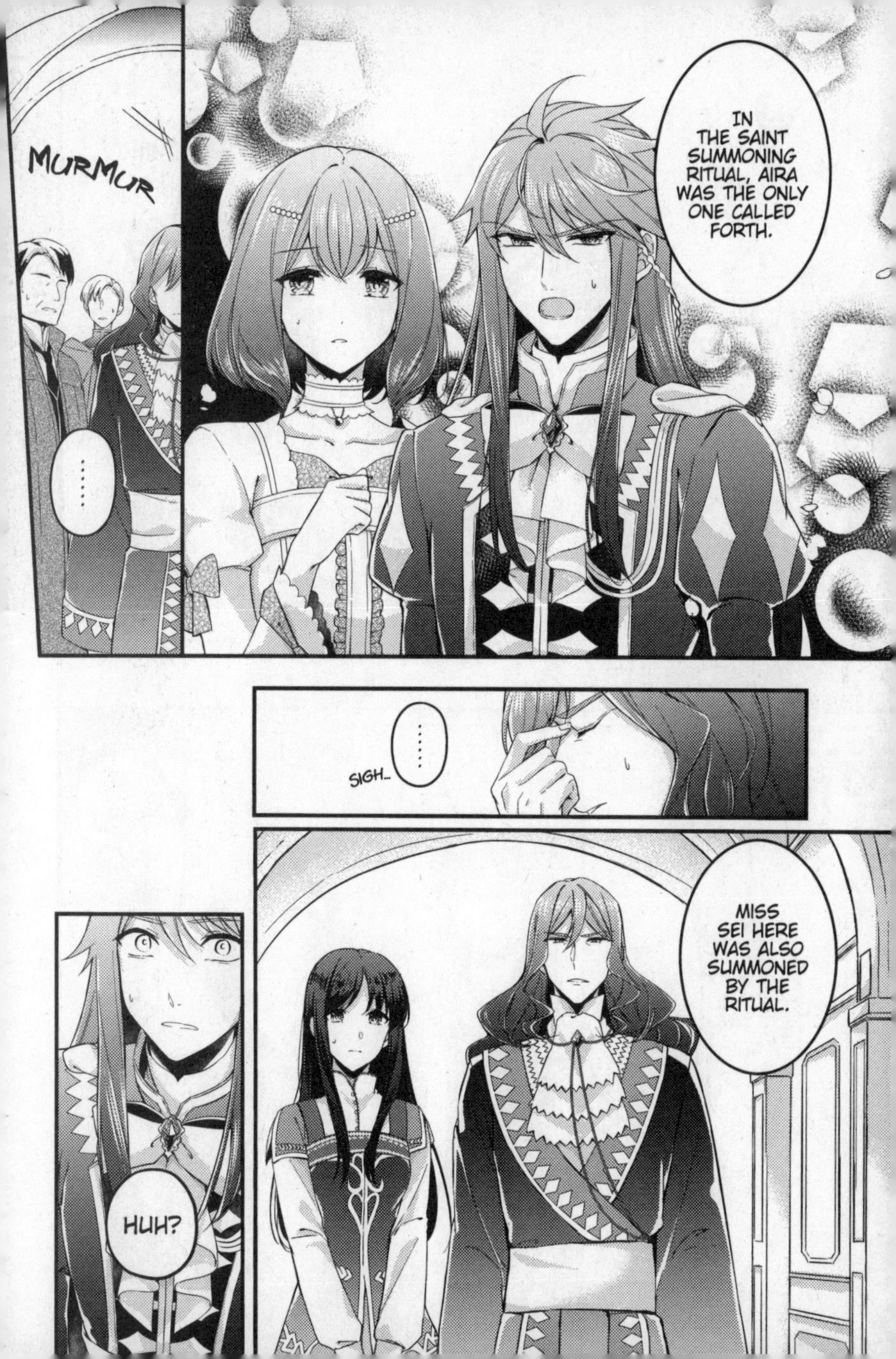
IN THE SAINT SUMMONING RITUAL, AIRA WAS THE ONLY ONE CALLED FORTH.
MURMUR
......
......
SIGH...
MISS SEI HERE WAS ALSO SUMMONED BY THE RITUAL.
HUH?

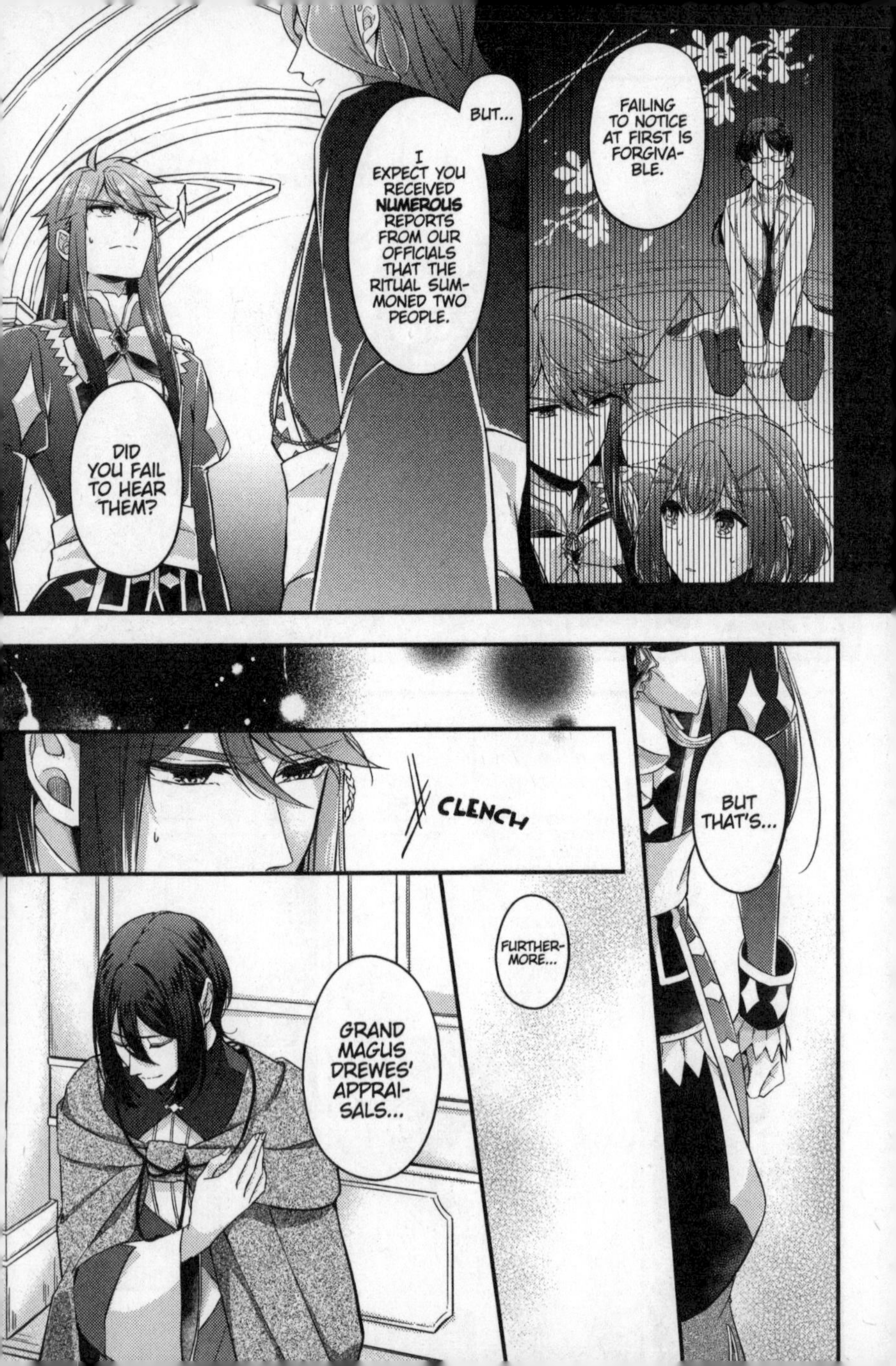
FAILING TO NOTICE AT FIRST IS FORGIVA-BLE.
BUT...
I EXPECT YOU RECEIVED **NUMEROUS** REPORTS FROM OUR OFFICIALS THAT THE RITUAL SUM-MONED TWO PEOPLE.
DID YOU FAIL TO HEAR THEM?
BUT THAT'S...
CLENCH
FURTHER-MORE...
GRAND MAGUS DREWES' APPRAI-SALS...

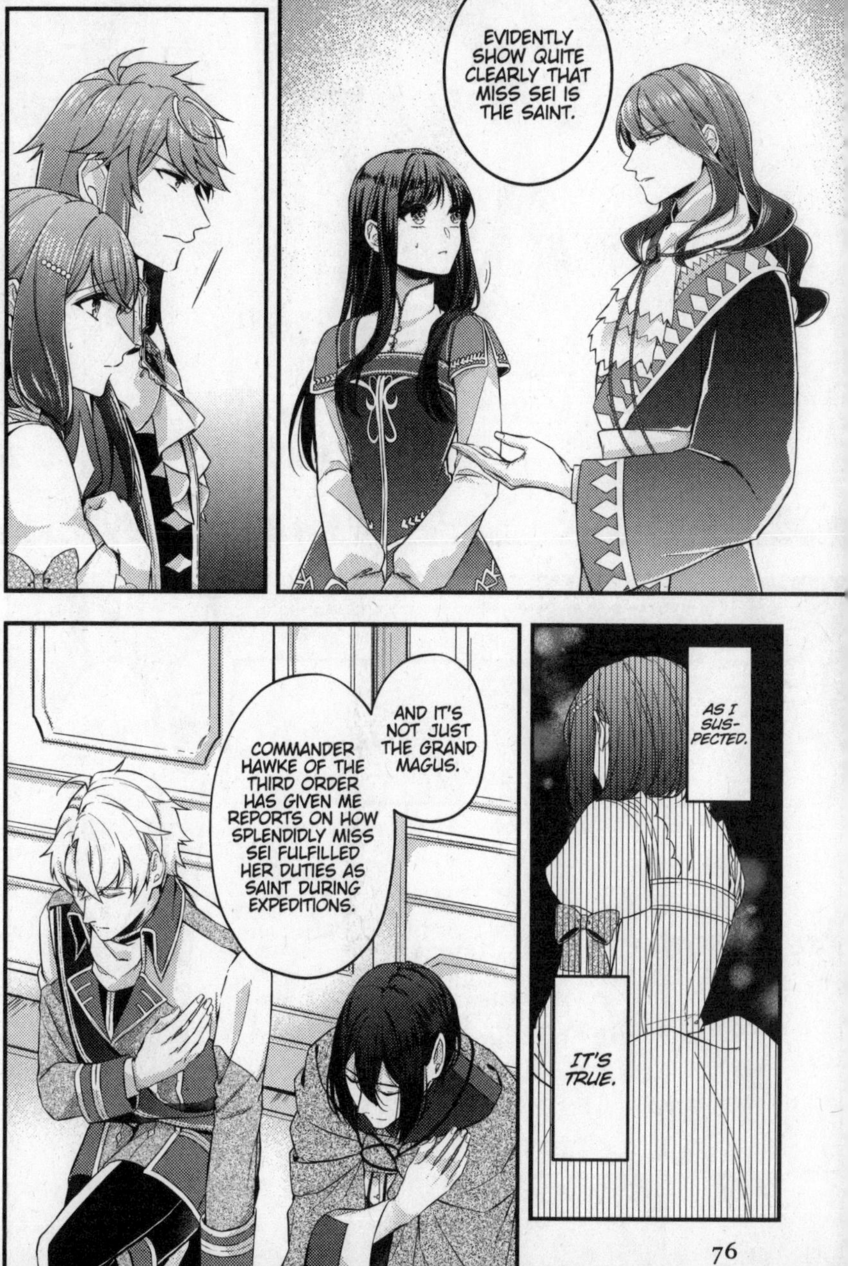
EVIDENTLY SHOW QUITE CLEARLY THAT MISS SEI IS THE SAINT.
AS I SUS-PECTED.
IT'S TRUE.
AND IT'S NOT JUST THE GRAND MAGUS.
COMMANDER HAWKE OF THE THIRD ORDER HAS GIVEN ME REPORTS ON HOW SPLENDIDLY MISS SEI FULFILLED HER DUTIES AS SAINT DURING EXPEDITIONS.

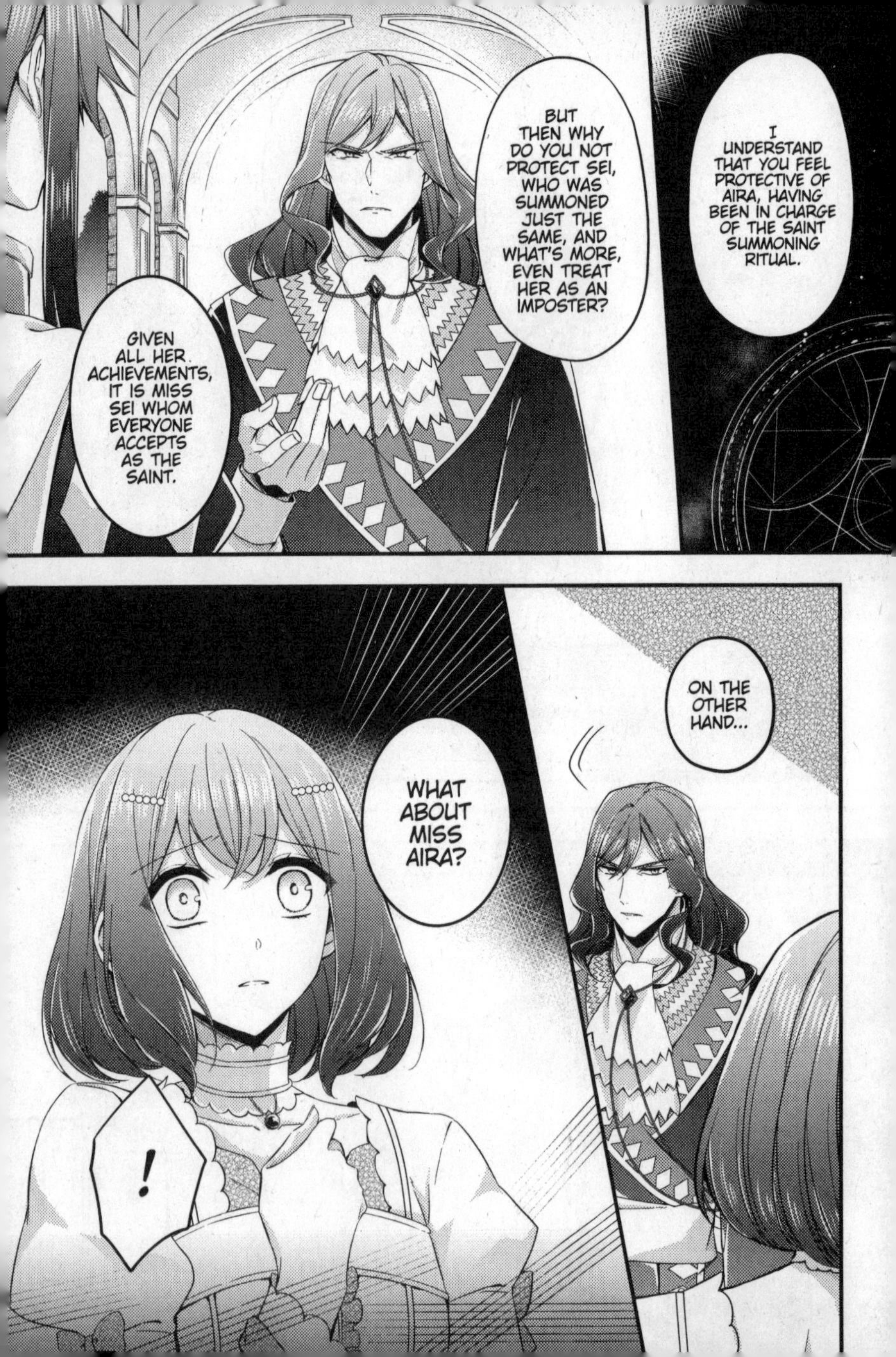
I UNDERSTAND THAT YOU FEEL PROTECTIVE OF AIRA, HAVING BEEN IN CHARGE OF THE SAINT SUMMONING RITUAL.
BUT THEN WHY DO YOU NOT PROTECT SEI, WHO WAS SUMMONED JUST THE SAME, AND WHAT'S MORE, EVEN TREAT HER AS AN IMPOSTER?
GIVEN ALL HER ACHIEVEMENTS, IT IS MISS SEI WHOM EVERYONE ACCEPTS AS THE SAINT.
ON THE OTHER HAND...
WHAT ABOUT MISS AIRA?
!

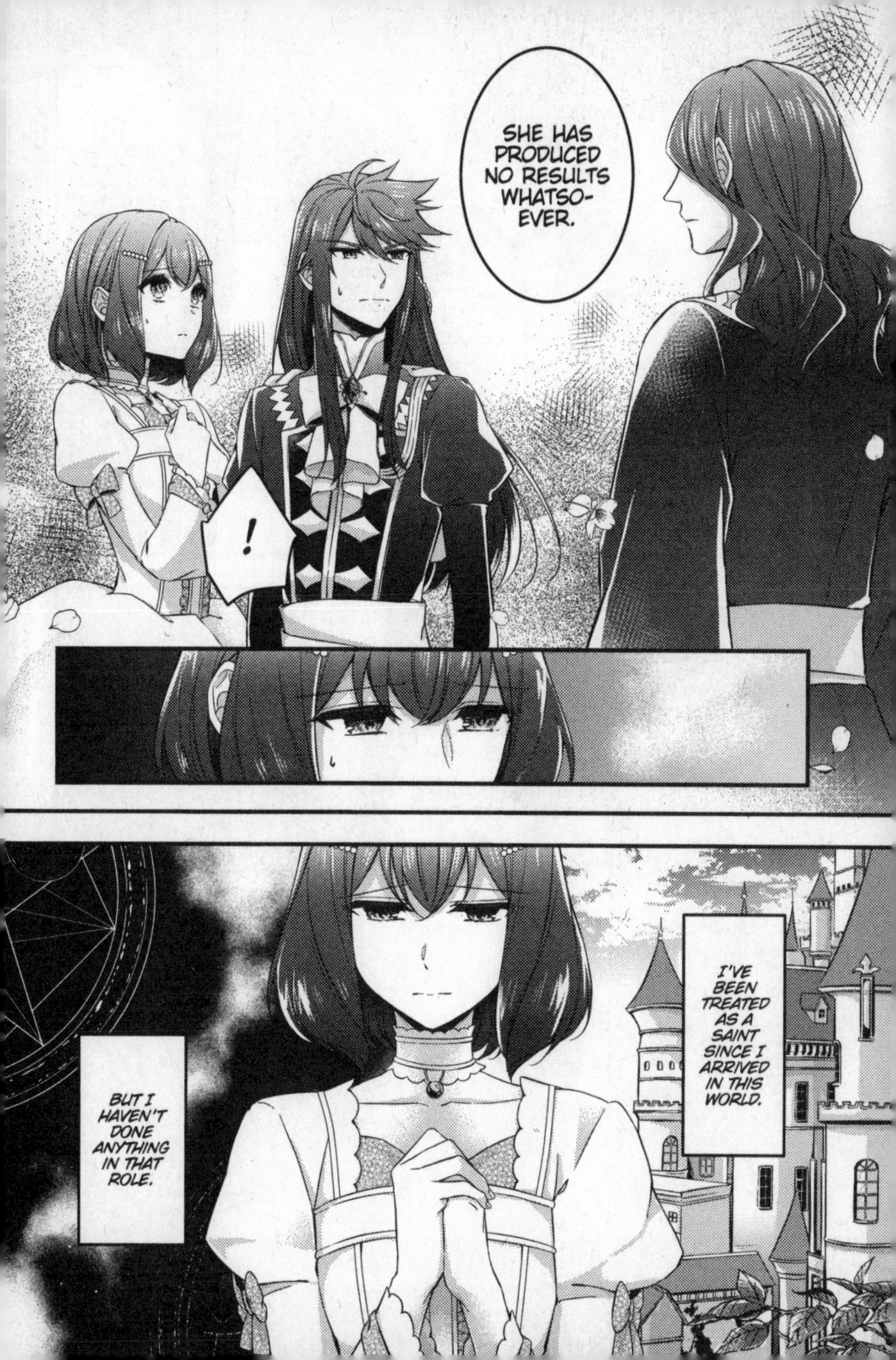
SHE HAS PRODUCED NO RESULTS WHATSO-EVER.
!
I'VE BEEN TREATED AS A SAINT SINCE I ARRIVED IN THIS WORLD.
BUT I HAVEN'T DONE ANYTHING IN THAT ROLE.

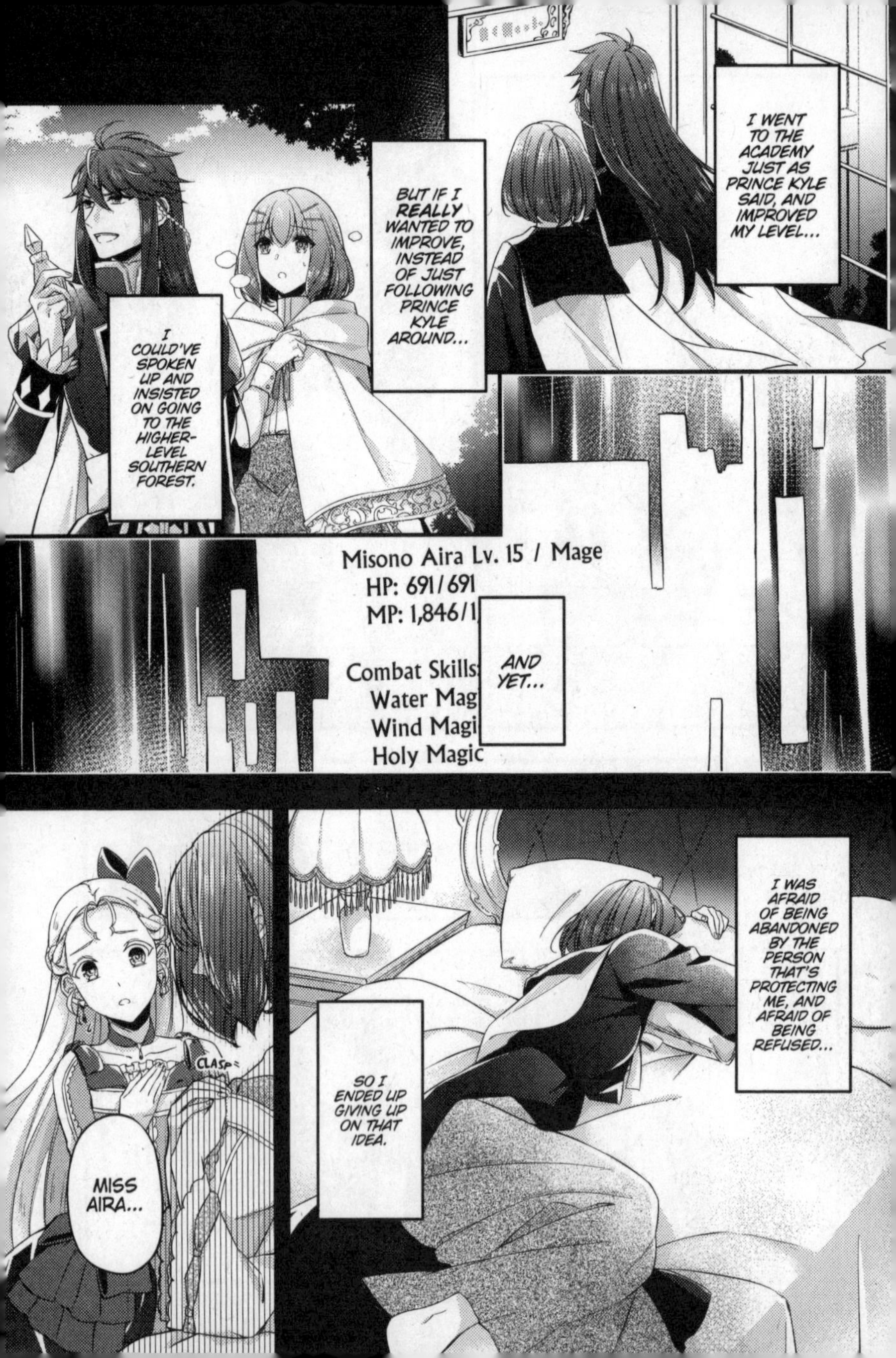
I WENT TO THE ACADEMY JUST AS PRINCE KYLE SAID, AND IMPROVED MY LEVEL...
BUT IF I REALLY WANTED TO IMPROVE, INSTEAD OF JUST FOLLOWING PRINCE KYLE AROUND...
I COULD'VE SPOKEN UP AND INSISTED ON GOING TO THE HIGHER-LEVEL SOUTHERN FOREST.
Misono Aira Lv. 15 / Mage
HP: 691/691
MP: 1,846/1
Combat Skills:
Water Mag
Wind Magi
Holy Magic
AND YET...
I WAS AFRAID OF BEING ABANDONED BY THE PERSON THAT'S PROTECTING ME, AND AFRAID OF BEING REFUSED...
SO I ENDED UP GIVING UP ON THAT IDEA.
CLASP
MISS AIRA...

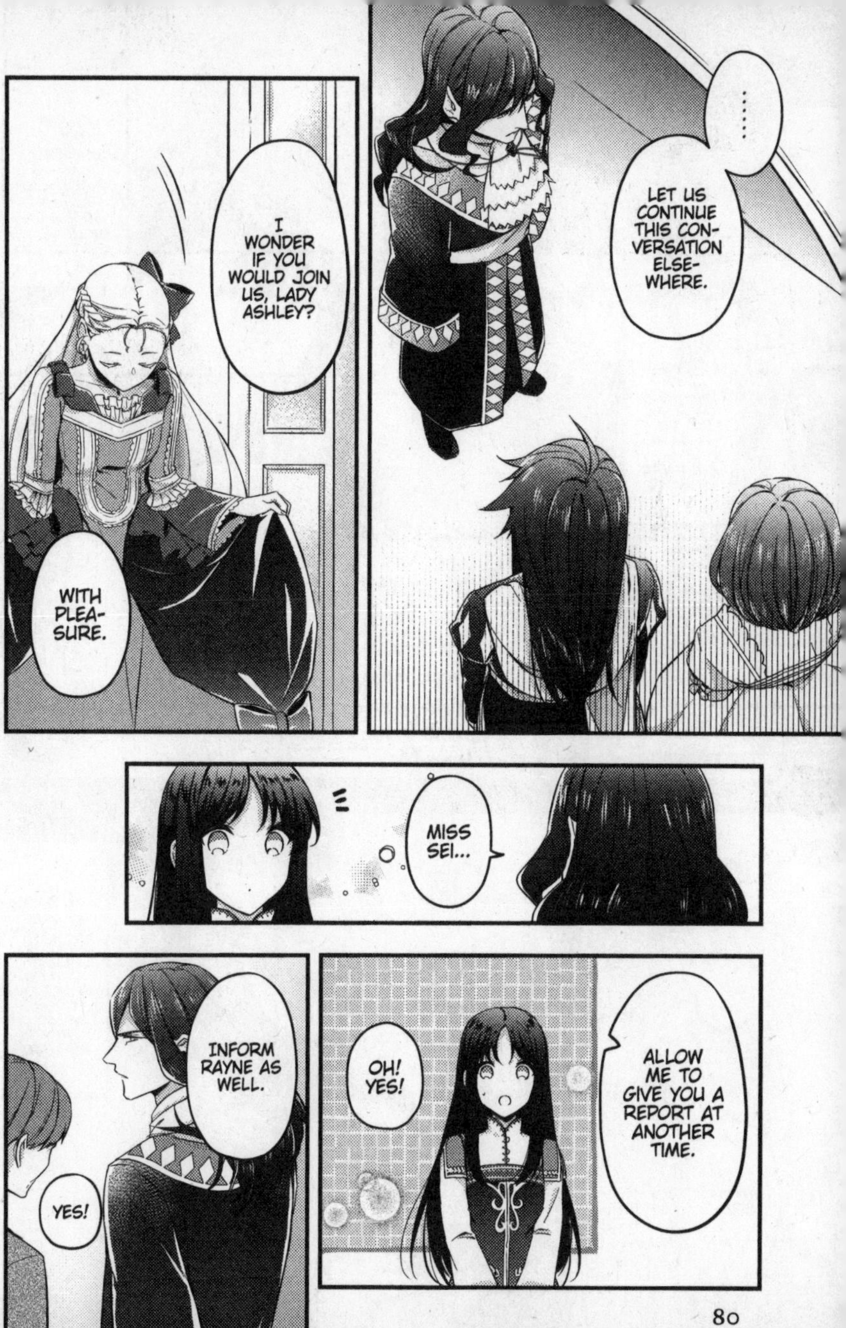
......
LET US CONTINUE THIS CON-VERSATION ELSE-WHERE.
I WONDER IF YOU WOULD JOIN US, LADY ASHLEY?
WITH PLEA-SURE.
MISS SEI...
ALLOW ME TO GIVE YOU A REPORT AT ANOTHER TIME.
OH! YES!
INFORM RAYNE AS WELL.
YES!

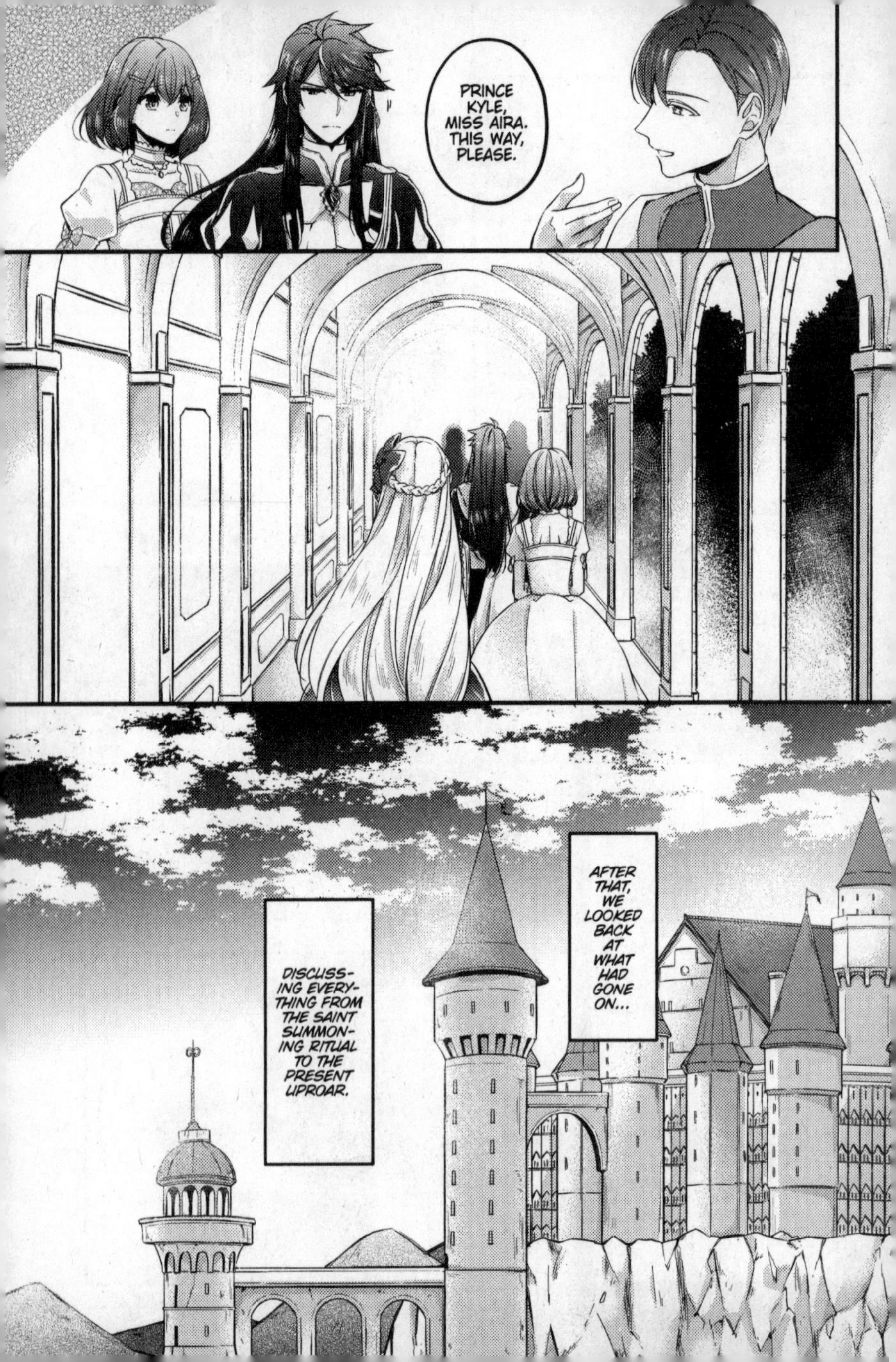
PRINCE KYLE, MISS AIRA. THIS WAY, PLEASE.
AFTER THAT, WE LOOKED BACK AT WHAT HAD GONE ON...
DISCUSSING EVERYTHING FROM THE SAINT SUMMONING RITUAL TO THE PRESENT UPROAR.

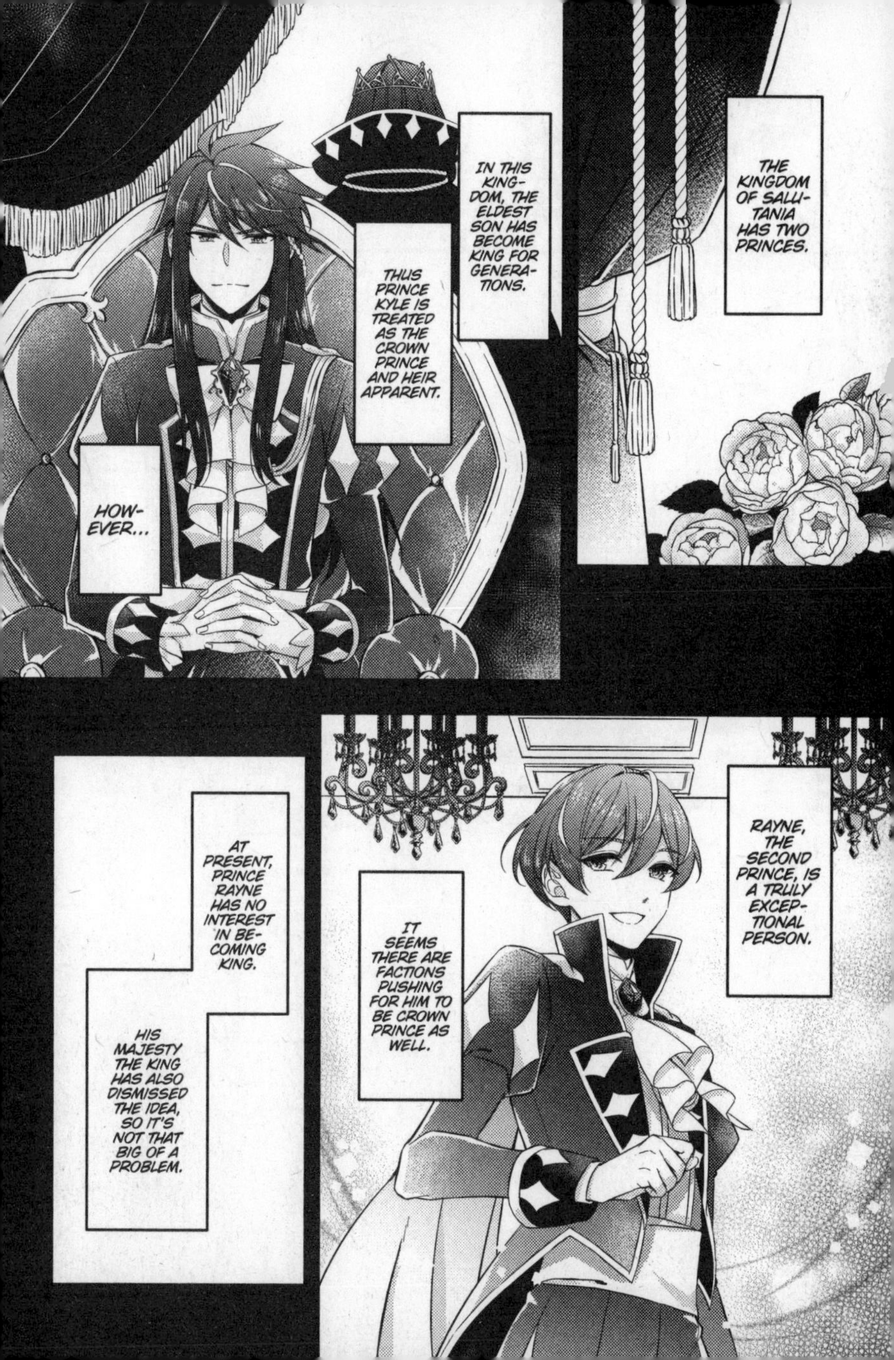
THE KINGDOM OF SALUTANIA HAS TWO PRINCES.
IN THIS KINGDOM, THE ELDEST SON HAS BECOME KING FOR GENERATIONS.
THUS PRINCE KYLE IS TREATED AS THE CROWN PRINCE AND HEIR APPARENT.
HOWEVER...
RAYNE, THE SECOND PRINCE, IS A TRULY EXCEPTIONAL PERSON.
IT SEEMS THERE ARE FACTIONS PUSHING FOR HIM TO BE CROWN PRINCE AS WELL.
AT PRESENT, PRINCE RAYNE HAS NO INTEREST IN BECOMING KING.
HIS MAJESTY THE KING HAS ALSO DISMISSED THE IDEA, SO IT'S NOT THAT BIG OF A PROBLEM.

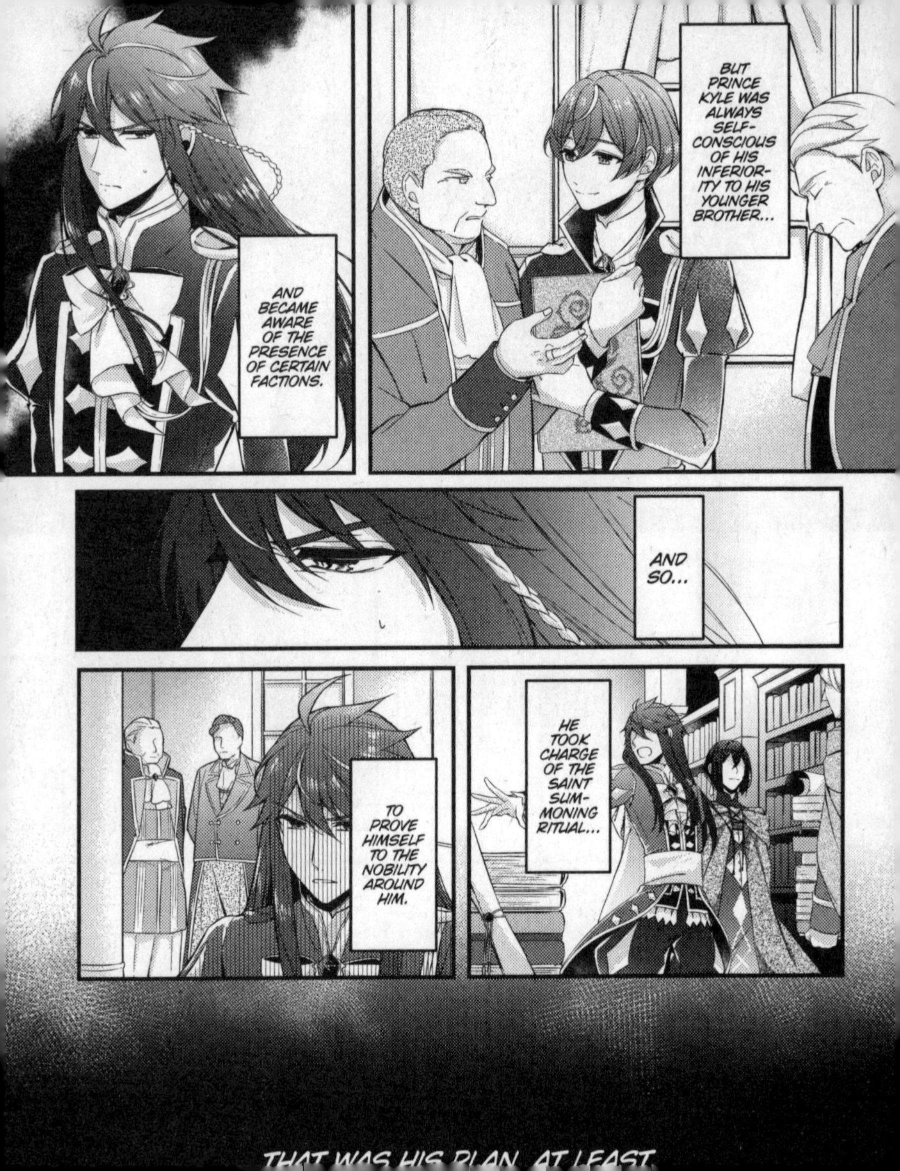
BUT PRINCE KYLE WAS ALWAYS SELF-CONSCIOUS OF HIS INFERIORITY TO HIS YOUNGER BROTHER...
AND BECAME AWARE OF THE PRESENCE OF CERTAIN FACTIONS.
AND SO...
HE TOOK CHARGE OF THE SAINT SUMMONING RITUAL...
TO PROVE HIMSELF TO THE NOBILITY AROUND HIM.
THAT WAS HIS PLAN, AT LEAST.

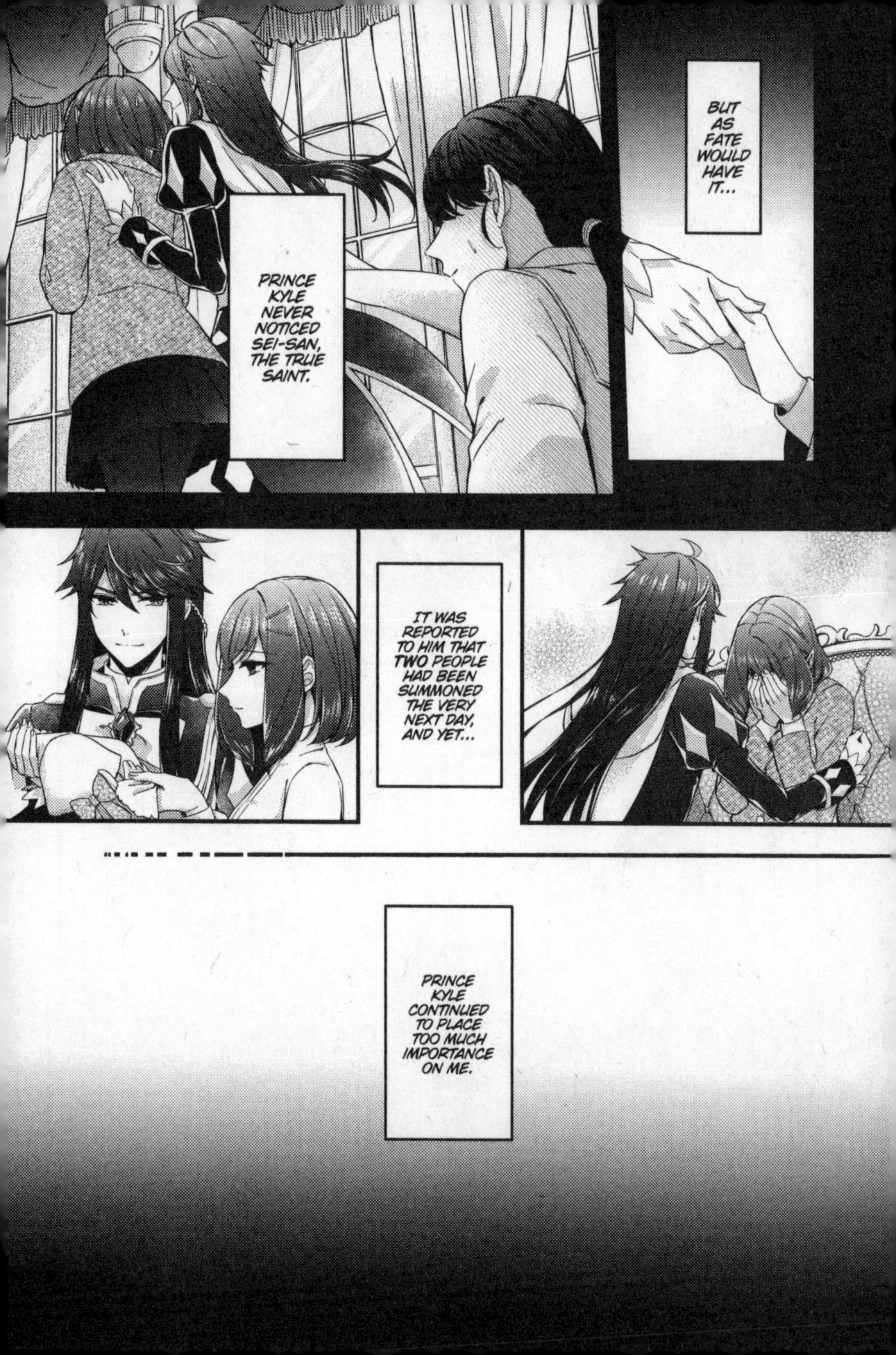
BUT AS FATE WOULD HAVE IT...
PRINCE KYLE NEVER NOTICED SEI-SAN, THE TRUE SAINT.
IT WAS REPORTED TO HIM THAT TWO PEOPLE HAD BEEN SUMMONED THE VERY NEXT DAY, AND YET...
PRINCE KYLE CONTINUED TO PLACE TOO MUCH IMPORTANCE ON ME.

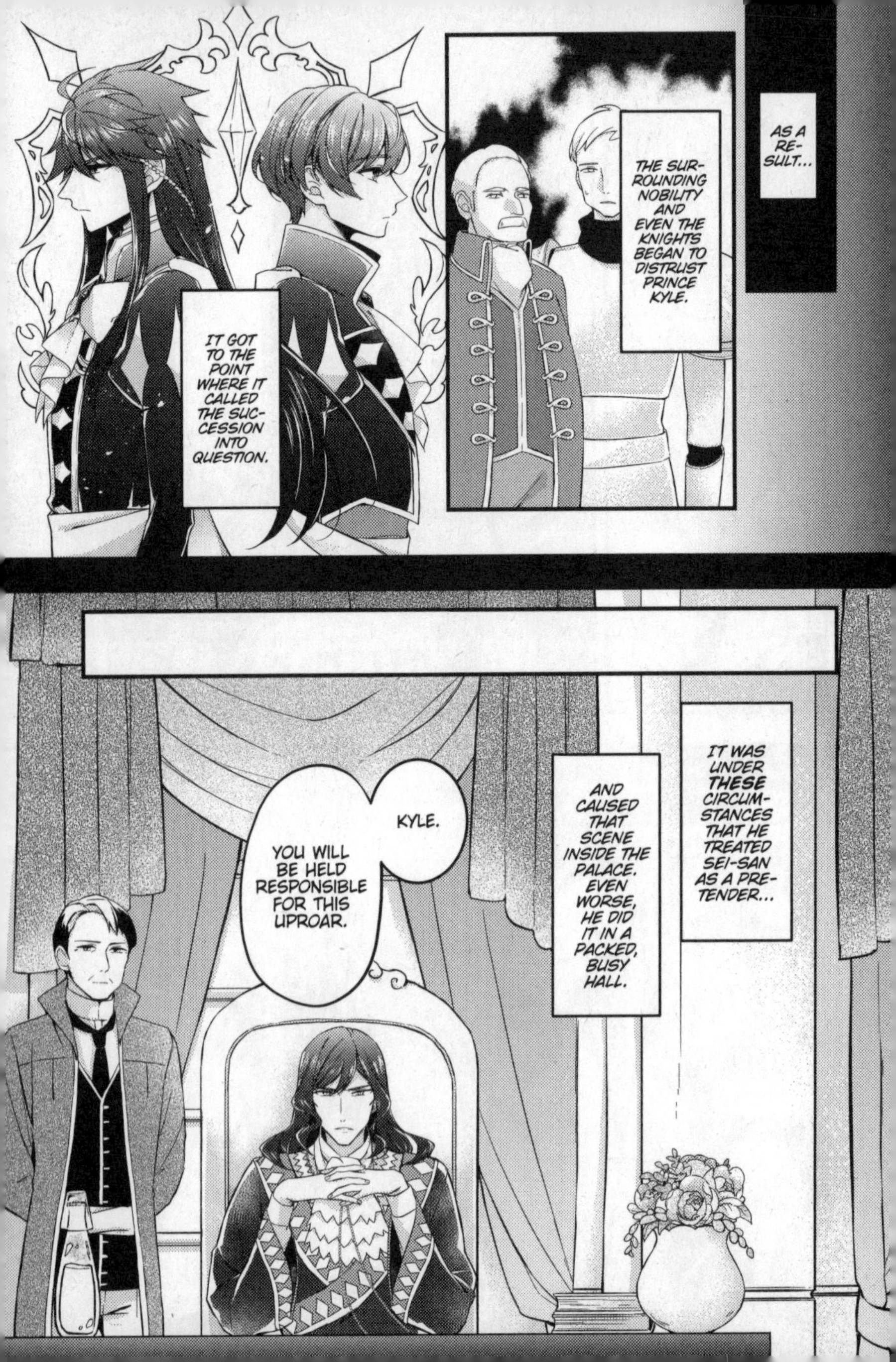
AS A RESULT...
THE SURROUNDING NOBILITY AND EVEN THE KNIGHTS BEGAN TO DISTRUST PRINCE KYLE.
IT GOT TO THE POINT WHERE IT CALLED THE SUCCESSION INTO QUESTION.
IT WAS UNDER **THESE** CIRCUMSTANCES THAT HE TREATED SEI-SAN AS A PRETENDER...
AND CAUSED THAT SCENE INSIDE THE PALACE. EVEN WORSE, HE DID IT IN A PACKED, BUSY HALL.
KYLE.
YOU WILL BE HELD RESPONSIBLE FOR THIS UPROAR.

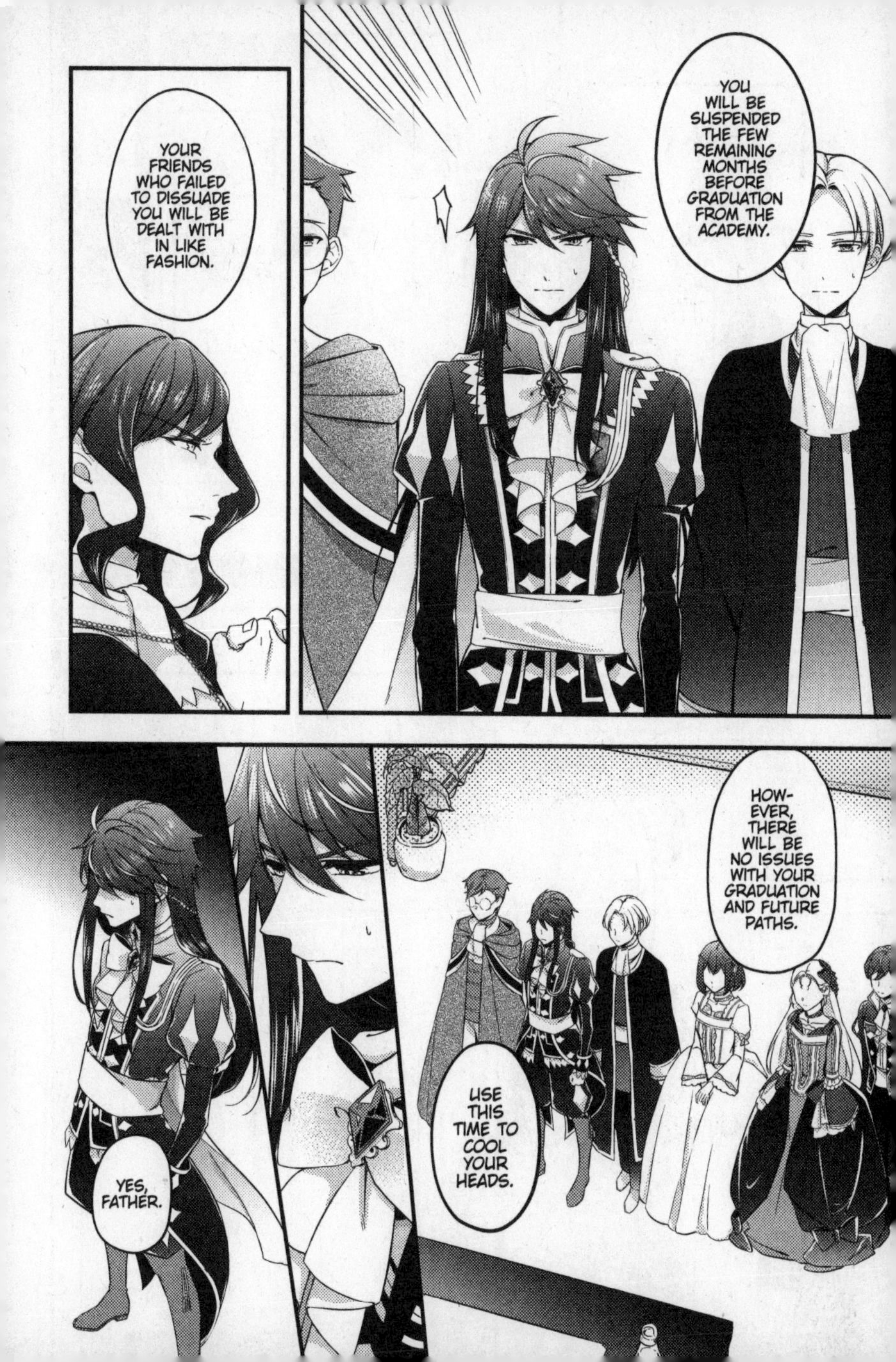
YOU WILL BE SUSPENDED THE FEW REMAINING MONTHS BEFORE GRADUATION FROM THE ACADEMY.
YOUR FRIENDS WHO FAILED TO DISSUADE YOU WILL BE DEALT WITH IN LIKE FASHION.
HOW-EVER, THERE WILL BE NO ISSUES WITH YOUR GRADUATION AND FUTURE PATHS.
USE THIS TIME TO COOL YOUR HEADS.
YES, FATHER.

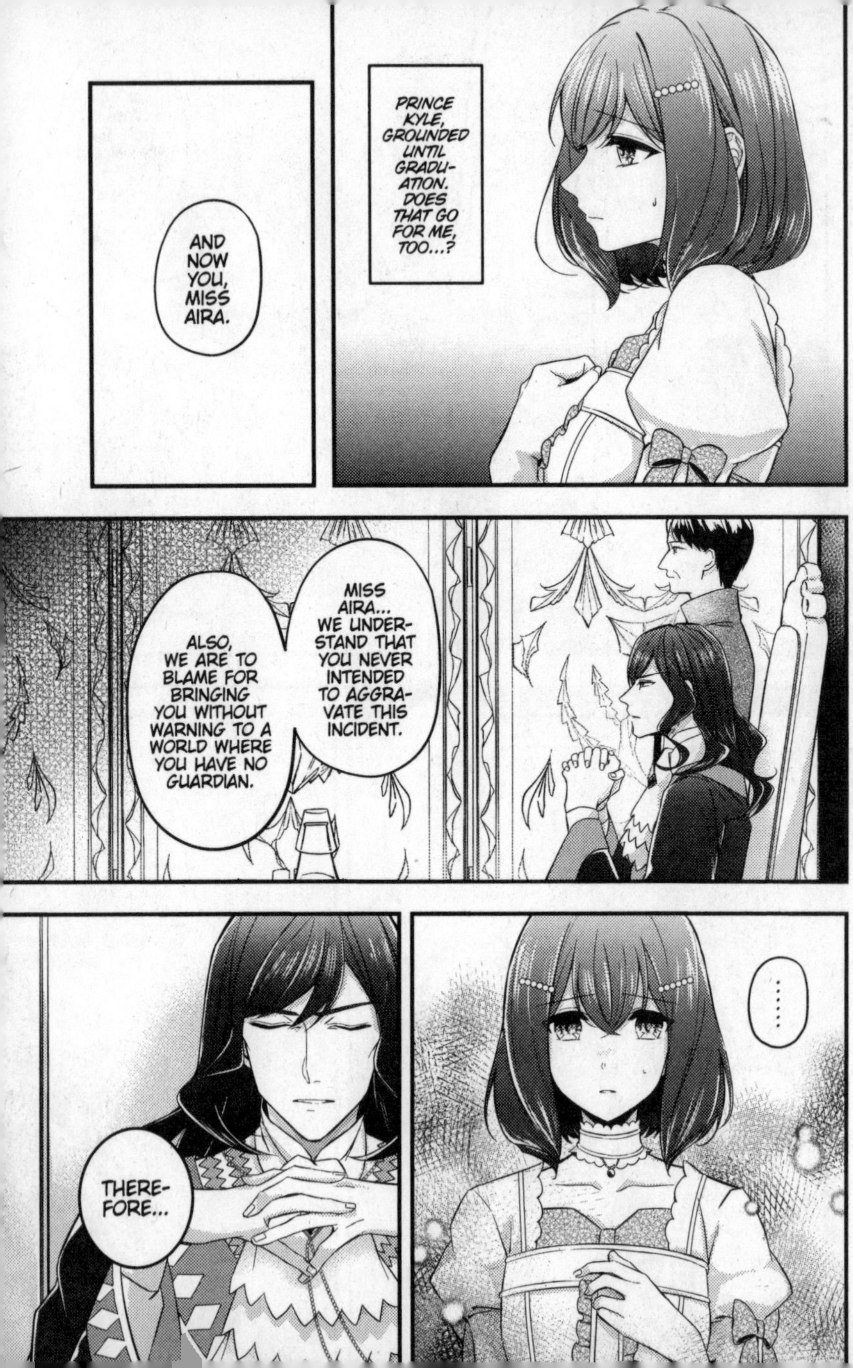
PRINCE KYLE, GROUNDED UNTIL GRADUATION. DOES THAT GO FOR ME, TOO...?
AND NOW YOU, MISS AIRA.
MISS AIRA... WE UNDERSTAND THAT YOU NEVER INTENDED TO AGGRAVATE THIS INCIDENT.
ALSO, WE ARE TO BLAME FOR BRINGING YOU WITHOUT WARNING TO A WORLD WHERE YOU HAVE NO GUARDIAN.
......
THEREFORE...

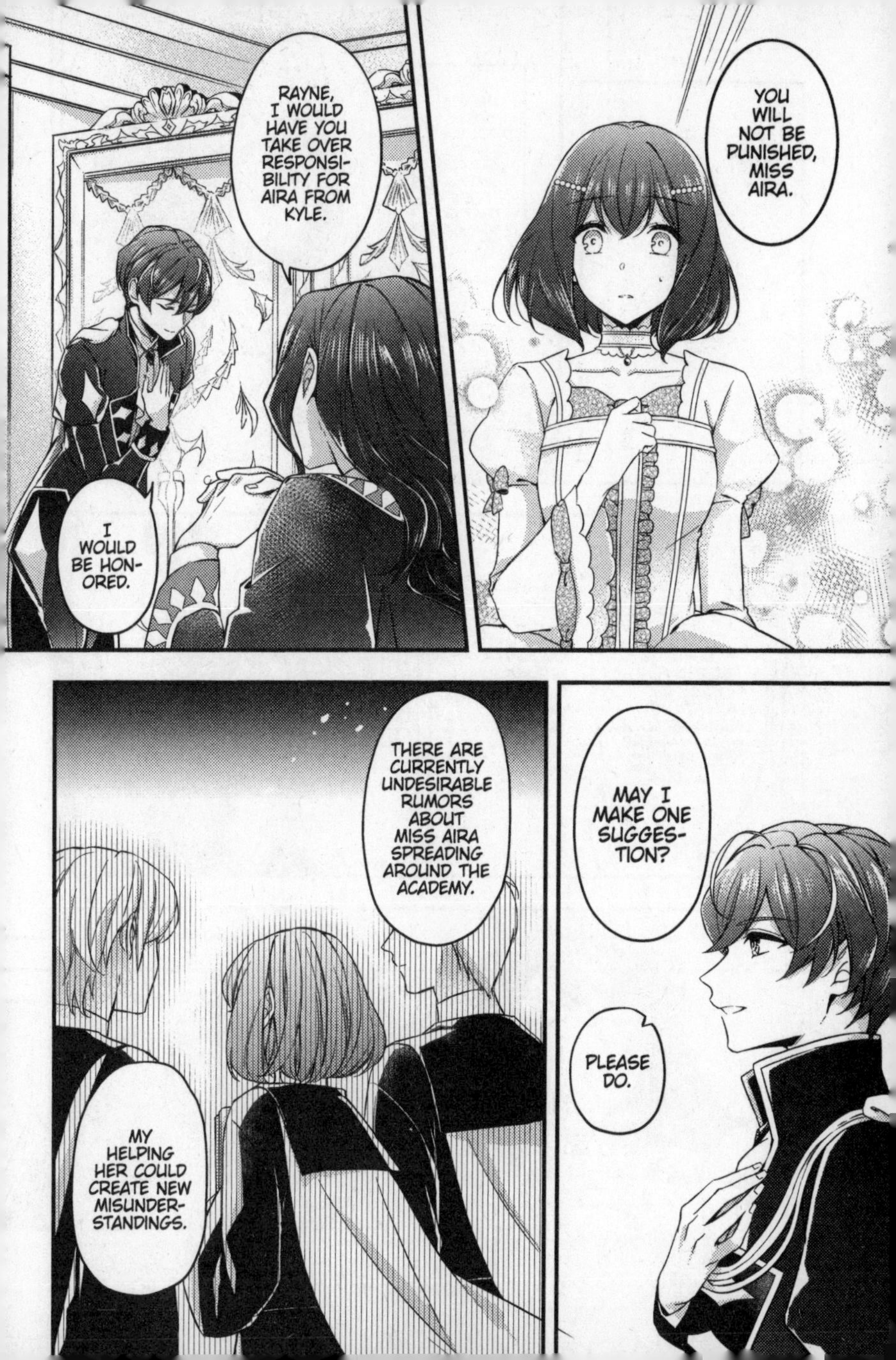
YOU WILL NOT BE PUNISHED, MISS AIRA.
RAYNE, I WOULD HAVE YOU TAKE OVER RESPONSIBILITY FOR AIRA FROM KYLE.
I WOULD BE HONORED.
MAY I MAKE ONE SUGGESTION?
PLEASE DO.
THERE ARE CURRENTLY UNDESIRABLE RUMORS ABOUT MISS AIRA SPREADING AROUND THE ACADEMY.
MY HELPING HER COULD CREATE NEW MISUNDERSTANDINGS.

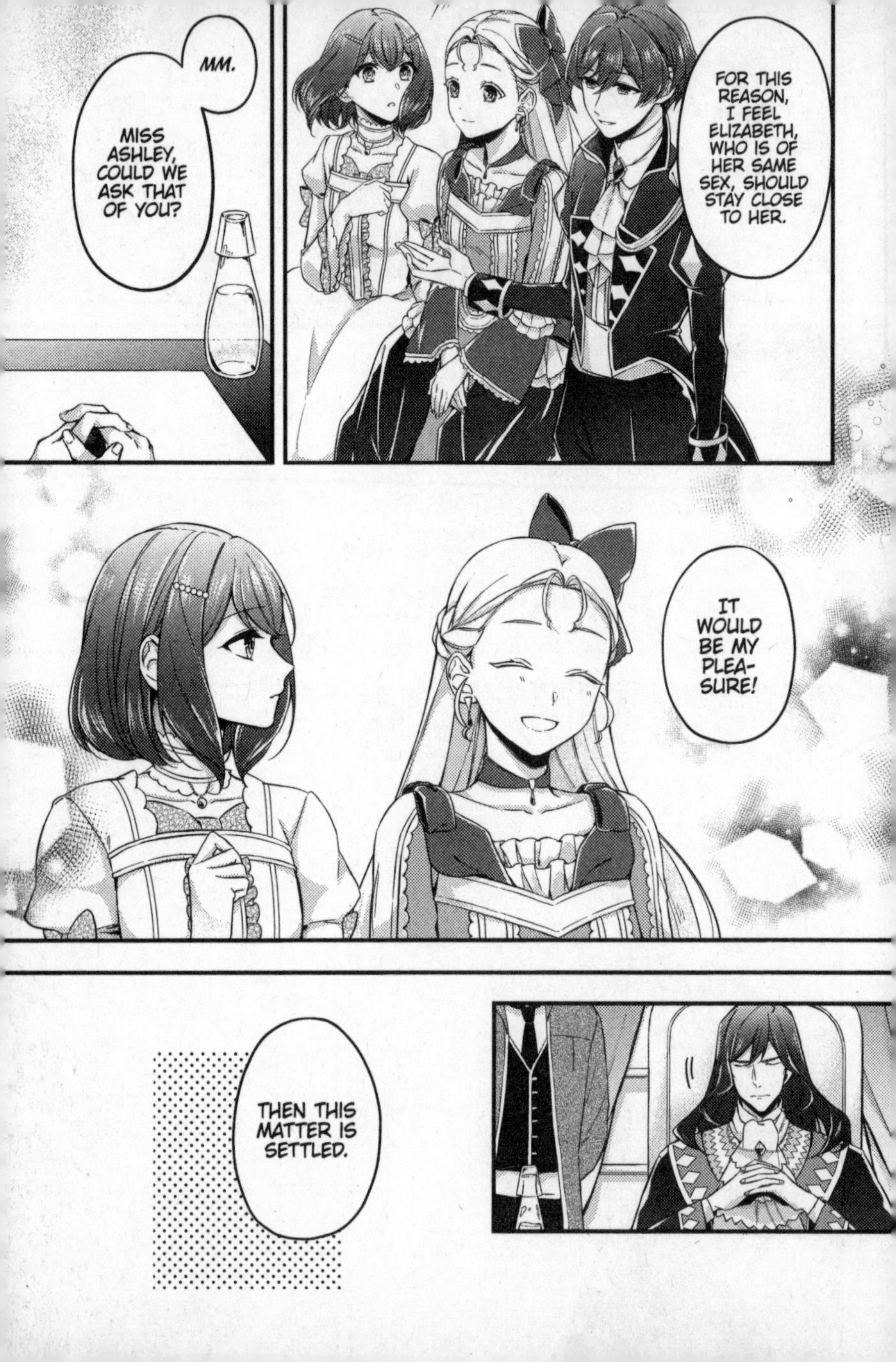
FOR THIS REASON, I FEEL ELIZABETH, WHO IS OF HER SAME SEX, SHOULD STAY CLOSE TO HER.
MM.
MISS ASHLEY, COULD WE ASK THAT OF YOU?
IT WOULD BE MY PLEA-SURE!
THEN THIS MATTER IS SETTLED.

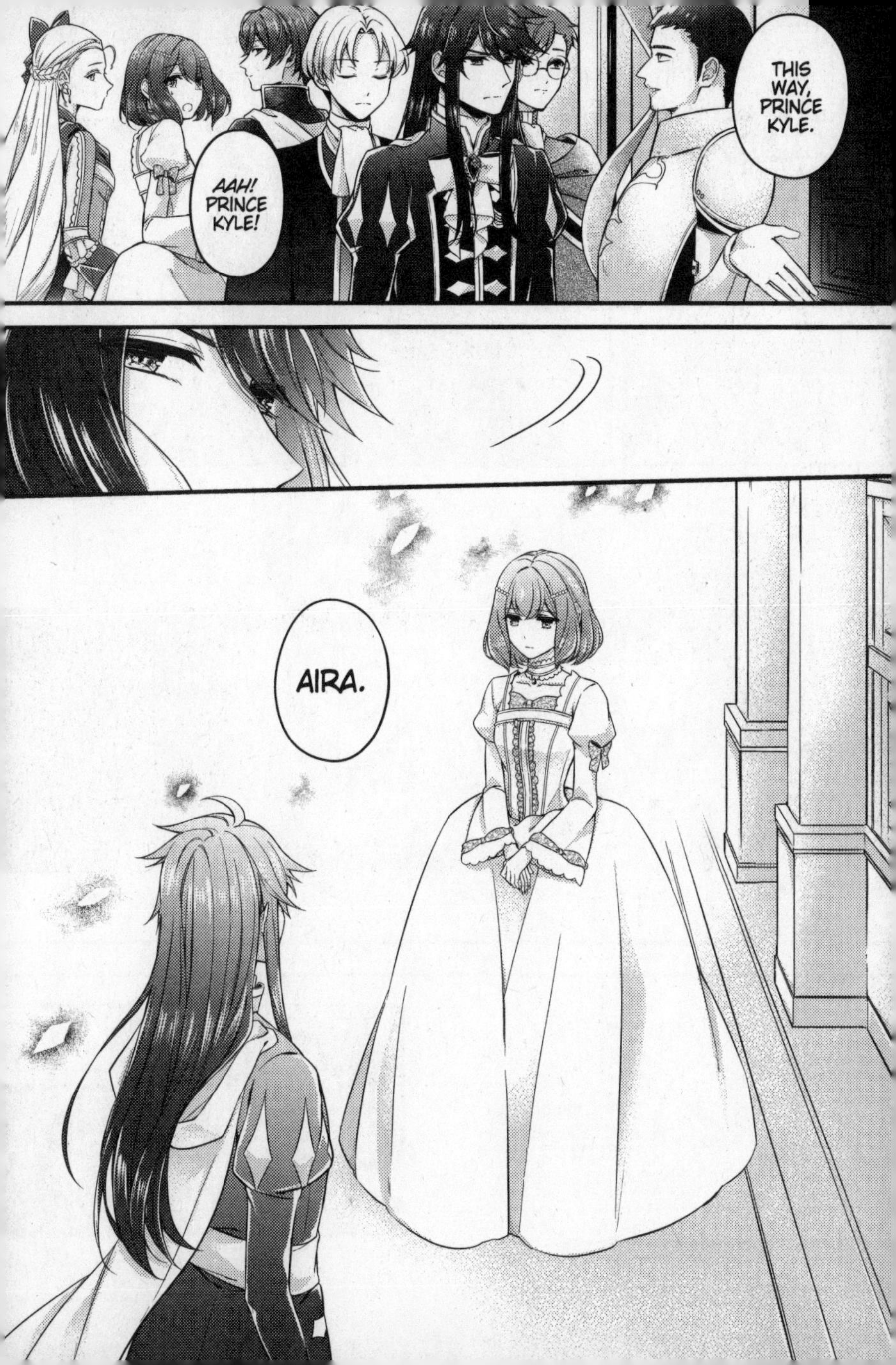
THIS WAY, PRINCE KYLE.
AAH! PRINCE KYLE!
AIRA.

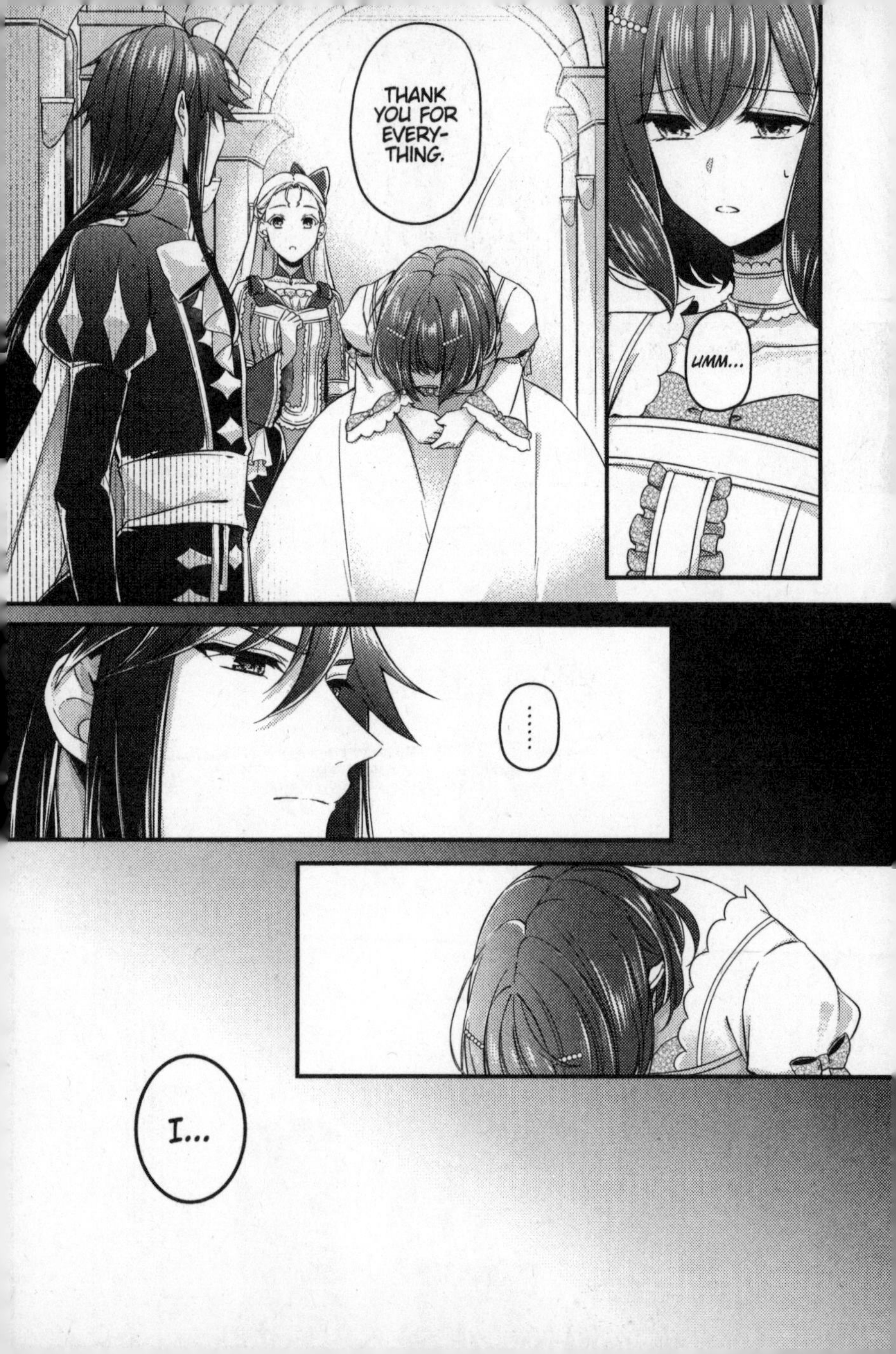
UMM...
THANK YOU FOR EVERY-THING.
......
I...

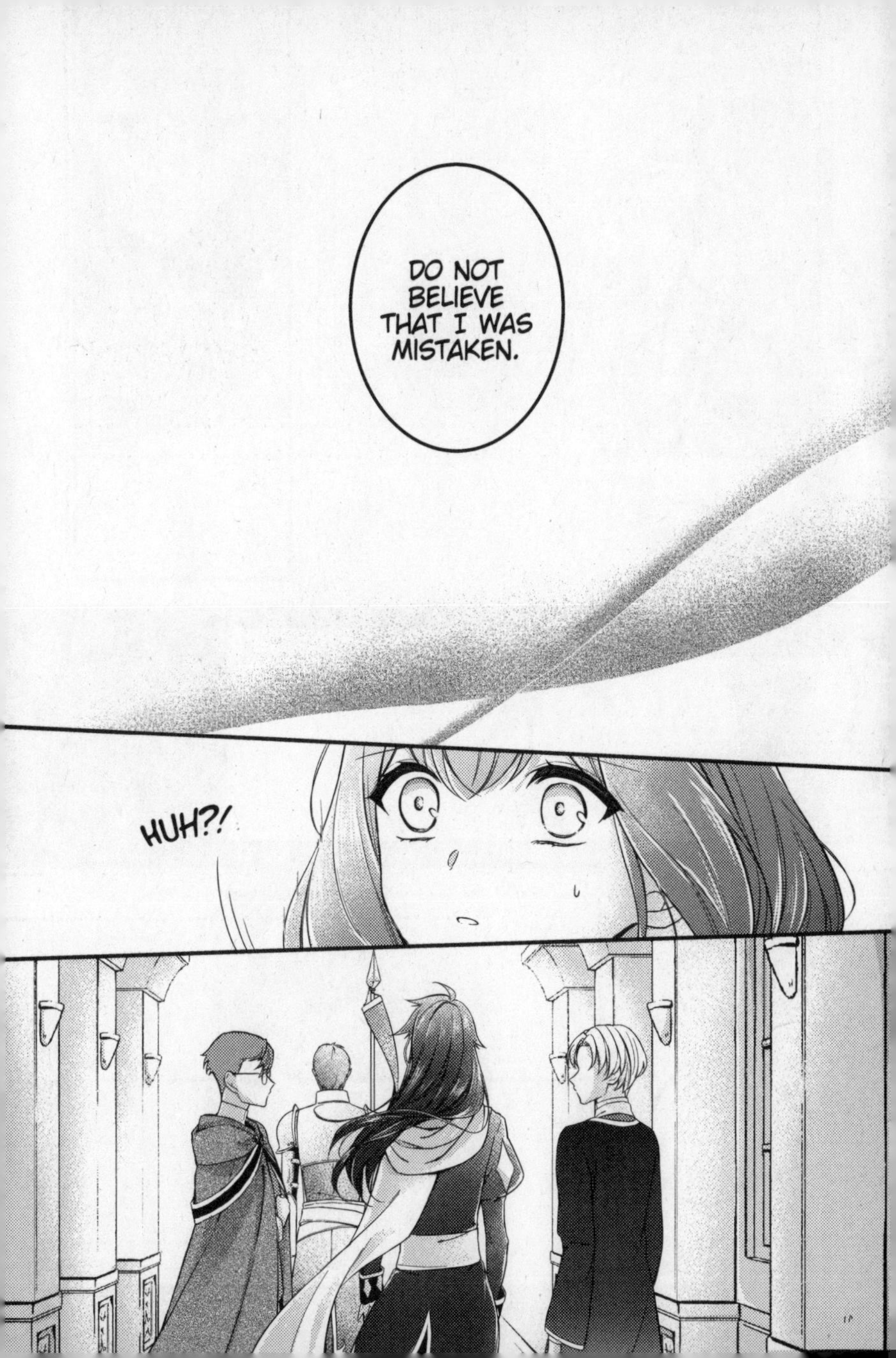
DO NOT BELIEVE THAT I WAS MISTAKEN.
HUH?!

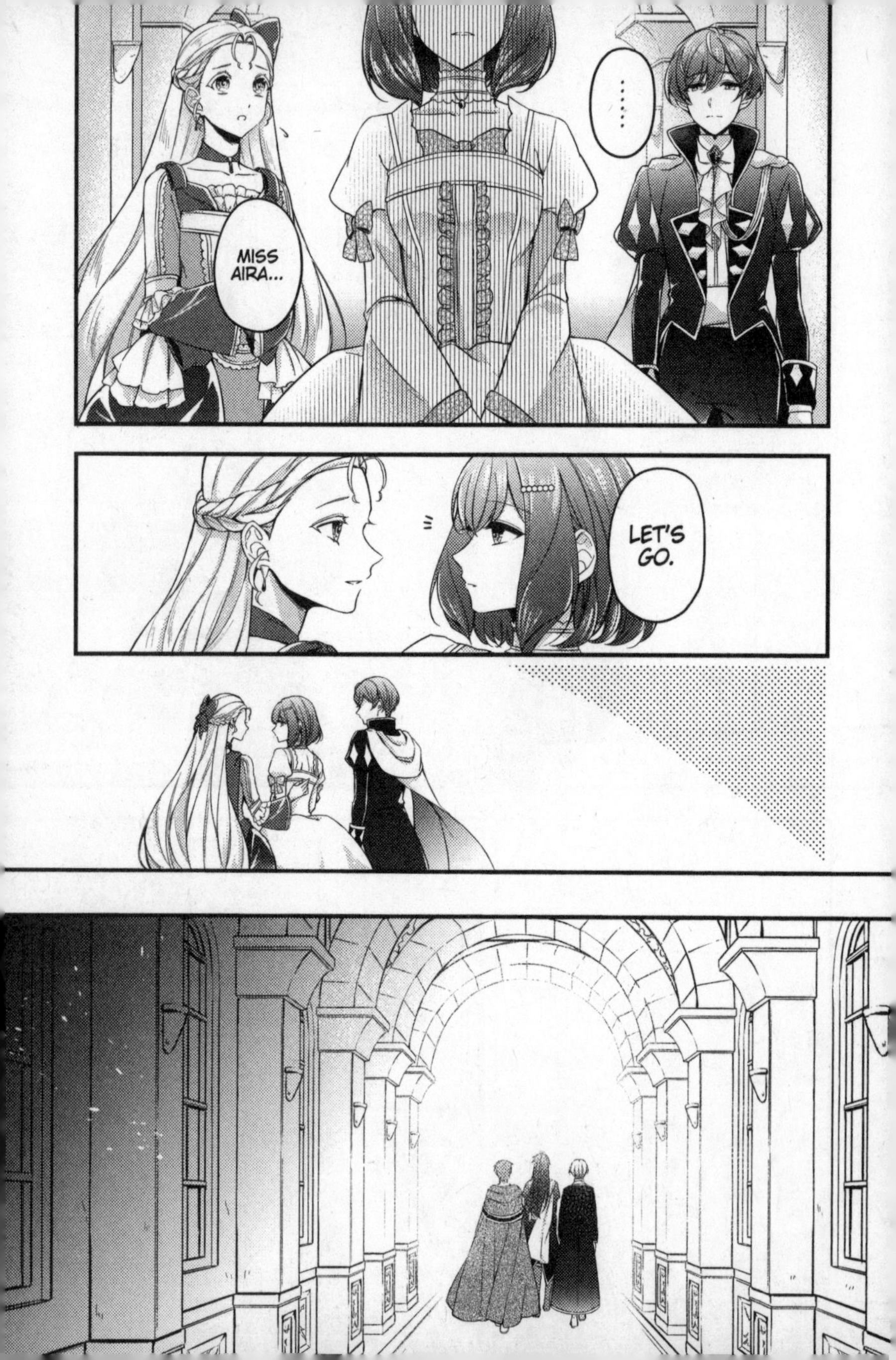
......
MISS AIRA...
LET'S GO.

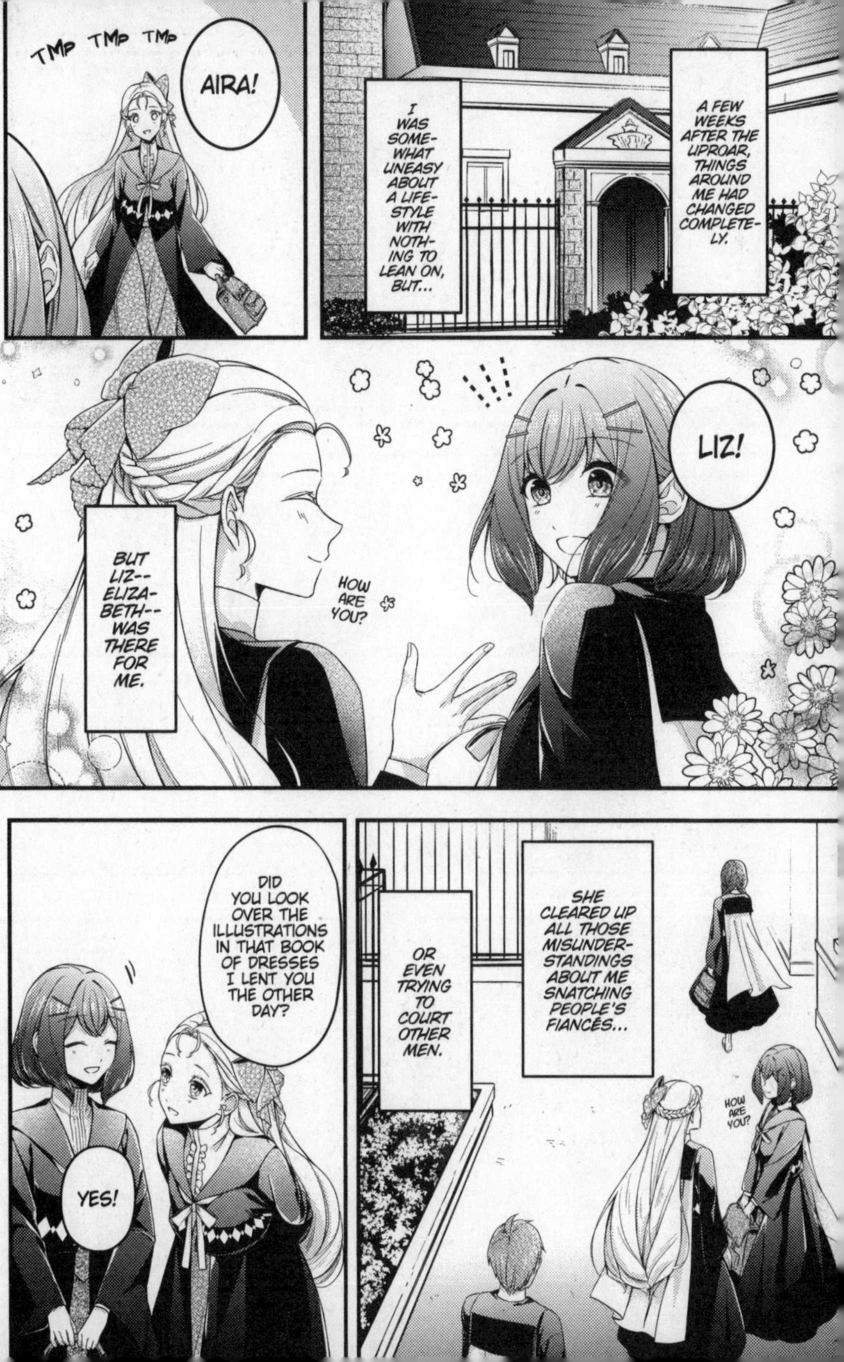
A FEW WEEKS AFTER THE UPROAR, THINGS AROUND ME HAD CHANGED COMPLETELY.
I WAS SOMEWHAT UNEASY ABOUT A LIFESTYLE WITH NOTHING TO LEAN ON, BUT...
TMP TMP TMP
AIRA!
LIZ!
BUT LIZ--ELIZABETH--WAS THERE FOR ME.
HOW ARE YOU?
SHE CLEARED UP ALL THOSE MISUNDERSTANDINGS ABOUT ME SNATCHING PEOPLE'S FIANCÉS...
OR EVEN TRYING TO COURT OTHER MEN.
HOW ARE YOU?
DID YOU LOOK OVER THE ILLUSTRATIONS IN THAT BOOK OF DRESSES I LENT YOU THE OTHER DAY?
YES!

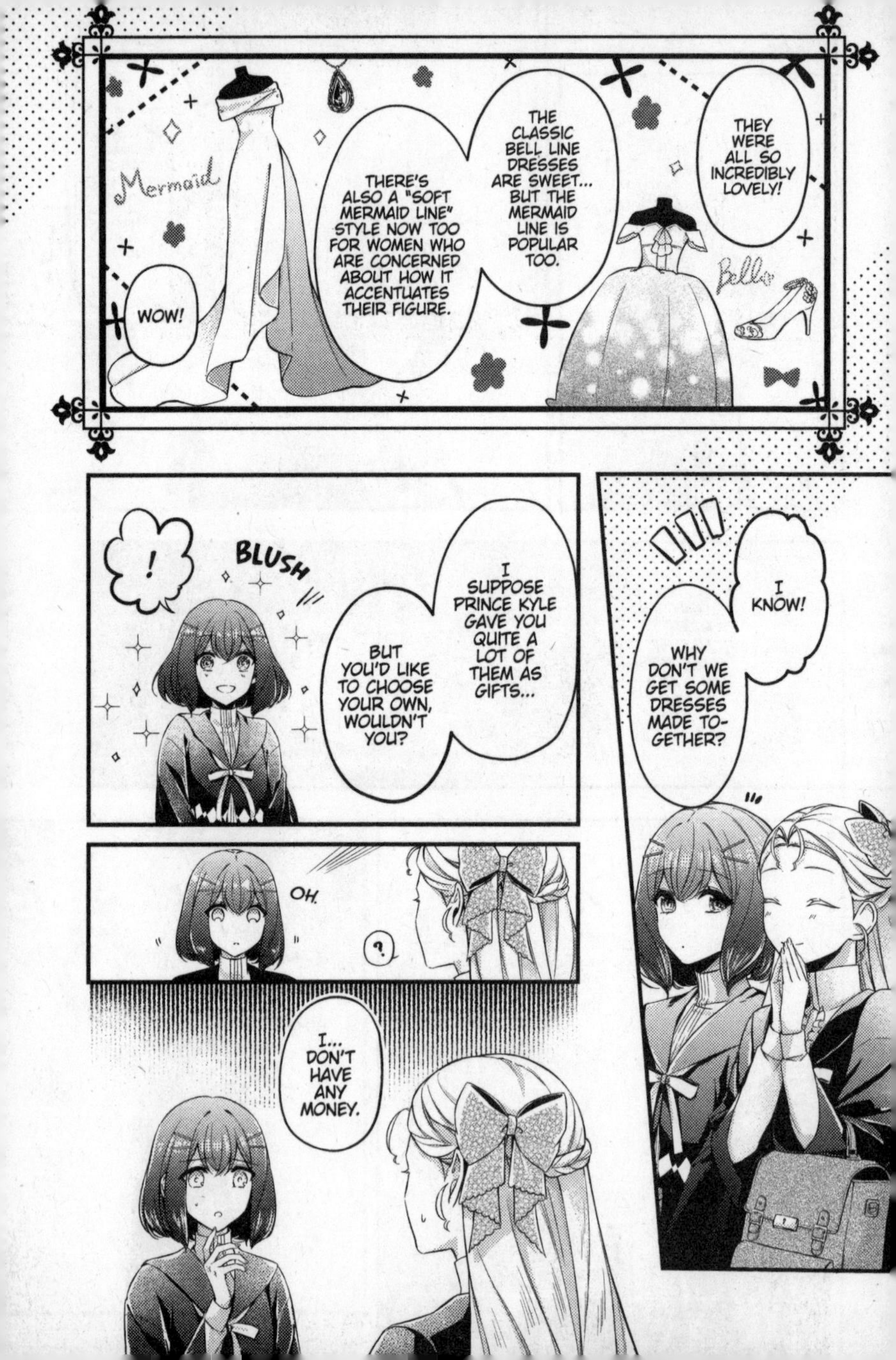
THEY WERE ALL SO INCREDIBLY LOVELY!
THE CLASSIC BELL LINE DRESSES ARE SWEET... BUT THE MERMAID LINE IS POPULAR TOO.
THERE'S ALSO A "SOFT MERMAID LINE" STYLE NOW TOO FOR WOMEN WHO ARE CONCERNED ABOUT HOW IT ACCENTUATES THEIR FIGURE.
Mermaid
WOW!
I KNOW!
WHY DON'T WE GET SOME DRESSES MADE TO-GETHER?
I SUPPOSE PRINCE KYLE GAVE YOU QUITE A LOT OF THEM AS GIFTS...
BUT YOU'D LIKE TO CHOOSE YOUR OWN, WOULDN'T YOU?
!
BLUSH
OH.
?
I... DON'T HAVE ANY MONEY.

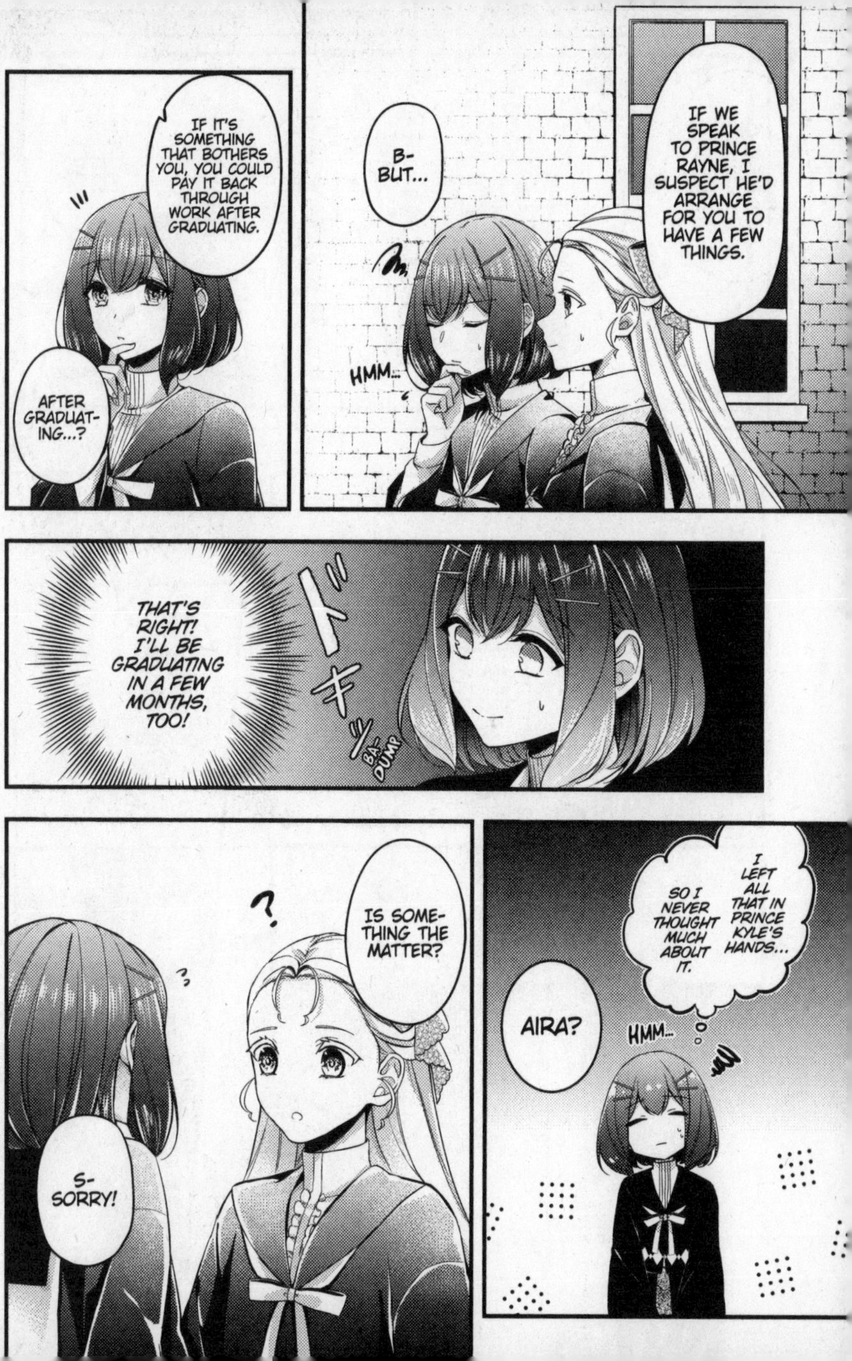
IF WE SPEAK TO PRINCE RAYNE, I SUSPECT HE'D ARRANGE FOR YOU TO HAVE A FEW THINGS.
B-BUT...
HMM...
IF IT'S SOMETHING THAT BOTHERS YOU, YOU COULD PAY IT BACK THROUGH WORK AFTER GRADUATING.
AFTER GRADUATING...?
THAT'S RIGHT! I'LL BE GRADUATING IN A FEW MONTHS, TOO!
BA-DUMP
I LEFT ALL THAT IN PRINCE KYLE'S HANDS...
SO I NEVER THOUGHT MUCH ABOUT IT.
HMM...
AIRA?
IS SOMETHING THE MATTER?
S-SORRY!

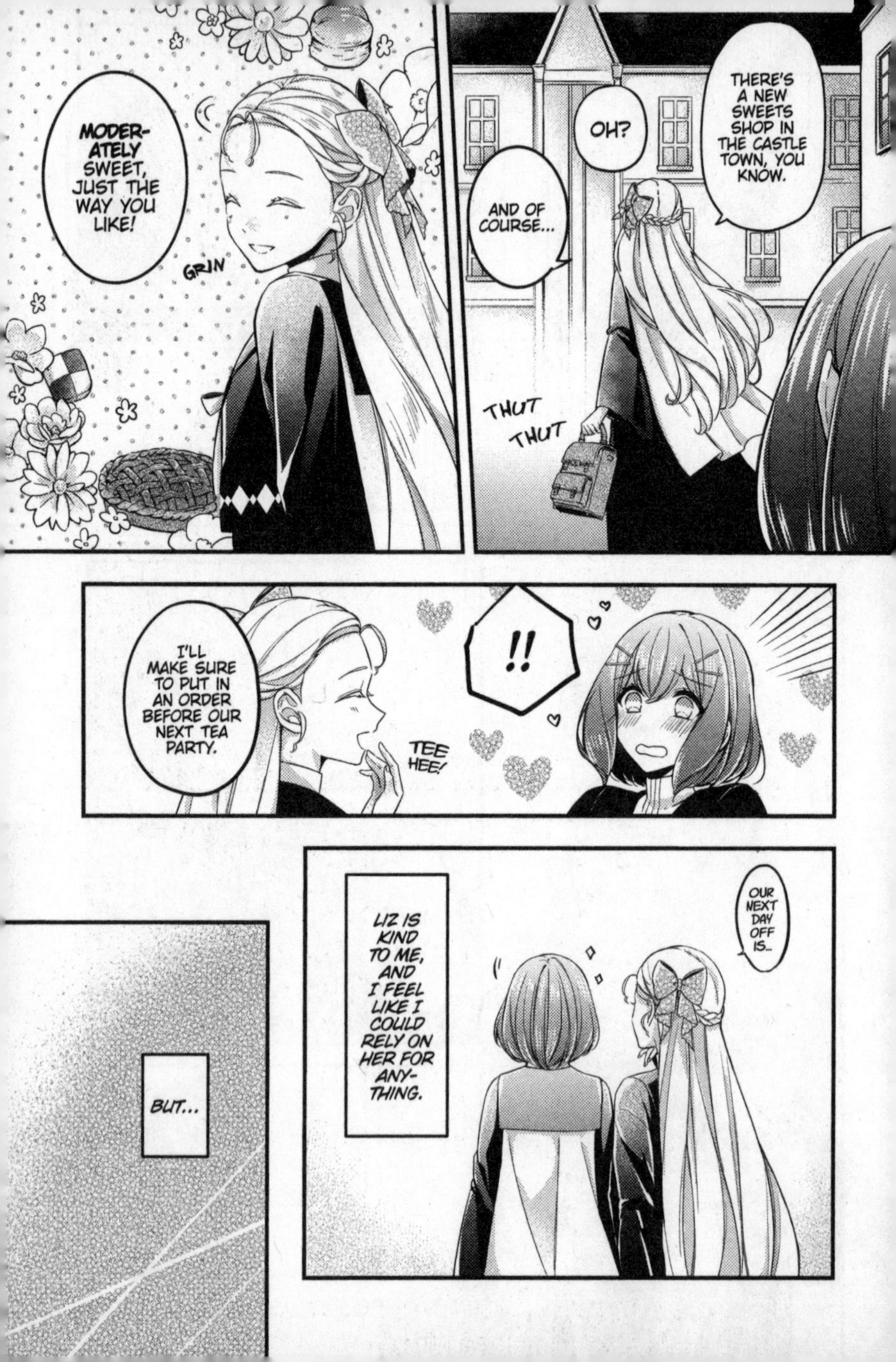
THERE'S A NEW SWEETS SHOP IN THE CASTLE TOWN, YOU KNOW.
OH?
AND OF COURSE...
THUT THUT
MODER-ATELY SWEET, JUST THE WAY YOU LIKE!
GRIN
!!
I'LL MAKE SURE TO PUT IN AN ORDER BEFORE OUR NEXT TEA PARTY.
TEE HEE!
OUR NEXT DAY OFF IS..
LIZ IS KIND TO ME, AND I FEEL LIKE I COULD RELY ON HER FOR ANY-THING.
BUT...

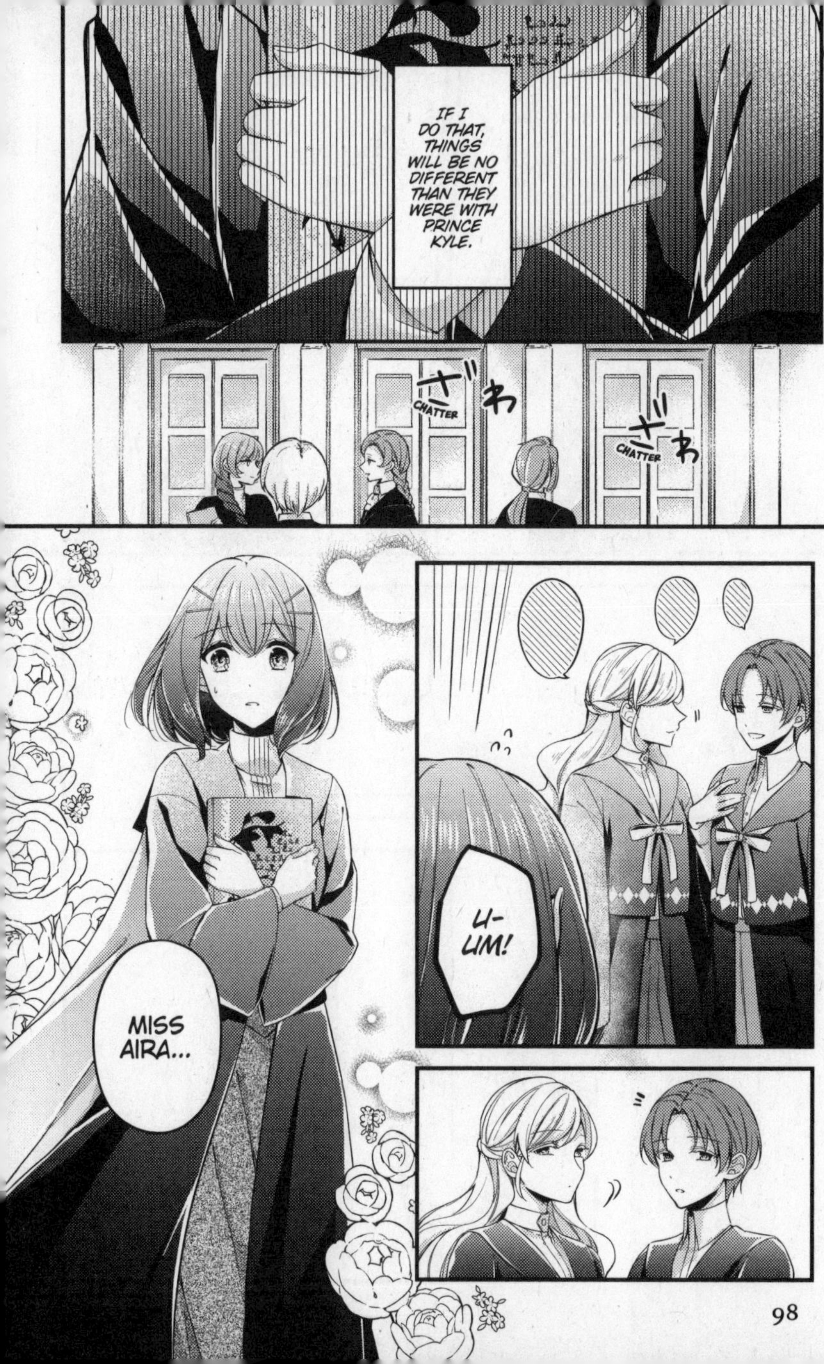

IF I DO THAT, THINGS WILL BE NO DIFFERENT THAN THEY WERE WITH PRINCE KYLE.
ざわ
CHATTER
ざわ
CHATTER
U-UM!
MISS AIRA...

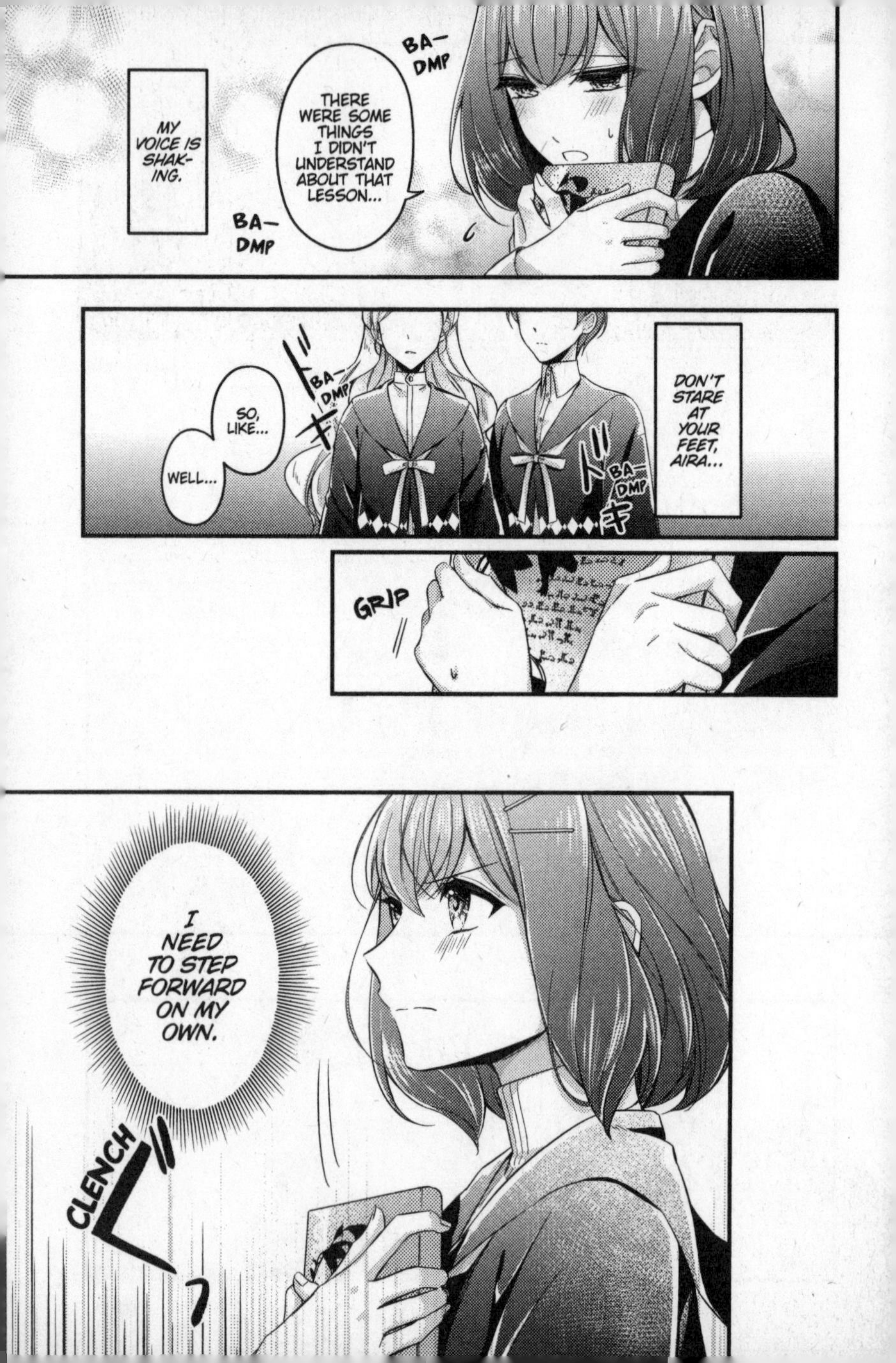
BA-DMP
THERE WERE SOME THINGS I DIDN'T UNDERSTAND ABOUT THAT LESSON...
BA-DMP
MY VOICE IS SHAK-ING.
DON'T STARE AT YOUR FEET, AIRA...
ドキ
BA-DMP
ドキ
BA-DMP
SO, LIKE...
WELL...
GRIP
I NEED TO STEP FORWARD ON MY OWN.
CLENCH

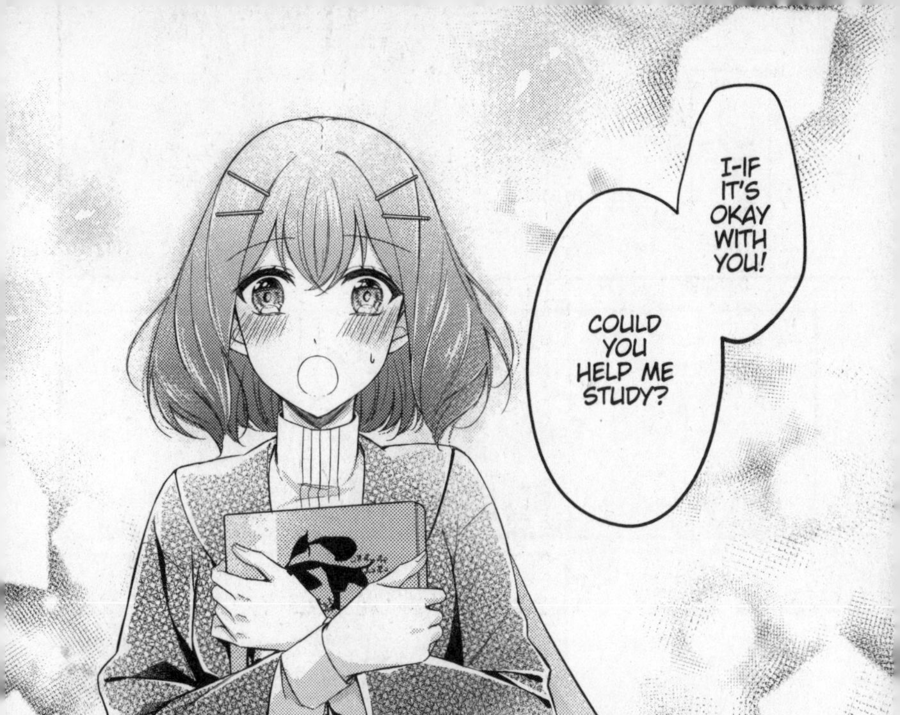
I-IF IT'S OKAY WITH YOU!
COULD YOU HELP ME STUDY?

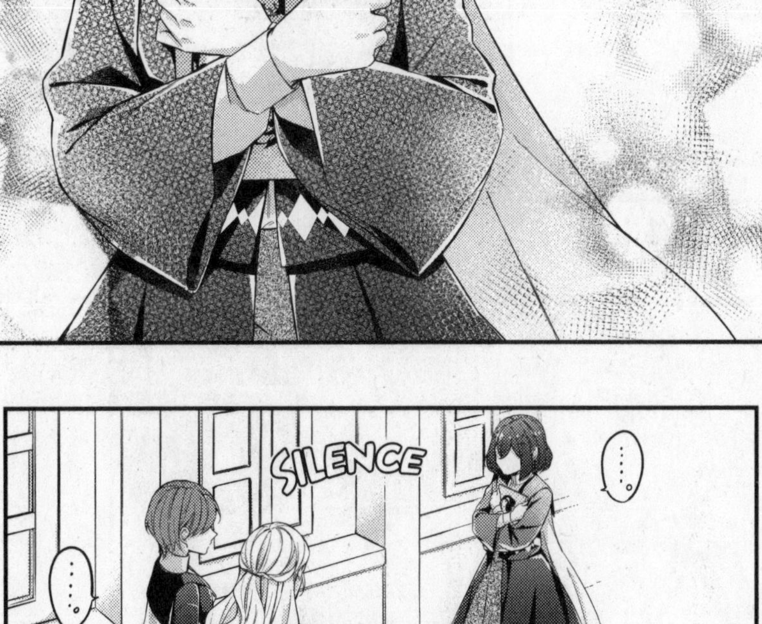
......
SILENCE
......

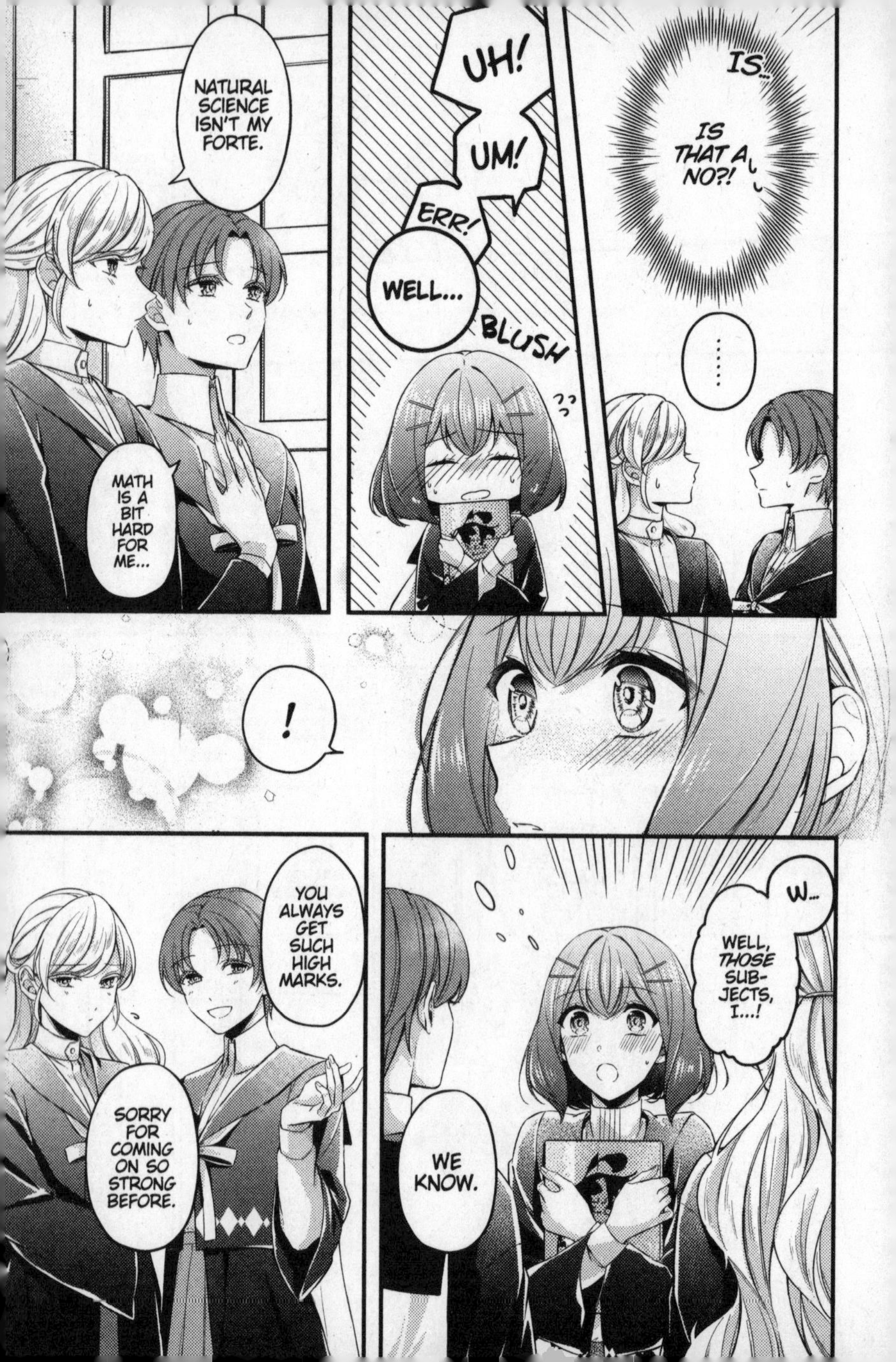
IS...
IS THAT A NO?!
......
UH!
UM!
ERR!
WELL...
BLUSH
NATURAL SCIENCE ISN'T MY FORTE.
MATH IS A BIT HARD FOR ME...
!
W...
WELL, *THOSE* SUB-JECTS, I...!
WE KNOW.
YOU ALWAYS GET SUCH HIGH MARKS.
SORRY FOR COMING ON SO STRONG BEFORE.

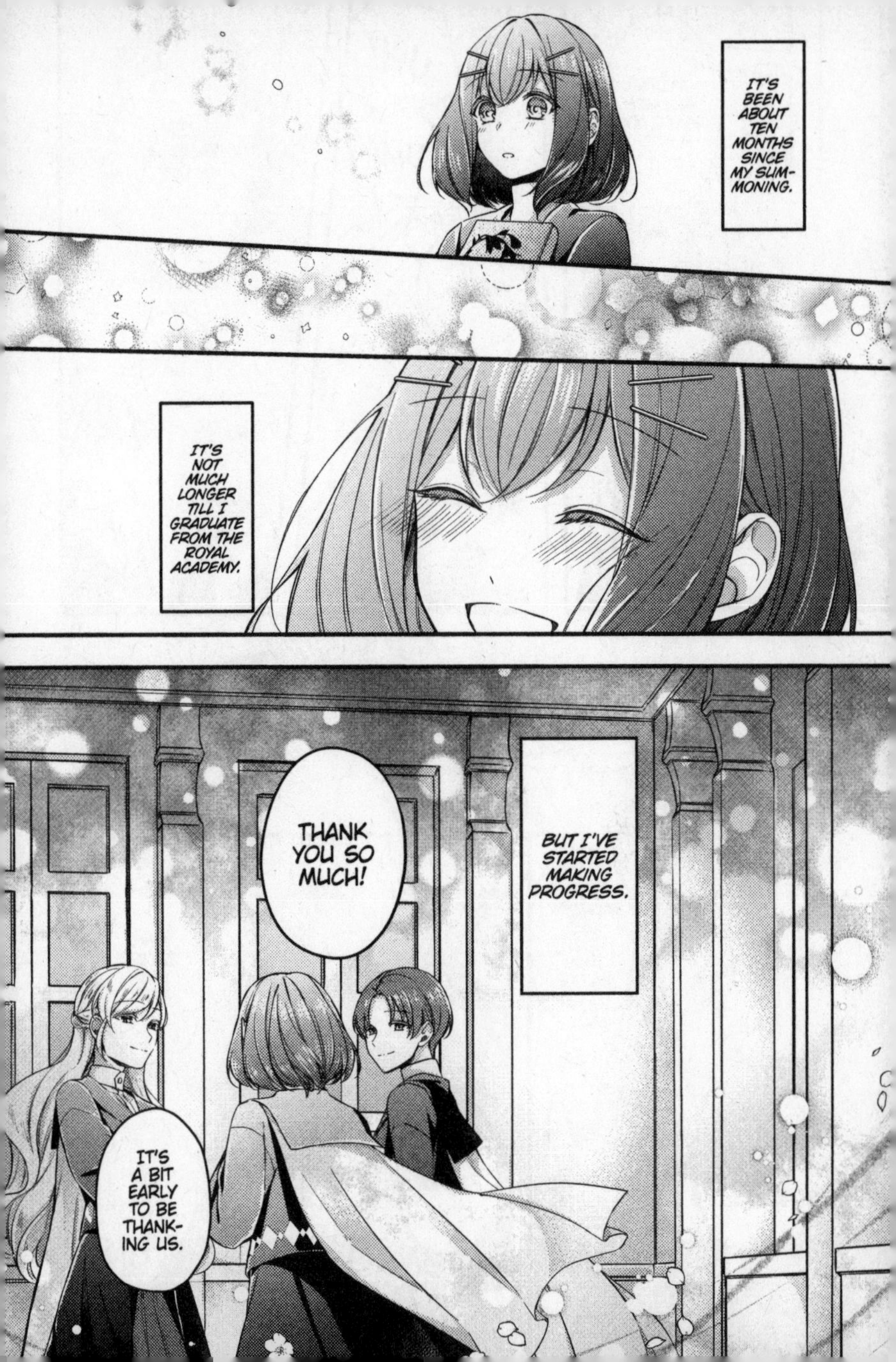
IT'S BEEN ABOUT TEN MONTHS SINCE MY SUMMONING.
IT'S NOT MUCH LONGER TILL I GRADUATE FROM THE ROYAL ACADEMY.
BUT I'VE STARTED MAKING PROGRESS.
THANK YOU SO MUCH!
IT'S A BIT EARLY TO BE THANKING US.

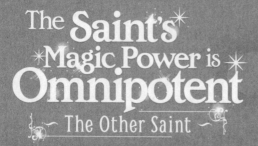

The Saint's
Magic Power is
Omnipotent
The Other Saint

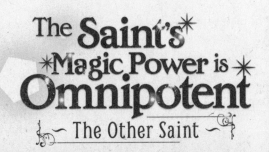

The Saint's
Magic Power is
Omnipotent
The Other Saint

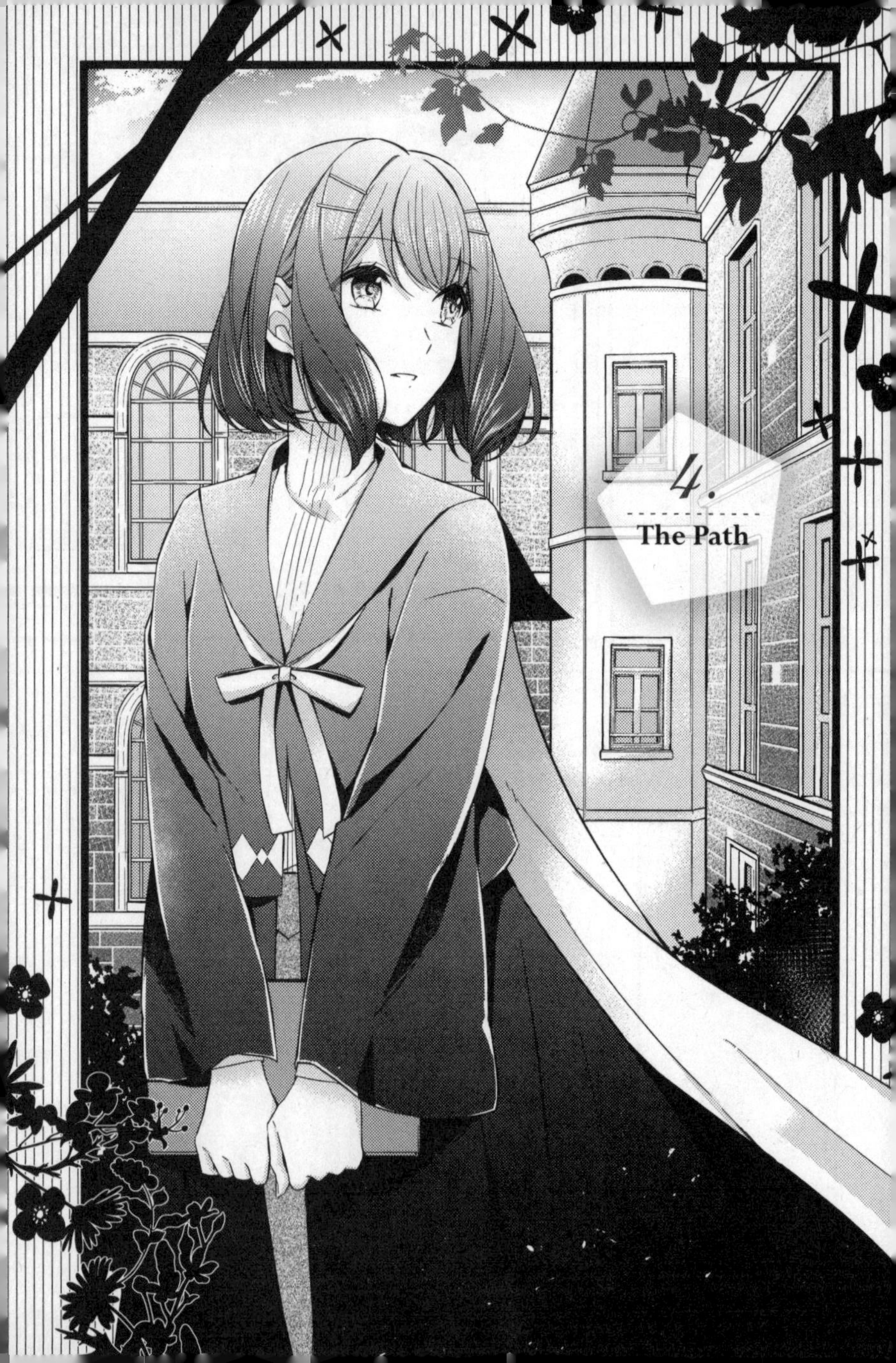
4.
The Path

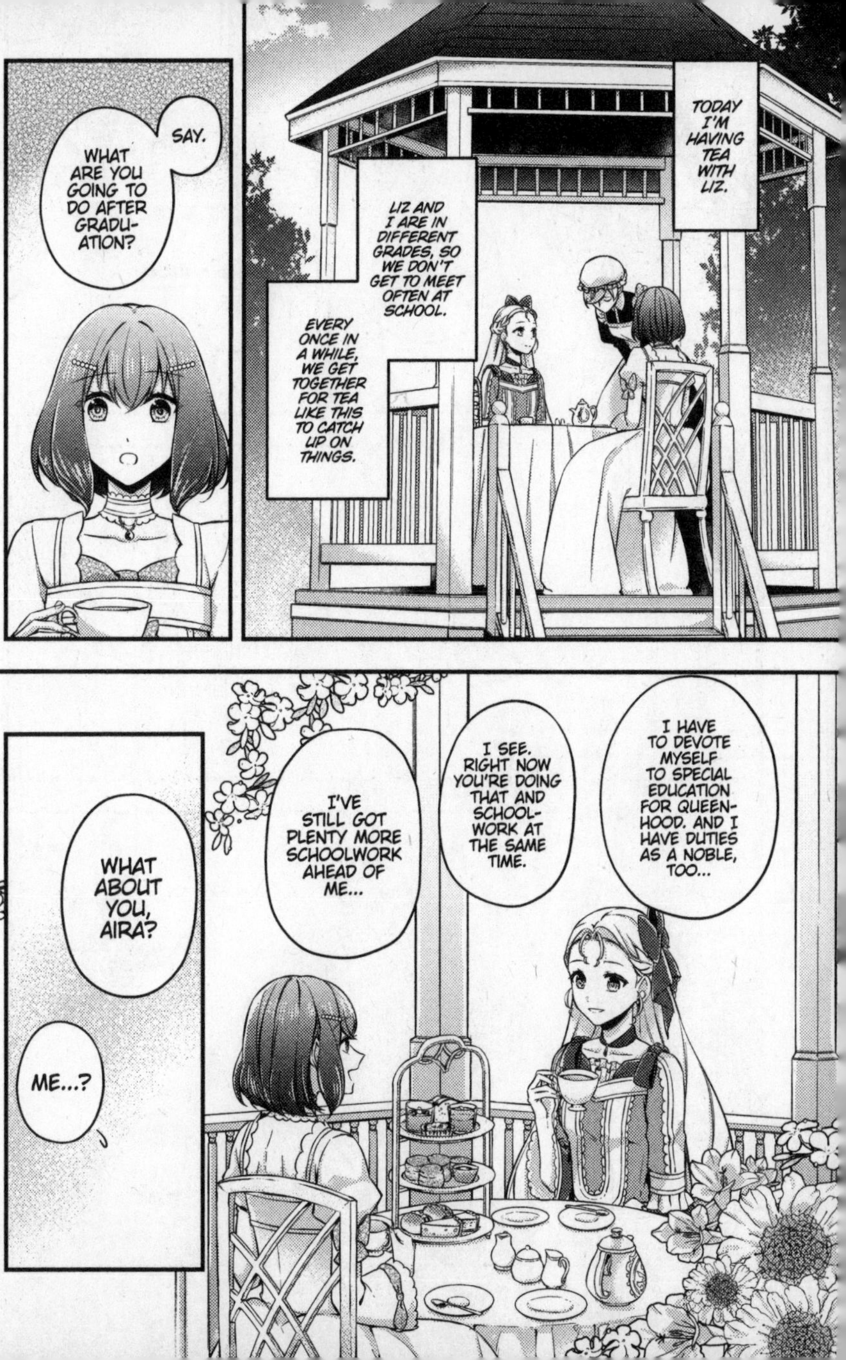
TODAY I'M HAVING TEA WITH LIZ.
LIZ AND I ARE IN DIFFERENT GRADES, SO WE DON'T GET TO MEET OFTEN AT SCHOOL.
EVERY ONCE IN A WHILE, WE GET TOGETHER FOR TEA LIKE THIS TO CATCH UP ON THINGS.
SAY.
WHAT ARE YOU GOING TO DO AFTER GRADUATION?
I HAVE TO DEVOTE MYSELF TO SPECIAL EDUCATION FOR QUEENHOOD. AND I HAVE DUTIES AS A NOBLE, TOO...
I SEE. RIGHT NOW YOU'RE DOING THAT AND SCHOOLWORK AT THE SAME TIME.
I'VE STILL GOT PLENTY MORE SCHOOLWORK AHEAD OF ME...
WHAT ABOUT YOU, AIRA?
ME...?

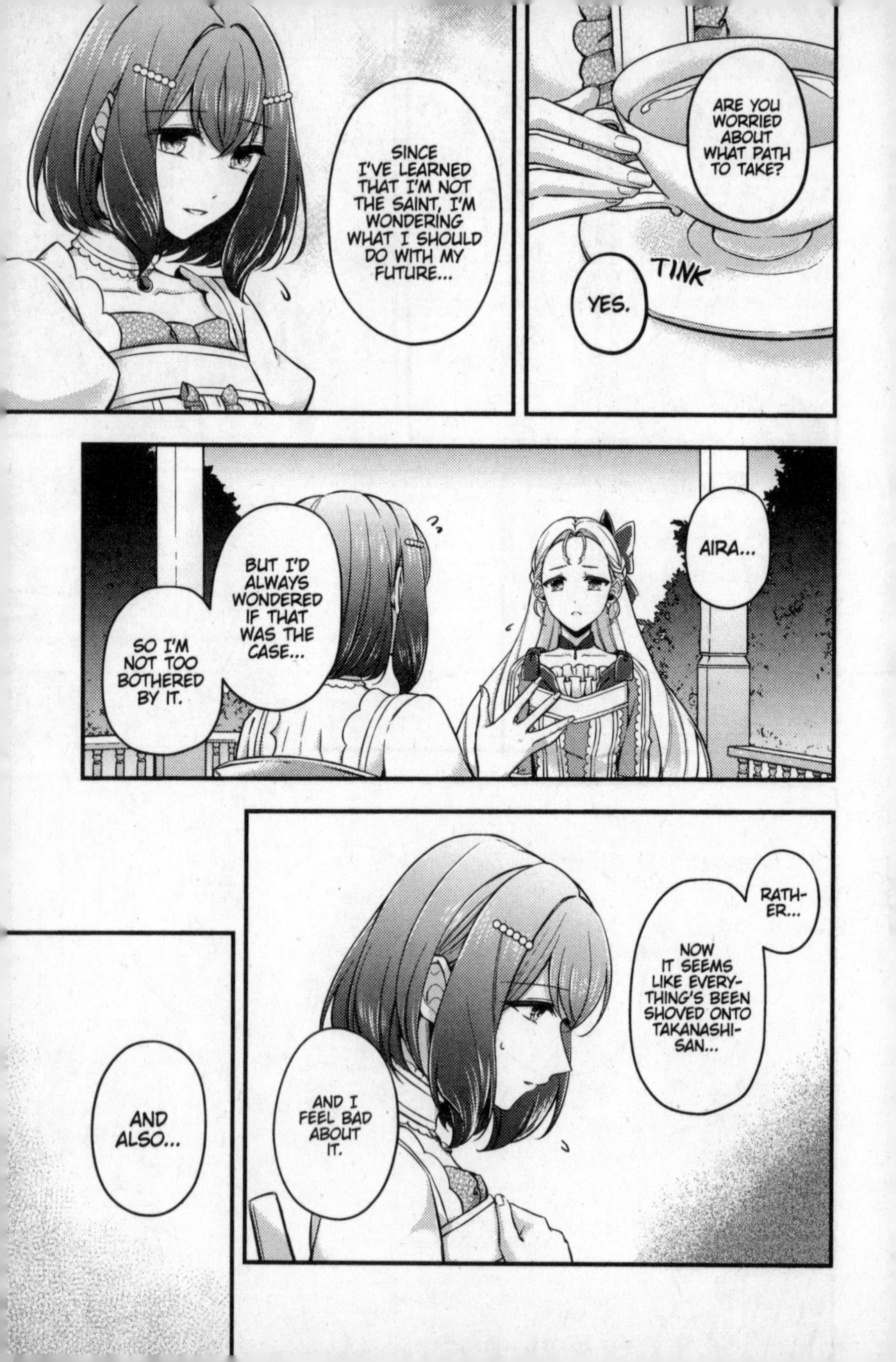
ARE YOU WORRIED ABOUT WHAT PATH TO TAKE?
TINK
YES.
SINCE I'VE LEARNED THAT I'M NOT THE SAINT, I'M WONDERING WHAT I SHOULD DO WITH MY FUTURE...
AIRA...
BUT I'D ALWAYS WONDERED IF THAT WAS THE CASE...
SO I'M NOT TOO BOTHERED BY IT.
RATH-ER...
NOW IT SEEMS LIKE EVERY-THING'S BEEN SHOVED ONTO TAKANASHI-SAN...
AND I FEEL BAD ABOUT IT.
AND ALSO...

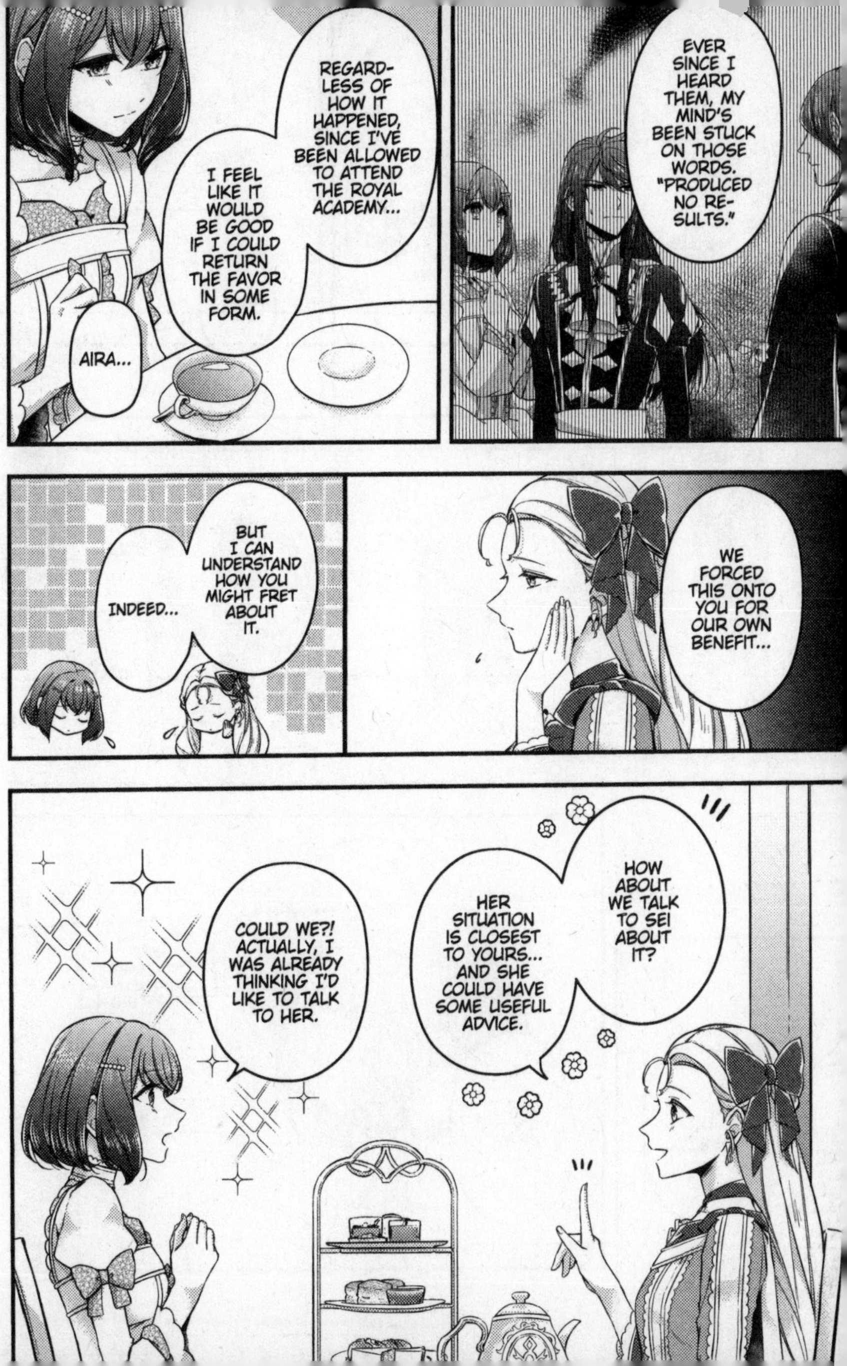
EVER SINCE I HEARD THEM, MY MIND'S BEEN STUCK ON THOSE WORDS. "PRODUCED NO RESULTS."
REGARDLESS OF HOW IT HAPPENED, SINCE I'VE BEEN ALLOWED TO ATTEND THE ROYAL ACADEMY...
I FEEL LIKE IT WOULD BE GOOD IF I COULD RETURN THE FAVOR IN SOME FORM.
AIRA...
WE FORCED THIS ONTO YOU FOR OUR OWN BENEFIT...
BUT I CAN UNDERSTAND HOW YOU MIGHT FRET ABOUT IT.
INDEED...
HOW ABOUT WE TALK TO SEI ABOUT IT?
HER SITUATION IS CLOSEST TO YOURS... AND SHE COULD HAVE SOME USEFUL ADVICE.
COULD WE?! ACTUALLY, I WAS ALREADY THINKING I'D LIKE TO TALK TO HER.

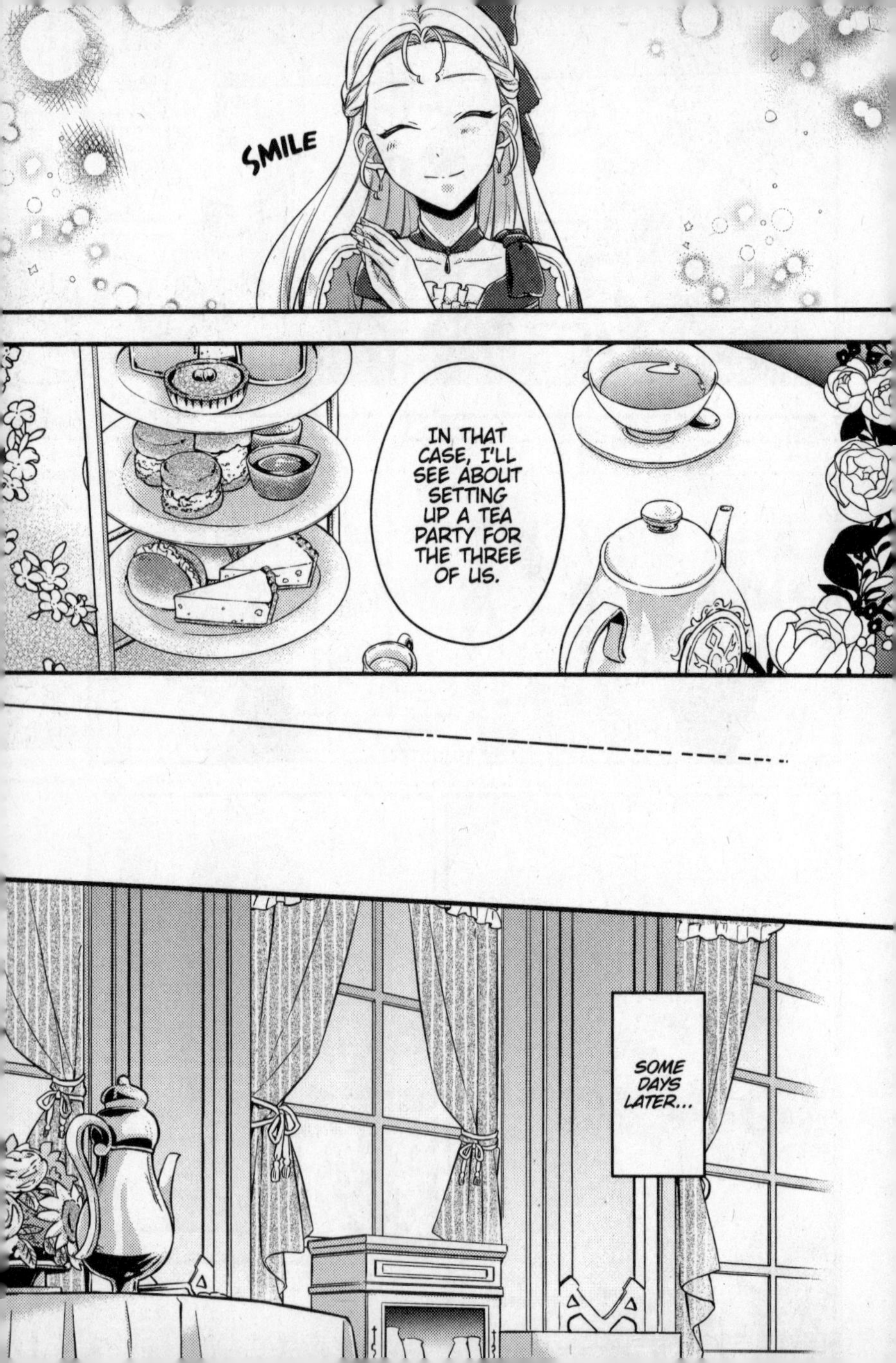
SMILE
IN THAT CASE, I'LL SEE ABOUT SETTING UP A TEA PARTY FOR THE THREE OF US.
SOME DAYS LATER...

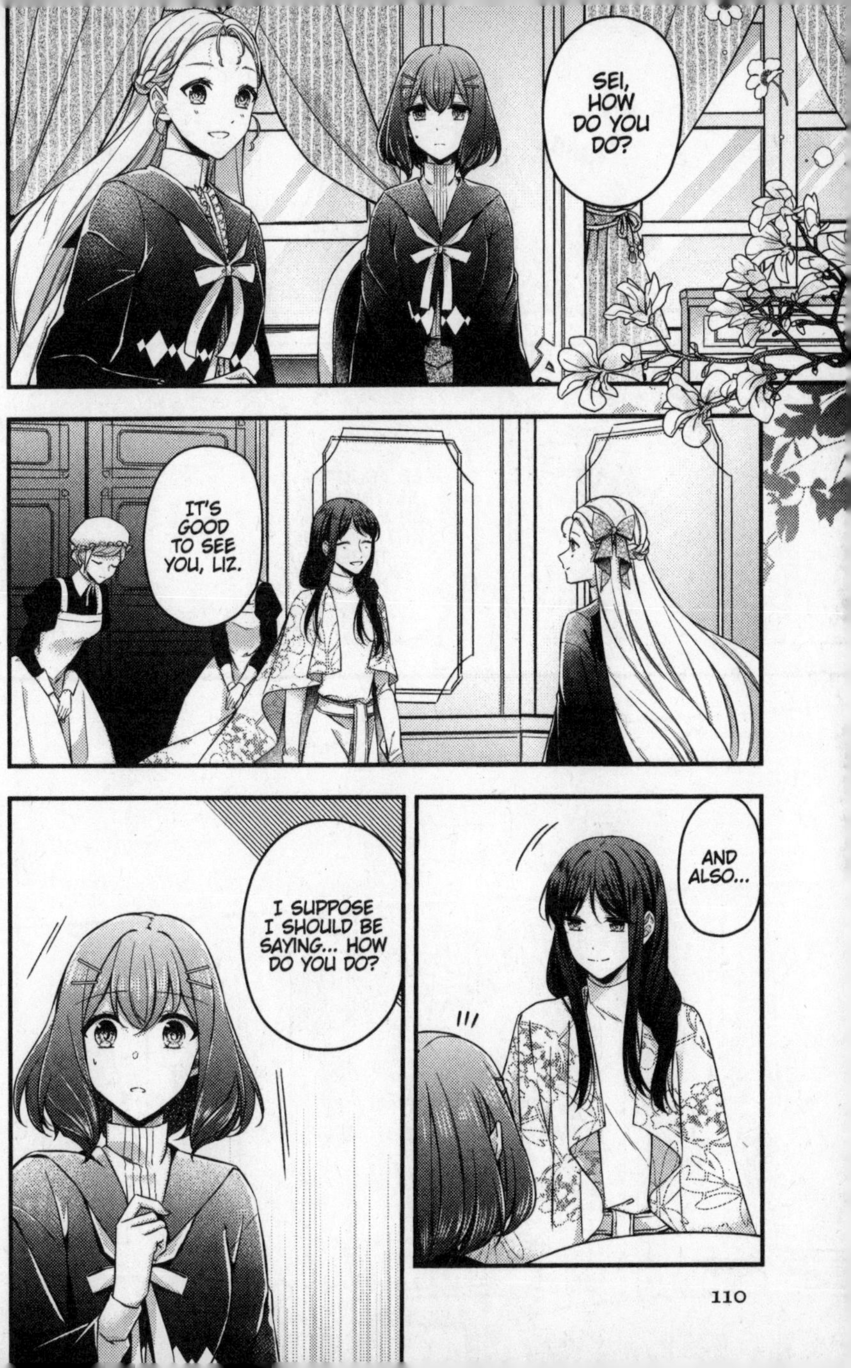
SEI, HOW DO YOU DO?
IT'S GOOD TO SEE YOU, LIZ.
AND ALSO...
I SUPPOSE I SHOULD BE SAYING... HOW DO YOU DO?

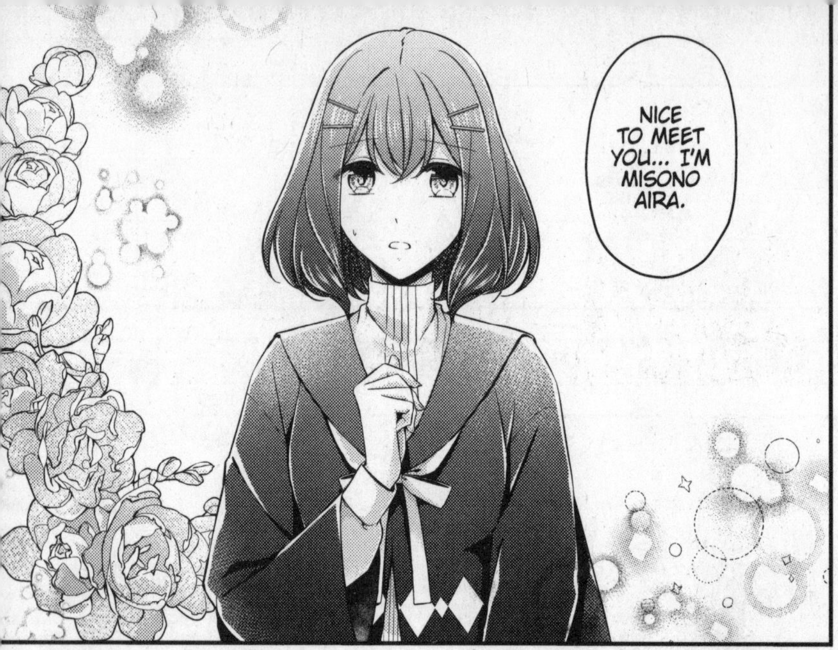
NICE TO MEET YOU... I'M MISONO AIRA.
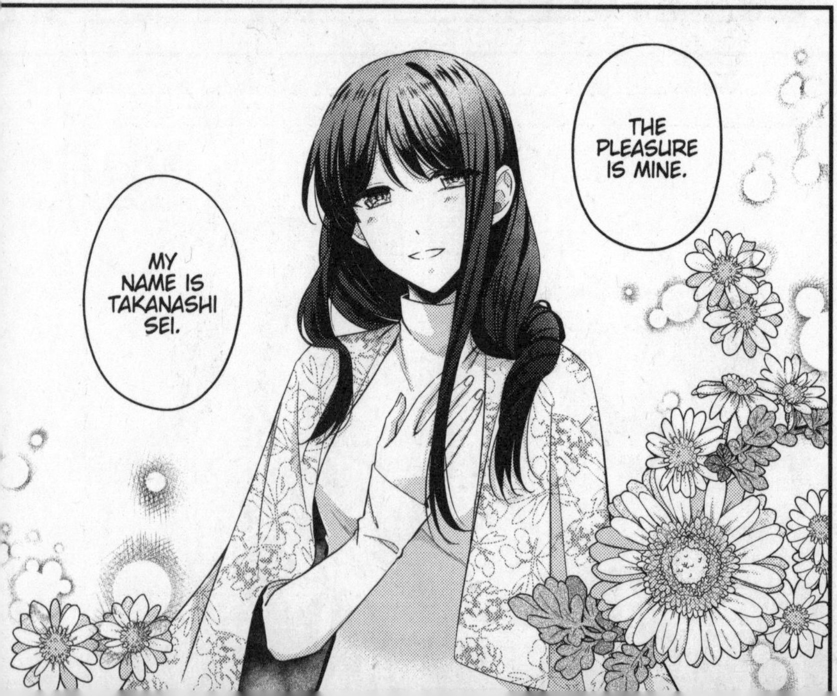
THE PLEASURE IS MINE.
MY NAME IS TAKANASHI SEI.

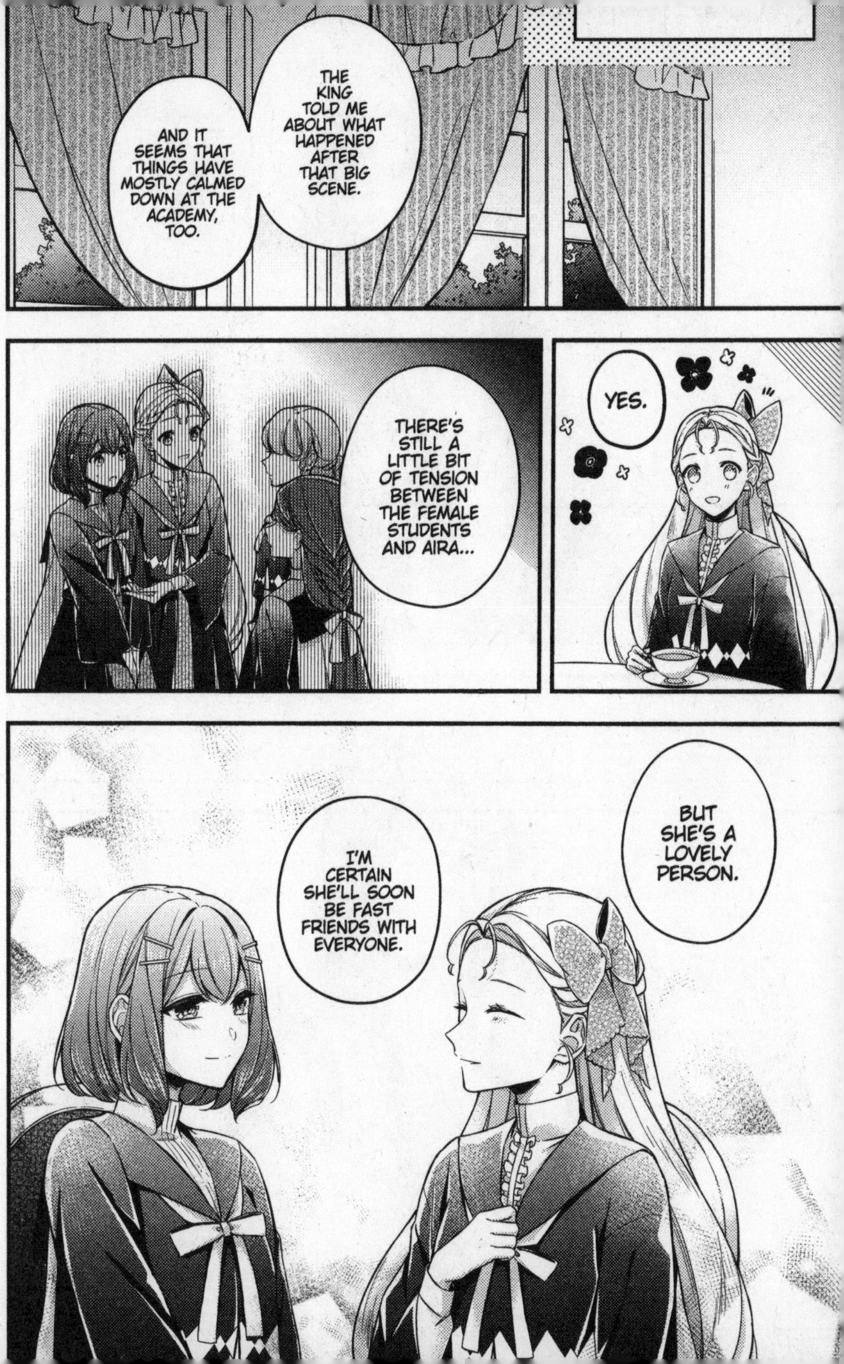
THE KING TOLD ME ABOUT WHAT HAPPENED AFTER THAT BIG SCENE.
AND IT SEEMS THAT THINGS HAVE MOSTLY CALMED DOWN AT THE ACADEMY, TOO.
YES.
THERE'S STILL A LITTLE BIT OF TENSION BETWEEN THE FEMALE STUDENTS AND AIRA...
BUT SHE'S A LOVELY PERSON.
I'M CERTAIN SHE'LL SOON BE FAST FRIENDS WITH EVERYONE.

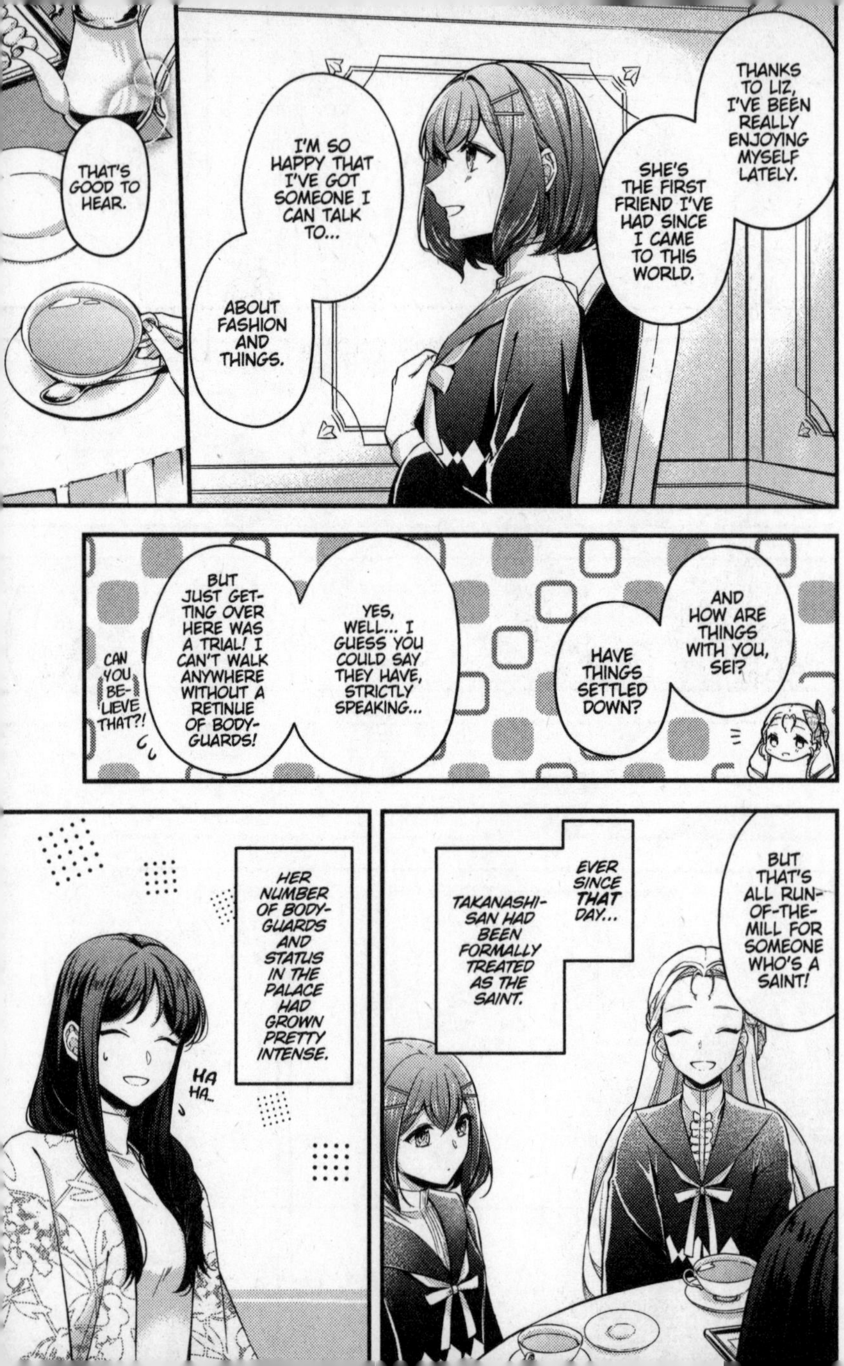
THANKS TO LIZ, I'VE BEEN REALLY ENJOYING MYSELF LATELY.
SHE'S THE FIRST FRIEND I'VE HAD SINCE I CAME TO THIS WORLD.
I'M SO HAPPY THAT I'VE GOT SOMEONE I CAN TALK TO...
ABOUT FASHION AND THINGS.
THAT'S GOOD TO HEAR.
AND HOW ARE THINGS WITH YOU, SEI?
HAVE THINGS SETTLED DOWN?
YES, WELL... I GUESS YOU COULD SAY THEY HAVE, STRICTLY SPEAKING...
BUT JUST GETTING OVER HERE WAS A TRIAL! I CAN'T WALK ANYWHERE WITHOUT A RETINUE OF BODYGUARDS!
CAN YOU BELIEVE THAT?!
BUT THAT'S ALL RUN-OF-THE-MILL FOR SOMEONE WHO'S A SAINT!
EVER SINCE *THAT* DAY...
TAKANASHI-SAN HAD BEEN FORMALLY TREATED AS THE SAINT.
HER NUMBER OF BODYGUARDS AND STATUS IN THE PALACE HAD GROWN PRETTY INTENSE.
HA HA...

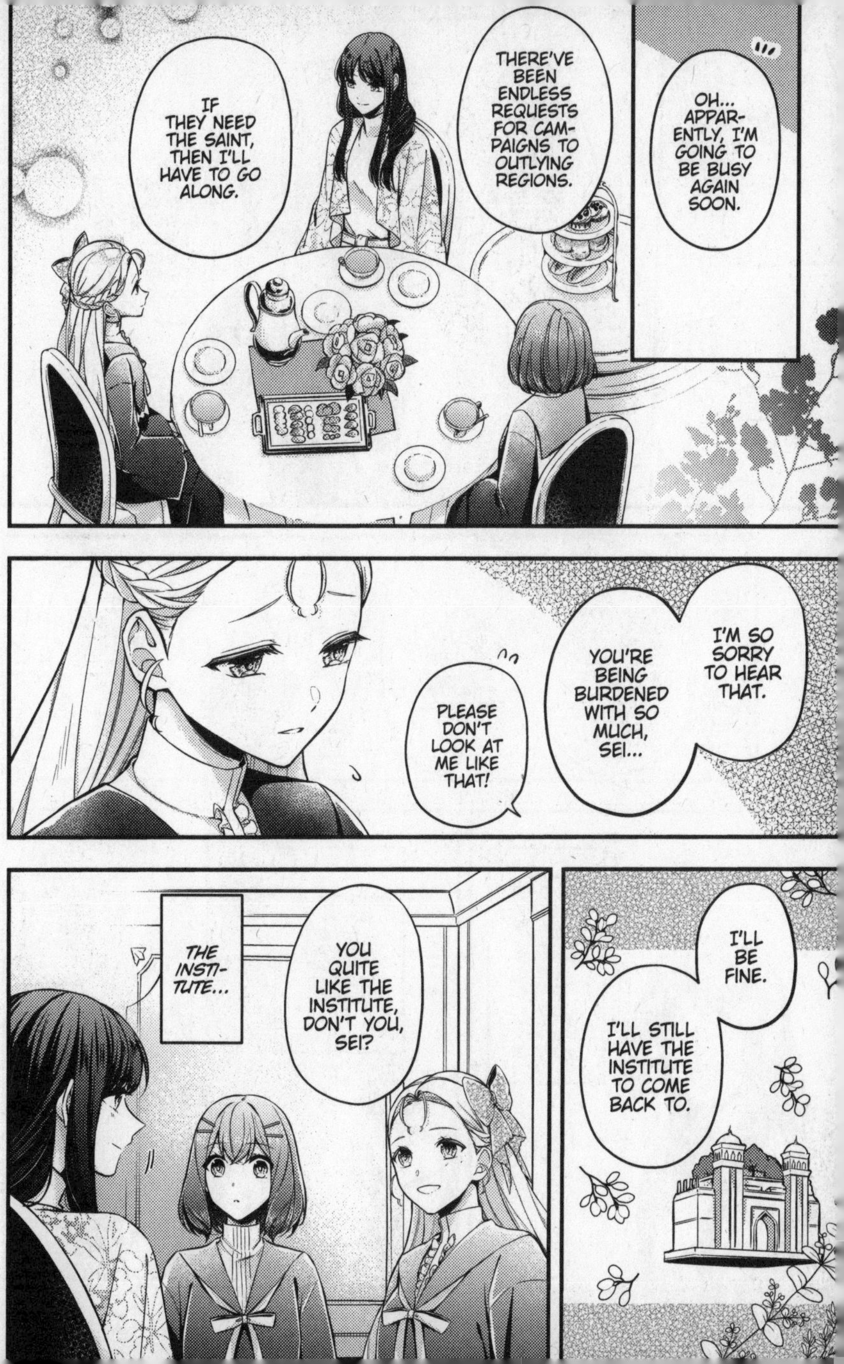
OH... APPARENTLY, I'M GOING TO BE BUSY AGAIN SOON.
THERE'VE BEEN ENDLESS REQUESTS FOR CAMPAIGNS TO OUTLYING REGIONS.
IF THEY NEED THE SAINT, THEN I'LL HAVE TO GO ALONG.
I'M SO SORRY TO HEAR THAT.
YOU'RE BEING BURDENED WITH SO MUCH, SEI...
PLEASE DON'T LOOK AT ME LIKE THAT!
I'LL BE FINE.
I'LL STILL HAVE THE INSTITUTE TO COME BACK TO.
YOU QUITE LIKE THE INSTITUTE, DON'T YOU, SEI?
THE INSTITUTE...

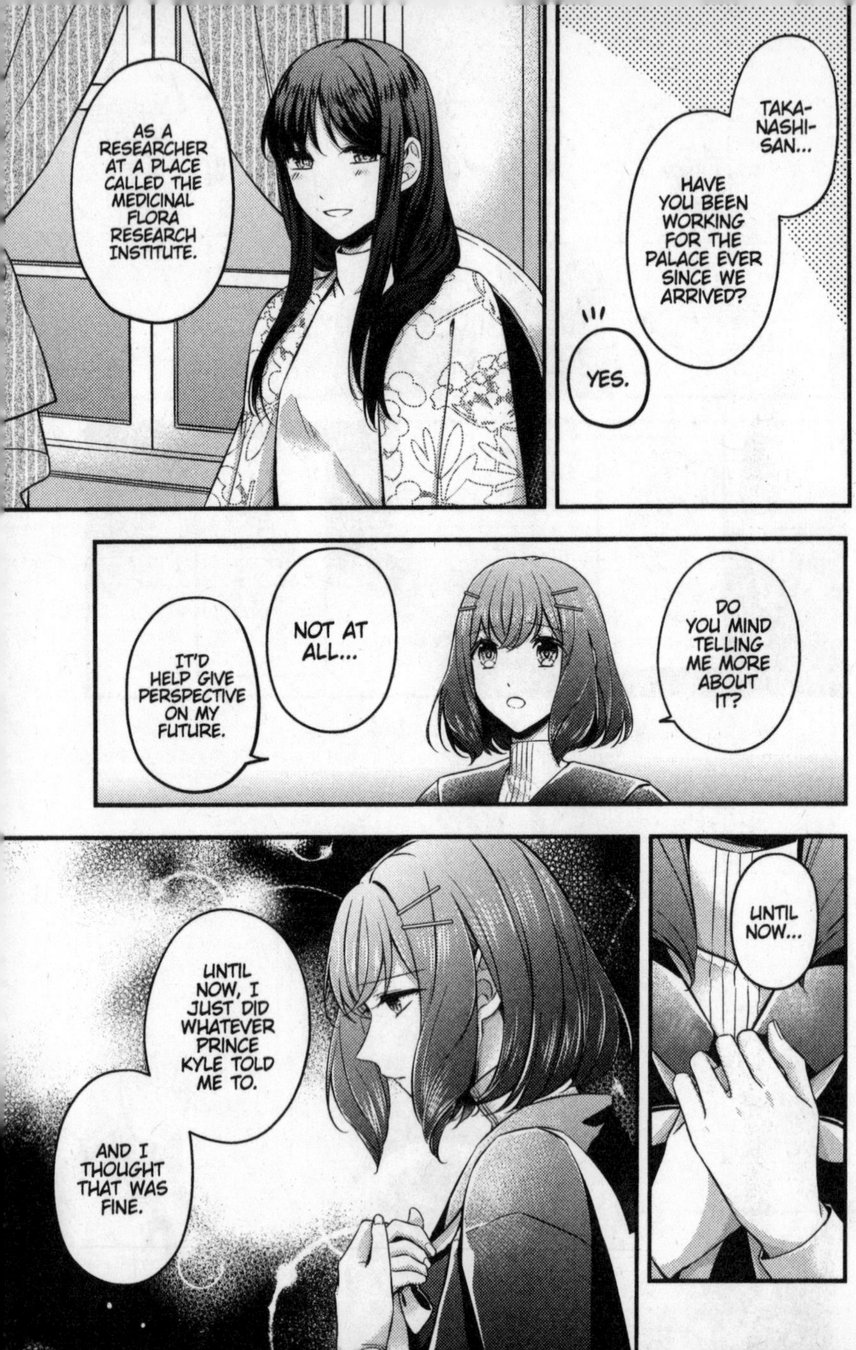
TAKA-NASHI-SAN... HAVE YOU BEEN WORKING FOR THE PALACE EVER SINCE WE ARRIVED?
YES.
AS A RESEARCHER AT A PLACE CALLED THE MEDICINAL FLORA RESEARCH INSTITUTE.
DO YOU MIND TELLING ME MORE ABOUT IT?
NOT AT ALL...
IT'D HELP GIVE PERSPECTIVE ON MY FUTURE.
UNTIL NOW...
UNTIL NOW, I JUST DID WHATEVER PRINCE KYLE TOLD ME TO.
AND I THOUGHT THAT WAS FINE.

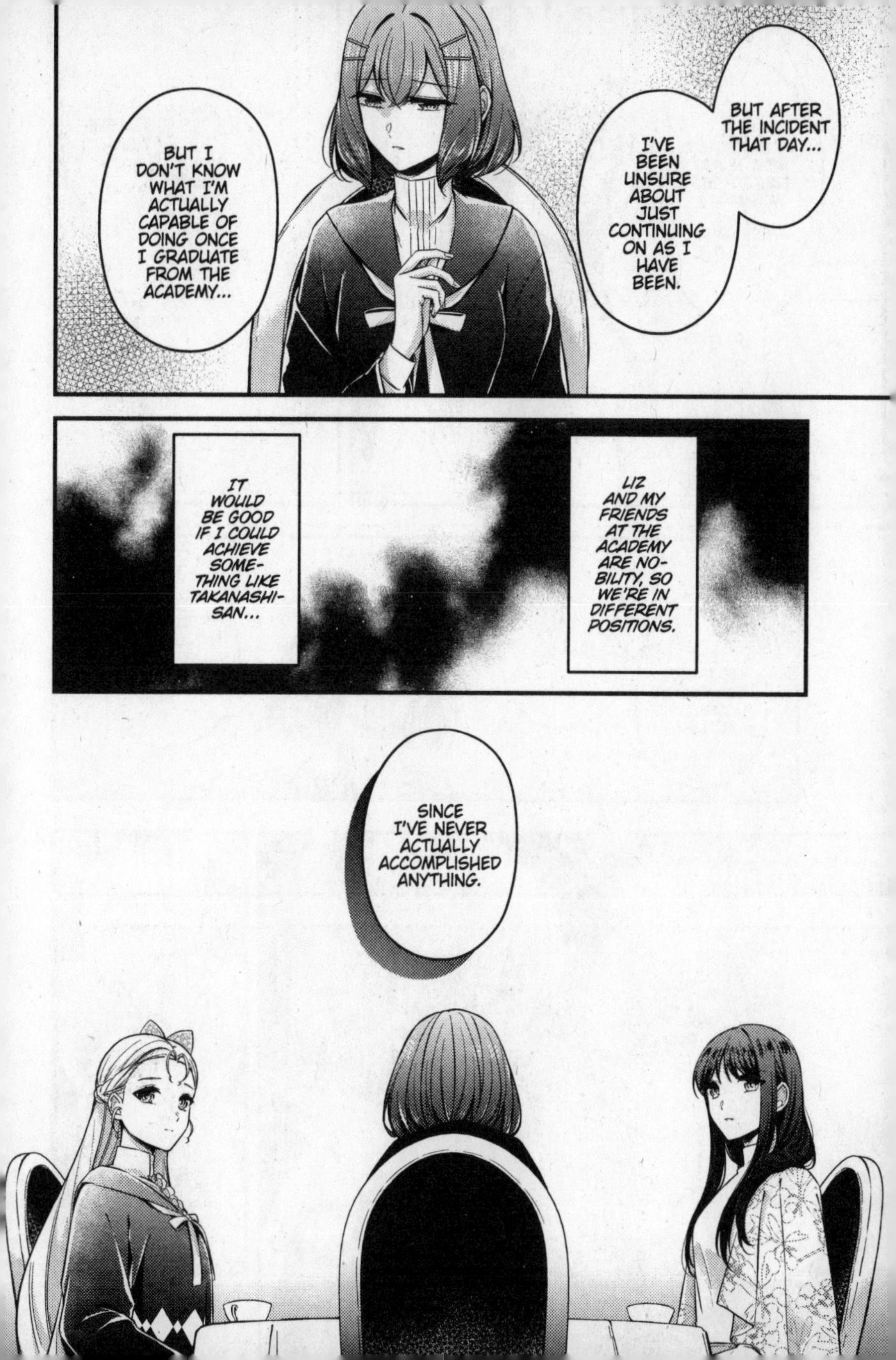
BUT AFTER THE INCIDENT THAT DAY...
I'VE BEEN UNSURE ABOUT JUST CONTINUING ON AS I HAVE BEEN.
BUT I DON'T KNOW WHAT I'M ACTUALLY CAPABLE OF DOING ONCE I GRADUATE FROM THE ACADEMY...
LIZ AND MY FRIENDS AT THE ACADEMY ARE NO-BILITY, SO WE'RE IN DIFFERENT POSITIONS.
IT WOULD BE GOOD IF I COULD ACHIEVE SOME-THING LIKE TAKANASHI-SAN...
SINCE I'VE NEVER ACTUALLY ACCOMPLISHED ANYTHING.

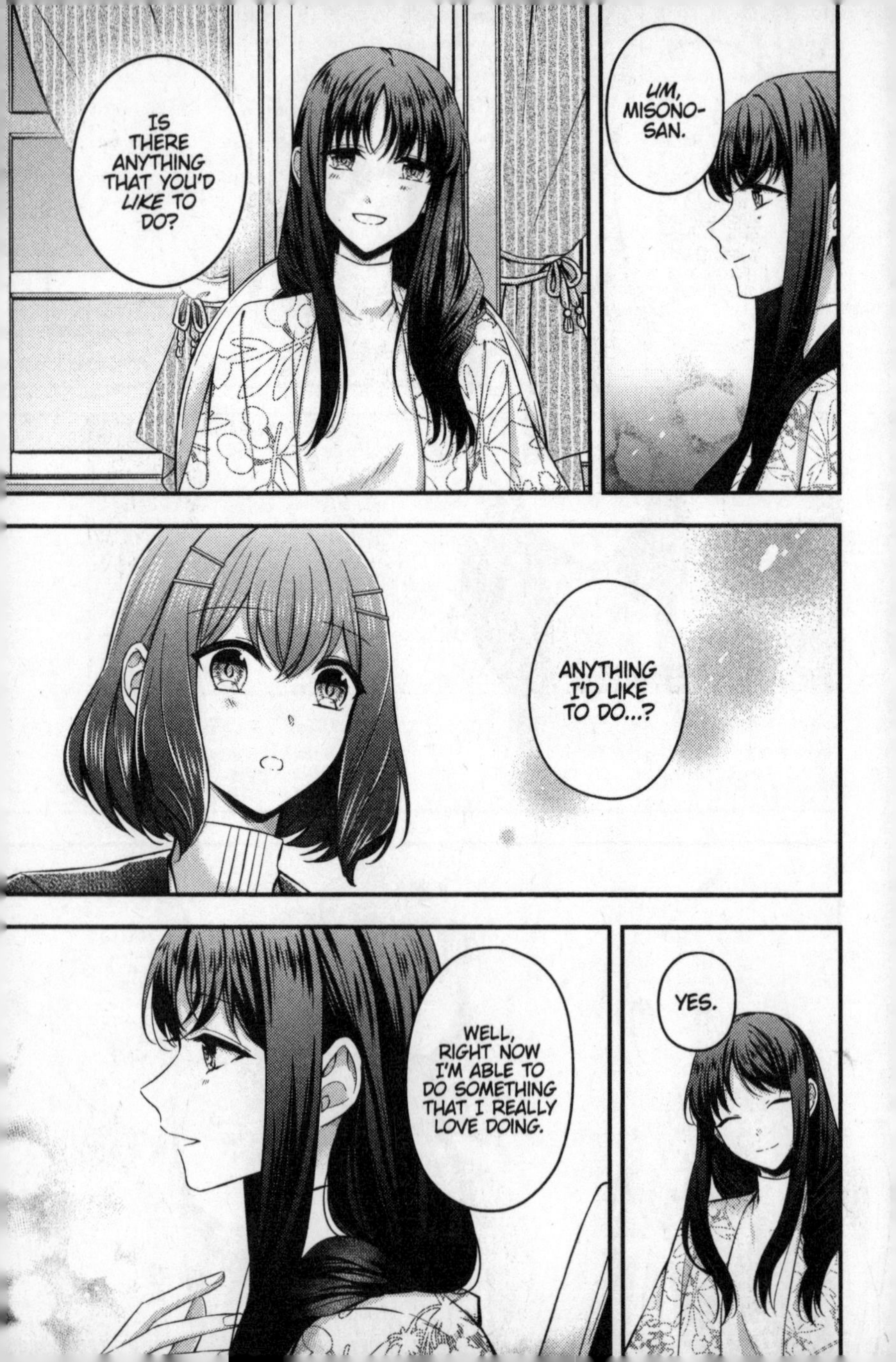
UM, MISONO-SAN.
IS THERE ANYTHING THAT YOU'D LIKE TO DO?
ANYTHING I'D LIKE TO DO...?
YES.
WELL, RIGHT NOW I'M ABLE TO DO SOMETHING THAT I REALLY LOVE DOING.

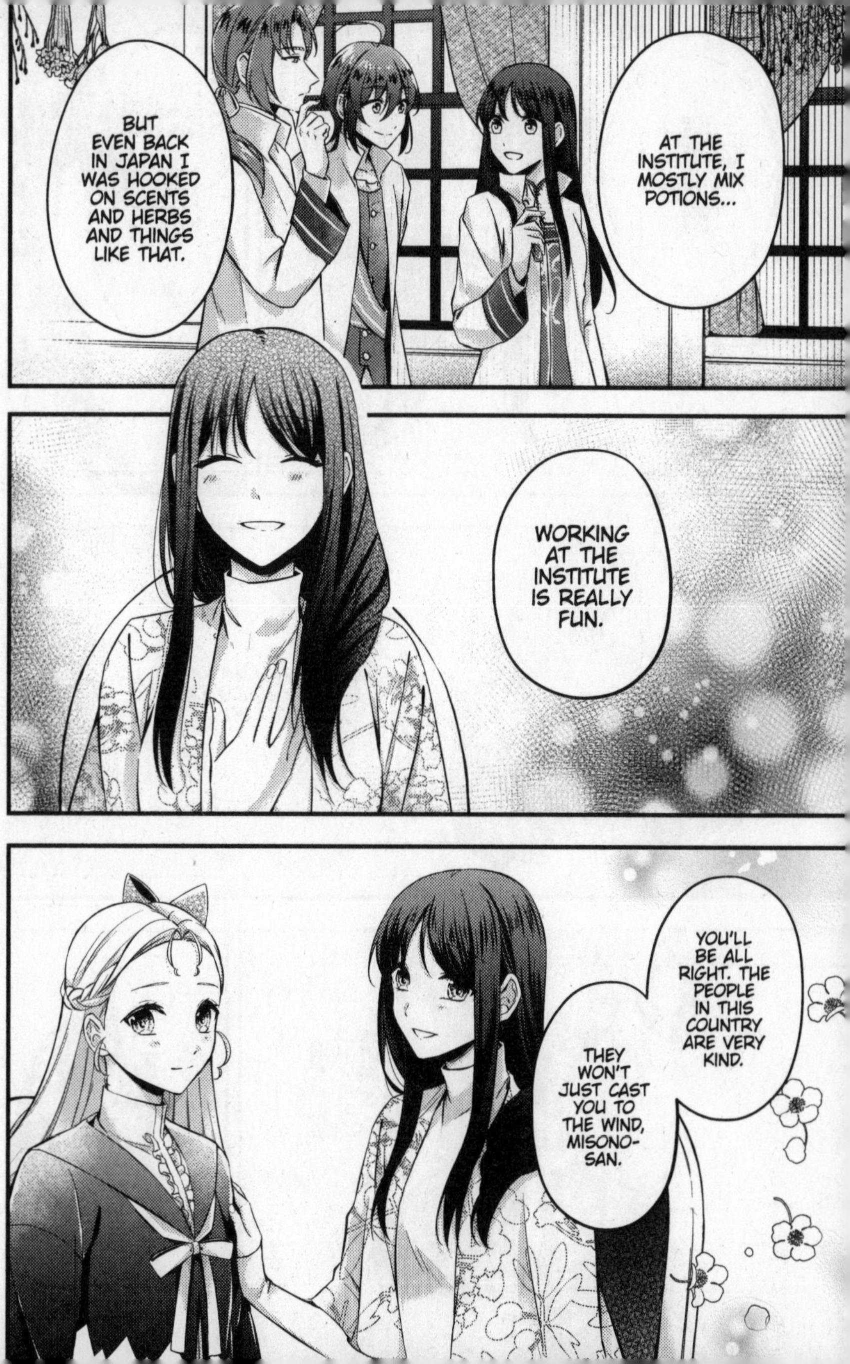
AT THE INSTITUTE, I MOSTLY MIX POTIONS...
BUT EVEN BACK IN JAPAN I WAS HOOKED ON SCENTS AND HERBS AND THINGS LIKE THAT.
WORKING AT THE INSTITUTE IS REALLY FUN.
YOU'LL BE ALL RIGHT. THE PEOPLE IN THIS COUNTRY ARE VERY KIND.
THEY WON'T JUST CAST YOU TO THE WIND, MISONO-SAN.

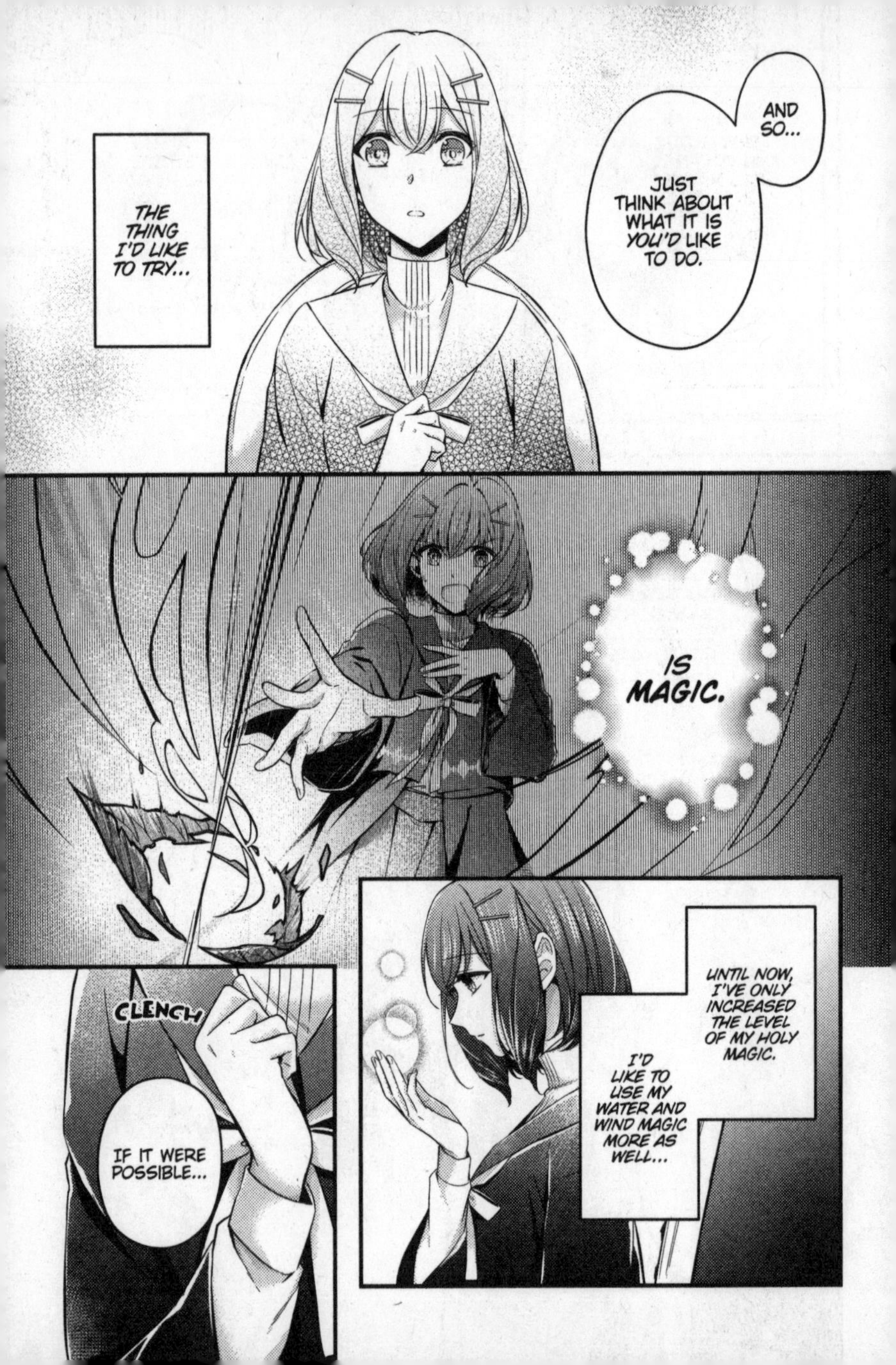
AND SO...
JUST THINK ABOUT WHAT IT IS YOU'D LIKE TO DO.
THE THING I'D LIKE TO TRY...
IS MAGIC.
UNTIL NOW, I'VE ONLY INCREASED THE LEVEL OF MY HOLY MAGIC.
I'D LIKE TO USE MY WATER AND WIND MAGIC MORE AS WELL...
CLENCH
IF IT WERE POSSIBLE...

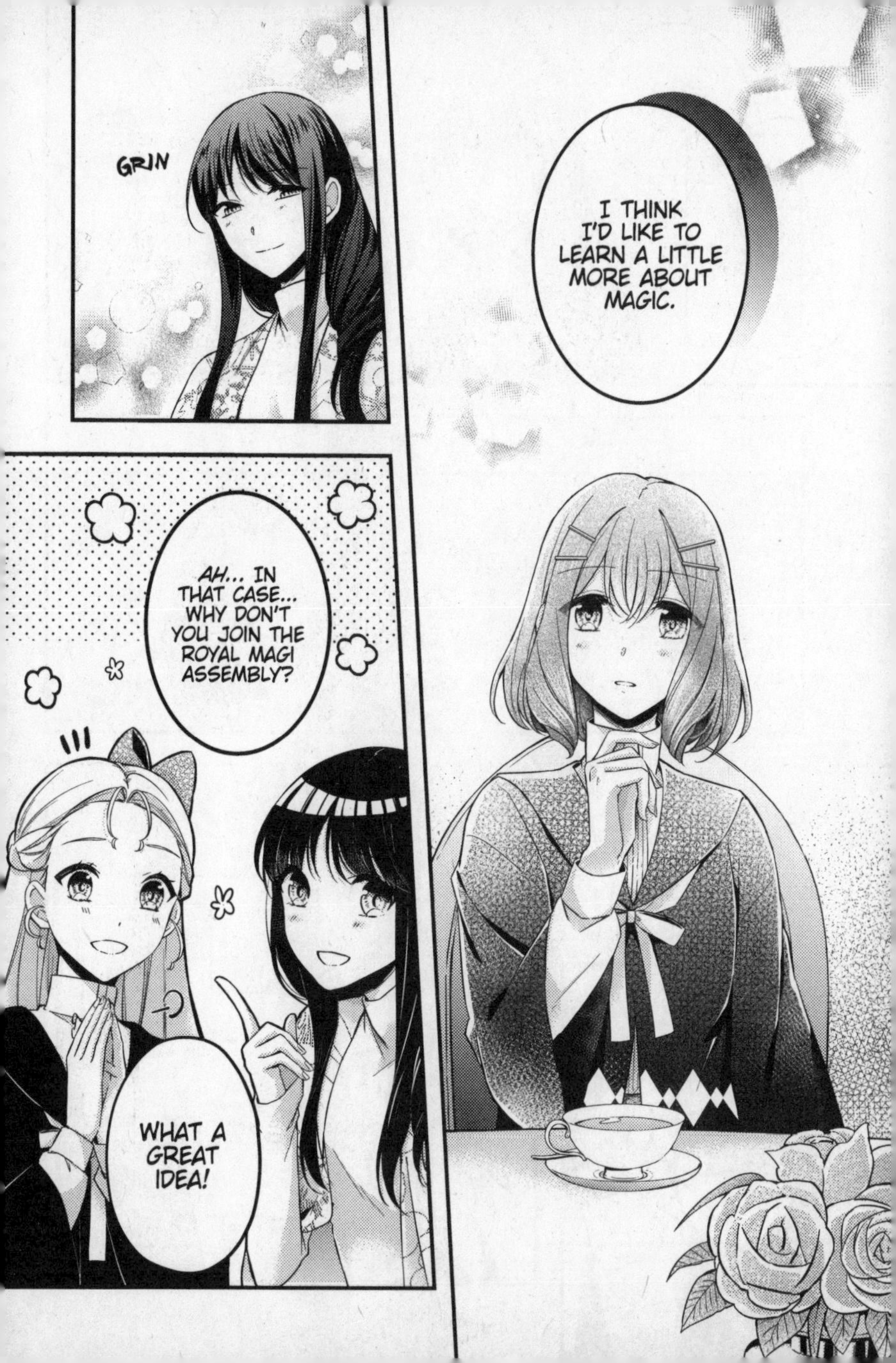
I THINK I'D LIKE TO LEARN A LITTLE MORE ABOUT MAGIC.
GRIN
AH... IN THAT CASE... WHY DON'T YOU JOIN THE ROYAL MAGI ASSEMBLY?
WHAT A GREAT IDEA!

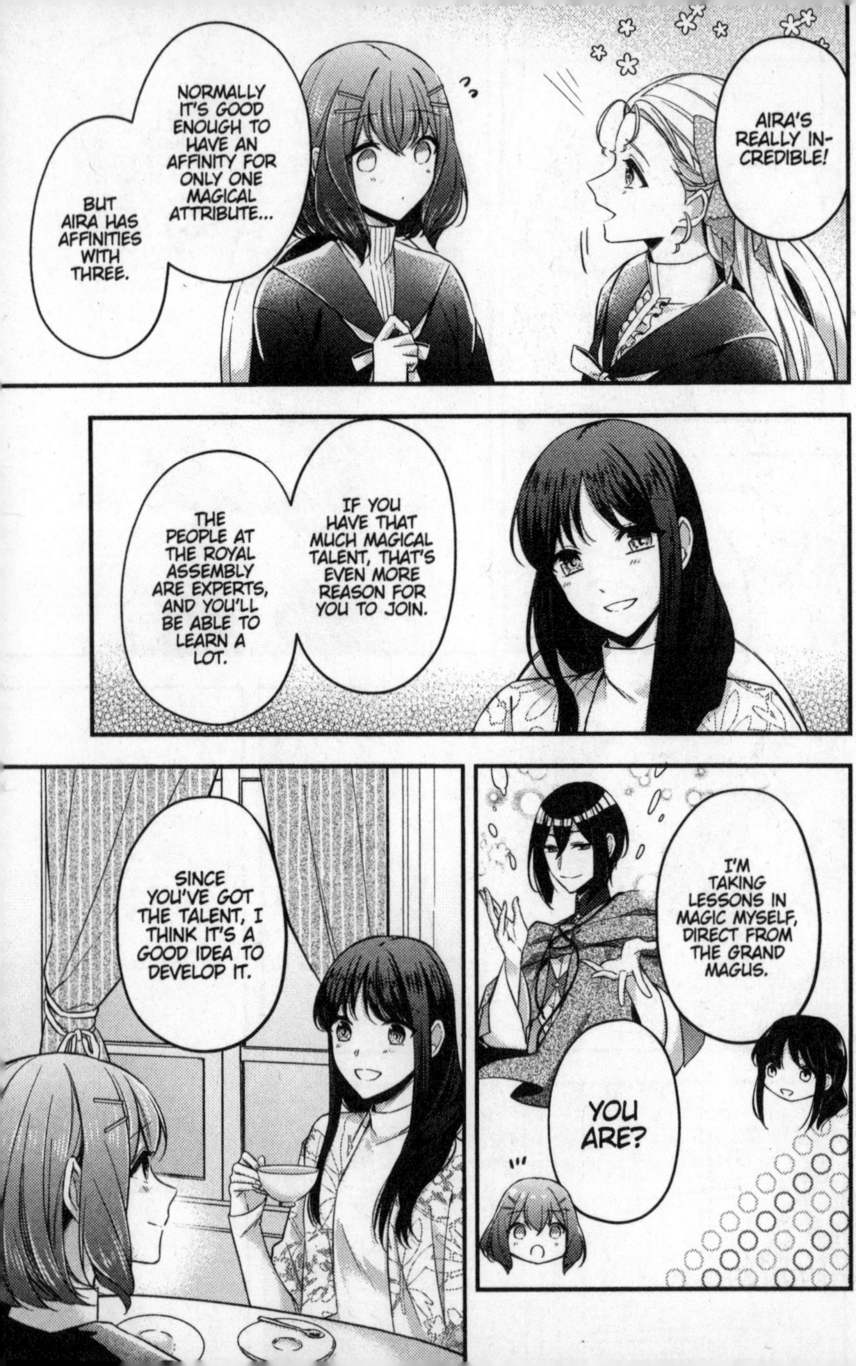
AIRA'S REALLY IN-CREDIBLE!
NORMALLY IT'S GOOD ENOUGH TO HAVE AN AFFINITY FOR ONLY ONE MAGICAL ATTRIBUTE...
BUT AIRA HAS AFFINITIES WITH THREE.
IF YOU HAVE THAT MUCH MAGICAL TALENT, THAT'S EVEN MORE REASON FOR YOU TO JOIN.
THE PEOPLE AT THE ROYAL ASSEMBLY ARE EXPERTS, AND YOU'LL BE ABLE TO LEARN A LOT.
I'M TAKING LESSONS IN MAGIC MYSELF, DIRECT FROM THE GRAND MAGUS.
YOU ARE?
SINCE YOU'VE GOT THE TALENT, I THINK IT'S A GOOD IDEA TO DEVELOP IT.

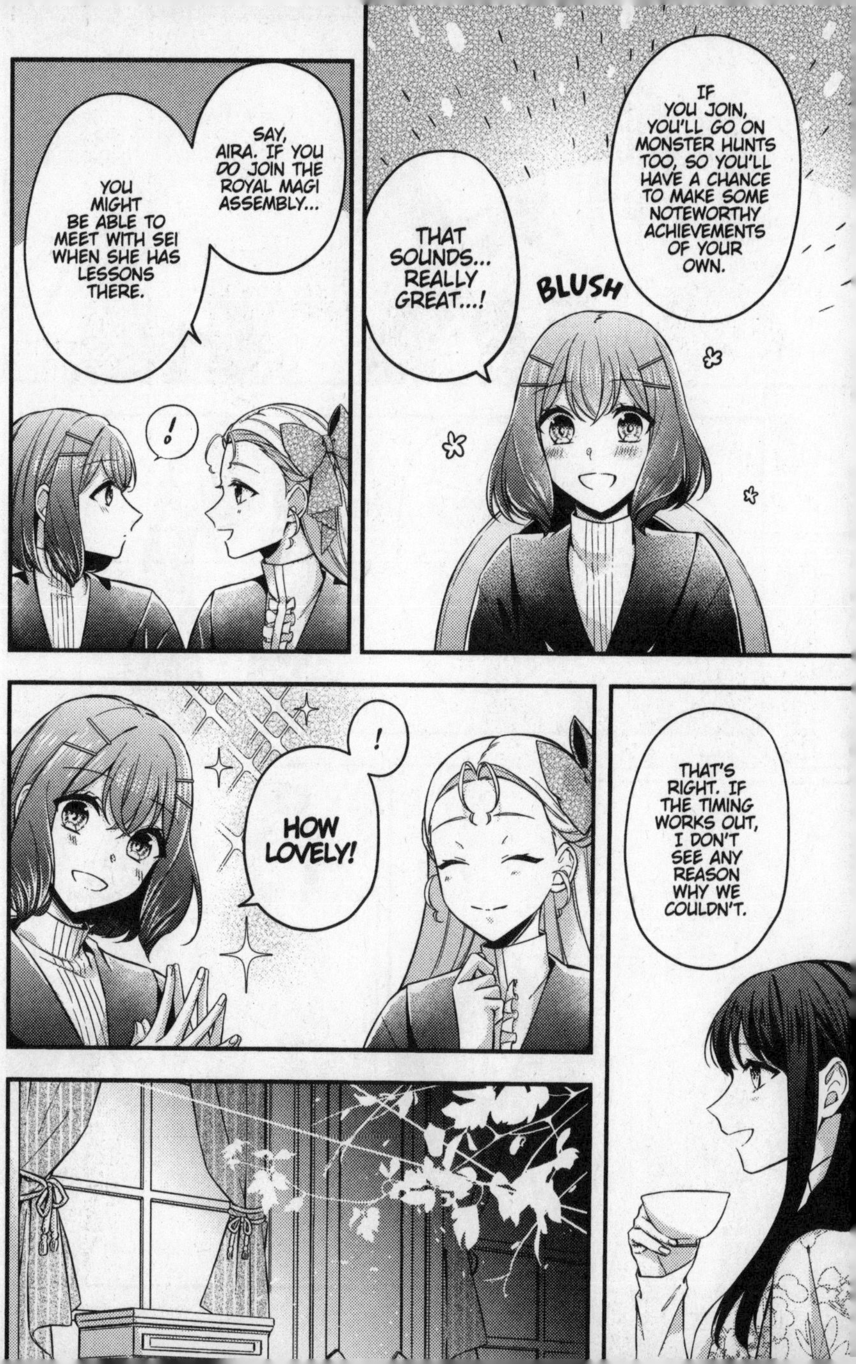
IF YOU JOIN, YOU'LL GO ON MONSTER HUNTS TOO, SO YOU'LL HAVE A CHANCE TO MAKE SOME NOTEWORTHY ACHIEVEMENTS OF YOUR OWN.
BLUSH
THAT SOUNDS... REALLY GREAT...!
SAY, AIRA. IF YOU DO JOIN THE ROYAL MAGI ASSEMBLY...
YOU MIGHT BE ABLE TO MEET WITH SEI WHEN SHE HAS LESSONS THERE.
!
THAT'S RIGHT. IF THE TIMING WORKS OUT, I DON'T SEE ANY REASON WHY WE COULDN'T.
!
HOW LOVELY!

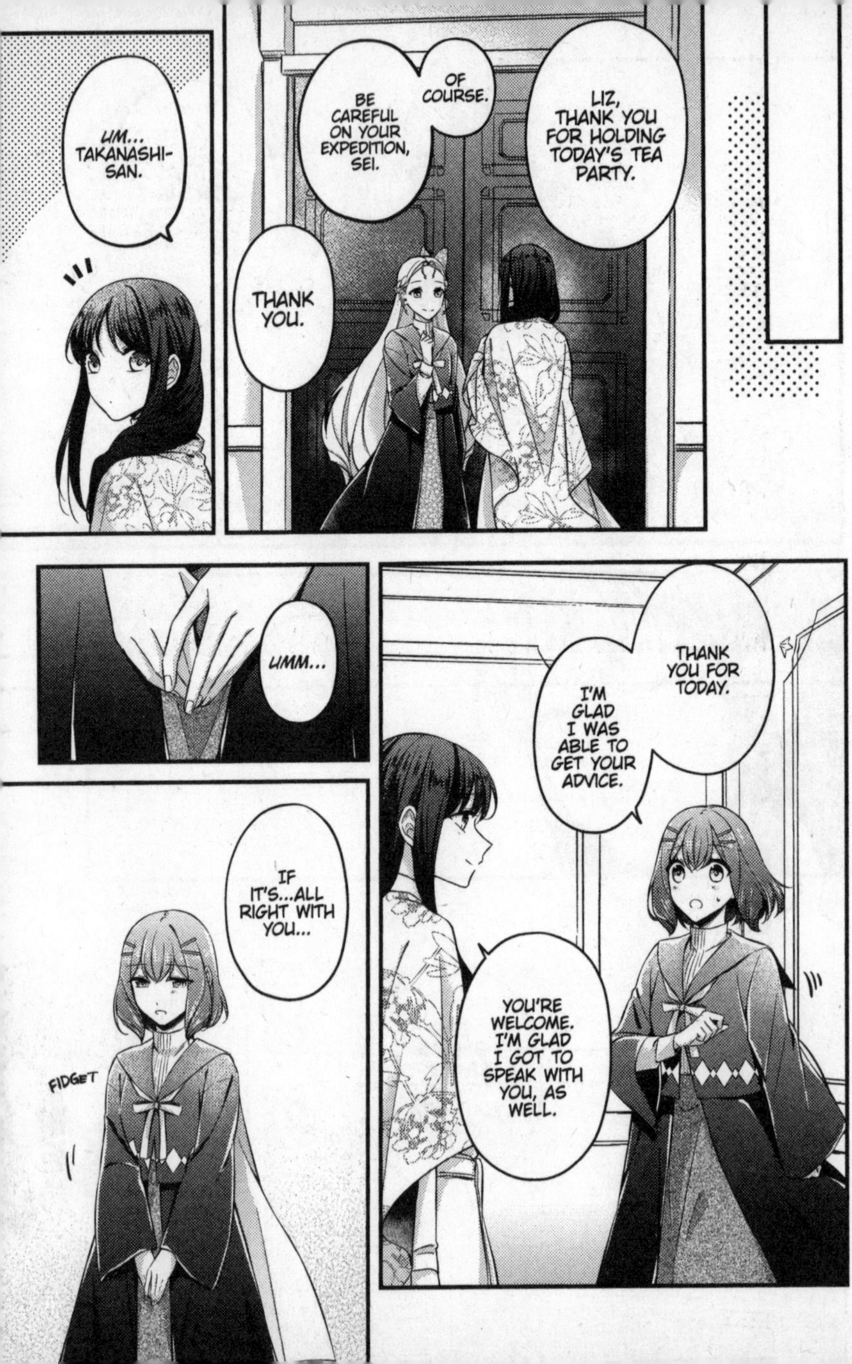
LIZ, THANK YOU FOR HOLDING TODAY'S TEA PARTY.
OF COURSE.
BE CAREFUL ON YOUR EXPEDITION, SEI.
THANK YOU.
UM... TAKANASHI-SAN.
THANK YOU FOR TODAY.
I'M GLAD I WAS ABLE TO GET YOUR ADVICE.
YOU'RE WELCOME. I'M GLAD I GOT TO SPEAK WITH YOU, AS WELL.
UMM...
IF IT'S...ALL RIGHT WITH YOU...
FIDGET

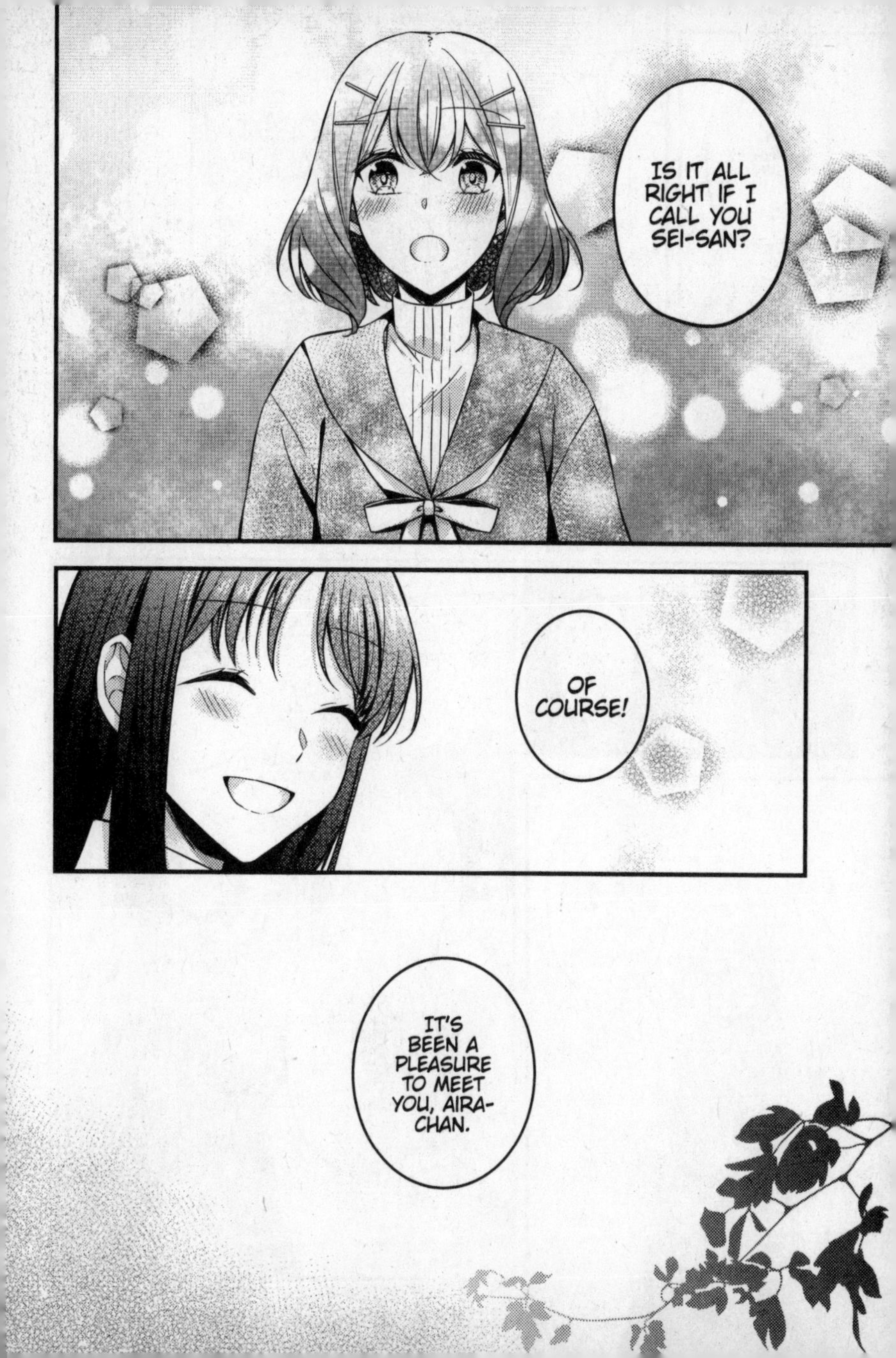
IS IT ALL RIGHT IF I CALL YOU SEI-SAN?
OF COURSE!
IT'S BEEN A PLEASURE TO MEET YOU, AIRA-CHAN.

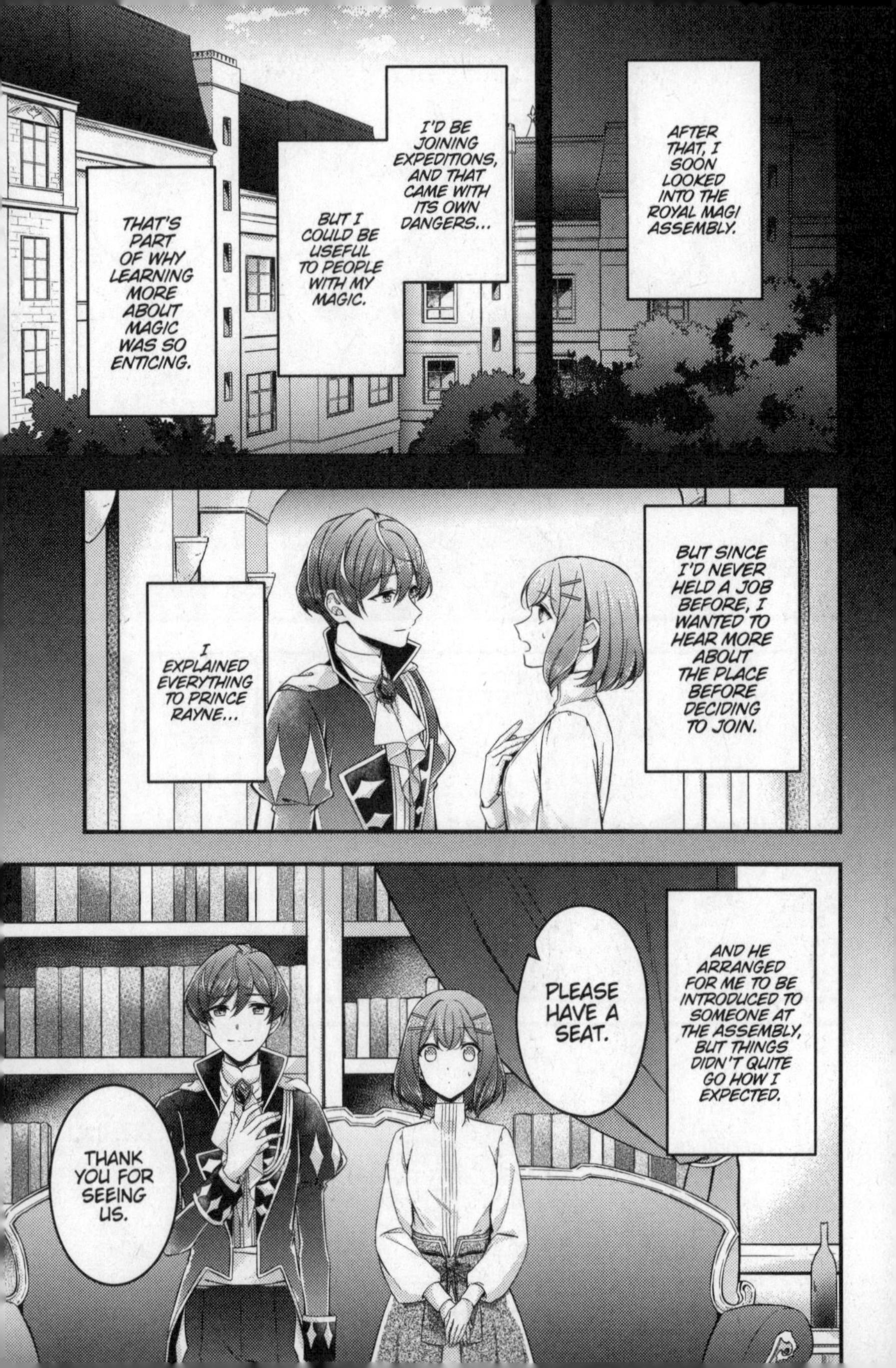
AFTER THAT, I SOON LOOKED INTO THE ROYAL MAGI ASSEMBLY.
I'D BE JOINING EXPEDITIONS, AND THAT CAME WITH ITS OWN DANGERS...
BUT I COULD BE USEFUL TO PEOPLE WITH MY MAGIC.
THAT'S PART OF WHY LEARNING MORE ABOUT MAGIC WAS SO ENTICING.
BUT SINCE I'D NEVER HELD A JOB BEFORE, I WANTED TO HEAR MORE ABOUT THE PLACE BEFORE DECIDING TO JOIN.
I EXPLAINED EVERYTHING TO PRINCE RAYNE...
AND HE ARRANGED FOR ME TO BE INTRODUCED TO SOMEONE AT THE ASSEMBLY, BUT THINGS DIDN'T QUITE GO HOW I EXPECTED.
PLEASE HAVE A SEAT.
THANK YOU FOR SEEING US.

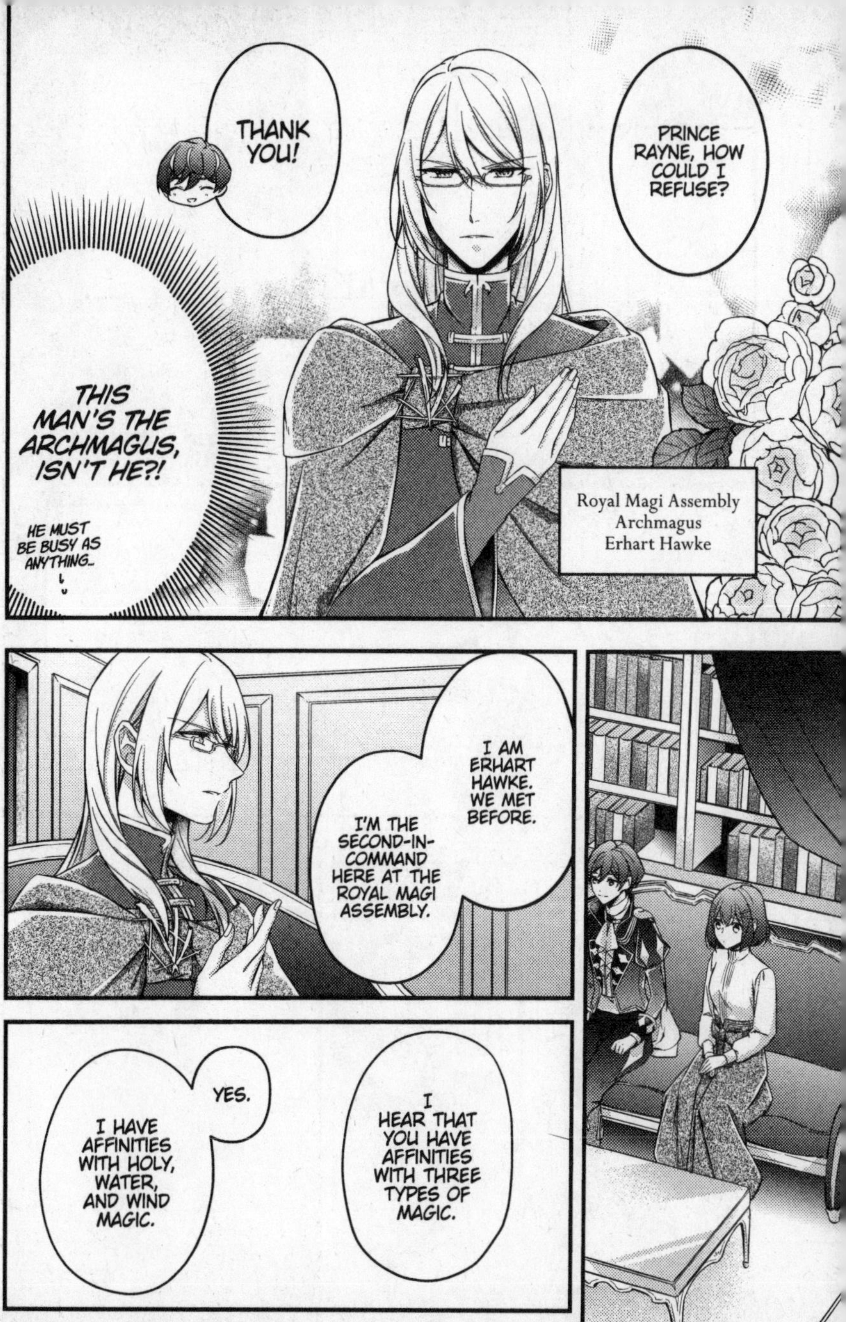
PRINCE RAYNE, HOW COULD I REFUSE?
THANK YOU!
THIS MAN'S THE ARCHMAGUS, ISN'T HE?!
Royal Magi Assembly Archmagus Erhart Hawke
HE MUST BE BUSY AS ANYTHING...
I AM ERHART HAWKE. WE MET BEFORE.
I'M THE SECOND-IN-COMMAND HERE AT THE ROYAL MAGI ASSEMBLY.
I HEAR THAT YOU HAVE AFFINITIES WITH THREE TYPES OF MAGIC.
YES.
I HAVE AFFINITIES WITH HOLY, WATER, AND WIND MAGIC.

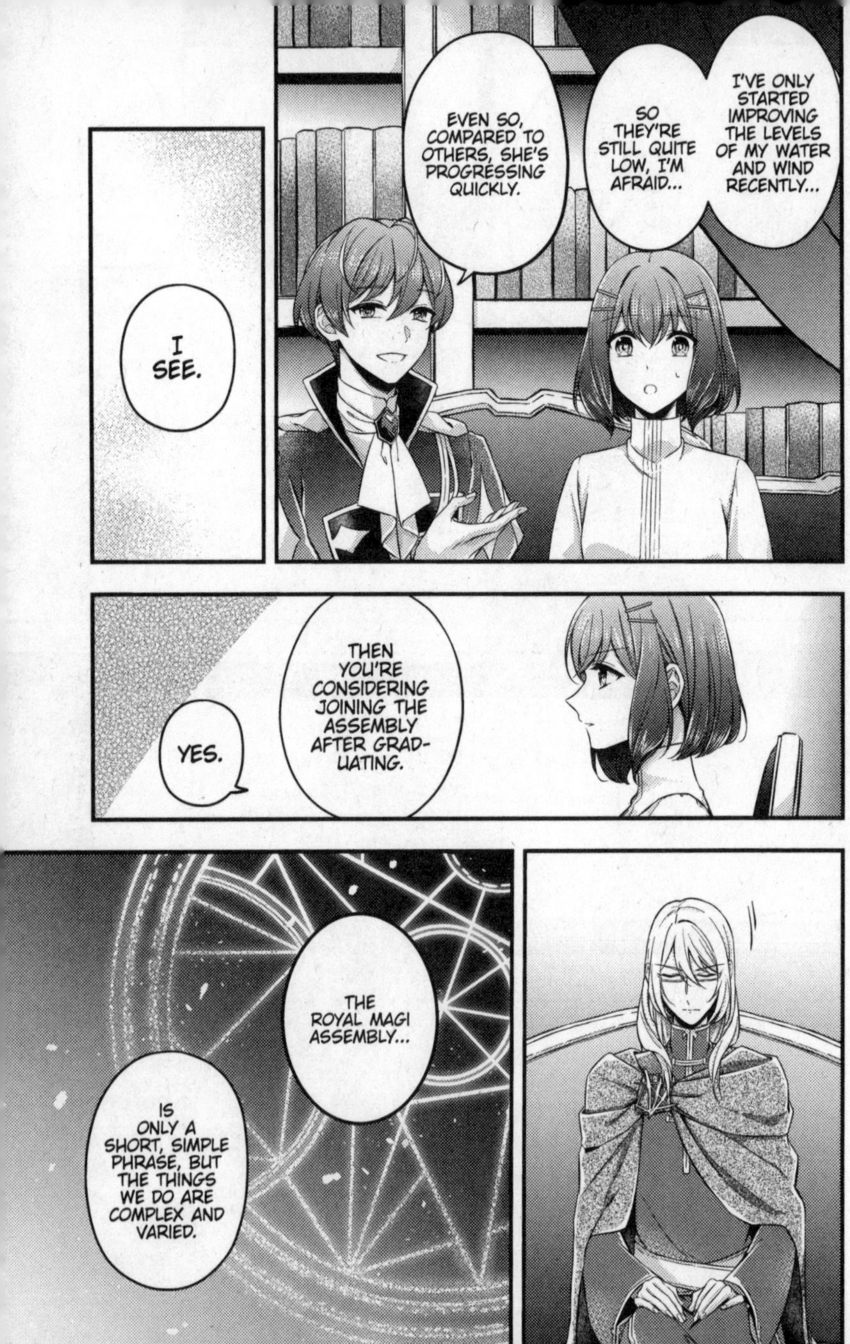
I'VE ONLY STARTED IMPROVING THE LEVELS OF MY WATER AND WIND RECENTLY...
SO THEY'RE STILL QUITE LOW, I'M AFRAID...
EVEN SO, COMPARED TO OTHERS, SHE'S PROGRESSING QUICKLY.
I SEE.
THEN YOU'RE CONSIDERING JOINING THE ASSEMBLY AFTER GRAD-UATING.
YES.
THE ROYAL MAGI ASSEMBLY...
IS ONLY A SHORT, SIMPLE PHRASE, BUT THE THINGS WE DO ARE COMPLEX AND VARIED.

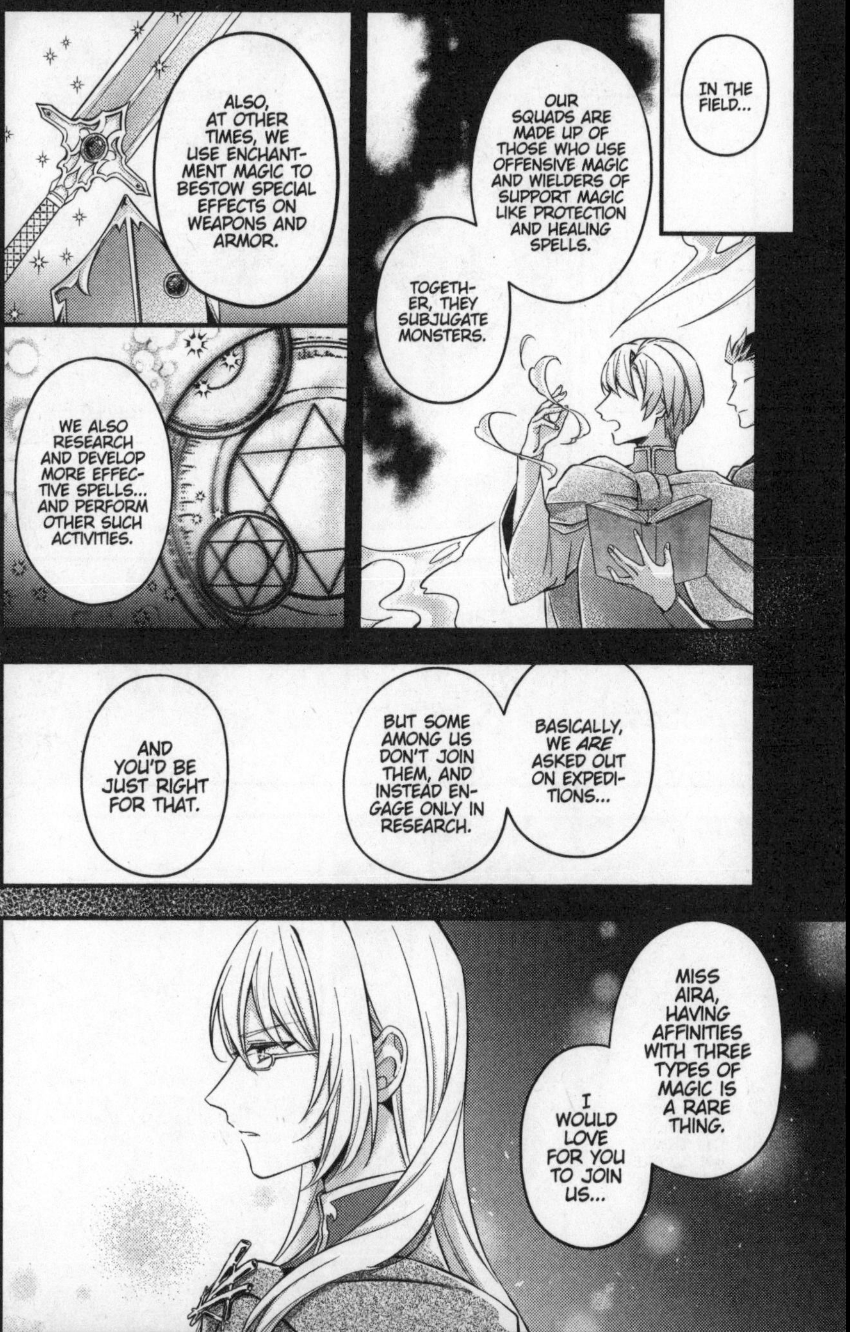
IN THE FIELD...
OUR SQUADS ARE MADE UP OF THOSE WHO USE OFFENSIVE MAGIC AND WIELDERS OF SUPPORT MAGIC LIKE PROTECTION AND HEALING SPELLS.
TOGETH-ER, THEY SUBJUGATE MONSTERS.
ALSO, AT OTHER TIMES, WE USE ENCHANT-MENT MAGIC TO BESTOW SPECIAL EFFECTS ON WEAPONS AND ARMOR.
WE ALSO RESEARCH AND DEVELOP MORE EFFEC-TIVE SPELLS... AND PERFORM OTHER SUCH ACTIVITIES.
BASICALLY, WE *ARE* ASKED OUT ON EXPEDI-TIONS...
BUT SOME AMONG US DON'T JOIN THEM, AND INSTEAD EN-GAGE ONLY IN RESEARCH.
AND YOU'D BE JUST RIGHT FOR THAT.
MISS AIRA, HAVING AFFINITIES WITH THREE TYPES OF MAGIC IS A RARE THING.
I WOULD LOVE FOR YOU TO JOIN US...

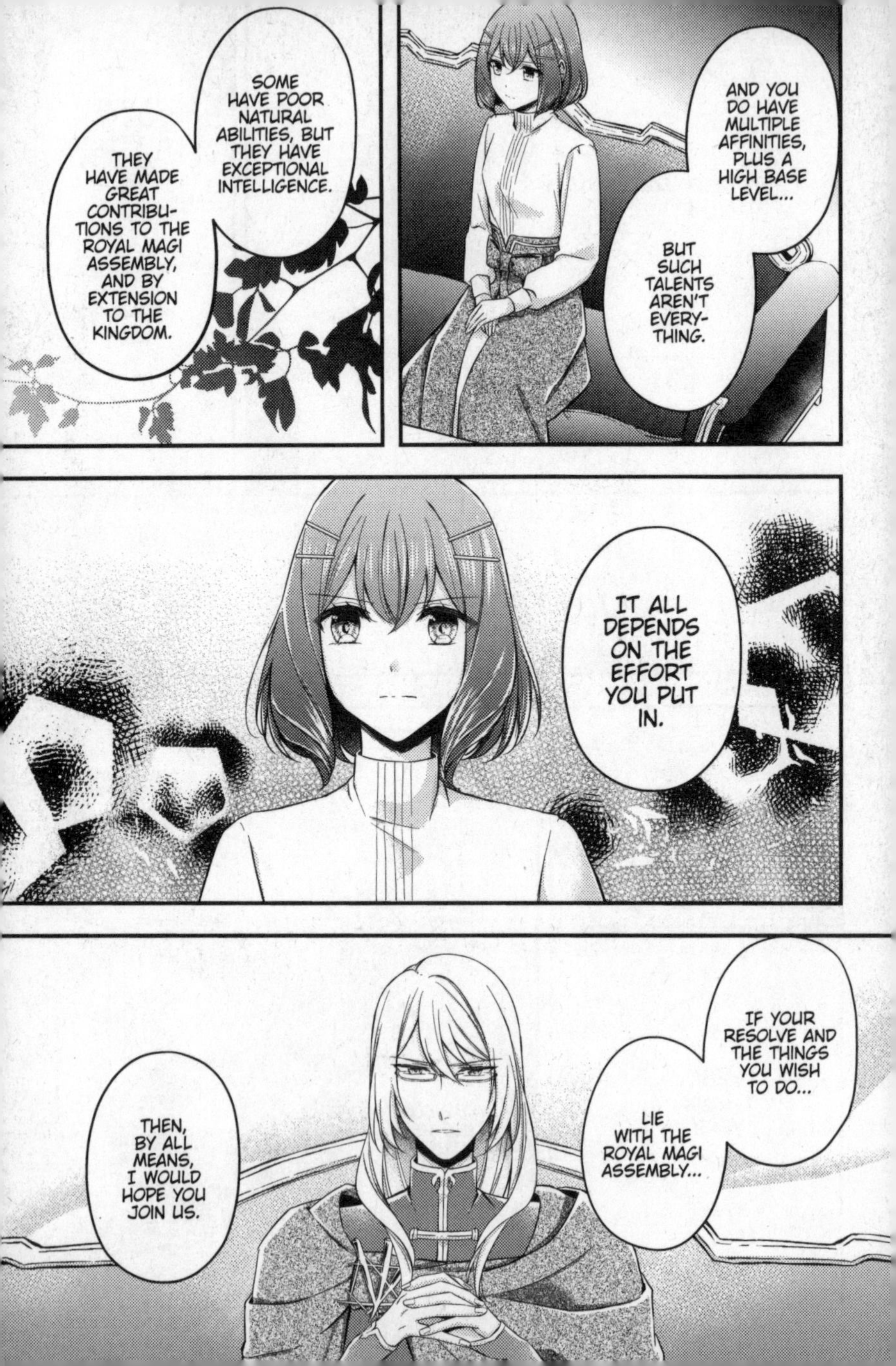
AND YOU DO HAVE MULTIPLE AFFINITIES, PLUS A HIGH BASE LEVEL...
BUT SUCH TALENTS AREN'T EVERYTHING.
SOME HAVE POOR NATURAL ABILITIES, BUT THEY HAVE EXCEPTIONAL INTELLIGENCE.
THEY HAVE MADE GREAT CONTRIBUTIONS TO THE ROYAL MAGI ASSEMBLY, AND BY EXTENSION TO THE KINGDOM.
IT ALL DEPENDS ON THE EFFORT YOU PUT IN.
IF YOUR RESOLVE AND THE THINGS YOU WISH TO DO...
LIE WITH THE ROYAL MAGI ASSEMBLY...
THEN, BY ALL MEANS, I WOULD HOPE YOU JOIN US.

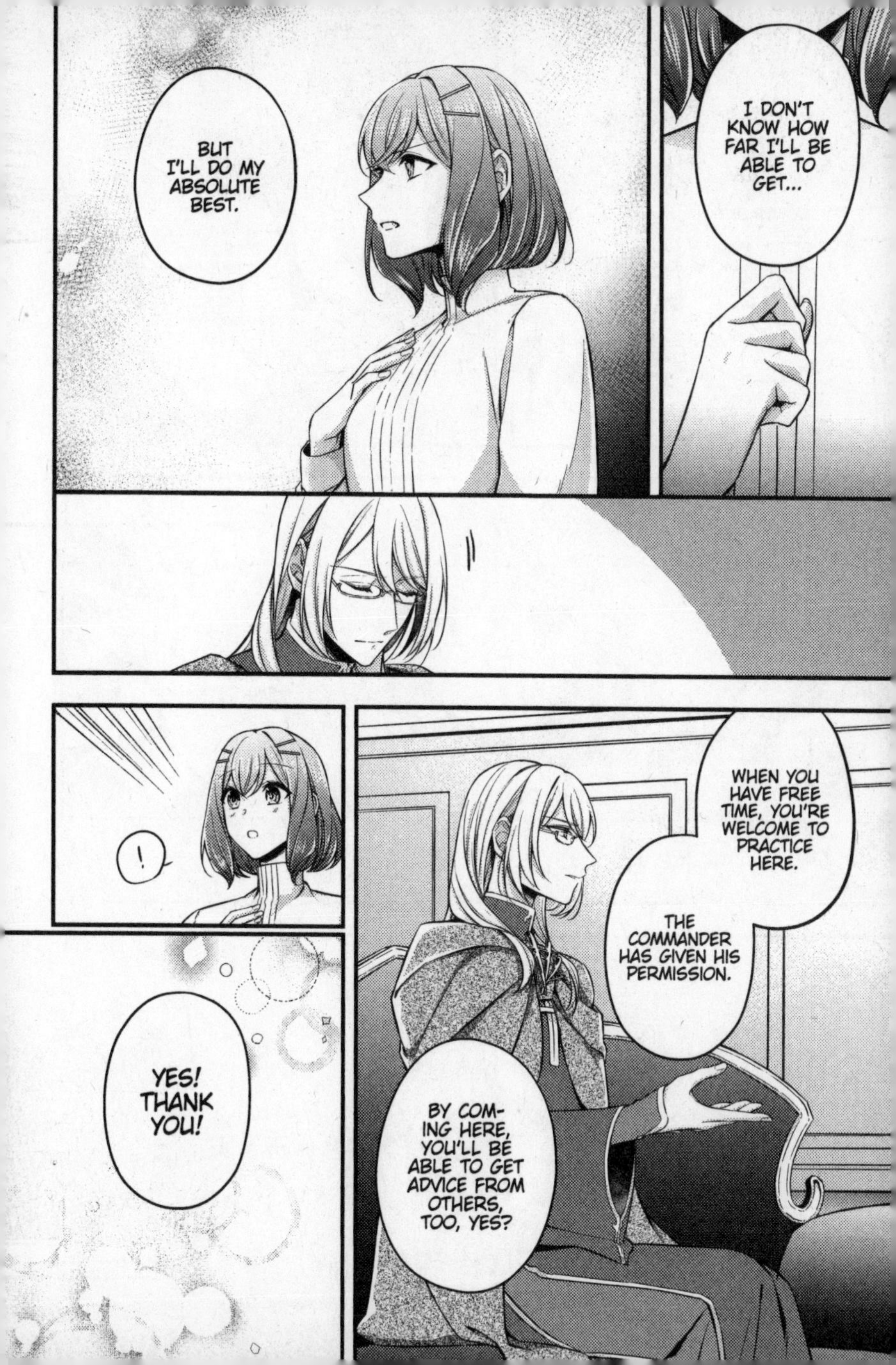
I DON'T KNOW HOW FAR I'LL BE ABLE TO GET...
BUT I'LL DO MY ABSOLUTE BEST.
WHEN YOU HAVE FREE TIME, YOU'RE WELCOME TO PRACTICE HERE.
THE COMMANDER HAS GIVEN HIS PERMISSION.
BY COM-ING HERE, YOU'LL BE ABLE TO GET ADVICE FROM OTHERS, TOO, YES?
!
YES! THANK YOU!

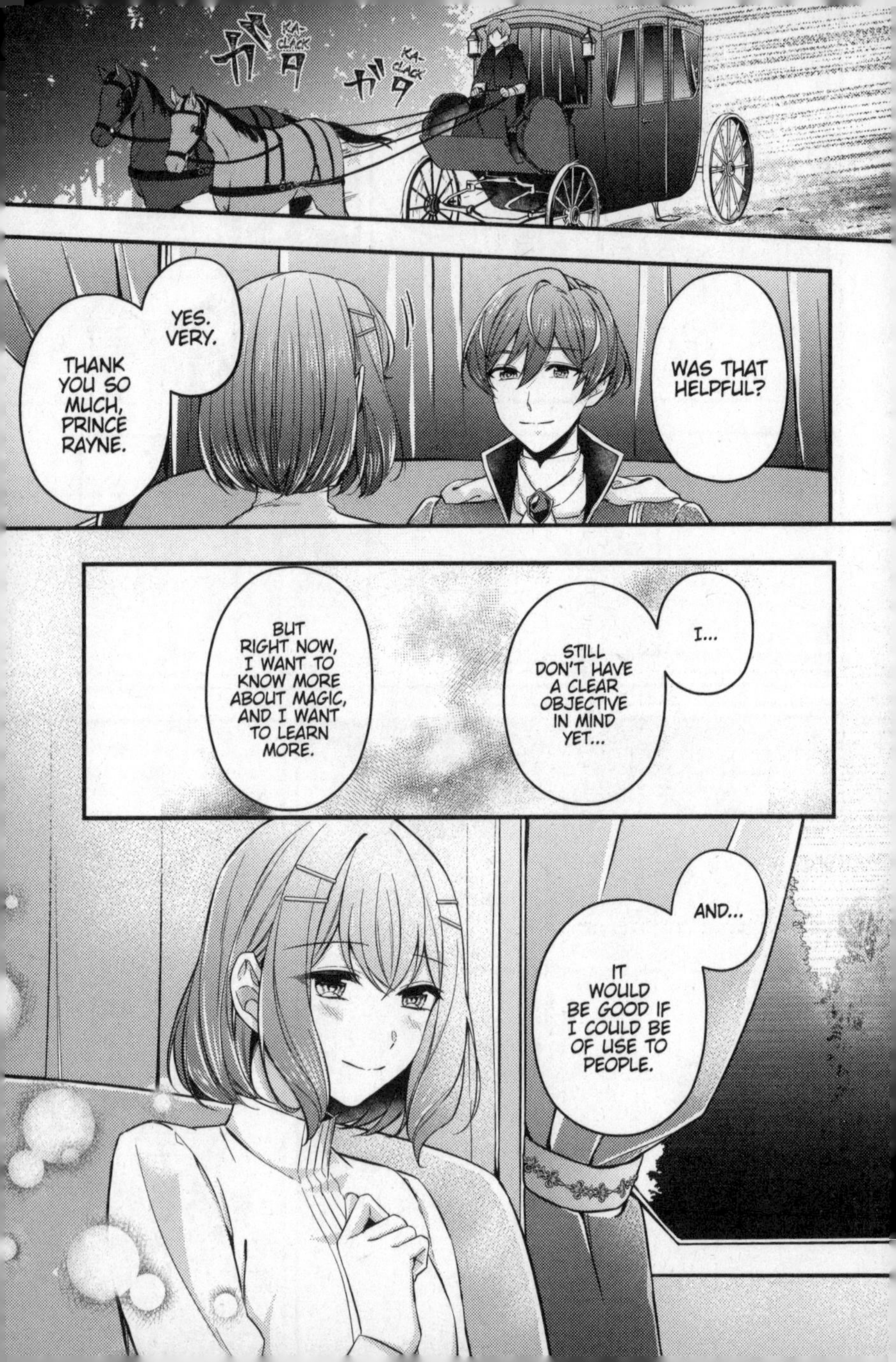
KA-CLACK
KA-CLACK
WAS THAT HELPFUL?
YES. VERY.
THANK YOU SO MUCH, PRINCE RAYNE.
I...
STILL DON'T HAVE A CLEAR OBJECTIVE IN MIND YET...
BUT RIGHT NOW, I WANT TO KNOW MORE ABOUT MAGIC, AND I WANT TO LEARN MORE.
AND...
IT WOULD BE GOOD IF I COULD BE OF USE TO PEOPLE.

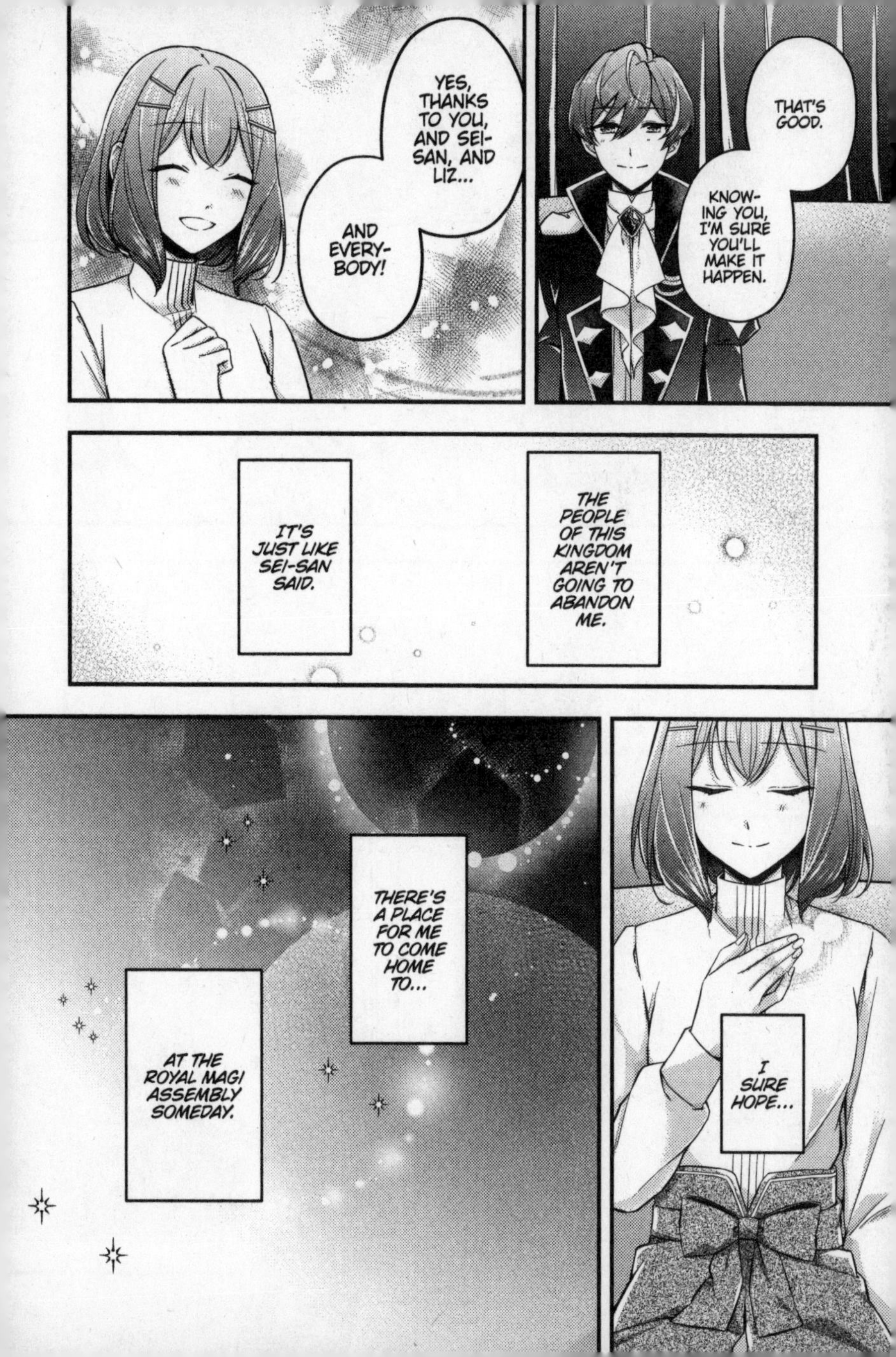
THAT'S GOOD.
KNOWING YOU, I'M SURE YOU'LL MAKE IT HAPPEN.
YES, THANKS TO YOU, AND SEI-SAN, AND LIZ...
AND EVERYBODY!
THE PEOPLE OF THIS KINGDOM AREN'T GOING TO ABANDON ME.
IT'S JUST LIKE SEI-SAN SAID.
I SURE HOPE...
THERE'S A PLACE FOR ME TO COME HOME TO...
AT THE ROYAL MAGI ASSEMBLY SOMEDAY.

The **Saint's**
Magic Power is
Omnipotent
The Other Saint

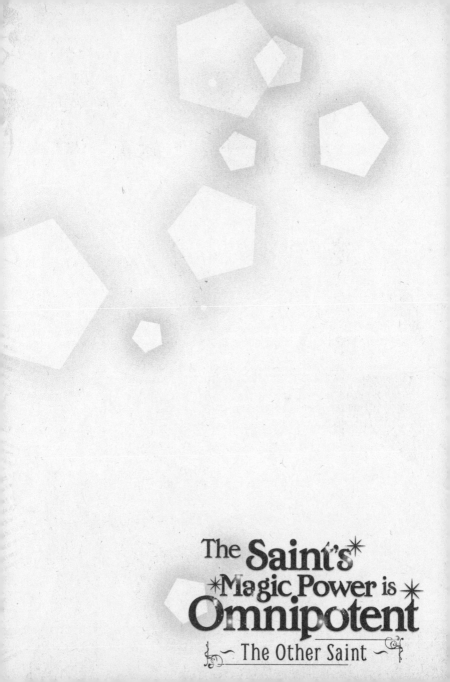

The Saint's
Magic Power is
Omnipotent
The Other Saint

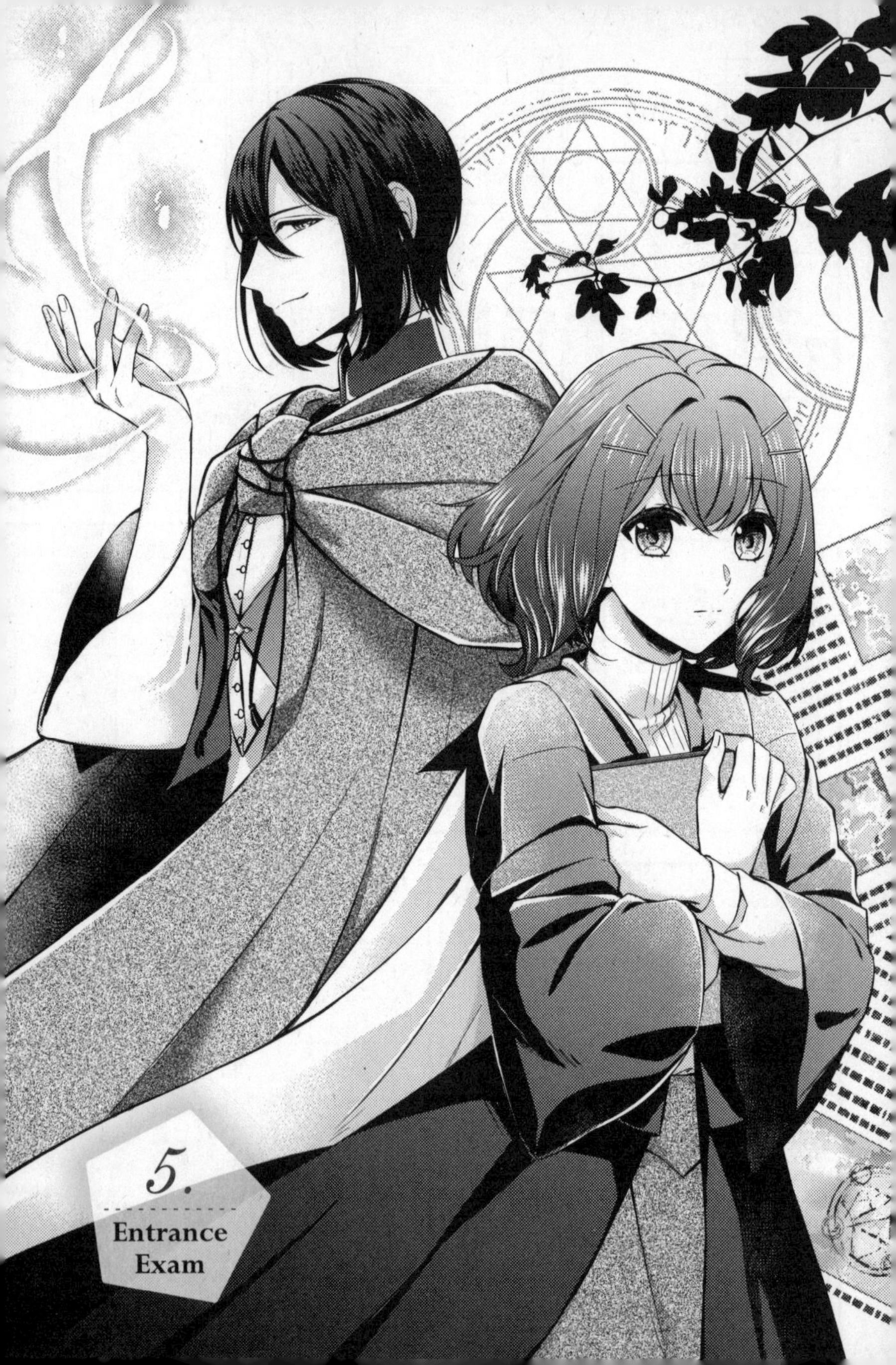
5.
Entrance
Exam

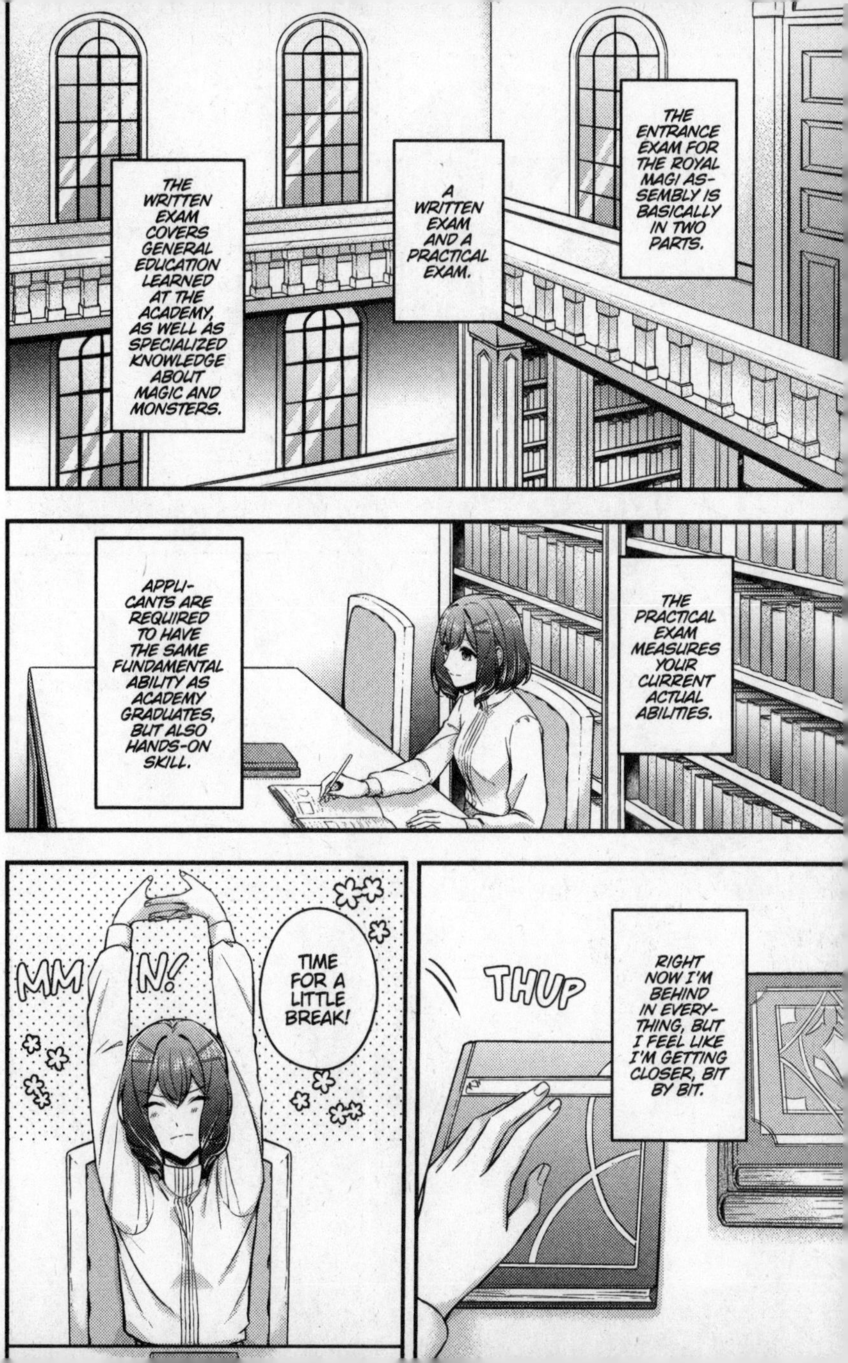
THE ENTRANCE EXAM FOR THE ROYAL MAGI AS-SEMBLY IS BASICALLY IN TWO PARTS.
A WRITTEN EXAM AND A PRACTICAL EXAM.
THE WRITTEN EXAM COVERS GENERAL EDUCATION LEARNED AT THE ACADEMY, AS WELL AS SPECIALIZED KNOWLEDGE ABOUT MAGIC AND MONSTERS.
THE PRACTICAL EXAM MEASURES YOUR CURRENT ACTUAL ABILITIES.
APPLI-CANTS ARE REQUIRED TO HAVE THE SAME FUNDAMENTAL ABILITY AS ACADEMY GRADUATES, BUT ALSO HANDS-ON SKILL.
RIGHT NOW I'M BEHIND IN EVERY-THING, BUT I FEEL LIKE I'M GETTING CLOSER, BIT BY BIT.
THUP
TIME FOR A LITTLE BREAK!
MMN!

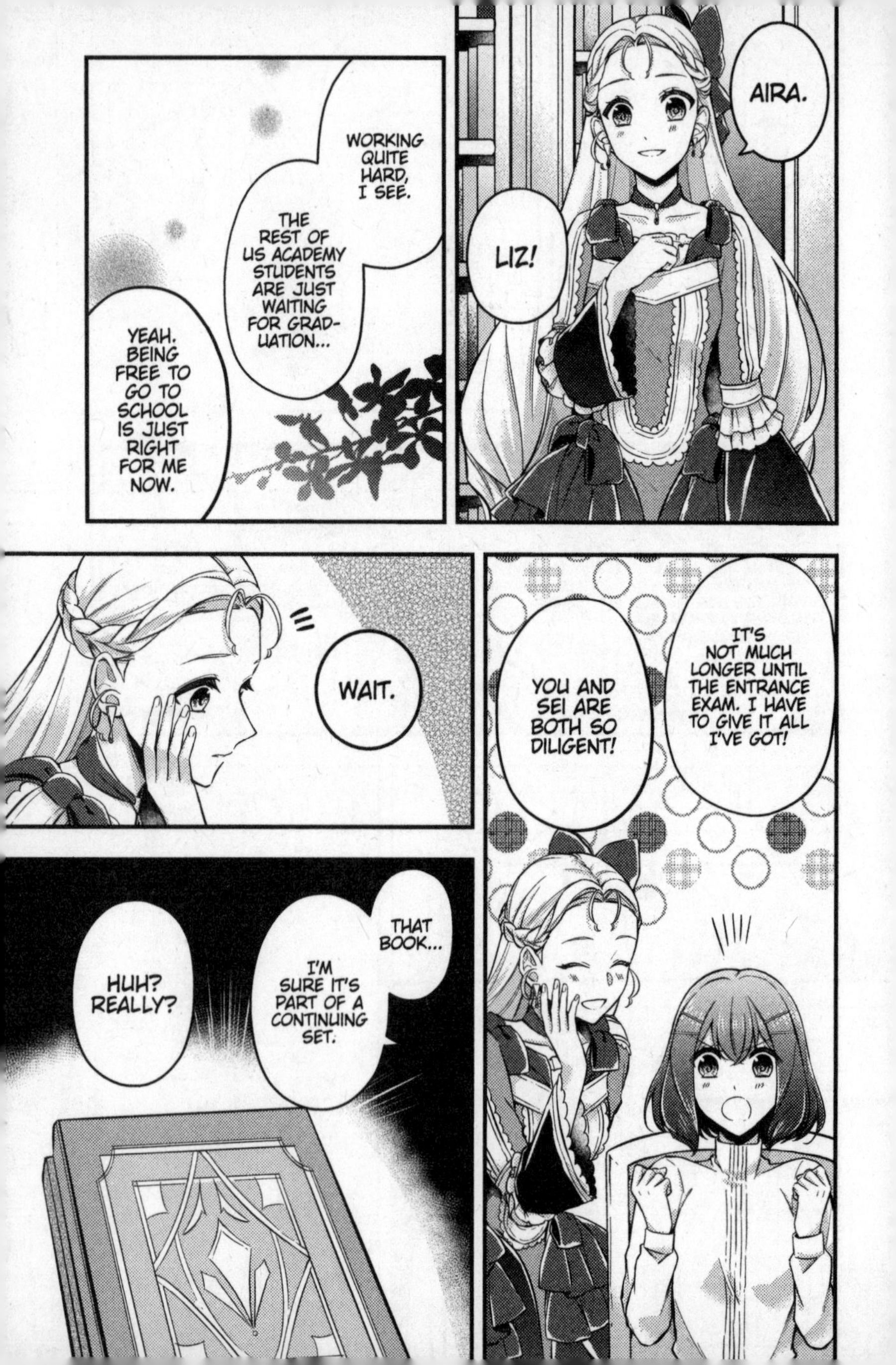
AIRA.
LIZ!
WORKING QUITE HARD, I SEE.
THE REST OF US ACADEMY STUDENTS ARE JUST WAITING FOR GRAD-UATION...
YEAH. BEING FREE TO GO TO SCHOOL IS JUST RIGHT FOR ME NOW.
IT'S NOT MUCH LONGER UNTIL THE ENTRANCE EXAM. I HAVE TO GIVE IT ALL I'VE GOT!
YOU AND SEI ARE BOTH SO DILIGENT!
WAIT.
THAT BOOK...
I'M SURE IT'S PART OF A CONTINUING SET.
HUH? REALLY?

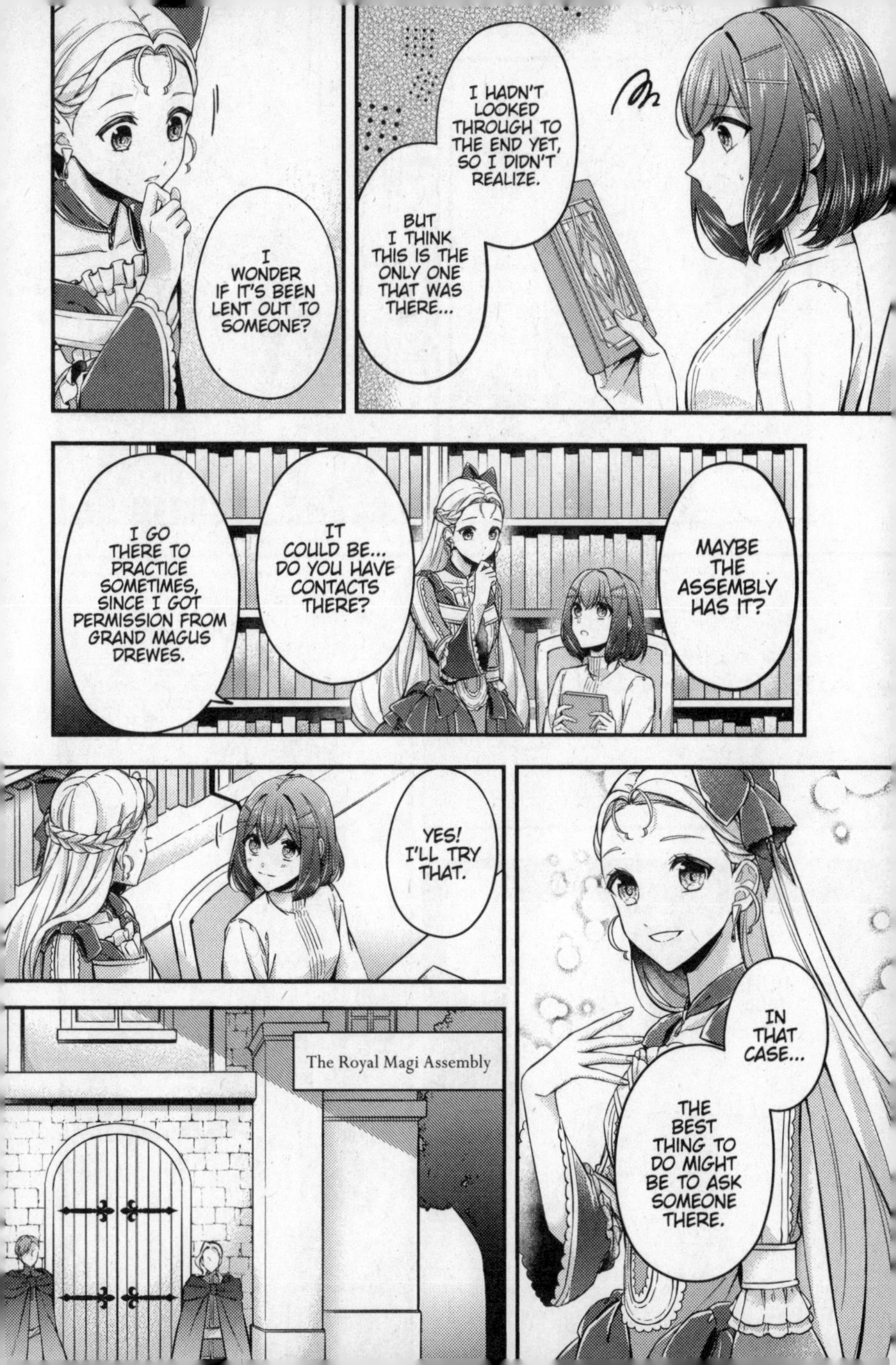
I HADN'T LOOKED THROUGH TO THE END YET, SO I DIDN'T REALIZE.
BUT I THINK THIS IS THE ONLY ONE THAT WAS THERE...
I WONDER IF IT'S BEEN LENT OUT TO SOMEONE?
MAYBE THE ASSEMBLY HAS IT?
IT COULD BE... DO YOU HAVE CONTACTS THERE?
I GO THERE TO PRACTICE SOMETIMES, SINCE I GOT PERMISSION FROM GRAND MAGUS DREWES.
IN THAT CASE...
THE BEST THING TO DO MIGHT BE TO ASK SOMEONE THERE.
YES! I'LL TRY THAT.
The Royal Magi Assembly

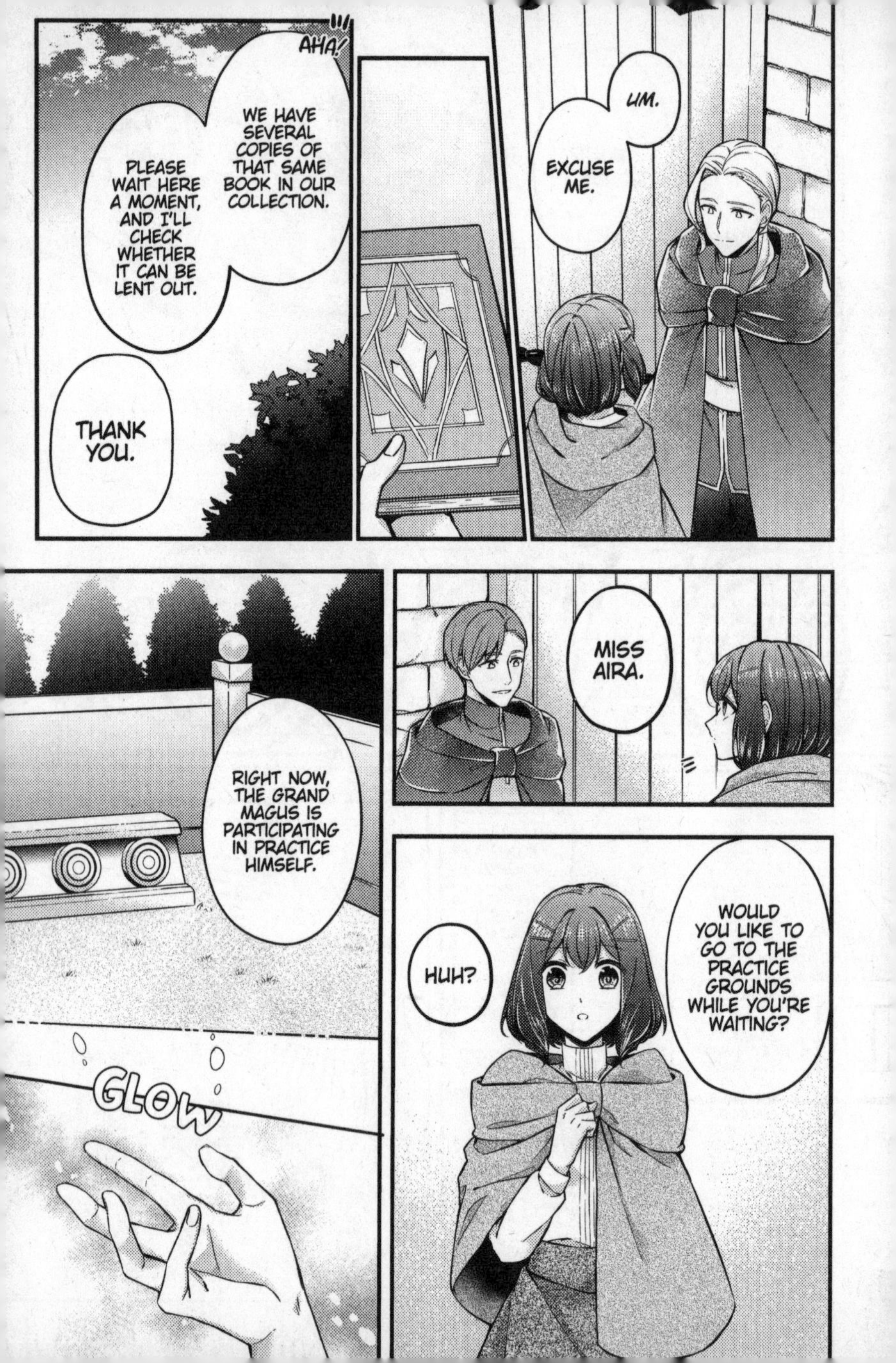
UM.
EXCUSE ME.
AHA!
WE HAVE SEVERAL COPIES OF THAT SAME BOOK IN OUR COLLECTION.
PLEASE WAIT HERE A MOMENT, AND I'LL CHECK WHETHER IT CAN BE LENT OUT.
THANK YOU.
MISS AIRA.
WOULD YOU LIKE TO GO TO THE PRACTICE GROUNDS WHILE YOU'RE WAITING?
HUH?
RIGHT NOW, THE GRAND MAGUS IS PARTICIPATING IN PRACTICE HIMSELF.
GLOW

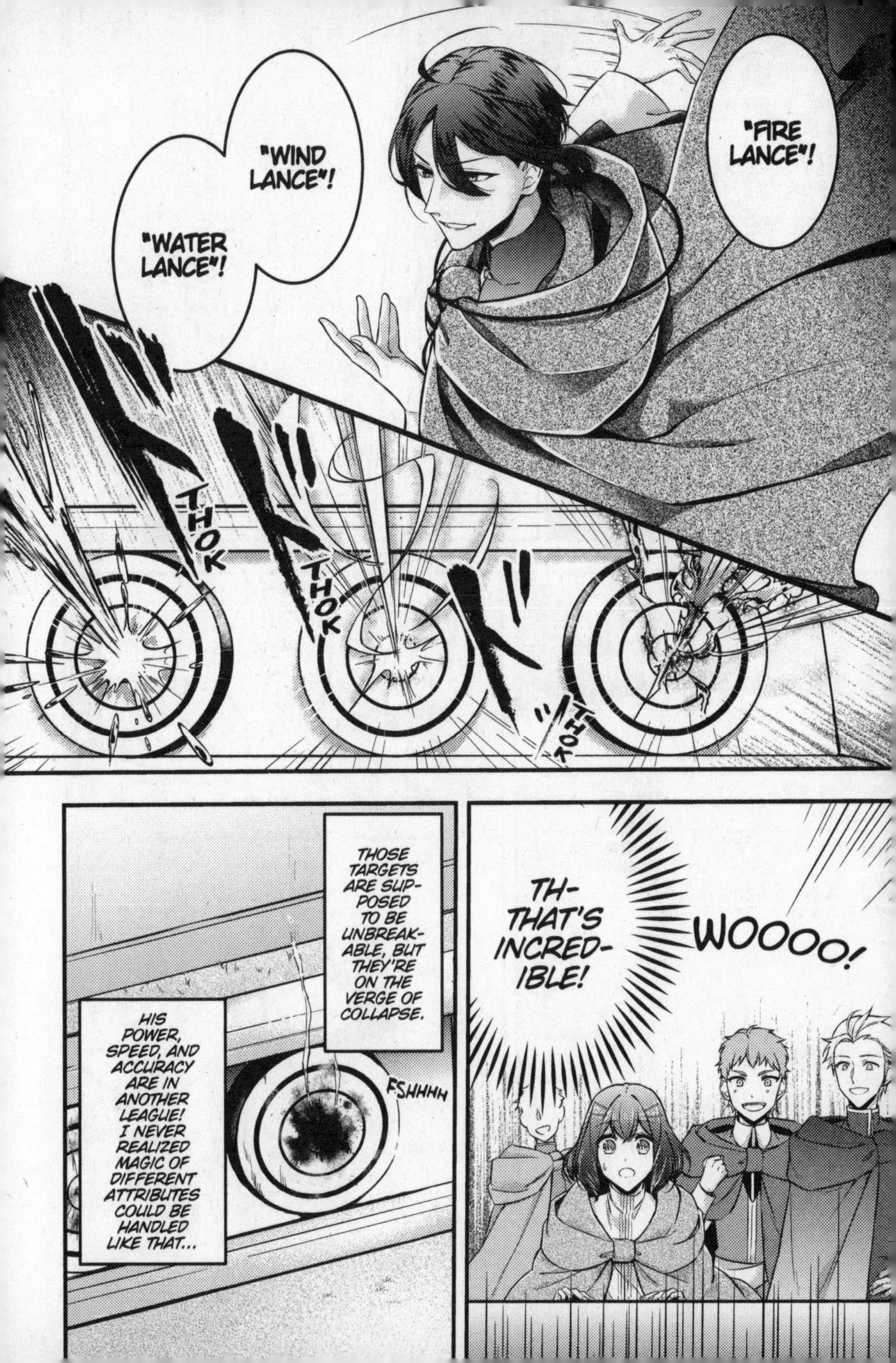
"FIRE LANCE"!
"WIND LANCE"!
"WATER LANCE"!
THOK
THOK
THOK
WOOOO!
TH-THAT'S INCREDIBLE!
THOSE TARGETS ARE SUPPOSED TO BE UNBREAKABLE, BUT THEY'RE ON THE VERGE OF COLLAPSE.
HIS POWER, SPEED, AND ACCURACY ARE IN ANOTHER LEAGUE! I NEVER REALIZED MAGIC OF DIFFERENT ATTRIBUTES COULD BE HANDLED LIKE THAT...
FSHHHH

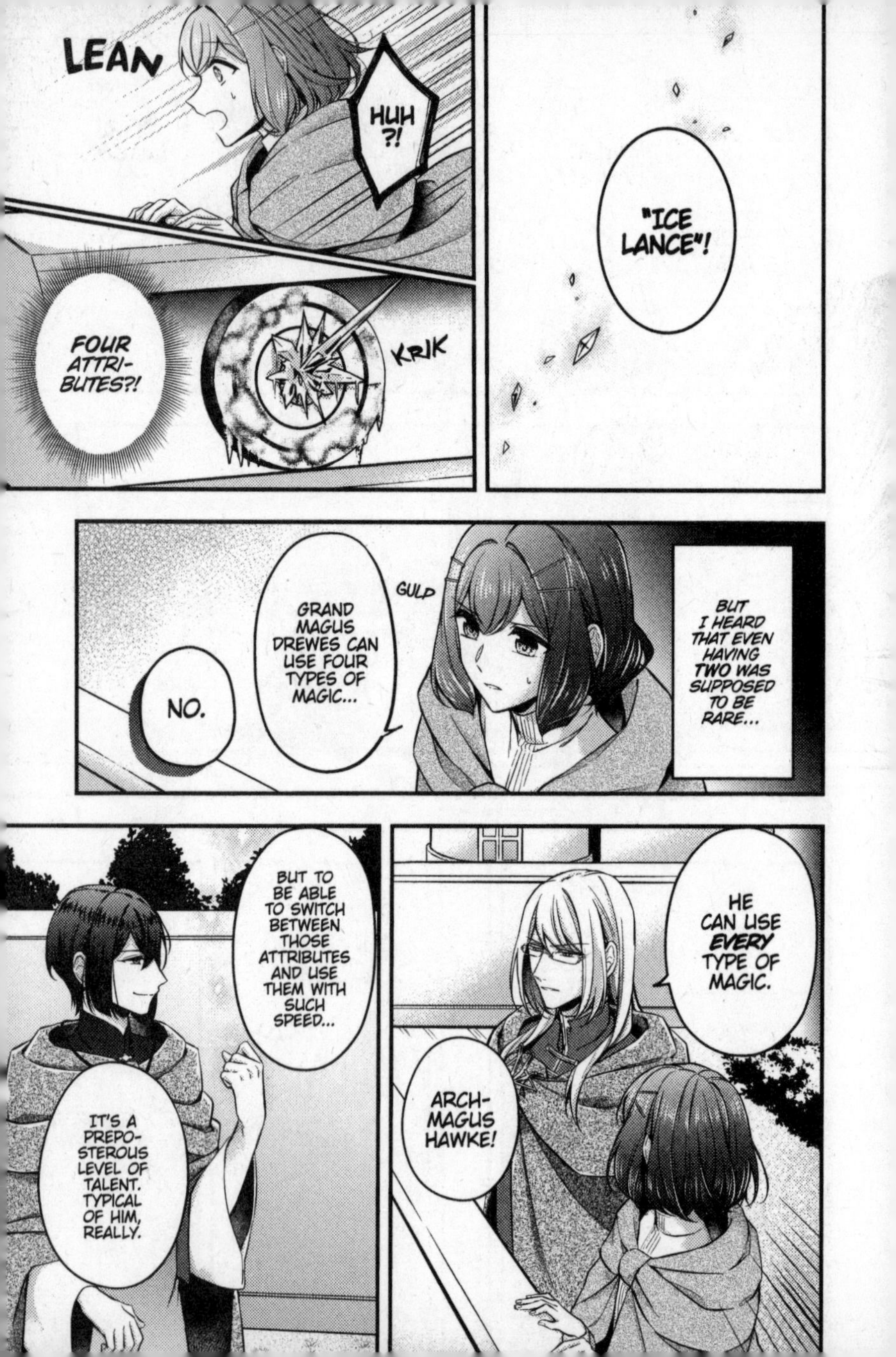
"ICE LANCE"!
HUH?!
LEAN
KRIK
FOUR ATTRIBUTES?!
BUT I HEARD THAT EVEN HAVING TWO WAS SUPPOSED TO BE RARE...
GULP
GRAND MAGUS DREWES CAN USE FOUR TYPES OF MAGIC...
NO.
HE CAN USE EVERY TYPE OF MAGIC.
ARCH-MAGUS HAWKE!
BUT TO BE ABLE TO SWITCH BETWEEN THOSE ATTRIBUTES AND USE THEM WITH SUCH SPEED...
IT'S A PREPOSTEROUS LEVEL OF TALENT. TYPICAL OF HIM, REALLY.

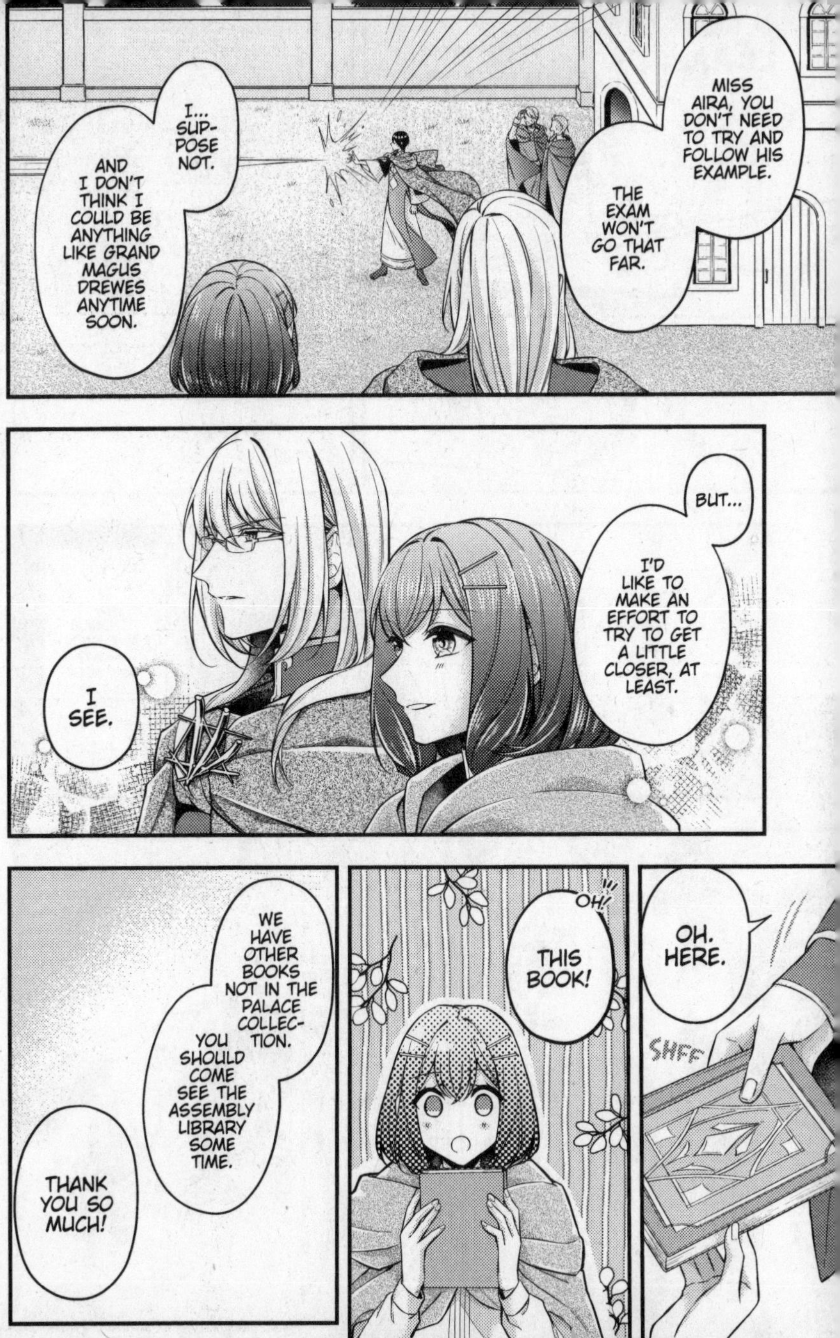
MISS AIRA, YOU DON'T NEED TO TRY AND FOLLOW HIS EXAMPLE.
THE EXAM WON'T GO THAT FAR.
I... SUP-POSE NOT.
AND I DON'T THINK I COULD BE ANYTHING LIKE GRAND MAGUS DREWES ANYTIME SOON.
BUT...
I'D LIKE TO MAKE AN EFFORT TO TRY TO GET A LITTLE CLOSER, AT LEAST.
I SEE.
OH. HERE.
SHFF
OH!
THIS BOOK!
WE HAVE OTHER BOOKS NOT IN THE PALACE COLLEC-TION.
YOU SHOULD COME SEE THE ASSEMBLY LIBRARY SOME TIME.
THANK YOU SO MUCH!

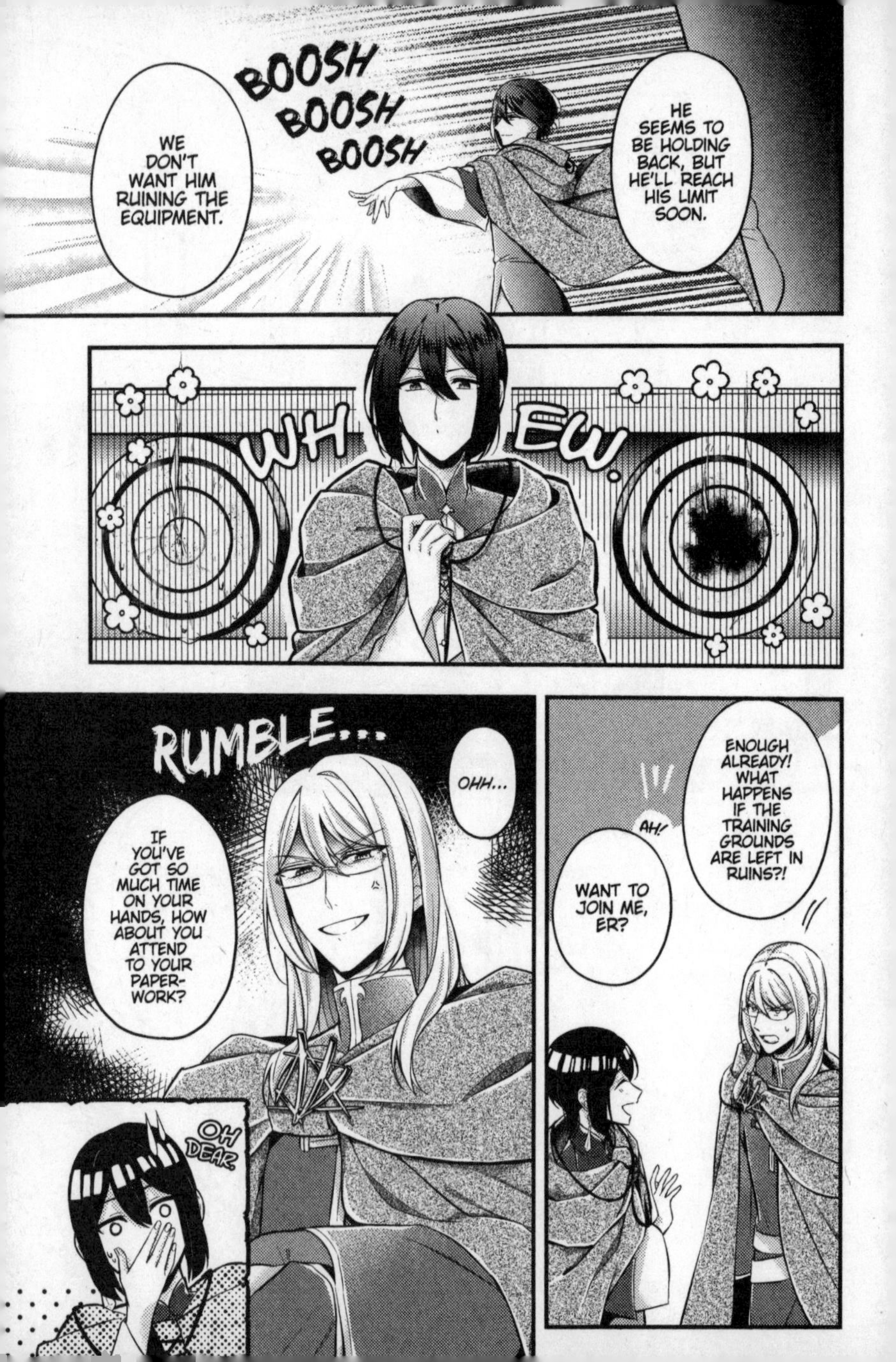
HE SEEMS TO BE HOLDING BACK, BUT HE'LL REACH HIS LIMIT SOON.
BOOSH BOOSH BOOSH
WE DON'T WANT HIM RUINING THE EQUIPMENT.
WHEW.
ENOUGH ALREADY! WHAT HAPPENS IF THE TRAINING GROUNDS ARE LEFT IN RUINS?!
AH!
WANT TO JOIN ME, ER?
RUMBLE...
OHH...
IF YOU'VE GOT SO MUCH TIME ON YOUR HANDS, HOW ABOUT YOU ATTEND TO YOUR PAPER-WORK?
OH DEAR

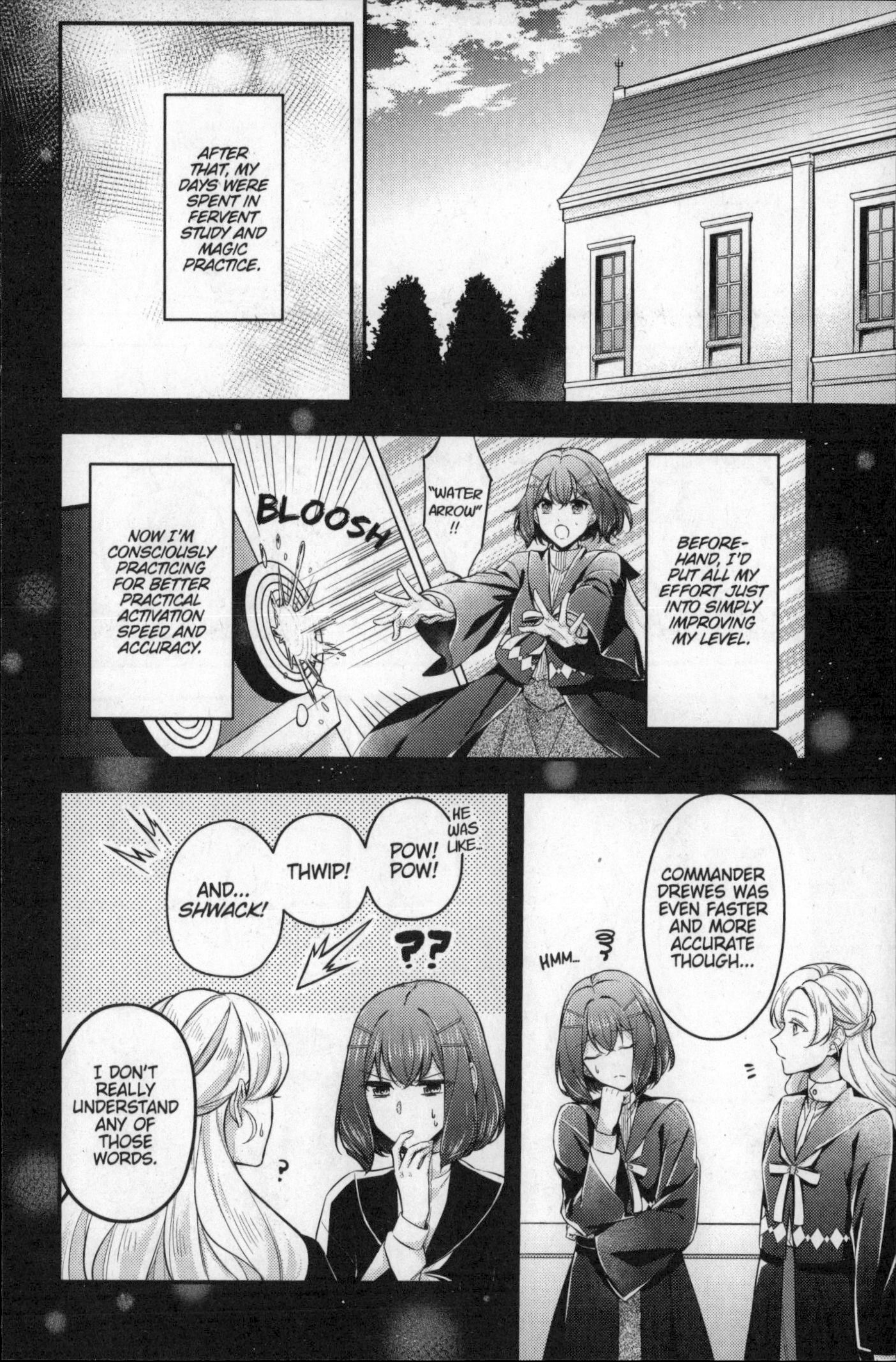
AFTER THAT, MY DAYS WERE SPENT IN FERVENT STUDY AND MAGIC PRACTICE.
BEFORE-HAND, I'D PUT ALL MY EFFORT JUST INTO SIMPLY IMPROVING MY LEVEL.
"WATER ARROW" !!
BLOOSH
NOW I'M CONSCIOUSLY PRACTICING FOR BETTER PRACTICAL ACTIVATION SPEED AND ACCURACY.
COMMANDER DREWES WAS EVEN FASTER AND MORE ACCURATE THOUGH...
HMM...
HE WAS LIKE...
POW! POW!
THWIP!
AND... SHWACK!
??
I DON'T REALLY UNDERSTAND ANY OF THOSE WORDS.
?

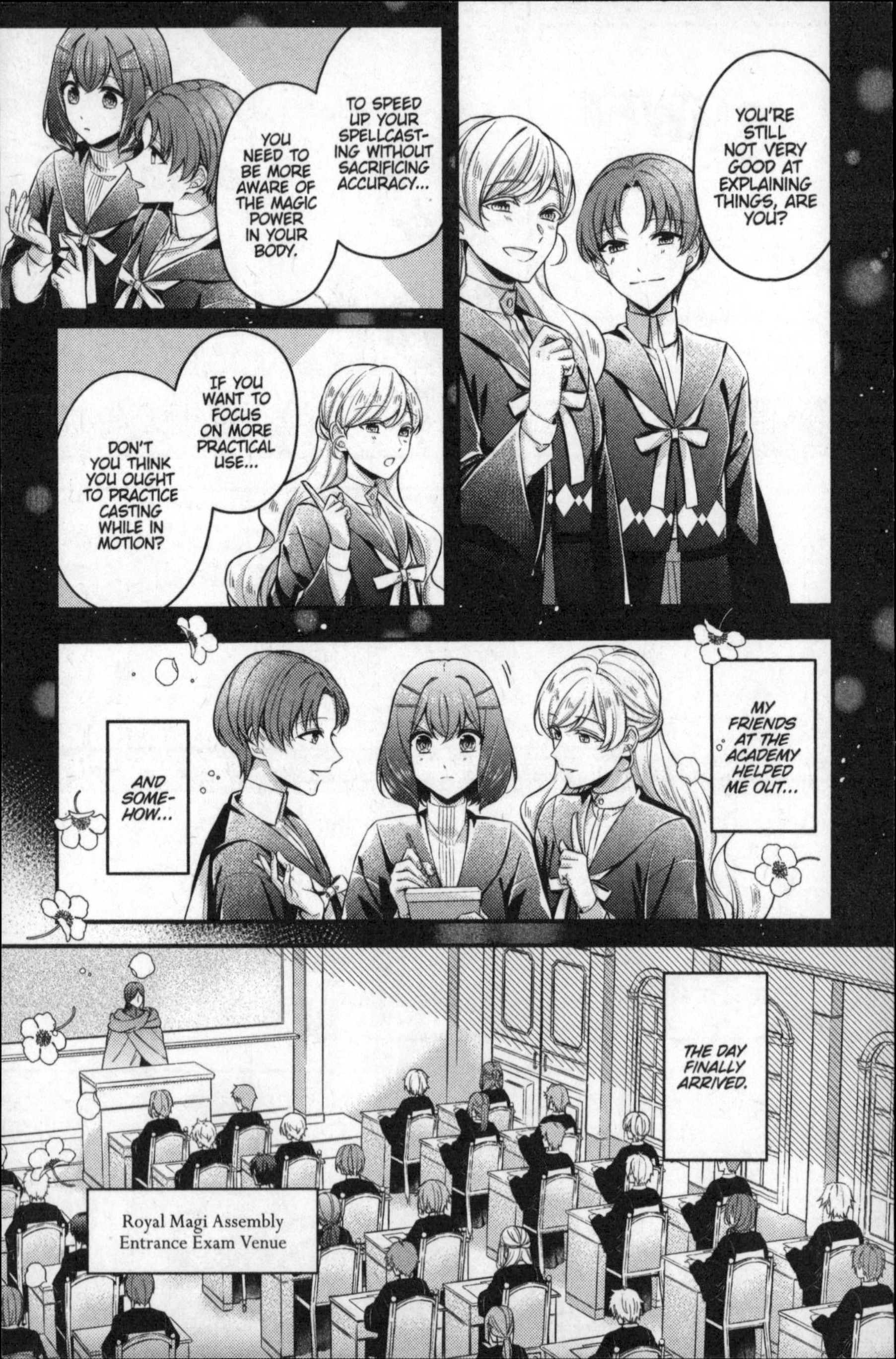
YOU'RE STILL NOT VERY GOOD AT EXPLAINING THINGS, ARE YOU?
TO SPEED UP YOUR SPELLCASTING WITHOUT SACRIFICING ACCURACY...
YOU NEED TO BE MORE AWARE OF THE MAGIC POWER IN YOUR BODY.
IF YOU WANT TO FOCUS ON MORE PRACTICAL USE...
DON'T YOU THINK YOU OUGHT TO PRACTICE CASTING WHILE IN MOTION?
MY FRIENDS AT THE ACADEMY HELPED ME OUT...
AND SOMEHOW...
THE DAY FINALLY ARRIVED.
Royal Magi Assembly Entrance Exam Venue

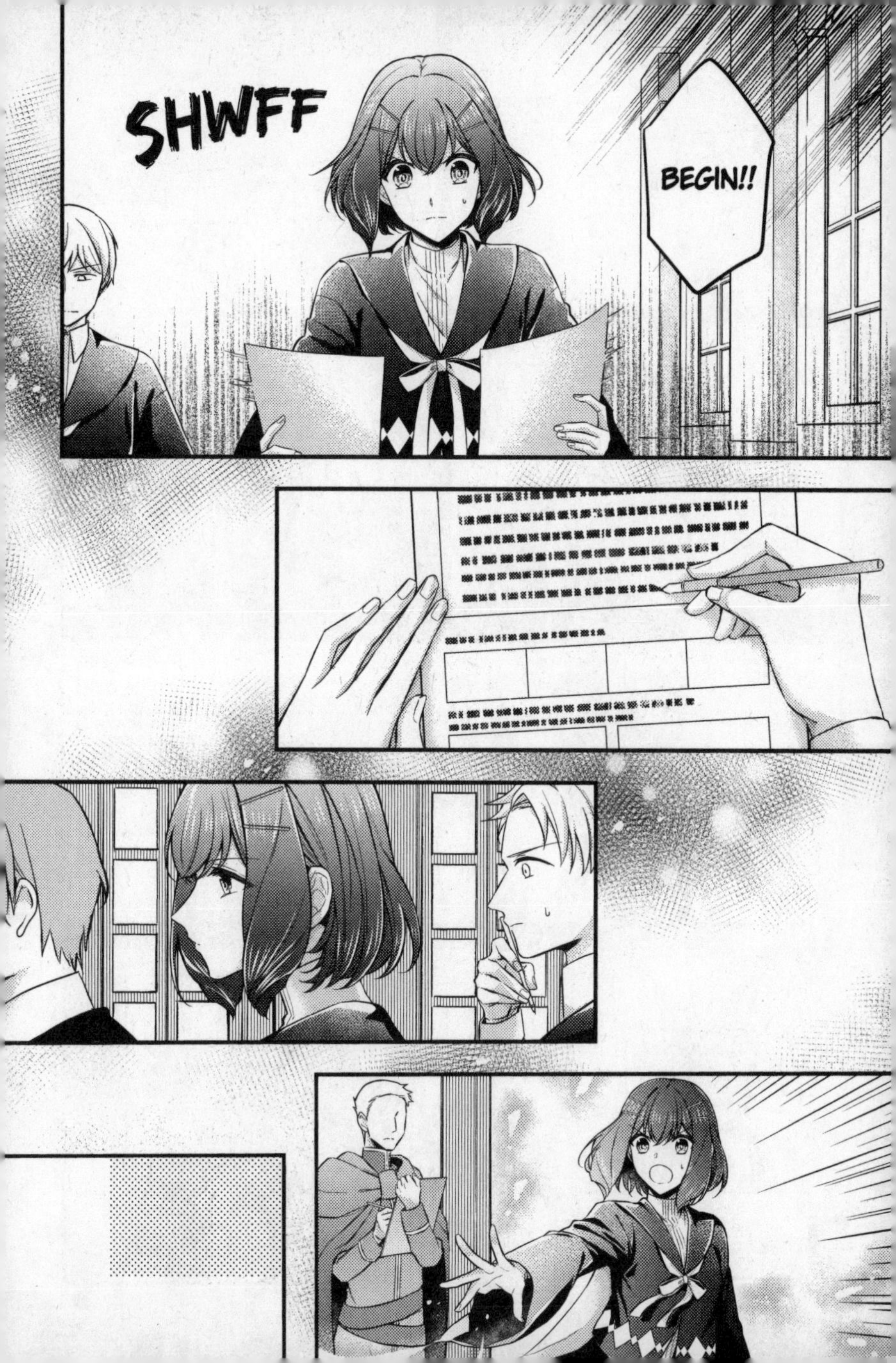
BEGIN!!
SHWFF

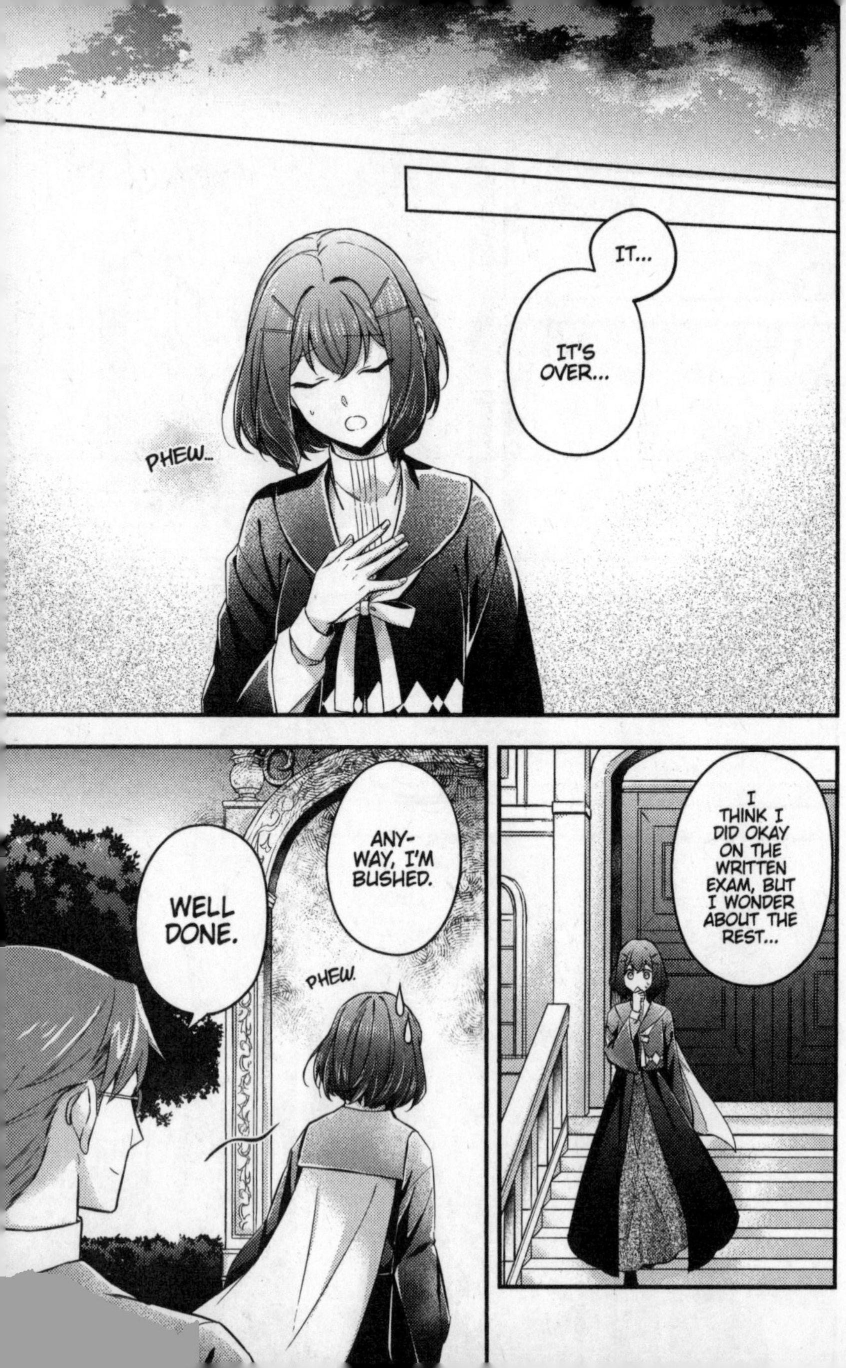
IT...
IT'S OVER...
PHEW...
I THINK I DID OKAY ON THE WRITTEN EXAM, BUT I WONDER ABOUT THE REST...
ANY-WAY, I'M BUSHED.
WELL DONE.
PHEW.

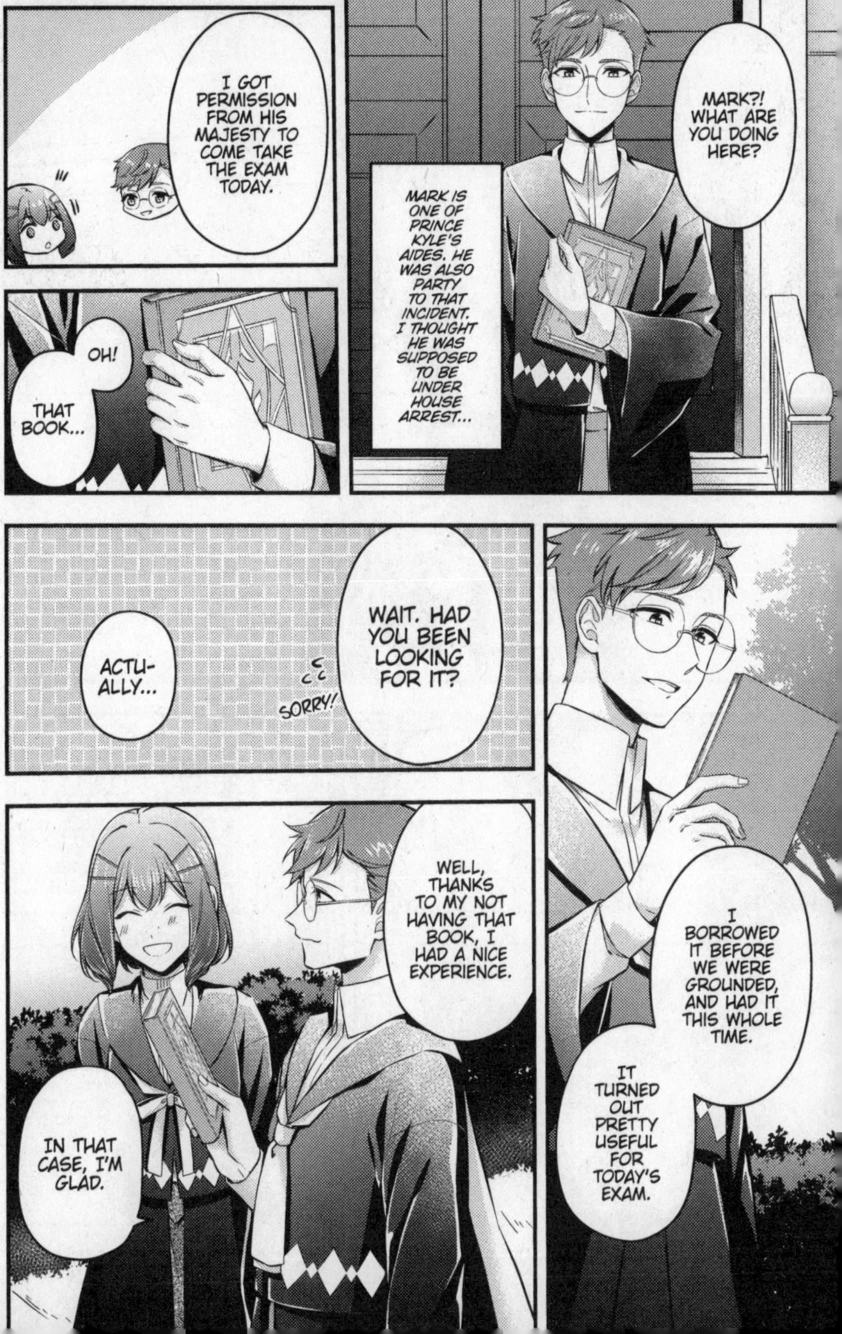
MARK?! WHAT ARE YOU DOING HERE?
MARK IS ONE OF PRINCE KYLE'S AIDES. HE WAS ALSO PARTY TO THAT INCIDENT. I THOUGHT HE WAS SUPPOSED TO BE UNDER HOUSE ARREST...
I GOT PERMISSION FROM HIS MAJESTY TO COME TAKE THE EXAM TODAY.
OH!
THAT BOOK...
I BORROWED IT BEFORE WE WERE GROUNDED, AND HAD IT THIS WHOLE TIME.
IT TURNED OUT PRETTY USEFUL FOR TODAY'S EXAM.
WAIT. HAD YOU BEEN LOOKING FOR IT?
SORRY!
ACTU-ALLY...
WELL, THANKS TO MY NOT HAVING THAT BOOK, I HAD A NICE EXPERIENCE.
IN THAT CASE, I'M GLAD.

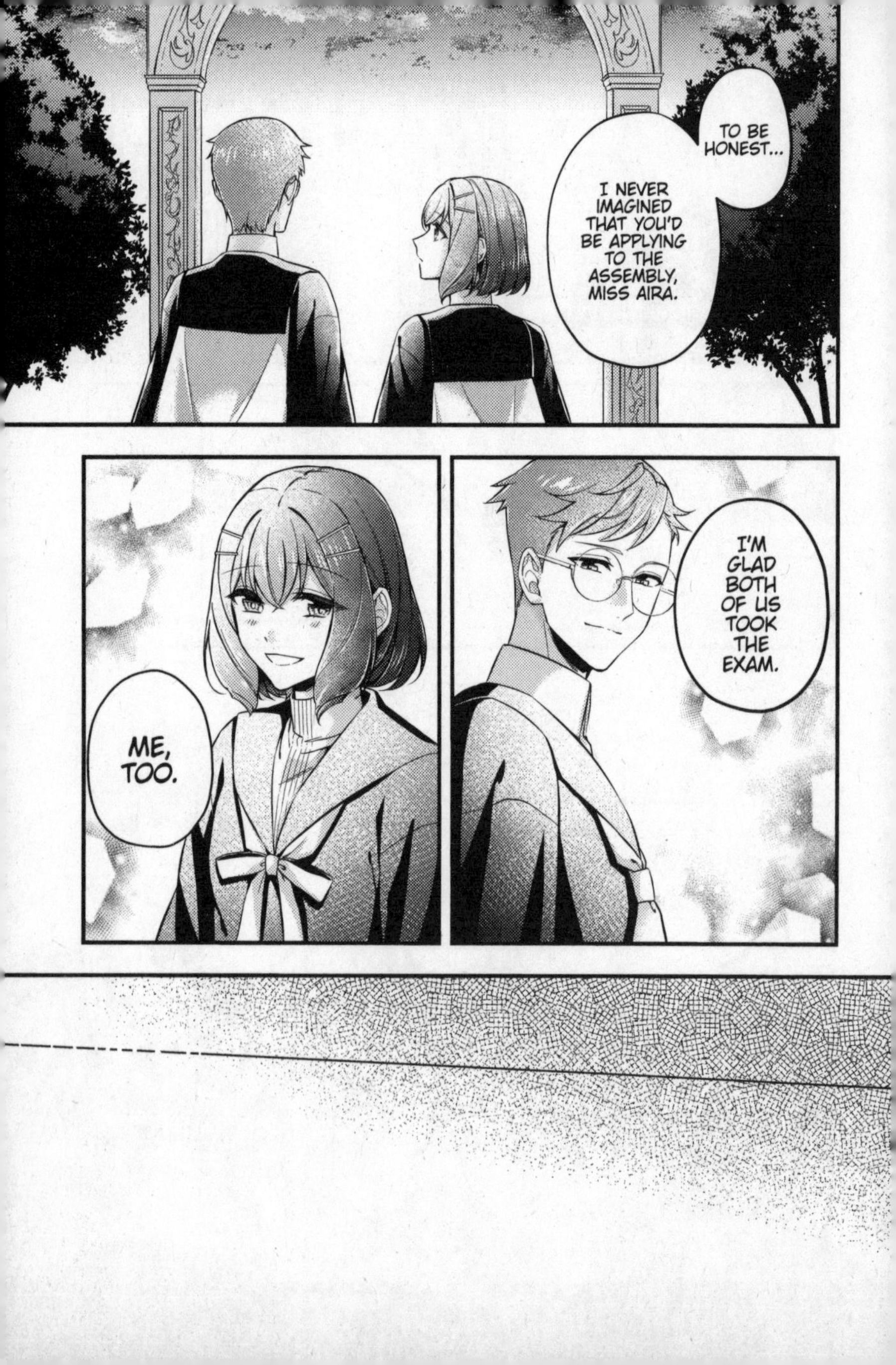
TO BE HONEST...
I NEVER IMAGINED THAT YOU'D BE APPLYING TO THE ASSEMBLY, MISS AIRA.
I'M GLAD BOTH OF US TOOK THE EXAM.
ME, TOO.

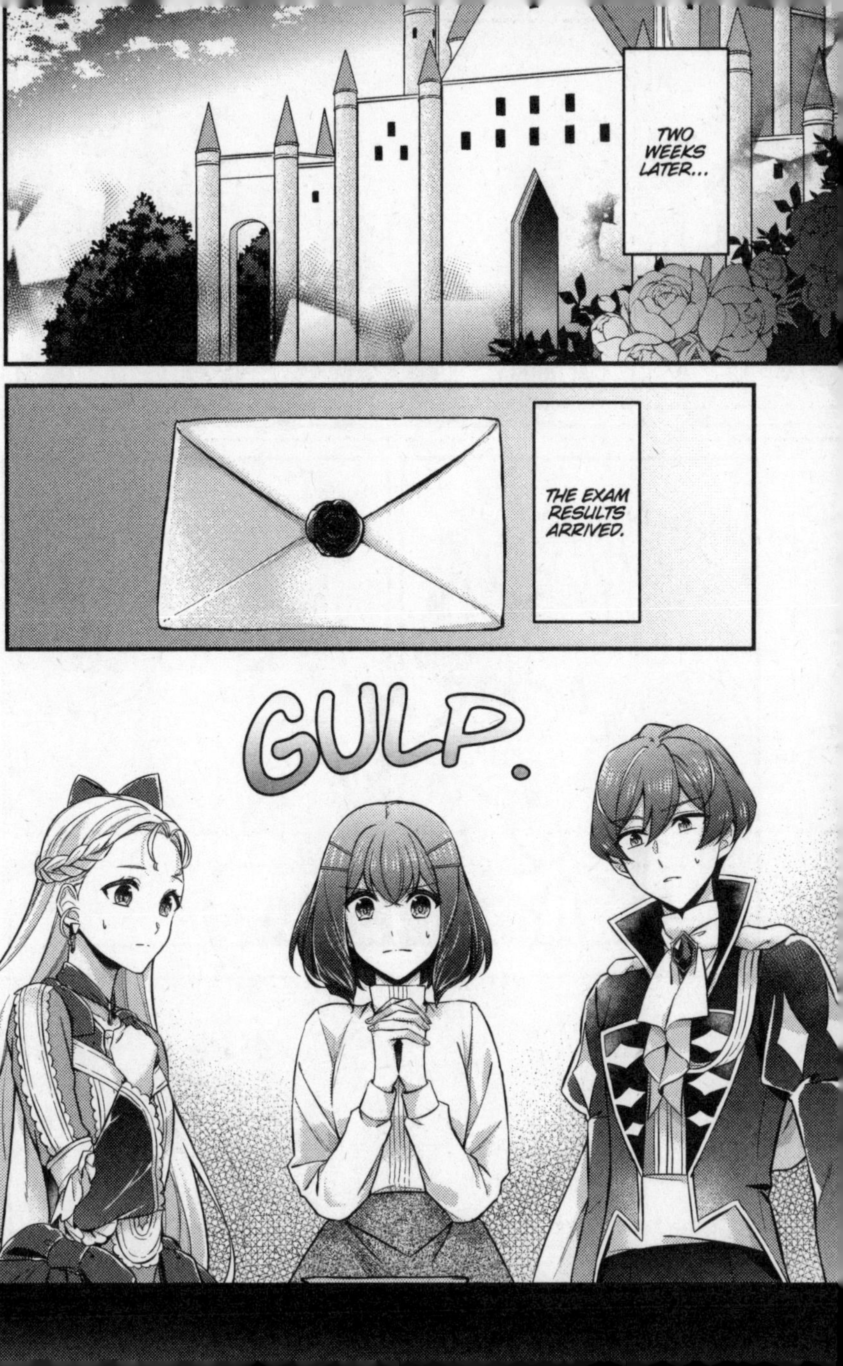
TWO WEEKS LATER...
THE EXAM RESULTS ARRIVED.
GULP.

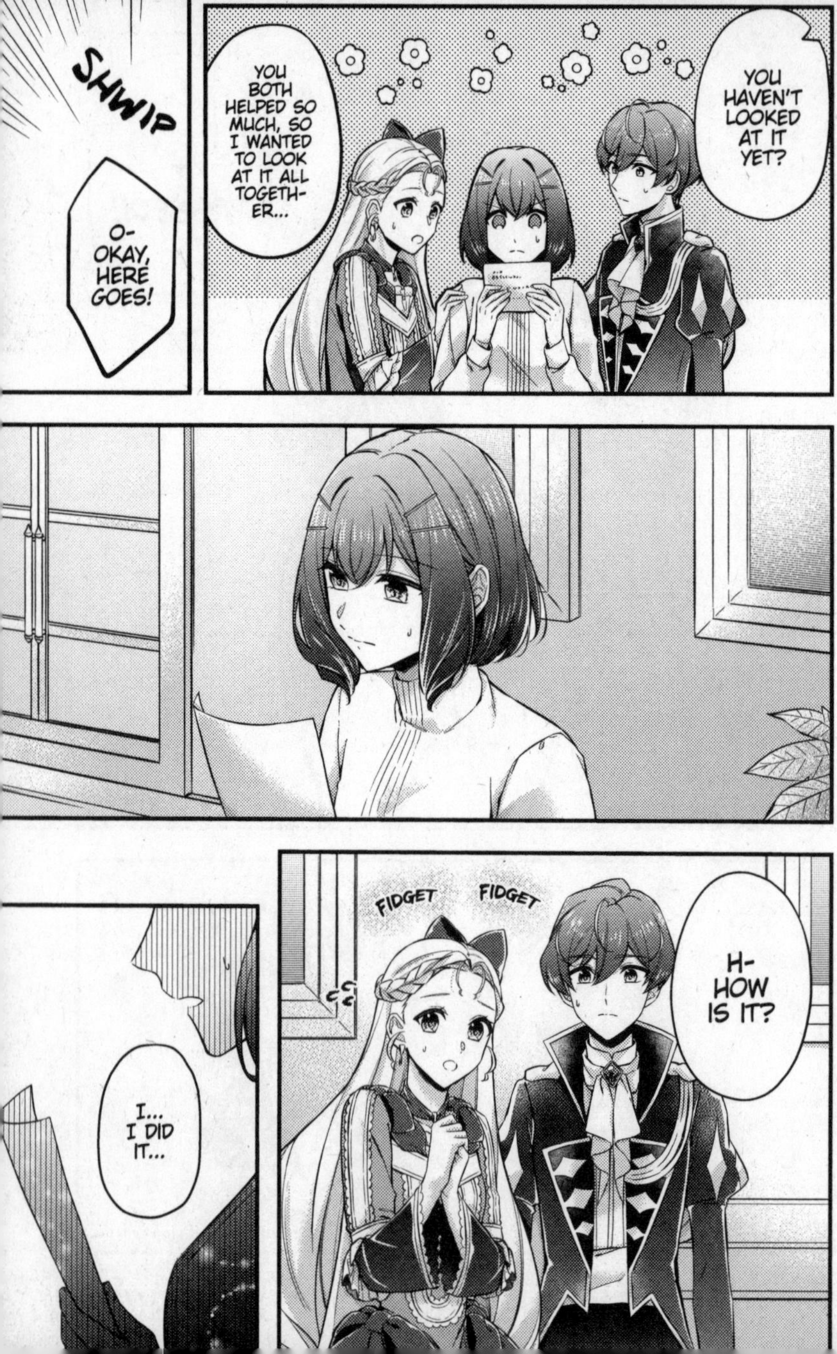
YOU HAVEN'T LOOKED AT IT YET?
YOU BOTH HELPED SO MUCH, SO I WANTED TO LOOK AT IT ALL TOGETH-ER...
SHWIP
O-OKAY, HERE GOES!
FIDGET FIDGET
H-HOW IS IT?
I... I DID IT...

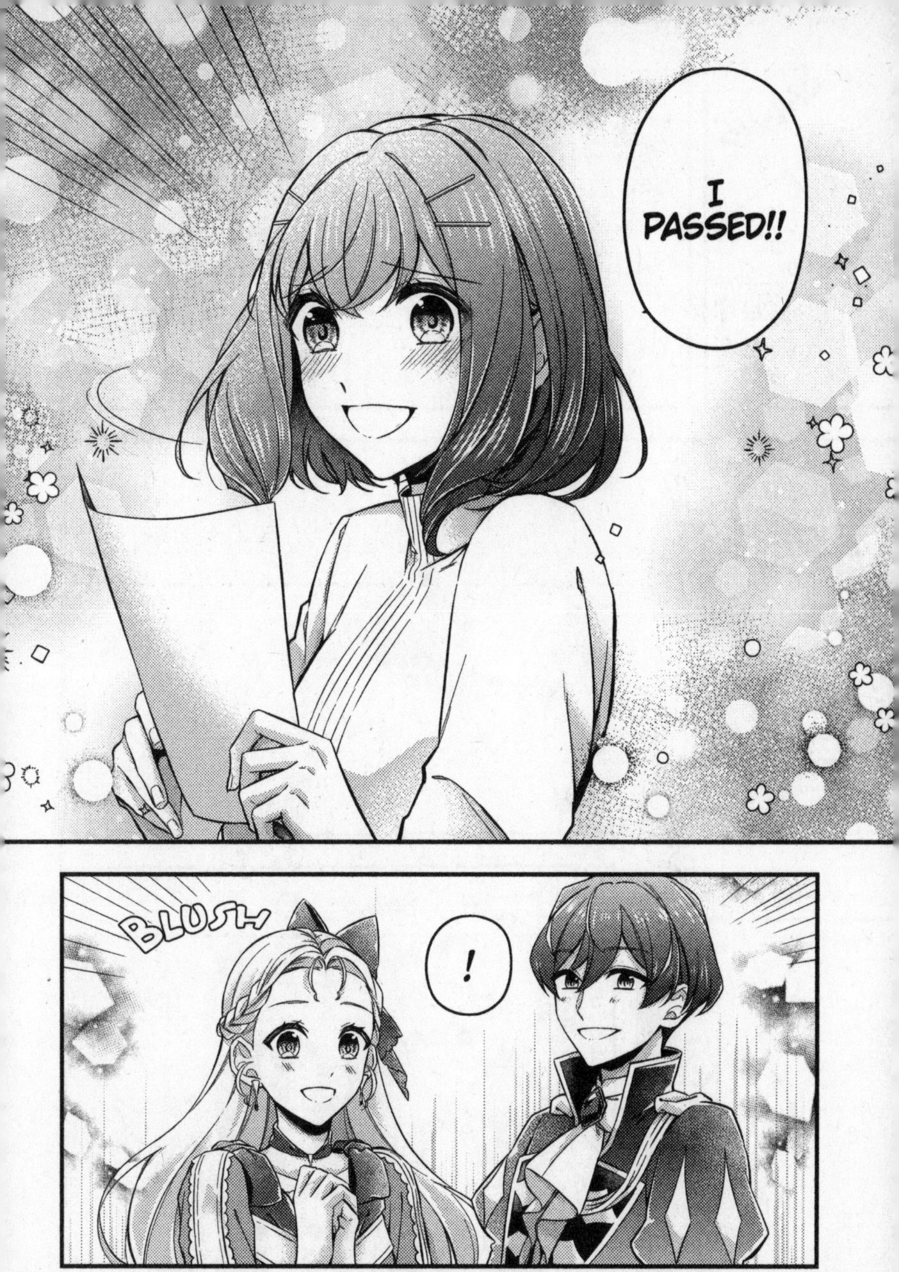
I PASSED!!
!
BLUSH

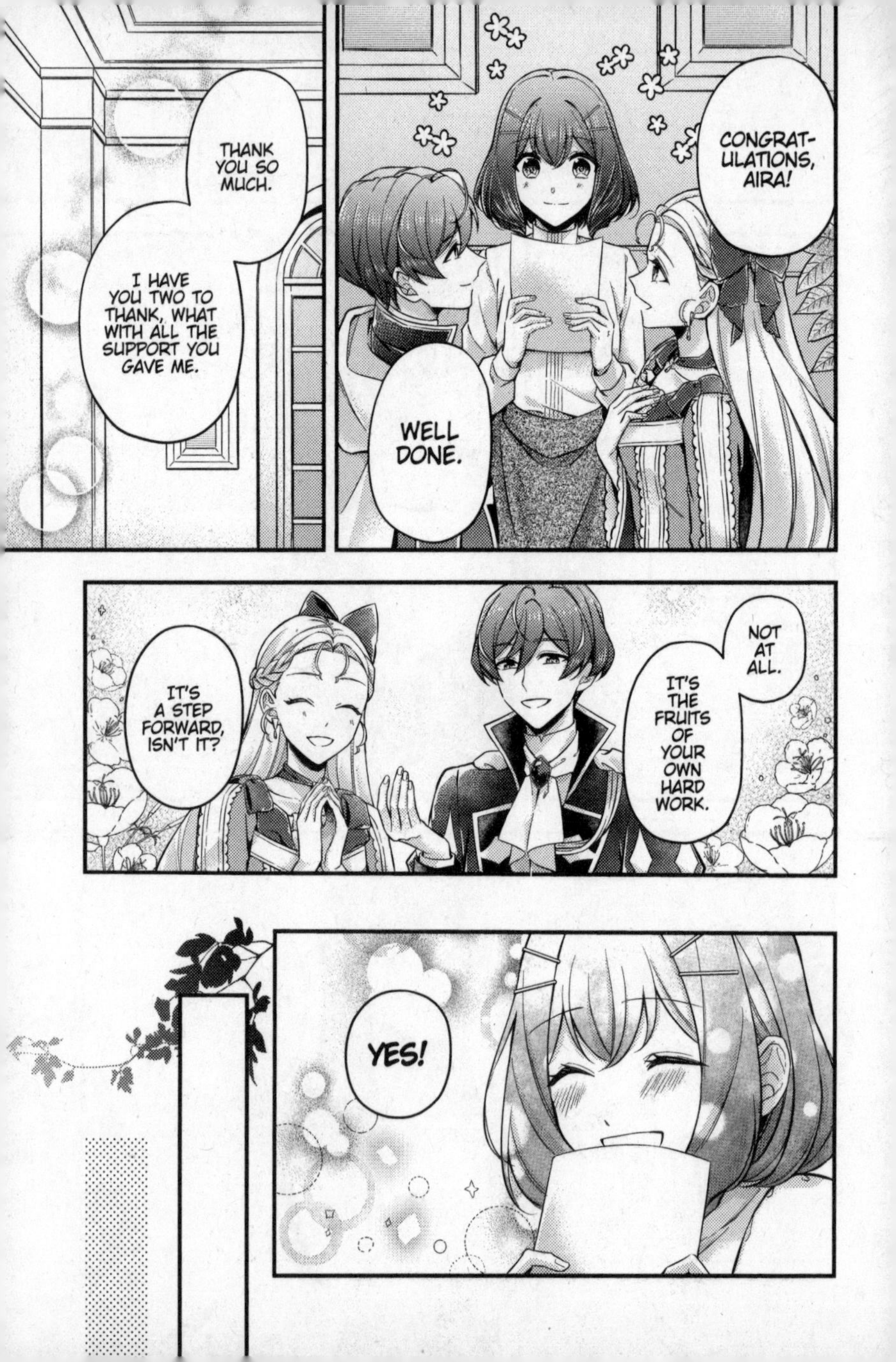
CONGRATULATIONS, AIRA!
WELL DONE.
THANK YOU SO MUCH.
I HAVE YOU TWO TO THANK, WHAT WITH ALL THE SUPPORT YOU GAVE ME.
NOT AT ALL.
IT'S THE FRUITS OF YOUR OWN HARD WORK.
IT'S A STEP FORWARD, ISN'T IT?
YES!

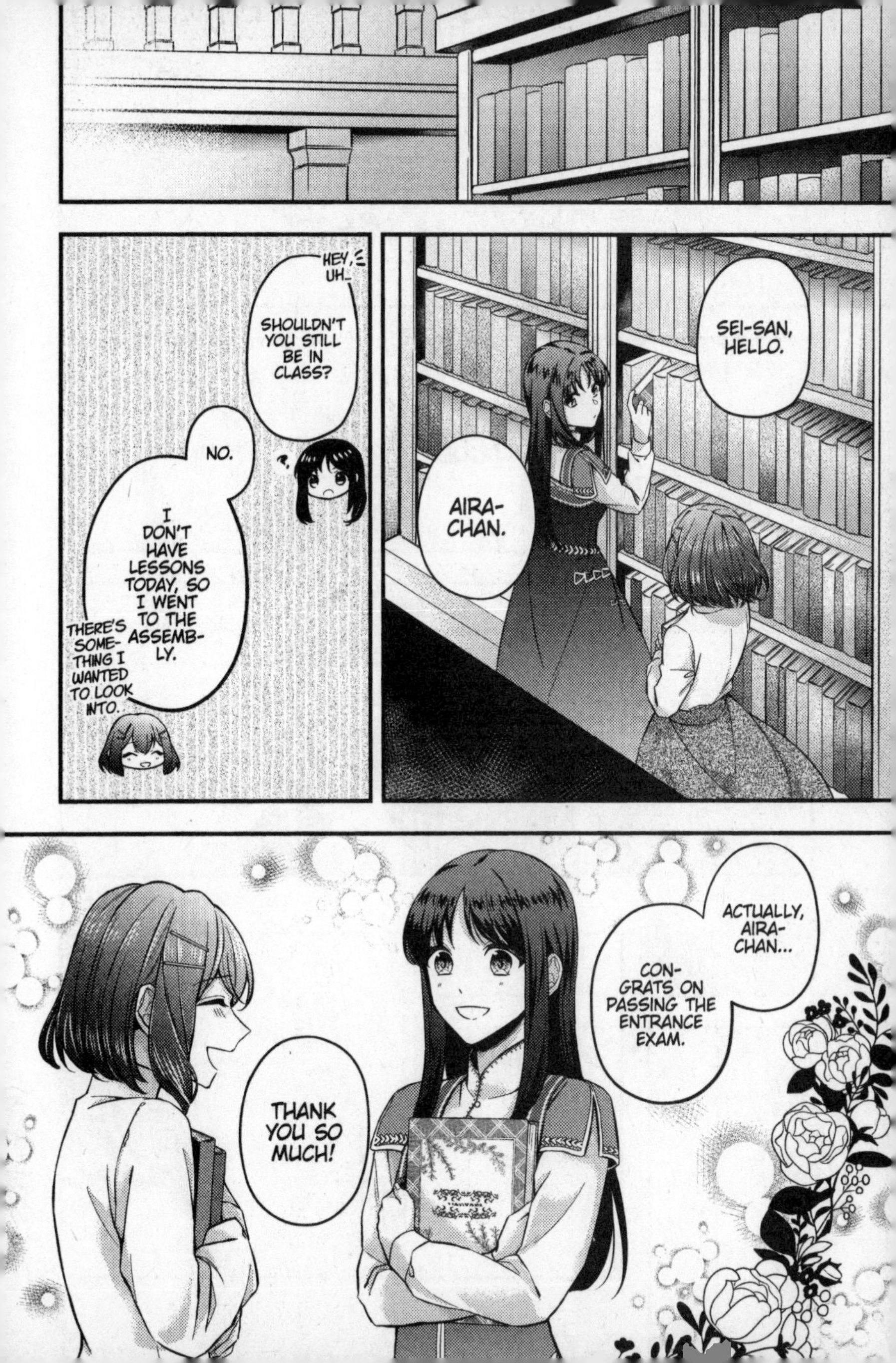
SEI-SAN, HELLO.
AIRA-CHAN.
HEY, UH...
SHOULDN'T YOU STILL BE IN CLASS?
NO.
I DON'T HAVE LESSONS TODAY, SO I WENT TO THE ASSEMBLY.
THERE'S SOMETHING I WANTED TO LOOK INTO.
ACTUALLY, AIRA-CHAN...
CONGRATS ON PASSING THE ENTRANCE EXAM.
THANK YOU SO MUCH!

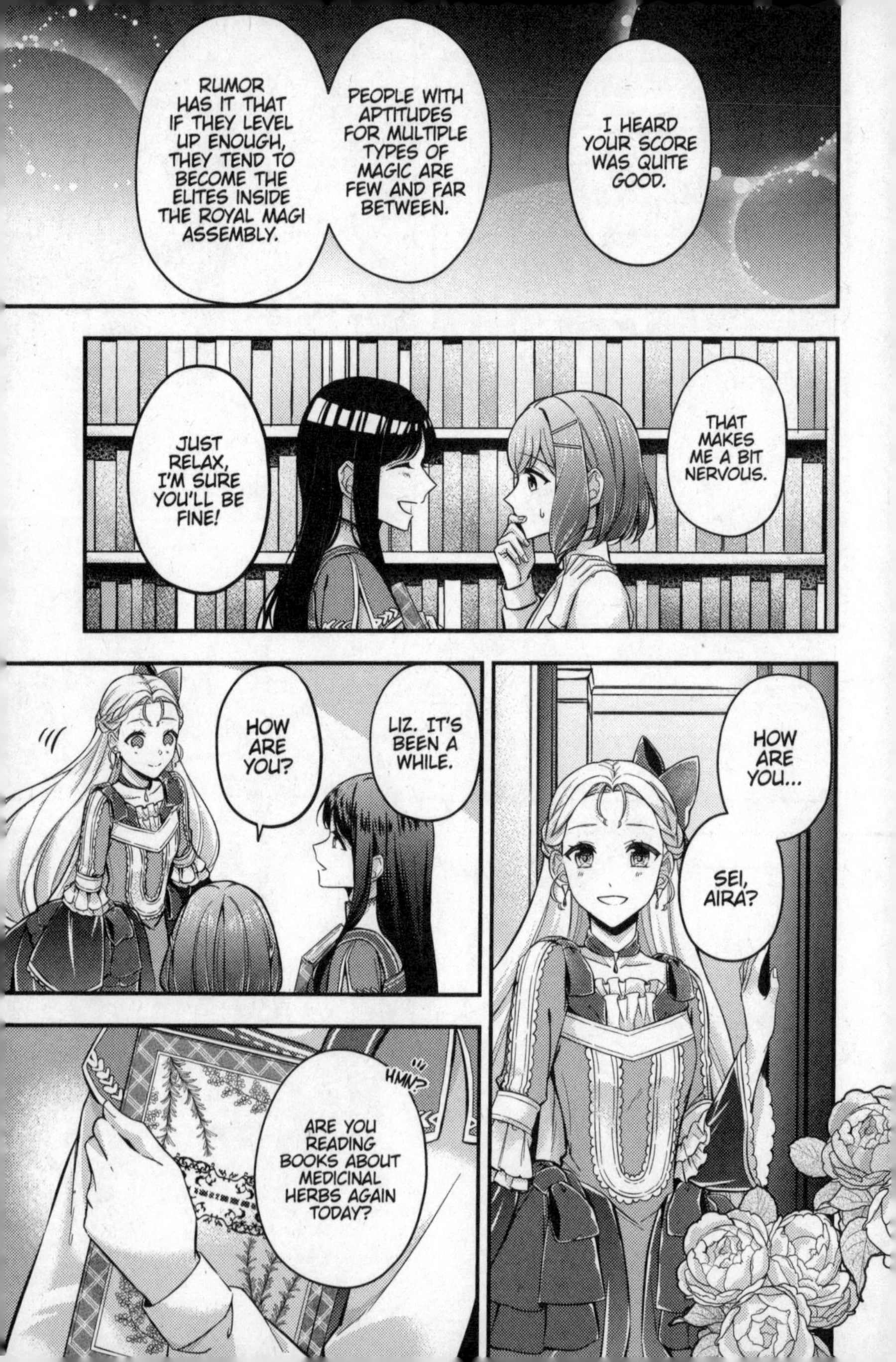
I HEARD YOUR SCORE WAS QUITE GOOD.
PEOPLE WITH APTITUDES FOR MULTIPLE TYPES OF MAGIC ARE FEW AND FAR BETWEEN.
RUMOR HAS IT THAT IF THEY LEVEL UP ENOUGH, THEY TEND TO BECOME THE ELITES INSIDE THE ROYAL MAGI ASSEMBLY.
THAT MAKES ME A BIT NERVOUS.
JUST RELAX, I'M SURE YOU'LL BE FINE!
HOW ARE YOU...
SEI, AIRA?
LIZ. IT'S BEEN A WHILE.
HOW ARE YOU?
HMN?
ARE YOU READING BOOKS ABOUT MEDICINAL HERBS AGAIN TODAY?

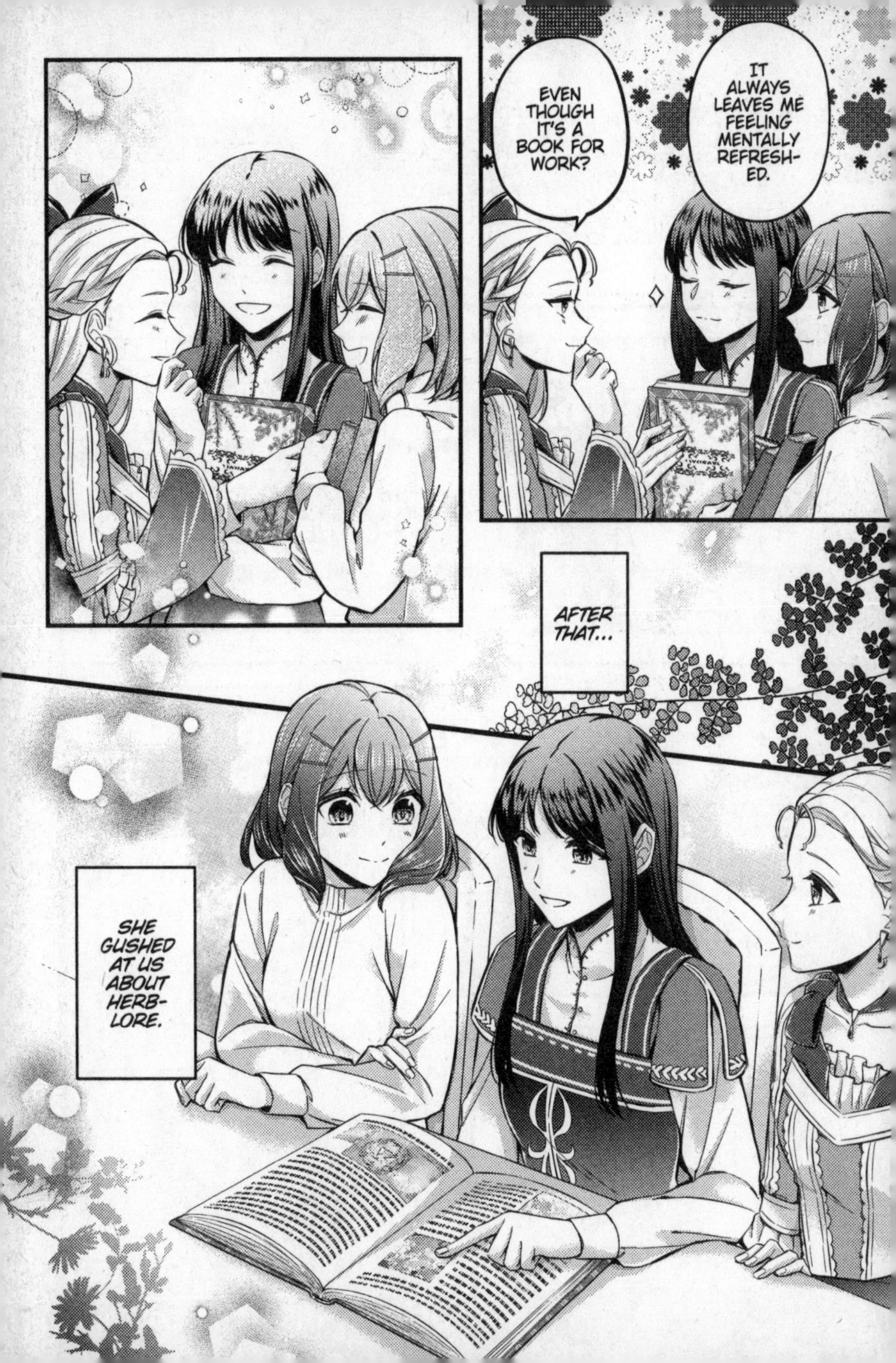
IT ALWAYS LEAVES ME FEELING MENTALLY REFRESH-ED.
EVEN THOUGH IT'S A BOOK FOR WORK?
AFTER THAT...
SHE GUSHED AT US ABOUT HERB-LORE.

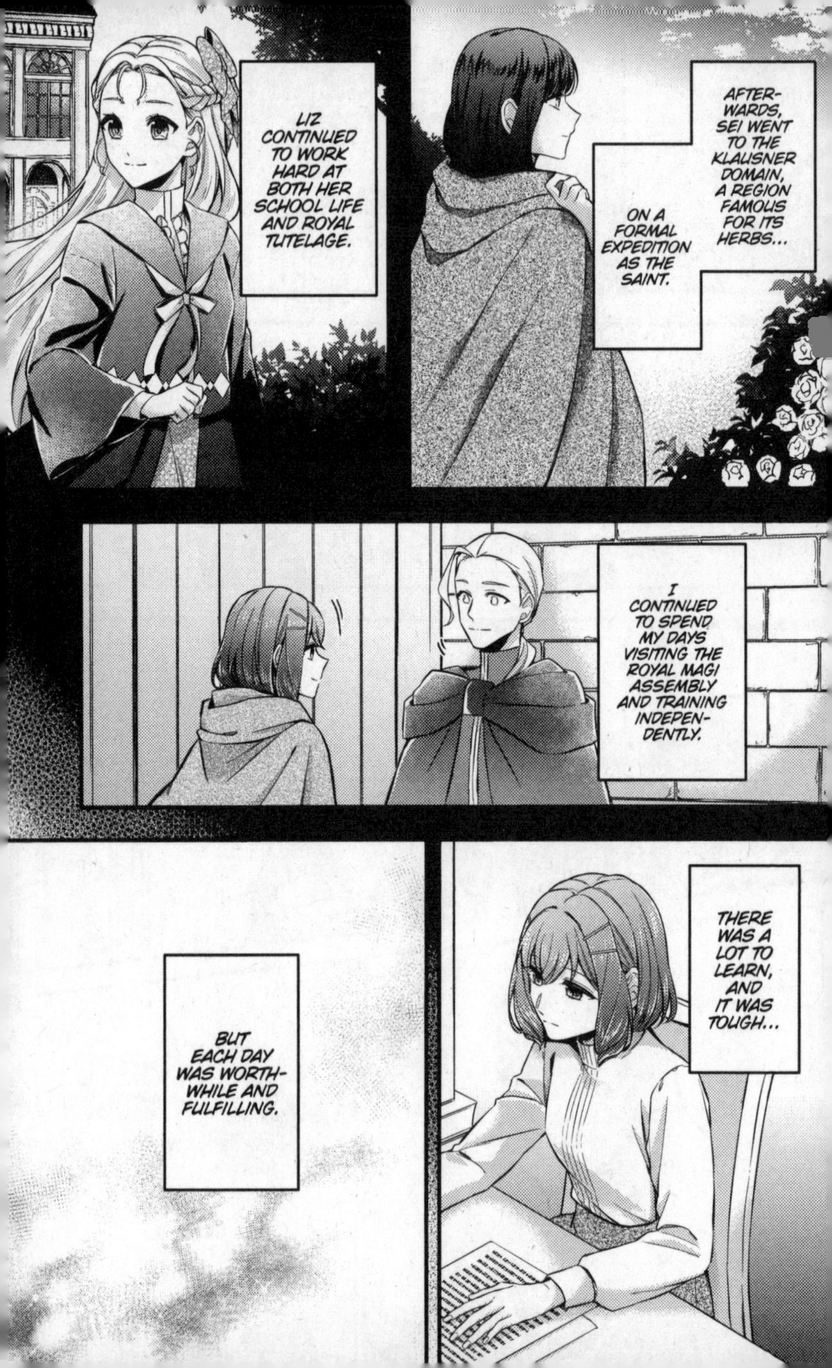
AFTERWARDS, SEI WENT TO THE KLAUSNER DOMAIN, A REGION FAMOUS FOR ITS HERBS...
ON A FORMAL EXPEDITION AS THE SAINT.
LIZ CONTINUED TO WORK HARD AT BOTH HER SCHOOL LIFE AND ROYAL TUTELAGE.
I CONTINUED TO SPEND MY DAYS VISITING THE ROYAL MAGI ASSEMBLY AND TRAINING INDEPENDENTLY.
THERE WAS A LOT TO LEARN, AND IT WAS TOUGH...
BUT EACH DAY WAS WORTHWHILE AND FULFILLING.

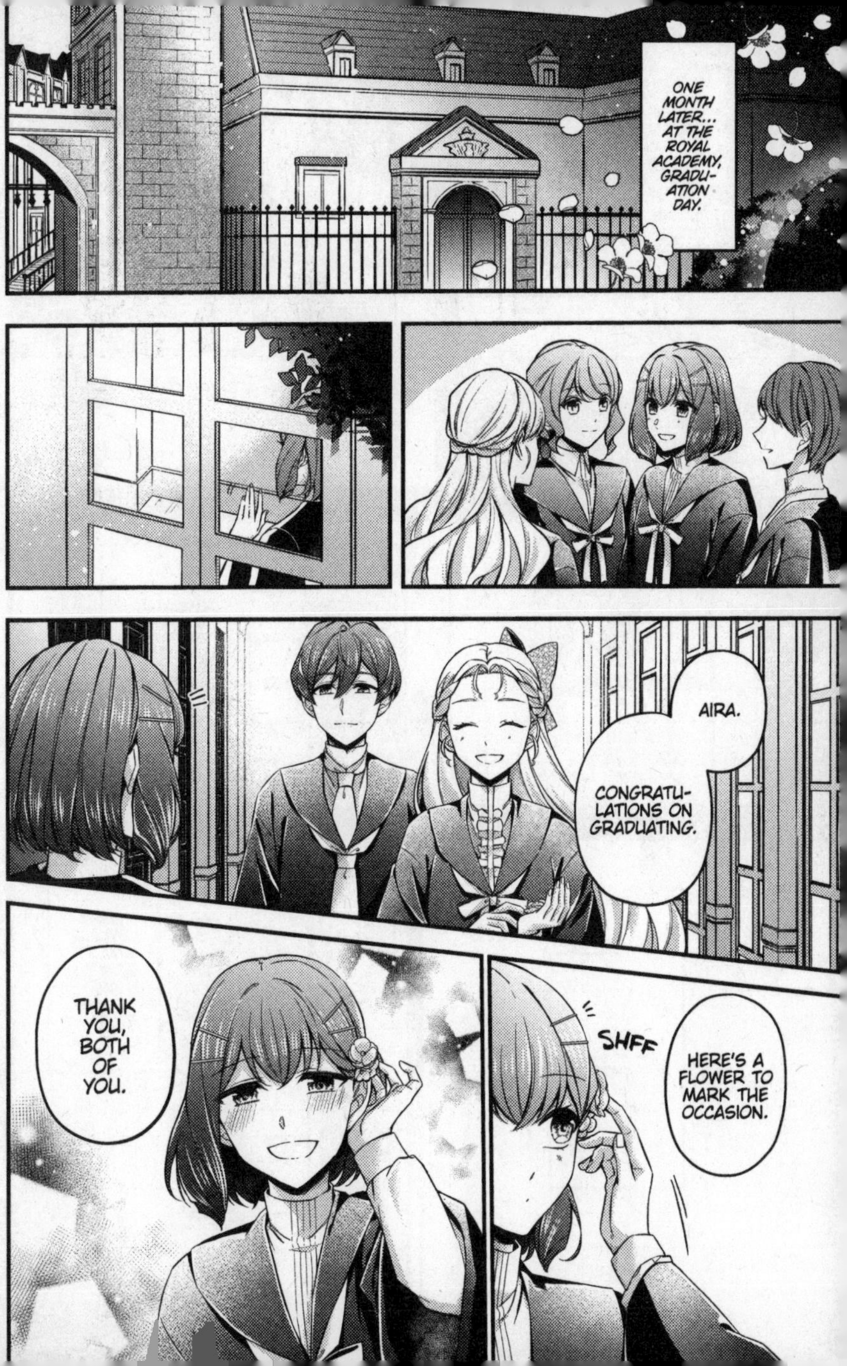
ONE MONTH LATER... AT THE ROYAL ACADEMY, GRADUATION DAY.
AIRA.
CONGRATULATIONS ON GRADUATING.
SHFF
HERE'S A FLOWER TO MARK THE OCCASION.
THANK YOU, BOTH OF YOU.

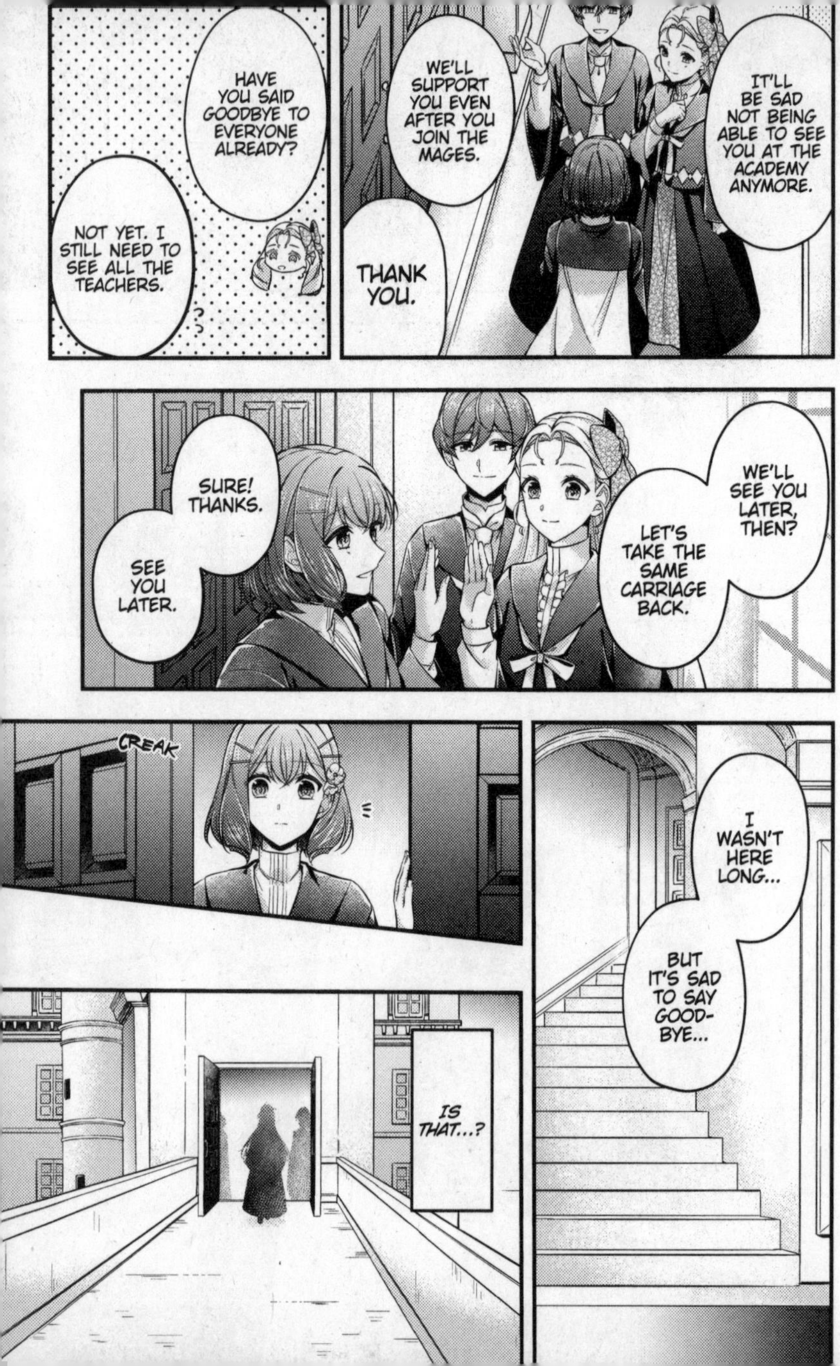
IT'LL BE SAD NOT BEING ABLE TO SEE YOU AT THE ACADEMY ANYMORE.
WE'LL SUPPORT YOU EVEN AFTER YOU JOIN THE MAGES.
THANK YOU.
HAVE YOU SAID GOODBYE TO EVERYONE ALREADY?
NOT YET. I STILL NEED TO SEE ALL THE TEACHERS.
WE'LL SEE YOU LATER, THEN?
LET'S TAKE THE SAME CARRIAGE BACK.
SURE! THANKS.
SEE YOU LATER.
I WASN'T HERE LONG...
BUT IT'S SAD TO SAY GOOD-BYE...
CREAK
IS THAT...?

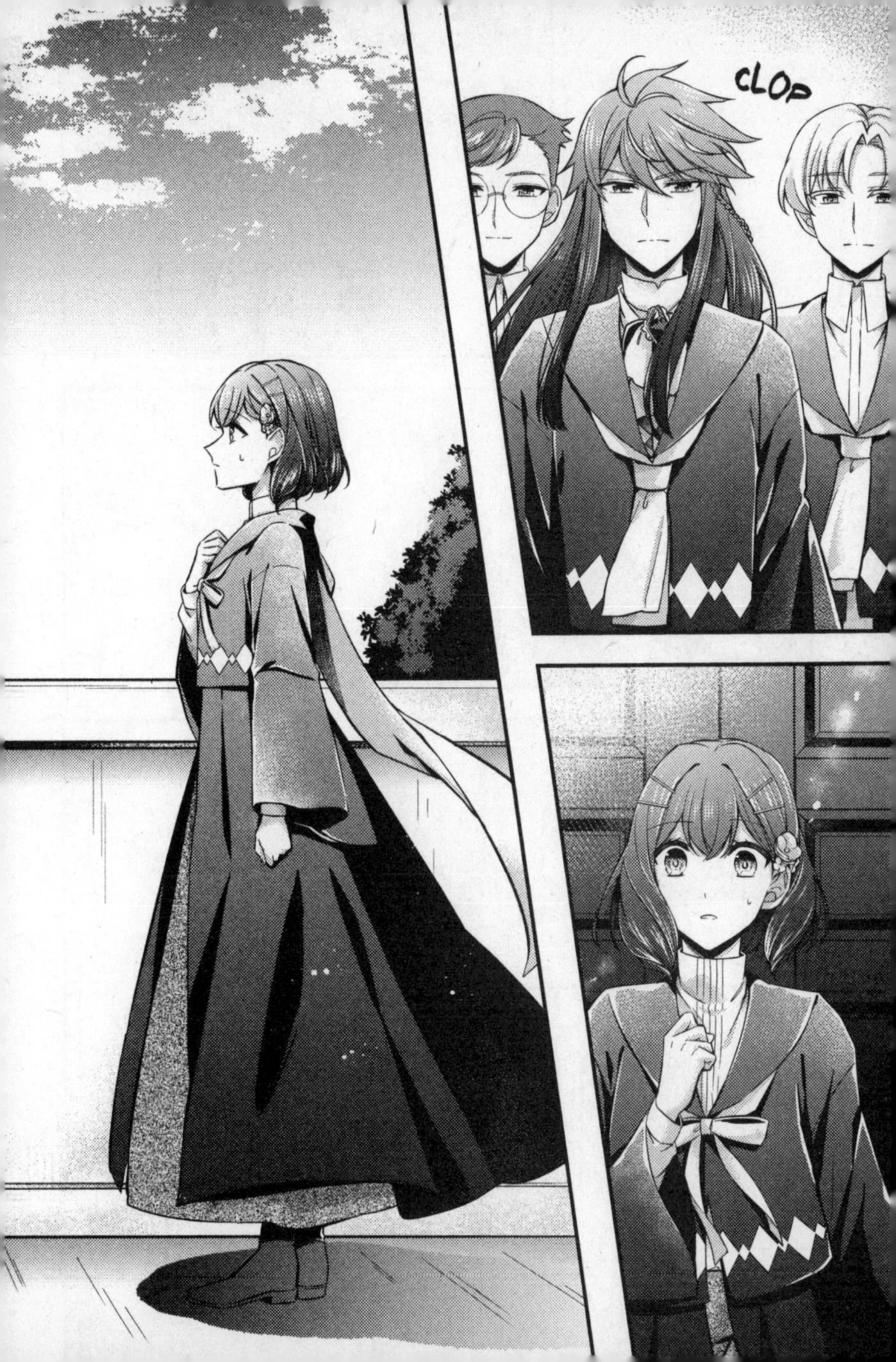
CLOP

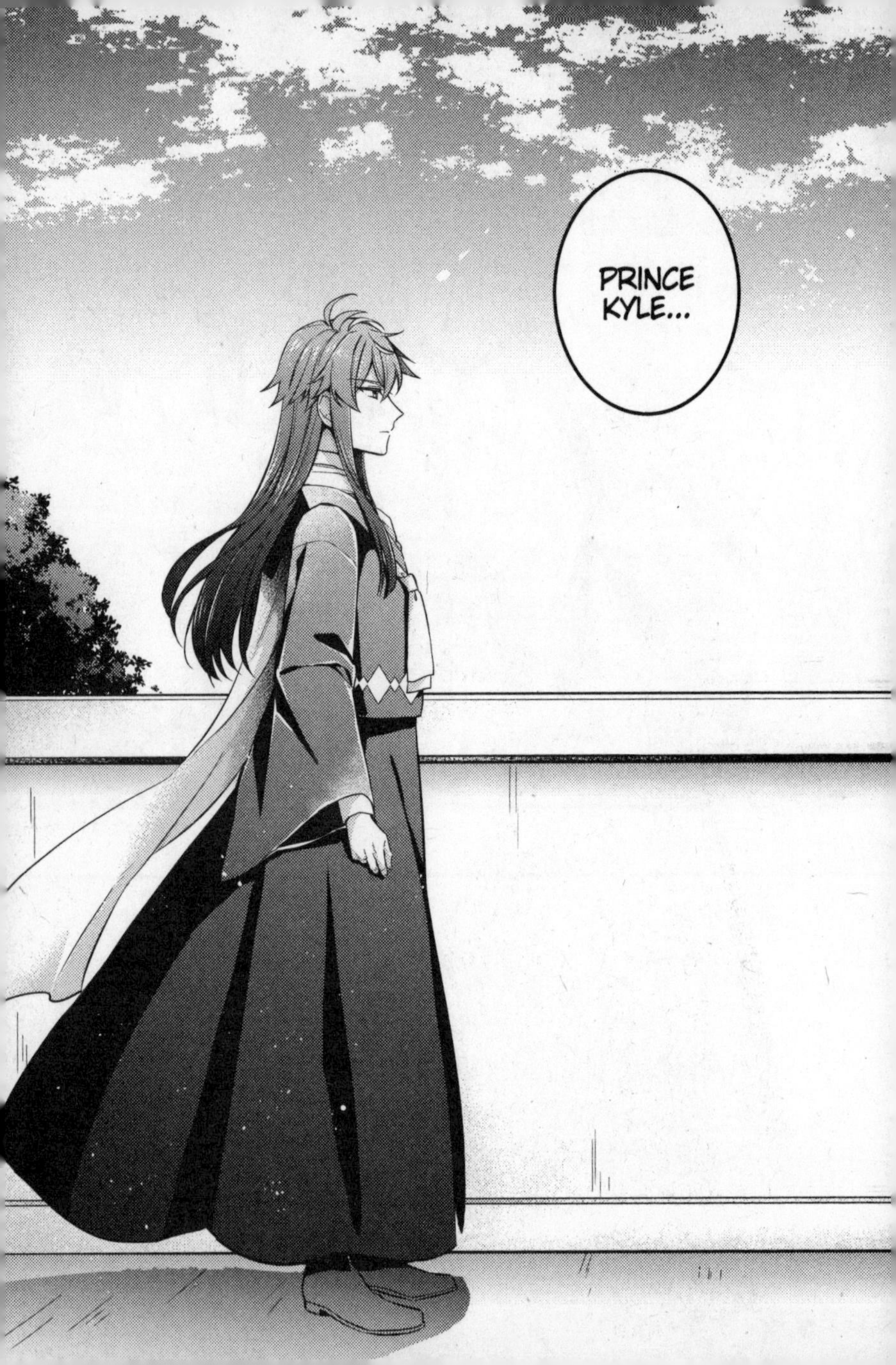
PRINCE KYLE...

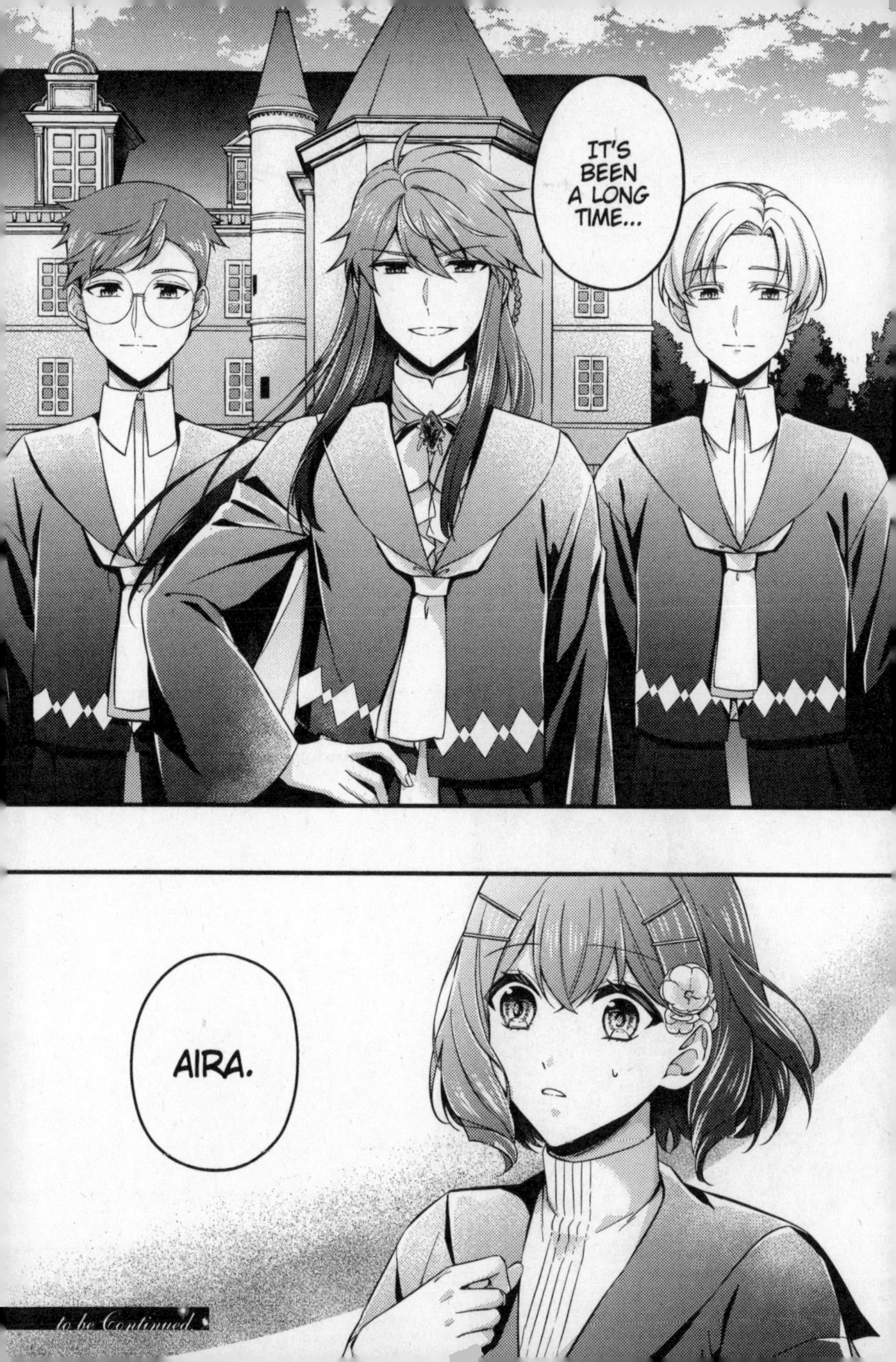
IT'S BEEN A LONG TIME...
AIRA.
to be Continued

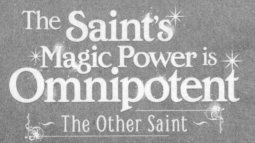

The Saint's
Magic Power is
Omnipotent
~ The Other Saint ~

The Saint's Magic Power is Omnipotent Original Creator's Commentary

Thank you very much for picking up *The Saint's Magic Power is Omnipotent: The Other Saint.* I'm the original creator of this series, Yuka Tachibana. This first started out as a novel I submitted to a website for aspiring novelists, and thanks to the support of many people, here we are at the publication of a spin-off manga volume. I must express my gratitude first to our web readers, and also Aoagu-sensei who handled the spin-off, the editors in charge, and everyone else involved. Thank you, truly.

When talk of a spin-off came up, I thought it would be a relatively simple matter, but once we started it was a big deal in many ways. Well, mainly for Ao-sensei. Since it was our first spin-off, I didn't know how to approach it, so I guess Ao-sensei must have worked very hard on it. Ao-sensei came up with the core story from square one, but first of all, there's no organized collection of material to work from. Most of the world-building material is only in my head. The one thing we had was the main books, so the world details are vague, and creating a story in those circumstances must have been very difficult, I believe. During the approval process I ended up pointing out tiny details, and I think those times must have been very troublesome. Ao-sensei saw Volume 1 through to publication without abandoning it, and for that I bow my head. Thanks to Ao-sensei we now have this tale of another lovely Saint. Thank you sincerely, Ao-sensei.

Finally, I would like to once again thank everyone who picked up this volume. I hope you all enjoy these tales of Aira, who isn't much depicted in the main story. Until next time.

Yuka Tachibana

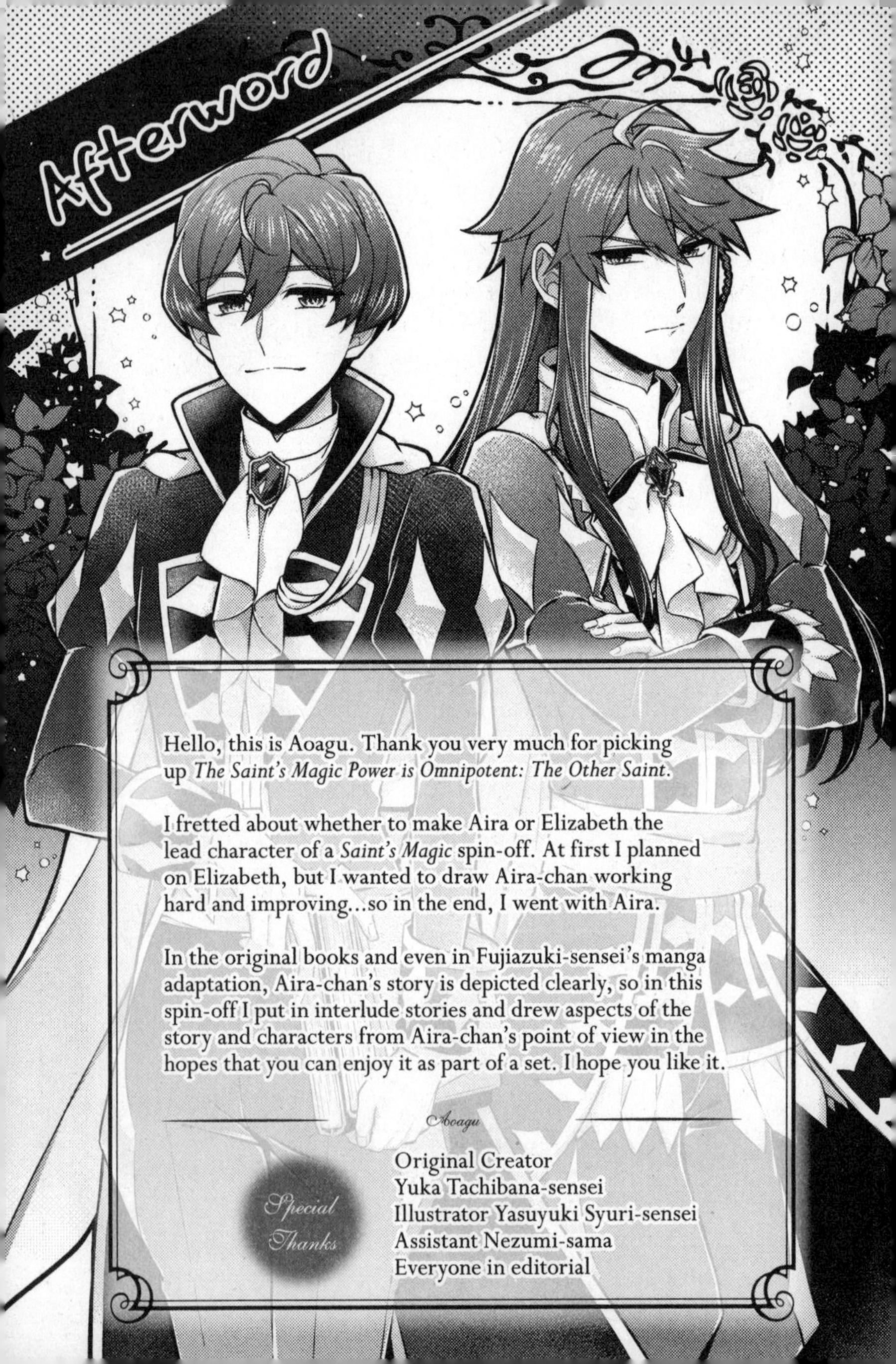

Afterword

Hello, this is Aoagu. Thank you very much for picking up *The Saint's Magic Power is Omnipotent: The Other Saint*.

I fretted about whether to make Aira or Elizabeth the lead character of a *Saint's Magic* spin-off. At first I planned on Elizabeth, but I wanted to draw Aira-chan working hard and improving...so in the end, I went with Aira.

In the original books and even in Fujiazuki-sensei's manga adaptation, Aira-chan's story is depicted clearly, so in this spin-off I put in interlude stories and drew aspects of the story and characters from Aira-chan's point of view in the hopes that you can enjoy it as part of a set. I hope you like it.

Aoagu

Special Thanks

Original Creator
Yuka Tachibana-sensei
Illustrator Yasuyuki Syuri-sensei
Assistant Nezumi-sama
Everyone in editorial

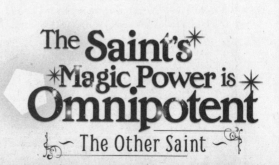

The Saint's
Magic Power is
Omnipotent
— The Other Saint —

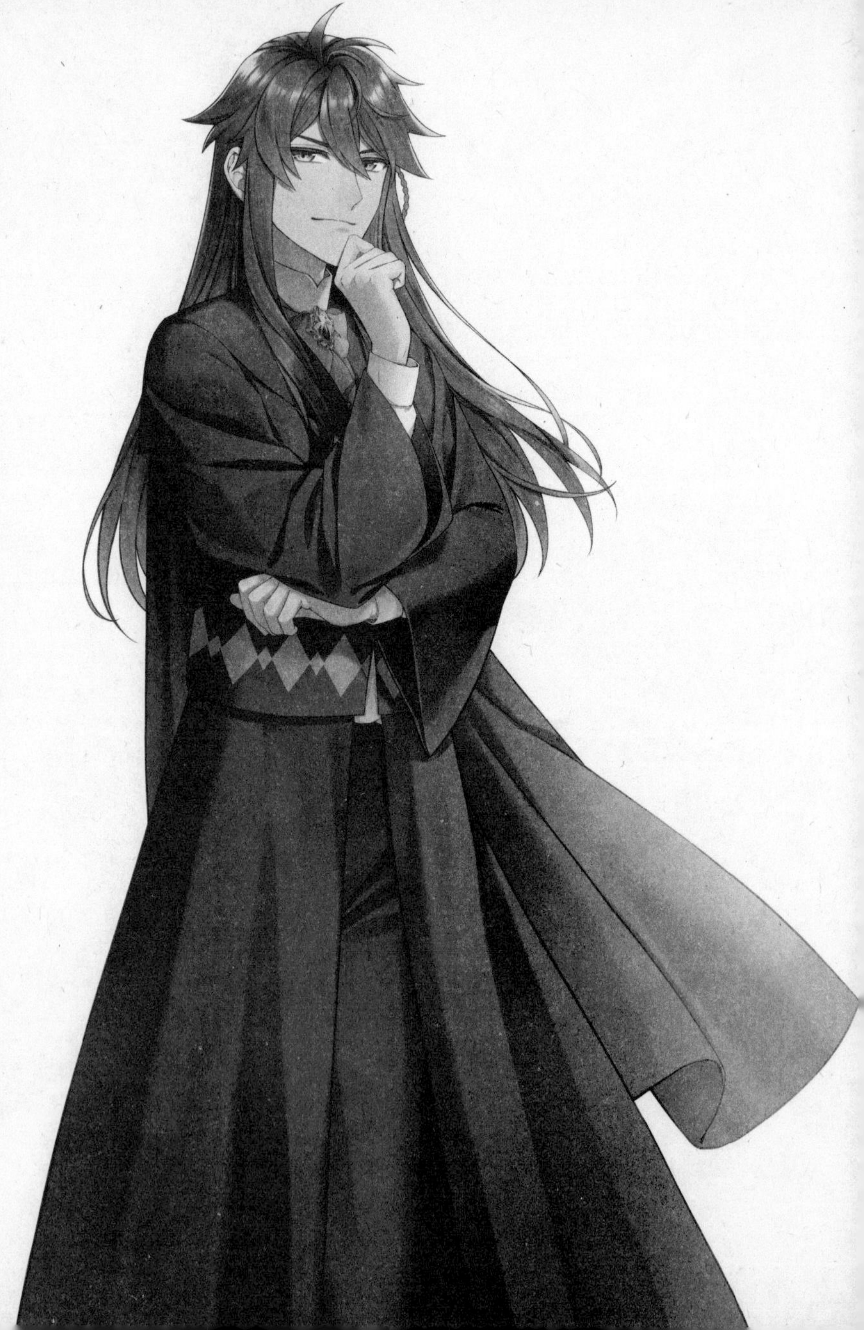

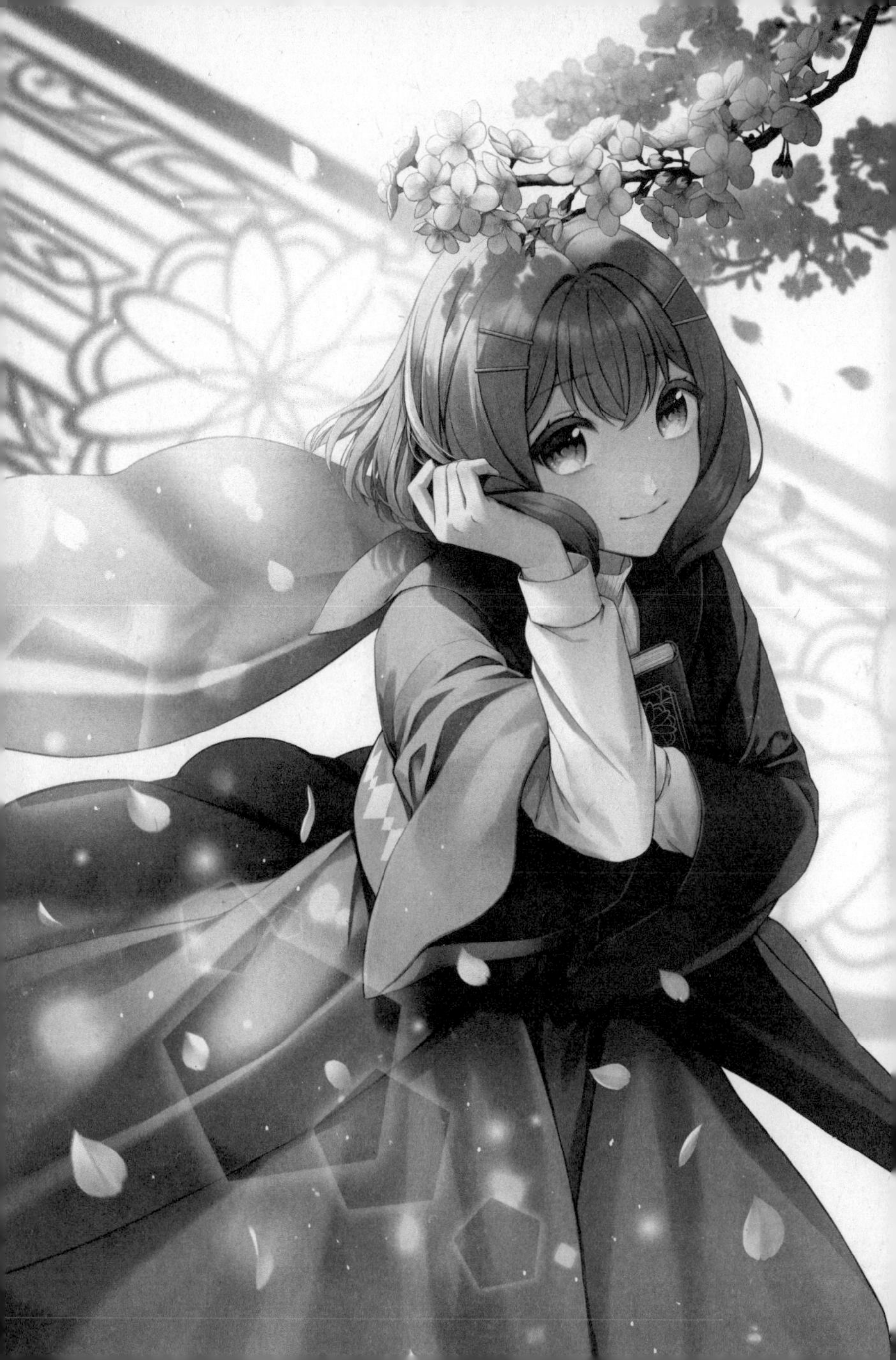

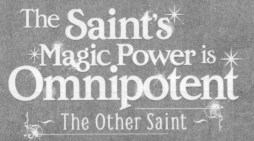

The **Saint's**
Magic Power is
Omnipotent
The Other Saint

The Saint's Magic Power is Omnipotent

~ The Other Saint ~

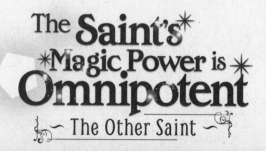

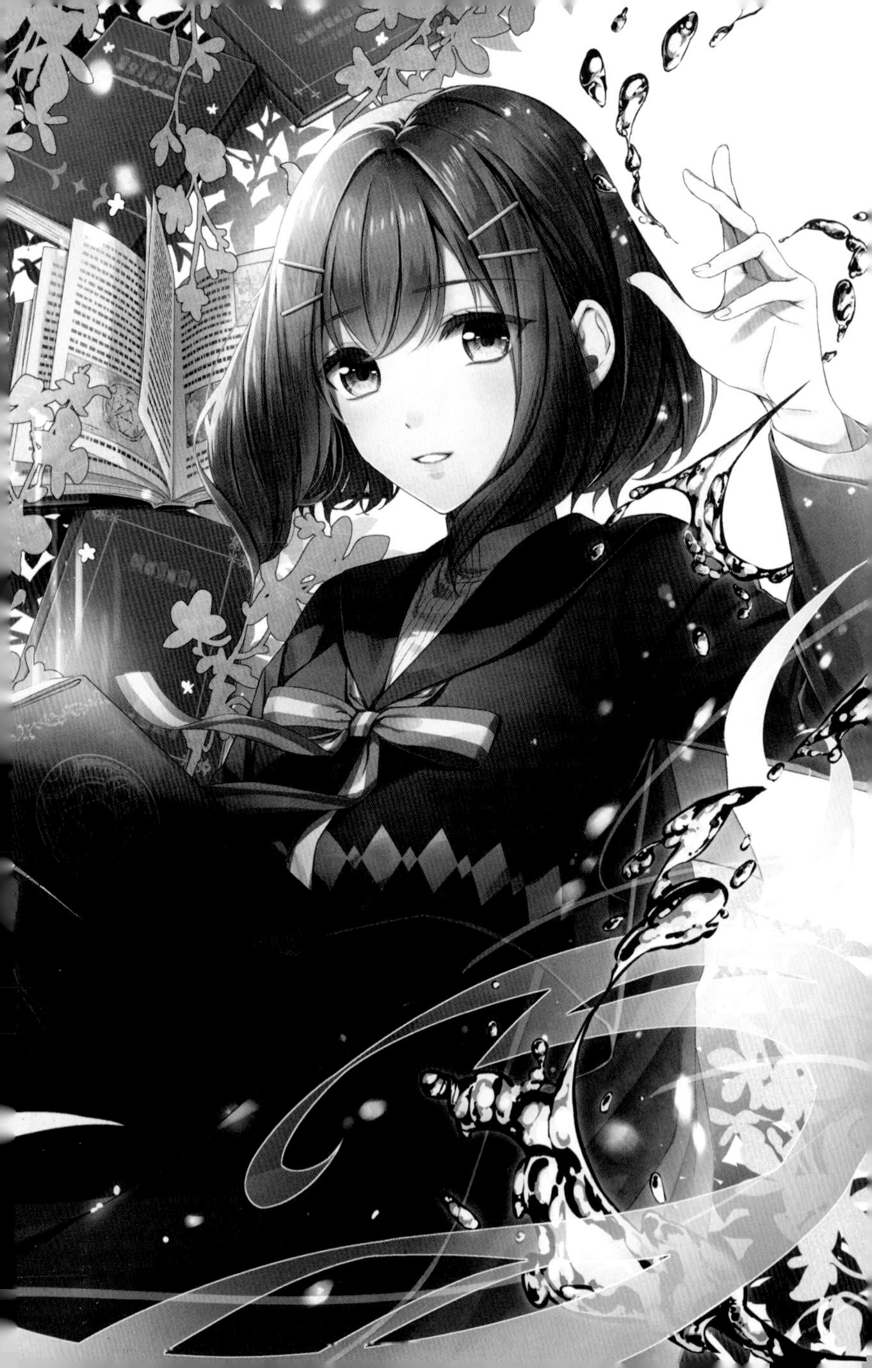

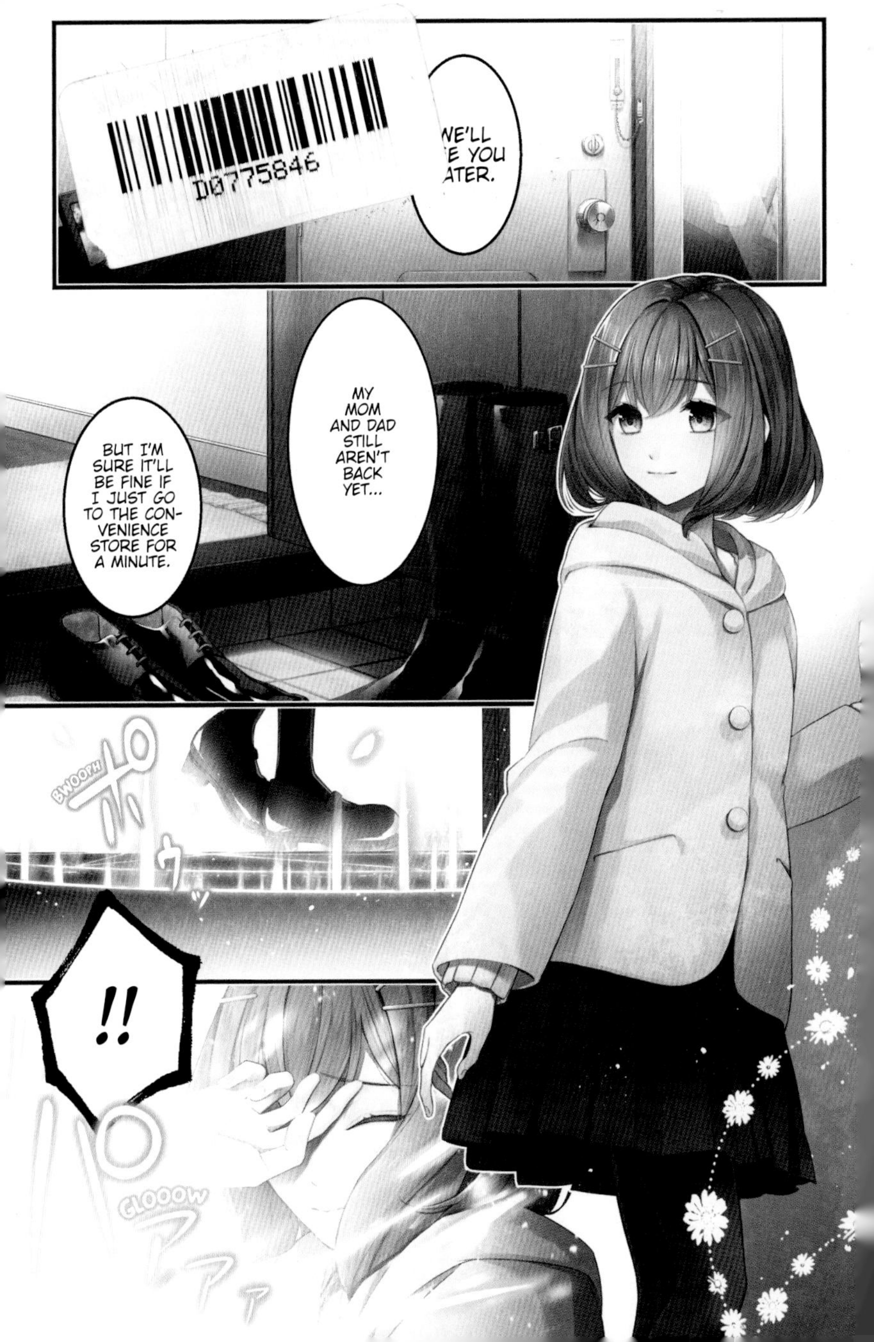
WE'LL
E YOU
ATER.
MY MOM AND DAD STILL AREN'T BACK YET...
BUT I'M SURE IT'LL BE FINE IF I JUST GO TO THE CON-VENIENCE STORE FOR A MINUTE.
BWOOPH
!!
GLOOOW